Labour's economic policies

1974–1979

Labour's economic policies
1974–1979

Michael Artis *and* David Cobham   *editors*

Manchester University Press
Manchester and New York

Distributed exclusively in the USA and Canada by St. Martin's Press

Published by Manchester University Press
Oxford Road, Manchester M13 9PL, UK
and Room 400, 175 Fifth Avenue,
New York, NY 10010, USA

*Distributed exclusively in the USA and Canada
by* St. Martin's Press, Inc.,
175 Fifth Avenue, New York, NY 10010, USA

British Library cataloguing in publication data
Labour's economic policies 1974–1979.
   1. Great Britain. Political parties: Labour Party (Great
Britain). Economic policies, history
   I. Artis, M. J. (Michael John) *1938–* II. Cobham, David
330.941

Library of Congress cataloging in publication data
Labour's economic policies 1974–1979 / edited by Michael Artis and
David Cobham.
    p.cm.
   Includes index.
   ISBN 0-7190-2264-9. – ISBN 0-7190-3438-8 (pbk.)
   1. Great Britain – Economic policy – 1974– 2. Labour Party (Great
Britain) I. Artis. Michael J. II. Cobham, David P.
HC256.6.L34 1991
338.941'009'047 – dc20   90-43507

ISBN 0 7190 2264 9 *hardback*
     0 7190 3438 8 *paperback*

Typeset in Great Britain
by Williams Graphics, Llanddulas, North Wales

Printed in Great Britain
by Bell & Bain Limited, Glasgow

Contents

Preface

The successive Labour governments which held power in the United Kingdom in the 1970s faced some unenviable problems. They operated in conditions of political weakness (not least in parliamentary terms) and in a difficult economic environment, and policy outcomes left much to be desired. While they have been castigated from the Left for their alleged failure to pursue true socialist objectives, the dominant political rhetoric of the 1980s highlighted the shortcomings of policy and caricatured the period as one of simply incompetent and irresponsible economic policy-making. In the light of the sharp recession of the early 1980s that caricature should always have seemed more than a little unfair, but the economic recovery that set in around the middle of the decade led to a reinforcement of the caricature. The aim of this book is to set the record straight. In fact, over the period in which the book has been in preparation, we have witnessed a return of many of the familiar British economic problems. The 1970s no longer seem so far away and the caricatures of the period are already beginning to seem less plausible descriptions of what went on.

To construct a book which would cover the whole gamut of economic policy it seemed appropriate to secure the services of expert authors to write individual chapters and the book is a compilation of sixteen chapters. The first is a narrative description of the period, reinforced by a calendar of events and a statistical appendix, whilst the last is a chapter of conclusions. The remaining chapters review the individual policy areas, starting with overall demand management policy.

Whilst the book is not intended to reflect an agreed line – and several differences of interpretation between different authors are to be found – it seemed right to ensure that these interpretations were confronted by one another and tested against the views of those who were influential as policy makers or advisers or were close to events in some capacity. Accordingly, the progress of preparation of the book was marked by two conferences, one for contributors only, held in September 1989 in Holly Royde Conference

Centre in Manchester, and the other, held in St. Catherine's College, Oxford in December 1989, at which the contributors' interpretations were presented before an audience of policy makers and others close to the events of the period. For providing finance for these conferences we are grateful to the Scottish Economic Society, the Nuffield Foundation, the Faculty of Economic and Social Studies at the University of Manchester and the Research Support Fund of Manchester University. For their helpful comments, but without implication, we should like to thank Lord Donoughue and the conference participants who included Sir Kenneth Berrill, Andrew Britton, Sir Alec Cairncross, Professor David Currie, Christopher Dow, Charles Goodhart, Sir Bryan Hopkin, William Keegan, Hans Liesner, Michael Posner, Anthony Seldon, Peter Shore and Sir Douglas Wass. Particular thanks go to Mark Wickham-Jones who not only painstakingly prepared the Calendar of Events but also carefully researched for us the numerous political biographies, memoirs and other accounts of the political developments of the period. Financial support from the Scottish Economic Society is also acknowledged in this connection. Kenneth Clark provided the subject and author indexes.

Last of all, we acknowledge a special debt of gratitude to Hilary Thornton whose assistance in the organisation of the enterprise (as well as in typing three chapter drafts) was invaluable and rendered with unfailing good humour.

Notes on contributors

Christopher Allsopp

Christopher Allsopp is Fellow in Economics at New College, Oxford, and Editor of *The Oxford Review of Economic Policy*. In 1973–74 he was Editor of the OECD *Economic Outlook*; in 1980–83 he was an adviser at the Bank of England. He has published widely on UK and international macroeconomic policy issues.

Michael Artis

Michael Artis is Professor of Economics at Manchester University. His chief professional interest is in macroeconomics, with special reference to monetary economics, macro modelling and forecasting and policy analysis. He contributed a chapter on Fiscal Policy to the book, edited by Wilfred Beckerman, on *The Labour Government's Economic Record 1964–70* (Duckworth, 1972).

Robin Bladen-Hovell

Robin Bladen-Hovell is Lecturer in Economics at the University of Manchester. He has worked extensively in the area of model-based macroeconomic policy appraisal. He is Assistant Editor of *The Manchester School* journal.

Alex Bowen

Alex Bowen is Head of Policy Analysis and Statistics at the National Economic Development Office, having worked previously at the LSE's Centre for Labour Economics and at Brunel University. He completed his Ph.D. at the Massachusetts Institute of Technology in 1983 and has been an adviser to the World Bank on labour market issues.

John Bowers

John Bowers is Reader in Applied Economics at the School of Business and Economic Studies, University of Leeds. He was 1966–70 Research Officer, National Institute of Economic and Social Research; and 1977–83 Associate Research Fellow, Industrial Relations Research Unit, University of Warwick. He has written and published widely on policy-related areas of applied microeconomics, particularly regional, environmental and labour market issues.

William Brown

William Brown is the Montague Burton Professor of Industrial Relations at the University of Cambridge. Previously he was Director of the Industrial Relations Research Unit at the University of Warwick. He has published on a number of aspects of collective bargaining and pay determination. During the 1970s his research was concerned with current developments in shop steward organisations, incomes policies, and Britain's changing bargaining structure.

David Cobham

David Cobham is Lecturer in Economics at St. Andrews University. He has specialised in UK monetary policy and control, but also has interests in international monetary economics, French monetary policy and financial markets. He was Houblon–Norman Research Fellow at the Bank of England in 1987.

Alan Gillie

Allan Gillie lectured in economics and economic statistics at the Universities of Durham and Leeds before moving to the Open University where he has been responsible for courses in public sector economics. He has chaired courses in the area of economics and government policy.

Peter M. Jackson

Peter M. Jackson is Professor of Economics and Director of the Public Sector Economics Research Centre, University of Leicester, and Research Director of the Public Finance Foundation, London. He has published on public sector economics and specialises in the analysis of public spending.

Robert Millward

Robert Millward is Professor of Economic History at the University of Manchester. He has published books and articles in the area of public sector economics and held a Chair in Economics at the University of Salford for fourteen years. Current research is concerned with the long-term development of the public enterprises and the service sector in the UK since the mid nineteenth century.

Paul Ormerod

Paul Ormerod is Director of Economics at the Henley Centre and Visiting Professor at Queen Mary and Westfield College, University of London. He was previously at the National Institute of Economic and Social Research and the Economist Intelligence Unit.

Malcolm Sawyer

Malcolm Sawyer is Professor of Economics at the University of York. One of his main areas of research interest is that of industrial economics, and he is the author of *Economics of Industries and Firms* (Croom Helm, 2nd edn, 1985). He has also written on empirical and theoretical aspects of inflation. Since 1987 he has been managing editor of *International Review of Applied Economics*.

Andrew G. Scott

Andrew Scott is Lecturer in Economics at Heriot-Watt University. He has published on Britain and the EMS, and the Economic Effects of 1992. He has acted as a consultant for the European Commission, producing two studies on Europe's external trade performance.

Mark Wickham-Jones

Mark Wickham-Jones is a Lecturer in the Department of Politics at the University of Bristol; he is researching the economic strategy of the Labour Party in the 1970s and his main teaching interests are in political economy.

George Zis

George Zis is Head of Department of Economics and Economic History at Manchester Polytechnic. He has published across the range of international monetary economics, including articles on the evolution of the sterling balances and the European Monetary System.

1 *Michael Artis and David Cobham*

The background

1 Introduction

Getting the context right is an essential element in policy appraisal. Policies not seen in context are likely to be misread, their objectives misunderstood and their effectiveness misstated. Irrelevant, or simply wrong, conclusions will be drawn. It is the purpose of this chapter to provide an account of the context in which the Labour government's policies were conceived and enacted. In the course of providing this background various questions inevitably arise, both about the policies actually pursued and about those that might have been pursued, but were not. Some of these issues are taken up, along with others, by the authors of subsequent chapters in the volume. We attempt an overall summary and appraisal in the last chapter of the book.

In formal economic analysis policy is represented by a mechanical rule for the adjustment of policy instruments in the light of circumstances (a 'feedback rule' in the parlance). This idea flows from the formal representation of economies as mathematical models and capitalises on the power of mathematical formalisation to clarify the policy problem. These tools can be used to provide information about the performance of policy and to provide the means of improvement. An example of this sort of analysis appears in Chapter 6 of this book (by Michael Artis and Robin Bladen-Hovell).

There is, however, much more to policy than this. First, an important dimension in policy omitted from the formal approach is that of creativity and policy innovation. Creative policy makers, recognising the institutional and political constraints on existing forms of policy should be expected to seek to undermine and loosen those constraints by building new institutions and devising new policy instruments. Stubborn policy problems place a premium on creative policy making of this kind. Second, even within those forms of policy to which the 'policy as application of a rule' approach more readily applies, such as conventional demand management policy, there exists a critical area of creative discretion. The conventional 'policy rule' analysis implicitly or explicitly assumes that the environment is essentially given and the trend of events is essentially known, but either or both of these conditions may be unfulfilled. Thus the question of interpreting the economic environment and predicting the trend of events both at home and abroad is hugely important. Of course this is an area in which good technical advice is vital (and its absence may be fatal) but it is not enough: for one thing, the experts differ in their opinions; for another, many of the most important possible future developments depend on political decisions, especially on decisions taken overseas. Associated with this is the vital question, where again good technical advice is important but not sufficient, of how to design policy so that it is robust to the realisation of the 'worst case'. Designing 'fair weather' policies is not enough because the weather cannot be relied upon. Finally, some policies more than others depend for their effectiveness on their political acceptability: the most obvious case in point is incomes policy. Political constraints may restrict the policy 'space', reducing available actions to a few, or they may be relaxed, offering the policy makers a wide choice of alternatives.

In the broad, then, the context of policy as we seek to describe it consists of the actual and perceived development of the domestic and the world economy, the perception of policy objectives, the performance character-istics of actual and alternative policy instruments under stress, and the constraints and opportunities represented by the balance of political forces. For a record of how things looked at the time the diaries and memoirs of active policy makers and accounts of the period based on interviews with them are indispensable material and these sources provide much of the evidence for what follows. A record of events – A Calendar of Economic Events – appears as Appendix A.[1]

2   On coming to office: the political inheritance

The Labour goverment assumed power on 4 March 1974 on the brink of the most testing economic crisis experienced by the Western economies for over two decades and in circumstances of industrial turmoil and political uncertainty.

A miners' overtime ban, which had been started on 12 November 1973 in support of a pay claim, together with the interruption of oil supplies and uncertainty about their future security, induced the Heath government to use its emergency powers to declare a restricted, three-day, working week. The government called the election on the theme of 'Who Rules?'. A substantial tradition of political folklore held that in an electoral contest in which this question was central, the government would always win. The Heath govern-ment sought to capitalise on this, but whether out of a perverse desire not to be taken for granted or for other reasons the electorate failed to endorse the expected result. Labour fought the election substantially on the basis that it could 'heal the wounds' inflicted by the Heath administration and was rewarded by being asked to form the next government, albeit without the mandate of an overall majority, for the election resulted in a hung parliament.

The circumstances of Labour's assumption of power had several significant implications. First, these circumstances were themselves essentially unexpected: the party was not well prepared for the task that lay ahead. During the period of opposition most of the running on economic policy formulation had been made by the Left with the result that the party's formal programme was of a kind that did not command the support of the leadership. Secondly, the 'healing of the wounds' was bound to imply, at best, a *perceived* capitulation to union strength, whatever steps might be taken to protest the contrary. More important, the three-day week and the election result were widely interpreted as evidence of the results of a policy of industrial 'confrontation' and of the public's verdict on such an approach. Finally, the government's political weakness obliged it to concentrate first on securing a more substantial mandate in an early successive election. These implications would not have been so serious had the scope of the crisis been limited to that of an industrial dispute, albeit a big and important one. But in fact Britain, along with other Western economies, was facing a major economic crisis as discussed in the next section.

In addition to the immediate economic pressures it was of course possible to identify some peculiarly British, supply-side, problems and structural economic weaknesses. However, although the party's existing economic policy document, *Labour's Programme 1973*, made this identification, it sought their rectification through intervention by way of extending public ownership, price control and planning agreements in a context given by its central political objective, 'to bring about a fundamental and irreversible shift in the balance of power and wealth in favour of working people' (Labour Party, 1973, pt. 1, p. 7).

The attitude struck in the document towards industry was minatory rather than persuasive or consensual; the Right of the Labour Party and most of the leadership were unhappy both with its general tone and with its specific recommendations (especially one which called for the public ownership of twenty-five top companies) and had no intention of carrying out very much of it. One result was that the leadership spent much time and resources both in opposition and subsequently in government battling against its own policy inheritance, at best a wasteful way of proceeding. The document also referred to a Social Contract between trade unions and the government which would create 'the right economic climate for money incomes to grow in line with production' (*ibid.*, p. 24). Measures specified as part of the Contract included price controls and subsidies, abolition of the Pay Board and repeal of the Heath government's Industrial Relations Act. Despite the strenuous efforts of the leadership, no promise of wage restraint was ever obtained from the TUC.[2] The campaign document issued for the election toned down some of the commitments which were felt to be politically embarrassing and in the election itself it was noted that Harold Wilson studiously avoided reference to many of the features of the programme.[3] He preferred instead to emphasise Labour's capacity to deal with the immediate crisis and the promise of the Social Contract.

Labour's political inheritance was not, therefore, an encouraging one. The union movement was in no immediate mood to concede wage restraint yet demanded delivery of the government's portion of the Social Contract while the formal policy programme contained an approach that stepped well beyond the limit of the consensual style with which most of the leadership felt happy. On the other hand, 'confrontation' had been tried and found wanting. A government which could negotiate with the trade unions might find the key to the resolution, both of the oil crisis and of Britain's longer-term economic problems. Thus its ability to deal constructively with the trade unions was emphasised by the new Labour government as the possible key to an alternative strategy.

3   The economic inheritance

There are two distinct aspects to the economic situation which the Labour government inherited: the international conjuncture and the specific effects of the policies pursued by the Heath government.

The year 1973 marked the peak of a boom in the world economy, an occasion of unprecedented synchronisation in economic activity in all the major economies. One consequence was a remarkable rise in world commodity prices, most notable of all being the fourfold rise in oil prices. The shock was novel in character and enormous in magnitude. The dependence of the Western economies on oil meant that there would be a drastic redistribution of real income from the consuming economies of the oil producers, a deficit in the collective balance of payments of the West *vis-à-vis* the oil producers, and a sharp twist in the inflation spiral. The crisis posed problems of an unprecedented character for forecasting, for domestic economic management and for international economic policy. At the same time the fixed exchange rate international monetary system which had provided the context for both demand management policy and nearly all thinking, by academics as well as policy makers, about macroeconomics for nearly three decades, had dissolved in early 1973. The full implications of the 'non-system' (Williamson, 1977) which took its place, initially by default but later by the intent of several major countries including the United States, were by no means immediately obvious.

Within the context of the world boom of 1972–73 the previous UK government had pursued exceptionally expansionary fiscal and monetary policies in the form of the 'Heath–Barber dash for growth', a strategy of creating and sustaining a high level of aggregate demand in the hope of encouraging a great leap in industrial investment, with favourable effects on productivity and growth. The result of these policies had been a rapid rate of economic expansion, a significant fall in unemployment and a marked deterioration of the current account together with a sterling crisis in June 1972 which led to the floating of the pound and substantial depreciation. The inflation rate had risen from 6–7% in mid-1972 to over 10% in late 1973, and the sterling depreciation meant that significant further price rises were already 'in the pipeline' in early 1974.

When the slowing down of the economic expansion during the course of 1973 (due essentially to capacity constraints) became increasingly clear, there was mounting pressure on the Heath government to change course. It finally did so in November and December 1973 when interest rates were raised to record levels, public expenditure cuts were announced and the 'corset' form of indirect control on bank lending was introduced. By this time, however, the oil price shock had arrived and the government was already involved in a major dispute with the miners.

4 The international economic context 1974–79

The context provided by other countries' policy adjustments during the period was not a particularly helpful one. In most countries the evidence of rising inflation before the oil crisis had already provoked a tightening of fiscal and monetary policies, and subsequent to the crisis a recession set in. Late in 1974 and in the first half of 1975 these tighter policies were eased somewhat but the ensuing (limited) recovery led many countries to withdraw in 1976 the stimulus applied in 1975 and monetary policies were generally tightened, too. These policies of 'restraint' carried on into 1977, but in late 1977 policy was relaxed in the USA, West Germany and Japan. In 1978 monetary and fiscal policies in all the major countries were expansionary but in 1979 policies were again tightened. It should be emphasised, however, that the variations in policy both through the period and across countries (excluding the UK) were relatively limited.

Table 1.1 shows the out-turns for the major macro-policy target variables for various groupings of countries. After the rapid expansion of 1973, GNP/GDP in the world economy stagnated in 1974 and 1975, but grew significantly during the rest of the period, albeit much more slowly than in the years before 1973. Unemployment rose slightly in 1974 and sharply in 1975; in the G-7 and in the OECD as a whole it then fell slightly towards the end of the period, but in the EC it rose in 1976 and 1977 and again slightly in 1978 and 1979. Inflation rose sharply in 1974 in all major countries except West Germany, and then fell back in most countries in 1975 and 1976; after a relatively small change in 1977 and a further fall in 1978 it rose again in 1979, partly in response to the second oil price shock. Most OECD countries experienced a strong current account

Michael Artis and David Cobham

Table 1.1   *The international economic environment*

	GDP/GNP growth %	Unemployment (standardised) %	Inflation %	Current account % GDP/GNP
G-7				
1973	6·1	3·4	7·5	0·3
4	0·1	3·7	13·3	−0·4
5	−0·3	5·4	11·0	0·5
6	4·9	5·4	8·0	0
7	4·1	5·4	8·1	0
8	4·6	5·1	7·0	0·4
9	3·6	4·9	9·3	−0·2
EC				
1973	6·0	2·9	8·7	0·4
4	2·0	3·0	13·5	−0·9
5	−1·2	4·3	13·5	0
6	4·7	5·0	11·3	−0·6
7	2·6	5·4	11·2	0
8	3·1	5·6	8·3	0·9
9	3·4	5·7	9·8	−0·2
Total OECD				
1973	6·1	3·3	7·8	0·4
4	0·6	3·5	13·4	−0·6
5	−0·2	5·2	11·3	0·1
6	4·7	5·3	8·7	−0·3
7	3·8	5·3	8·9	−0·4
8	4·2	5·2	7·8	0·2
9	3·4	5·1	9·7	−0·4
UK				
1973	7·3	3·0	9·2	−1·3
4	−1·9	2·9	16·0	−3·8
5	−0·9	4·3	24·2	−1·4
6	2·8	5·6	16·5	−0·8
7	2·3	6·0	15·8	−0·1
8	3·7	5·9	8·3	0·6
9	2·7	5·0	13·4	−0·3

Note: Figures for the UK from domestic sources (e.g. *Economic Trends*) are slightly
    different, particularly for GDP growth in 1978 − see Appendix B.
Source: OECD *Economic Outlook*, June 1989, Tables R1, R17, R 11 and R20.

deterioration in 1974 followed by a recovery before renewed deterioration in 1979.

Thus the international context in which the UK economy was to operate during this period was much less propitious than that of the 1960s, with lower growth, higher unemployment, higher inflation, and larger current account imbalances in the early part of the period at least.

The UK's own experience, also shown in Table 1.1, included sharp falls in GDP in 1974 and 1975 followed by four years of moderate growth; a rise in unemployment to a record level in 1977 succeeded by a limited fall; four years of double-digit inflation peaking in 1975 and declining to 8·3% in 1978 before rising again (partly under the influence of the VAT increase in the June 1979 Budget of the new Conservative government); and four years of gradually falling balance of payments deficit succeeded by a small surplus in 1978 and a return to deficit in 1979. Economic policy itself, however, needs to be examined more closely.

5 Policy narrative

The course of policy over the period of the Labour governments can be divided roughly into five phases. In the first, the government moved quickly to deal with the immediate crisis but generally adopted a 'steady as she goes' strategy in the run-up to the election of October 1974. In the second, the government moved gradually towards a tightening of fiscal policy and the introduction of a specific incomes policy (the £6 pay limit). In the third phase, from early 1976 to early 1977, the principal concern was the prolonged sterling crisis of March to November 1976, with which were associated a further severe tightening of fiscal policy, the IMF loan and the introduction of formal monetary targets. The fourth phase, from early 1977 to mid-1978, saw a gradual recovery of the economy and the relaxation of policy. The final phase involved reflationary policy measures and growing disagreement over pay policy which culminated in the renewed industrial turmoil of the 'Winter of Discontent', followed shortly by the election defeat of May 1979.

5.1 *The run-up to October 1974*
In the period immediately after the oil price shock, understanding of its full implications was slow to spread; whilst Donoughue's assessment surely exaggerates the position,[4] it seems fair to say that at the time the full dimensions of the 'crisis' were not appreciated. There was a tendency to identify the crisis with the miners' dispute and the short working week, for which an 'immediate' solution could be found, and to underestimate the more deep-seated problems resulting from both the oil price shock and the Heath–Barber expansion.

The new government moved very quickly to deal with the immediate crisis, settling the miners' pay dispute on 6 March and so ensuring a rapid end to the three-day week. Action was quickly begun to repeal the Industrial Relations Act.

A dominant theme of the period was the securing of a more formalised Social Contract which would govern the development of wage bargaining after the expiry of the incomes policy inherited from the Heath government. Stage III of that policy had provided for cost-of-living compensation payments to be made as the inflation rate triggered various thresholds. This policy had been devised at a time when the official view of inflation prospects was a relatively sanguine one and the threshold device was expected to lower wage claims by taking care of the exaggerated expected inflation component in them. The commodity price boom and oil price increases now threatened to convert this device into a mechanism for accelerating inflation, and the first threshold payment was triggered in May. A number of steps were taken to dampen the rise in prices by regulation (a freeze on rents was imposed) and by subsidy (on food), and by the end of June negotiations had hardened the form of the Social Contract, which was formally published shortly before the end of July. It provided for wage increases to match the cost-of-living increases with exceptions for the low-paid and invited responsible unions to modify their claims in the light of the government's policies and the effect of these on the 'social wage'. At the same time, statutory price controls were retained.

The final form of the Social Contract did not afford strong reason to suppose that it would provide a reliable bulwark against inflation without further development. But the priority given to its construction to date and the government's insistence on maintaining the rigour of Stage III of the inherited incomes policy gave some promise that this further development might in fact take place.

The theme of the Social Contract underlay the budgetary policies of the period. Whilst the first (March) Budget provided promises of a wealth tax and capital transfer tax to come it also provided immediately for food subsidies to be increased; in July's Budget VAT rates were cut, food subsidy expenditure was increased further and the regional employment premium was doubled. There was no suggestion at this time regarding to what extent public expenditure programmes would be a necessary part of the adjustment process; indeed in the March Budget, which was thought to be more or less neutral, the Treasury forecast a significant fall in the PSBR from the 1973/74 level without any expenditure cuts. Finally, in October, the Chancellor clarified to the International Monetary Fund meetings his view that an extension of the oil surplus-recycling facility was needed to protect activity levels.

The outlines of a strategy for dealing with the crisis thus seemed to emerge by this time as the following: the inflation threat would be contained by a combination of statutory price control and voluntary wage restraint;

the deflation threat would be averted by a combination of borrowing to finance the balance of payments deficit and encouragement for other countries to do the same; at home, deflationary demand management actions could be averted. The package as a whole embodied a high level of risk. It was uncertain what other countries would do, or to what extent the foreign exchange markets would finance a UK balance of payments deficit; it was certainly not clear that wage bargaining in Britain would in the event conform to the needs of the time. An avowedly deflationary policy, on the other hand, would put in jeopardy the possible development of the Social Contract. It might be said that high-risk though the strategy was, there was in fact no viable alternative available to the government. It may be that the realisation of this on the part of senior policy makers and the accompanying realisation that the key to success lay in the willingness of the unions to develop the Social Contract account for what it is easy to mistake from the description of events attributed to Donoughue in Whitehead (1985)[5] as unreasonable insouciance. After all, the evidence does confirm, on the contrary, that there was a great deal of negotiation over the Social Contract and that ministers attached high importance to the success of these endeavours.[6] The deliberate construction of budgetary policy to promote the Social Contract provided another important example of the new approach.

The General Election was called for 10 October, and a Labour government was re-elected, this time with an overall majority, though only of 3.

5.2 *Deflation and the £6 pay limit*

The need for measures to restrain the rate of inflation had become increasingly clear. Even before the October election the damaging effect of inflation on corporate profitability and liquidity had manifested itself; the pace of price increases exposed companies to substantial tax liabilities on their nominal gains from holding stocks. This particular consequence of inflation was dealt with in the Chancellor's November budget when tax relief for stock appreciation gains was brought in. But inflation itself continued to gather pace. The annual rate of wage increase, which had been 13½% in the first quarter of the year, had risen to over 18% by the third. In its November 1974 *Review* the National Institute of Economic and Social Research forecast that the annual rate of wage inflation would rise to 20% in 1975, which proved in the event to be a sizeable underestimate (cf. Fig. 1.1). Early in the new year in fact, the National Union of Mineworkers (NUM) received a much publicised increase of 35%. Speeches vainly urging a measure of wage restraint appeared from Jack Jones as early as October, and later from Len Murray and Denis Healey.

These developments threatened a balance of payments crisis and occasioned Denis Healey's first deflationary budget in April 1975, when income tax was raised and a higher rate of VAT introduced and cuts were

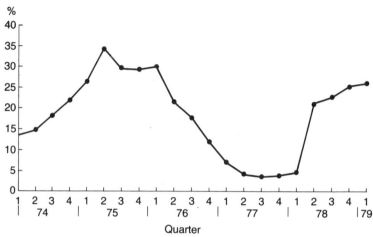

Fig. 1.1

announced in public expenditure and in food subsidies. To emphasise the new direction, the Chancellor shortly afterwards took the opportunity to mention that further deflationary adjustments might be called for.

The foreign exchange rate began to slide in May, culminating in a sharp decline at the end of June in spite of Bank of England intervention. The correction of this crisis came in the form of a speech from Denis Healey on 1 July which, first and foremost, promised a commitment to the restraint of wages. The precise form of this commitment was to be announced later. The Cabinet had already decided, earlier in June, to introduce a pay policy of some kind and set about considering three forms of policy – a statutory policy and two types of voluntary agreement (Donoughue, 1987). Union leaders became aware that a statutory policy was one of the options under consideration.

One of the alternatives considered by Cabinet was a proposal for a flat-rate increase. Such a proposal could capitalise upon the suggestion of such a policy already put into the public arena by Jack Jones in May, and in commanding his support also obtained the assent of Hugh Scanlon and eventually the TUC as a whole by majority vote. The agreement was to limit annual pay increases to £6 per week. Flanking their voluntary agreement on wages, formally delivered by the TUC on 9 July, were measures of price control, the whole put forward in White Paper form on 11 July. This inaugurated the beginnings of a phase of apparently successful counter-inflation policy (cf. Figs 1.1 and 1.2).

The period from the election to the breaking of the crisis in the summer of 1975 was important also for the birth and, some would say, the strangulation of Labour's industrial policy. It is made very clear in Whitehead's account of the matter (Whitehead, 1985) that the Prime Minister's strategy

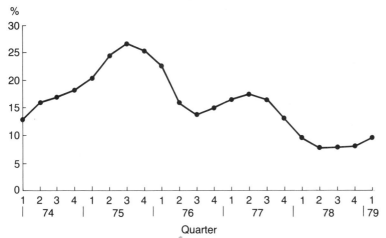

Fig. 1.2

was to remove some of the features of Labour's industrial policy inheritance that were felt to be most difficult. To this end, implementation was delayed until after the October election; a White Paper *The Regeneration of British Industry* was prepared for August in which the Prime Minister intervened strongly. Earlier plans were seen in this to have been watered down (Whitehead, 1985). Legislation was not pursued until February 1975. This provided for voluntary planning agreements and for a National Enterprise Board; by the time this was set up, cumulating industrial and financial problems meant that the NEB's funds were already pledged in large part to adjustment assistance, British Leyland being among the first beneficiaries. The government had also renegotiated the terms of the UK's membership of the EEC, and the outcome of the EEC referendum on 5 June gave Harold Wilson the opportunity to reshape his Cabinet. The resultant move of Tony Benn from Industry to Energy and his succession by Eric Varley was widely seen, both at the time and later, as a demotion for him and as the final blow to the hopes of those who saw in Industry Policy a vehicle for radical intervention in the economy.[7]

Thus the period from the October election to the end of the following June, a space of only eight months, saw a shift in macro policy, the development of a serious wage policy and the effective jettisoning of the industrial policy promoted by the Labour Party in opposition. However, the putting-in-place of an effective wages policy with the £6 pay limit was not sufficient in itself to create a viable economic strategy. Something also had to be done to correct the balance of public and private expenditure. Progress on this aspect of the strategy began immediately – indeed, in the July crisis-correction statements, Denis Healey had already revealed his intention to use the device of cash limits to control public expenditure. In November the

Chancellor confirmed that the new device of 'cash limits' would be used, and a substantial round of cuts was agreed for announcement in February 1976.

Although the conclusion of the £6 pay limit with the TUC inaugurated a new and successful phase of wage restraint, the news from the balance of payments and industrial front remained poor throughout the rest of this phase. In an endeavour to slow down the rise in unemployment the government introduced in August 1975 the first of its direct labour market measures, the temporary employment subsidy (TES). The combination of balance of payments deficit, concern for inflation and rising unemployment lent encouragement to talk both inside and outside the Cabinet of import controls, conceived of as a means of squaring the circle, or as an international bargaining counter.

5.3   *The 1976 sterling crisis and further deflation*

On 5 March 1976, there was a particularly sudden decline in sterling, promoted, so it was said, by a sale by the Bank of England on an already falling market. This rumour, not unnaturally, resulted in further downward pressure (Whitehead, 1985, pp. 182–4). The evidence now available does confirm that a decision had been taken in February that some fall in sterling would be desirable, and it does appear that there was something about the Bank's intervention which gave rise to the rumour, even if the facts were not quite as the rumour suggested.[8] Harold Wilson resigned as Prime Minister on 16 March, to be succeeded by James Callaghan. Against this background the budget of April 1976, which made a number of changes in tax allowances and expenditures conditional upon negotiation of a Stage Two of the pay policy which would limit wage rises to 3%, did not stop a further decline of the pound on the exchanges.[9] In June, a large credit was received from the Bank for International Settlements; in July, a further large cut in public spending together with the introduction of a money supply target was announced. These developments may have delayed but did not prevent a further convulsion in the foreign exchange market from occurring in September, to which the Chancellor felt obliged to respond on the 29th by announcing that the UK had applied for an IMF stand-by loan.[10] This announcement should have reassured markets that the UK would not introduce import controls and would respond by further deflationary measures; even so, sterling fell further (cf. Fig. 1.3) before the details of the agreement with the IMF were eventually announced in December. In that agreement, additional public expenditure cuts for the years 1977/78 and 1978/79 were made. That the resultant policy package contained an element of overkill, as it appeared to policy makers at the time, is suggested by the fact that less than half of the IMF loan was ever drawn whilst there was a subsequent rapid recovery of the economy and the exchange rate; within six months of receiving the loan and after a year of prolonged decline in sterling and political tension within the government and labour movement more generally, the

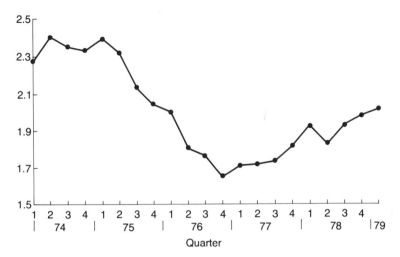

Fig. 1.3

government found itself fighting to prevent or slow down an unwelcome appreciation in the exchange rate.

The process of obtaining Cabinet approval for these cuts caused the government severe political problems. The Cabinet discussions reviewed both the 'siege economy' alternative economic strategy put forward by Tony Benn and the 'import controls as blackmail' argument put forward by Tony Crosland. Whereas Denis Healey had been able to argue for the earlier rounds of expenditure cuts by appealing to the need to 'leave room' for a turn-round in the external accounts without tax increases, the additional cuts under consideration from October onwards appeared to be demanded essentially for the sake of preserving confidence in the foreign exchange markets. For a time, Tony Crosland argued that in these circumstances the UK should blackmail the IMF into providing easy credit by threatening the use of import controls, with little or no further decline in public expenditure.[11] Whether or not such a manoeuvre could have succeeded is in the realm of political, not economic, speculation; in any case, Crosland withdrew the argument at the last minute in favour of supporting the Prime Minister. The latter, having failed to find alternative financial support from EEC quarters, had determined to satisfy the IMF and the United States, whose Secretary to the Treasury, William Simon, took a considerable interest in the correction of the British crisis. The process of negotiation with the IMF appeared to yield some concessions, though of course these may have been allowed for in advance. The final agreement, in any case, called for additional cuts of £1 billion in 1977/78 and £1·5 bn in 1978/79 together with the sale of £0·5 bn of BP shares.

By the new year of 1977 the British government possessed a tight grip on the economy, with good prospects for a real recovery based on a transformation of the external accounts. The exchange rate was set low enough to provide a spur to export activity, wage inflation was controlled by Stage Two of the pay policy, public expenditures had been cut back. However the government paid a high political price for this. It was not able to carry the labour movement at large with it in the cutting of public expenditure to the extent that it had been able to do in the formation of its wage policy (towards which, however, the TUC renewed its commitment). The political Left of the party was by this time thoroughly disillusioned with the government, the option of its Alternative Economic Strategy having been decisively rejected. Donoughue (1987, p. 100) also adds the point that 'the IMF Agreement formally entrenched monetarism in Labour's economic policy-making, although it really only made public what was already happening in Whitehall'; this is the monetarism for which Fforde (1983) has suggested the alternative label 'monetarily-constrained Keynesianism'.

5.4   *Recovery and reflation*
The securing of the IMF loan calmed the foreign exchanges and the financial markets (which now bought gilts as heavily as they had earlier tried to sell them) and was pursued by a period of falling inflation, strengthening balance of payments and economic recovery. The government did not draw more than half the loan in the first place and avoided accelerating its repayment on the grounds that this would encourage an unwanted appreciation of the exchange rate. Already, in January, the Chancellor was able to promise tax cuts and to relax monetary policy.

The Chancellor had announced in January that his tax cuts would be conditional on securing an extension of the pay policy and he was joined by the Prime Minister in February in stressing the necessity for a third year of pay restraint. Ministers spent a great deal of time in attempts to persuade the unions to agree to a formal Stage Three. In the union movement, however, the call for a return to free collective bargaining was spreading. In the March Budget the Chancellor stipulated that the tax concessions he proposed (reducing the standard rate of tax from 35% to 33%) were conditional on an extension of the pay policy. A norm of 4–5% was suggested.

As union conferences proceeded and negotiations took place it became apparent that no such norm could be maintained; instead, a figure of 10% became current. The July Budget was accordingly framed in terms of this target, the standard rate being reduced to 34%, not 33% as first promised. Through the price control system firms conceding pay rises (earnings increases) of more than 10% were to be penalised. Whilst unions did not formally concede the 10% limit, it nevertheless seemed to be informally accepted that wage restraint was still needed, and the unions did formally confirm the '12-month rule' (that wage settlements should not occur more frequently than once a year). Events were to show that in a majority of cases from August to the end of the year the 10% limit was not breached. The relaxation of the target thus seemed well judged: a threatened unhinging of the pay policy was averted.

In October, the Chancellor introduced a reflationary budget, whilst the policy of keeping the exchange rate low was abandoned as favourable sentiment led to large capital inflows which threatened to swamp the new-found money supply targets. By the year's end the fruits of recovery became apparent; unemployment started to fall, inflation was well down on the levels of the previous year, and the balance of payments position had strengthened. The favourable economic conditions of 1977 continued into 1978: the annual rate of inflation fell below 10% in February for the first time since October 1973.

5.5 *Discontent and dissolution*

These successes could not conceal the fragility of the pay policy agreement, however. The Prime Minister saw the key to sustaining the recovery with lower inflation as being the return to a more formal pay policy with a lower norm. In January 1978, apparently in the face of Treasury scepticism (Whitehead, 1985), he had spoken of 5% wage rises by 1979.[12]

However, the recovery itself, with the quickening of labour demand associated with it, was also tending to undermine the informal limit on pay increases. Neither unions nor employers favoured a toughening of pay policy. For some unions the narrowing of skill differentials was the important issue, for others simply the fact that real rates of pay had declined over the period of pay policy hitherto. The public-sector unions complained of the deterioration of their position *vis-à-vis* the private sector. The TUC General Council failed to agree on a formal policy; the CBI opposed sanctions on firms that broke the guidelines.

Nevertheless, the government published its plan for Stage Four in July, setting a limit of 5% on pay deals from August with sanctions on employers breaking the limit. Union opposition to the policy was repeated at the Labour Party Conference. In August, unions at Fords had put in a claim exceeding 5%; in November, after a prolonged strike, they received an award of 16·5%. The government blacklisted the company as a result. This turned out to be the test case that broke the policy. A House of Commons vote on 13 December defeated the government as Labour leftwingers joined the opposition. The sanctions were withdrawn.

Without union support for wage restraint and without effective sanctions to keep employers in line, the government had little power to influence wage settlements except in the public sector where it was the employer. So were created the conditions for the Winter of Discontent. Public-sector unions, left behind by private-sector wage claims, began to campaign for higher wages. Although the government attempted to retrieve its policy by agreeing in January 1979 a package of concessionary adjustments and bought off a number of threatened strikes in both private and public sectors it nevertheless incurred a damaging series of strikes including those of hospital workers and council manual workers.

It is widely agreed that the Winter of Discontent cost the government valuable votes in the election in May in which it was defeated.

6   The structure of the book

The preceding narrative is designed to provide a basic chronological account of the period as a background to the more analytical work that follows; its emphasis on incomes policy and macroeconomic issues reflects the headline concerns of the times. These questions are examined in greater depth in the next five chapters. Chris Allsopp (Chapter 2) looks at the 'high-level' issues of the design and performance of macro policy, while David Cobham (Chapter 3) focuses on monetary policy and Paul Ormerod (Chapter 4) on incomes policy. Peter Jackson (Chapter 5) analyses the government's record on public expenditure. Michael Artis and Robin Bladen-Hovell (Chapter 6) provide a macroeconometric model-based evaluation of the government's policies.

The international aspects of policy are examined in more detail by George Zis (Chapter 7), who focuses on the issue of the sterling balances and on the government's decision not to join the exchange rate mechanism of the European Monetary System, and Andrew Scott (Chapter 8), who reviews the government's overall record in relation to the European Community.

On the supply side, Robert Millward (Chapter 9) looks at the performance of the nationalised industries over the period and at the government's contribution to it. Malcolm Sawyer (Chapter 10) discusses the government's industrial policy, from the roles played by the National Enterprise Board, the sector working parties and selective assistance, to the three major nationalisations undertaken. He then discusses (in Chapter 11) the government's prices policies, in their earlier counter-inflationary phase and their later 'efficiency audit' phase.

Alex Bowen (Chapter 12) examines the various labour market policies introduced at different times, including policies on training and equal opportunities as well as those designed to generate or protect employment. William Brown (Chapter 13) discusses the industrial relations record, from the government's legislative measures through its own behaviour as employer to its actions with respect to the political context of industrial relations. Alan Gillie (Chapter 14) investigates policies on redistribution, through both cash benefits and taxation. John Bowers (Chapter 15) looks at the rise and fall of regional policy and evaluates its success.

In Chapter 16 the editors attempt to provide an overall appraisal of the period. The volume concludes with two appendices, a calendar of events prepared by Mark Wickham-Jones and a selection of basic statistics.

Notes

1 The authors are greatly indebted to Mark Wickham-Jones, now Lecturer in Politics at the University of Bristol, who not only assembled the Calendar but also provided us with comprehensive digests of the leading political accounts of the period.

2 Mrs Castle recounts the proceedings of a meeting of the TUC–Labour Party Liaison Committee on 4 January 1974 in which Len Murray (then General Secretary of the TUC) bluntly stated the opposition of the TUC to any commitment on incomes policy. Harold Wilson is reported to have settled for less: 'What we need is more the creation of a mood than a compact' (Castle, 1980, p. 20). It was the most he could hope to obtain at the time.

3 See Butler and Kavanagh (1975, p. 125) who noted of Wilson's campaign speeches that 'he mentioned "Socialism" only twice and rarely referred to the wealth tax and public ownership'.

4 Donoughue (1987) remarks that 'Looking back what is striking about that election campaign [February 1974] is how few participants from any side fully understood the true significance of the recent energy crisis – perhaps only Edward Heath in the government and Harold Lever on the Labour side' (p. 40).

5 According to Whitehead (1985, p. 128), Donoughue remembered 'the almost complete absence of discussion of economic policy ... the Cabinet never really discussed economic policy before the October election'. He also recalled that one Treasury official claimed to be waiting for the crisis to burst before anything would be done. See also Donoughue (1987, p. 51).

6 Mrs Castle's diaries (Castle, 1980) for the period provide an eloquent testimony to this.

7 Tony Benn himself (1982, p. 29) indicts the subsequent crisis as being manipulated (or manufactured?) to complete the process. 'The economic crisis following the referendum was in my opinion masterminded to create the atmosphere in which it was possible to get agreement to a pay policy and drop industrial policy.'

8 The Bank denied that it sold on a falling market though it is true that it intervened to prevent a rise in sterling on 4 March and the market took the message (Whitehead, 1985, p. 184). Denis Healey has referred to 'this technical accident or mistake by the Bank of England' as 'responsible for the acceleration of the trend', adding 'it wasn't the whole thing' (Whitehead, *ibid.*).

9 In fact, Stage Two, timed to begin in August, comprised a 4·5% limit on pay rises combined with a minimum weekly pay increase of £2·50 and a maximum of £4·00.

10 On the previous day Callaghan had made his famous speech to the Labour Party Conference attacking conventional policies of reflation.

11 Susan Crosland quotes her husband as having suggested some cosmetic cuts and the sale of some BP shares, after which the government should call the Americans' and the IMF's bluff and say that if more were required the result would be a siege economy. 'As the IMF was even more passionately opposed to protectionism than it was attached to monetarism, this threat would be sufficient to persuade the IMF to lend the money without unacceptable conditions' (Crosland, 1982, p. 378).

12 According to Whitehead (1985) the Chancellor, too, was prepared to go for a low norm: 'we were carried away by the degree of success we'd already had' (p. 277).

References

Benn, A. (1982), *Parliament, People, and Power*, Verso, London.

Butler, D., and Kavanagh, D. (1975), *The British General Election of February 1974*, Macmillan, London.

Castle, B. (1980), *The Castle Diaries, 1974–1976*, Weidenfeld & Nicolson, London.

Crosland, S. (1982), *Tony Crosland*, Jonathan Cape, London.

Department of Industry (1974), *The Regeneration of British Industry*, Cmnd 5710.

Donoughue, B. (1987), *Prime Minister: The Conduct of Policy under Harold Wilson and James Callaghan*, Jonathan Cape, London.

Fforde, J. (1983), 'Setting monetary objectives', *Bank of England Quarterly Bulletin*, June.

Labour Party (1973), *Labour's Programme 1973*.

Whitehead, P. (1985), *Writing on the Wall*, Michael Joseph, London.

Williamson, J. (1977), 'The international monetary non-system', in M. J. Artis and A. R. Nobay (eds), *Studies in Modern Economic Analysis*, Blackwell, Oxford.

Macroeconomic policy: design and performance

1 Introduction

Many myths have grown up round the experience of the 1974–79 Labour government's period of office. Thus, in popular political discussion, it is often regarded as a failure by the Left and as a disaster by the Right. Overall performance, measured by growth and productivity, was poor with little growth in living standards. Unemployment stepped up towards the then politically unthinkable level of 5% during the recession and remained at roughly that level thereafter. In terms of the government's own objectives this was failure. One view is that this shows that stronger, more radical measures were needed. But more influential politically is the claim that policy in the 1970s was irresponsible: inflation was extraordinarily high at the beginning of the period and rising at the end. Public deficits were at record peacetime levels. And, most damaging of all, there was a spectacular run on sterling in 1976 with recourse to borrowing from the IMF and the signing of the Letter of Intent.

This view of macroeconomic irresponsibility contrasts with the results of many professional analyses of monetary and fiscal policy over the period. To start with, there is a factor of mitigation: the legacy of the Heath government's dash for growth combined with the first oil crisis meant that the starting point was one of extraordinary difficulty. Perhaps policy needed to be short term and reactive in a situation of crisis management. Second, there is a question about what macroeconomic policy, however well designed, can be expected to achieve. A naive answer from the 1960s might have been 'almost everything'. From the standpoint of the early 1990s more modesty is appropriate. Perhaps macroeconomic policy is blamed for more deeply rooted failures – of supply and competitiveness – which originated elsewhere, and which are discussed in other chapters of this book.

But if this more favourable view about what policy was and could have been is taken, there remains an extremely difficult puzzle. What was it that accounted for the run on sterling in 1976? Even with hindsight it is not easy to explain. And what are the lessons for policy in the future?

There are two other questions which bear importantly on the continuing policy debate. One concerns the extent to which the policies associated with the succeeding Thatcher government actually originated earlier. Monetary targets and concern for the PSBR were in evidence from 1976 onwards (indeed, concern for the PSBR dates from the Jenkins period in the late 1960s). Another concerns the legacy of the 1974–79 government to its successors. In particular, how bad was the situation with regard to inflation?

The plan of this chapter is as follows. The next section provides a brief overview of the changing policy framework from the rather muddled crisis management of 1974 through the change in policy of 1976 and the attempts at growth in the late 1970s. The emphasis is on the perception of the policy framework: how the various aspects of policy fitted together. Section 3 looks at fiscal policy, evaluating the claim that policies towards the deficit were irresponsible. Section 4 provides a brief overview of changing attitudes towards monetary policy, a theme taken up in more detail in the next chapter. Section 5 examines the puzzling episode of 1976. Section 6 considers the similarities and differences between the strategy followed after 1976 and the subsequent MTFS. Section 7 considers the legacy. Section 8 presents some conclusions.

2   The changing policy framework

The context in which the Labour government came into power has been described in Chapter 1. With a hung parliament and the need to call a further election (which took place in the autumn) they faced not only the consequences of the miners' strike and the three-day week, but also the effects of the Heath–Barber boom (including the monetary overhang from Competition and Credit Control and the secondary banking crisis) as well as the international oil crisis. The major price hike, quadrupling the price of oil, occurred on 23 December 1973 and was starting to feed through as the Labour government was elected. The threshold system of compensation for inflation of Stage III of Heath's pay policy was in operation, and was not removed until the autumn of 1974.

The problems posed by the oil price rise *per se* were similar to those faced by other developed oil-importing countries. There was effectively no oil production in 1973, though the major discoveries had been made and the rise in production from about 1976 onwards could be foreseen. The mechanical impact of the oil price rise on the balance of payments and on the price level, at about 3% of GDP, was of similar magnitude to that in other European countries and in Japan. The difficulties posed came on top of demand and commodity price inflation and serious problems of wage push and industrial unrest.

The Labour government's position on international issues was to favour co-operative, offsetting, action to lessen the risk of serious world recession, and to promote official intervention in the recycling process. These attitudes affected domestic policy responses, but carried clear risks if other countries saw things differently or failed to co-operate. It was simply not possible for a country such as the UK to remain out of line and to grow whilst other countries went into recession (Healey, 1989).

This is one of the reasons why the initial strategy in 1974 appeared muddled and sometimes contradictory. But domestic policy also seemed to lack a clear basis. In public pronouncements the need was seen for some deflation – to offset excess demand – but beyond that it was maintained that the 'trade-off' was very unfavourable and that a strategy of deflation and rising unemployment would be costly if not actually counterproductive. The initial budget was slightly contractionary in terms of the conventional budget arithmetic. This policy was effectively reversed by budgetary help to the corporate sector in late 1974, as pressure on company finances built up and recession took hold.

A novel feature of the oil impact was the imposed and effectively unavoidable swing in the current account of the balance of payments. Clearly this called for restraint internationally. As far as domestic policy is concerned, a simple analysis of the flow of funds or sectoral balances – Table 2.1 – brings out the tautological truth that the impact had to fall on some domestic sector. With households protected by thresholds (and tending to save more as a response to inflation and uncertainty) and the government initially not prepared to raise its *ex ante* deficit the impact was bound to fall on the company sector, which swung predictably to large deficit. Pressure on the company sector led, in the UK as in many other countries, to destocking and labour shedding in late 1974 (and, internationally, to the onset of world recession). In a mechanical sense, the pressure was relieved by 1975 as corporations went back to small surplus and the public deficit rose. This involved specific budgetary help to the corporate sector as well as the operation of the automatic stabilisers which swelled the deficit as recession intensified. The budget deficit (General Government) rose in 1975 and 1976 to about 5% of GDP, a figure comparable with that experienced by most other major OECD countries. (The Public Sector deficit rose further as nationalised industries moved into deficit and the PSBR rose even more.)

The rise in inflation was substantially worse in the UK than in most other countries. One of the main reasons for this was the operation of the threshold payments. In the first half of 1974, forecasting inflation was effectively a matter of predicting how many thresholds would be triggered in a given time period. Wage inflation peaked at over 30% per annum. The maintenance of these agreements – whatever the political pressures – was an economic disaster.

From 1975, the Labour government's strategy relied heavily on the Social Contract – a non-statutory incomes policy – and its successors. A particularly simple form was adopted initially which had the feature of fixed rises

Table 2.1 *Sectoral balances: 1973–80 (% GDP)*

	Public[a]	Private[a]			Overseas[a b]	Memorandum items	
		Total	Persons	Industrial & commercial companies		Net trade in oil	PSBR
1973	−3·8	3·2	2·9	0·3	1·5	−1·7	5·6
1974	−5·7	0·4	4·0	−3·1	4·0	−4·7	7·7
1975	−7·2	4·6	4·8	–	1·5	−3·5	9·6
1976	−6·7	3·5	4·1	−0·5	0·7	3·4	7·1
1977	−4·2	4·1	3·4	0·4	0·1	−2·3	3·8
1978	−5·0	5·2	4·6	0·7	−0·1	−1·4	5·0
1979	−4·4	4·1	4·8	−0·8	0·4	−0·6	6·5
1980	−4·7	5·9	6·5	−0·1	−1·3	–	5·1

Notes:
[a] Figures do not add to zero due to residual error in National Accounts.
[b] Apart from sign, equals Current Account deficit plus net capital transfers.
Sources: Economic Trends; Net Trade in Oil from Allsopp and Rhys (1989).

for most workers and hence implied a progressive narrowing of differentials – one of the reasons for later breakdown. This policy, combined with a tighter demand management policy and a reduced commitment to a rapid return to full employment, was apparently successful: wage inflation tumbled down to reach about 8% in 1977. (Average earnings, 3rd quarter 1977 on a year earlier: wage rates declined even further.) Price rises fell quickly too, helped by favourable movements in world commodity prices as the rapid world upswing in 1976 petered out into 1977.

It is, of course, highly controversial as to how much this fall owed to the incomes policy as opposed to other forces, such as the increase in unemployment and its higher level, commodity price developments, and the pressure on company profits. The point that needs to be brought out here, however, is the bearing this policy choice has on the macroeconomic framework. With the main thrust of counter-inflation policy centred on a form of incomes policy, the role of macroeconomic policy is to be consistent with the other aspects of strategy – or, beyond that, to lean, or err, in the direction of tightness or disinflation. (This contrasts with the central role assigned to financial policy in the 1980s.) It also has the less happy implication that if incomes restraint fails, the whole strategy falls apart or at least would have to be very substantially modified. This, indeed, is what happened in 1978/79 with the 'Winter of Discontent'.

Though it is probably fair to say that the emphasis of counter-inflation policy remained on incomes policy throughout the period, it is important to stress that this involved major changes in other aspects of macroeconomic policy as well. Public expenditure needed to be reined in, in line with reduced growth prospects, and – especially difficult for a Labour government – the commitment to a rapid fall in unemployment to pre-oil-crisis levels had to be shelved, or at least postponed.

In fact, there was a major change in the framework of policy – or policy regime – half-way through the period of office, surrounding the sterling crisis of 1976 and the signing of the IMF Letter of Intent in December. Prior to that crisis, one important strand of policy appeared to be to seek a competitive pound (or at least to acquiesce in downward movements) as an aid to the longer-term health of industry. A competitive exchange rate was also seen, at least in part, as a way of managing demand (and supply) which did not require budgetary action. Indeed, a successful strategy of export-led expansion would, it was argued, reduce the need for deficit finance, swelling revenues and cutting expenditures. Unfavourable aspects of a low exchange rate, especially in setting off inflation, would be dealt with by incomes restraint.[1]

There was a period in 1976 when the broad lines of this strategy appeared to be succeeding. The world economy was expanding again: wages and prices were coming under control and industry was extremely cost-competitive. The balance of payments deficit had fallen to 0·8% of GDP. North Sea oil was expected (indeed was certain) to build up rapidly from 1977 onwards. Despite this there was a series of sterling crises through 1976 and the major run on the pound in the last quarter. This experience is further discussed below.

The Letter of Intent which accompanied the IMF loan negotiated in December spelt out targets for Public Borrowing and Domestic Credit Expansion. A monetary objective of a somewhat informal kind had already been introduced in July 1976: from 1977 onwards announced targets for M3 (later, £M3) and for the Public Sector Borrowing Requirement (PSBR) were an important part of government strategy. These IMF measures were probably mainly important as a signal of the government's intentions. They showed a willingness to divert the instruments of policy (especially public expenditure) towards external exchange rate objectives and marked the end of a period of confusion. They also marked a shift in priority towards giving precedence to counter-inflation policy. The conversion away from a 'low' exchange rate policy was not, however, initially complete. There was a spectacular turn-round in international sentiment in 1977 with strong capital inflows. Upward pressure on the exchange rate was resisted by intervention and large reductions in the interest rate. The policy was abandoned in October when the exchange rate was uncapped for fear of the monetary consequences of the inflows, including very low real interest rates.

From that period, the exchange rate was in effect left to market forces whilst attention was directed to domestic indicators of the thrust of financial policy − £M3 and the PSBR. Though on the back burner, the desire for a competitive exchange rate was still present − as a glance at the government's Green Paper on the EMS makes clear. Financial targets tended to be seen as guideposts to markets of the thrust of monetary and fiscal policy, whilst the main weight of countering inflation continued to fall on incomes policy. The political attractions of such a package deal, especially to the monetary authorities, are evident.

3 Fiscal policy

As noted, one of the outstanding characteristics of the 1970s is the high levels of the public-sector deficit, both absolutely and in relation to GDP. More than any other numbers, these high figures are responsible for the impression of macroeconomic irresponsibility that is an abiding political legacy. They are, moreover, sometimes used, rather informally, to demonstrate the purported ineffectiveness of fiscal policy: even these high deficits seemed to have little effect on activity.

Subsequent research has shown just how misleading these raw figures for the PSBR really are. There are a number of different reasons for adjusting or reinterpreting the figures: some are economic, some more crudely a matter of accounting practice. The scale of the problem, however, is indicated by just one observation. Despite apparent deficits, national debt as a proportion of GDP went on falling steadily over the period (Table 2.2), suggesting if anything, fiscal tightness rather than laxity.

Amongst the conventional reasons for adjusting the figures for the PSBR or other measures of the deficit is the normal one of the dependence of the deficit on the state of the cycle: part of the rise in the deficit, for example between 1973 and 1975, was due to the rise in unemployment and the reduction in the tax base as recession developed. Cyclically adjusted figures correct for this and are in principle a better, if crude, indicator of dis-cretionary changes in public expenditure programmes and tax schedules. The figures for the General Government deficit in Table 2.2 suggest that a substantial portion of the rise in the mid-1970s can be accounted for in this way. Indeed, the figures indicate a fiscal relaxation of no less than 6·6% of GDP between 1970 and 1973, with little change thereafter through the 1970s (apart from a tightening in 1977) until the equally large change in the opposite direction at the beginning of the 1980s (a positive swing in the structural balance between 1979 and 1982 of 6·5% of GDP).

This, however, is not the end of the story. We have already noted that the oil price impact was of the order of 3% of GDP in 1974. As far as the effect on the private sector is concerned (and it is the private sector that is supposed to react to the financial consequences) the oil price rise looks like an indirect tax rise of 3% of GDP. An offsetting public sector policy would have been to raise the deficit in the short run by this amount (preferably in a price-lowering way). Against this counterfactual, fiscal policy in 1974 was strongly contractionary. We have already noted that the impact was on companies – a major cause of the ensuing recession.[2]

A further factor, well known at the time, was the behaviour of private-sector savings and financial asset accumulation – which rose in the 1970s. The reasons for this are further discussed below. If, however, for the moment, we take this as an exogenous factor it would justify higher equilibrium public sector deficits. The rise in savings was commonly ex-plained, at the time, in terms of the erosion of wealth or financial assets (Townend, 1976) or in terms of other, less specified, results of inflation.[3]

This leads on to the most important adjustment of all. The distortions to public-sector deficit figures and to other sectoral balances due to inflation were first studied in a systematic way by Taylor and Threadgold (1979). Their calculations showed that the possible distortions due to inflation and the accounting practices of National Income statisticians were enormous: so large that they could turn the deficit figures of the mid-1970s into substan-tial surpluses. Here in essence was the resolution of the apparent paradox that high public borrowing coincided with reductions in debt ratios over time.

Much work has been done since on refining the concepts and figures for inflation adjustment. A selection of figures appear in Table 2.2. As can be

Table 2.2 *Indicators of fiscal stance (% GDP)*

	General government financial balance	Structural balance[a]	Inflation adjustment[b]		Inflation adjusted structural balance[c]			Debt/GDP ratio[d]
			I	II	III	IV	V	
1970	3·0	3·0	5·2	2·3	6·5	3·6	5·0	66·2
1971	1·5	1·6	5·5	2·0	5·4	1·6	3·3	58·3
1972	−1·2	−0·8	4·8	2·0	2·7	−0·1	1·3	55·4
1973	−2·6	−3·6	5·4	2·2	0·6	−2·6	−1·0	48·8
1974	−3·7	−3·7	11·1	3·1	5·4	−2·6	1·4	42·5
1975	−4·5	−3·2	11·2	2·9	5·3	−3·0	1·1	41·1
1976	−4·9	−3·4	5·9	3·1	0·7	−2·1	−0·7	43·5
1977	−3·1	−1·7	6·4	3·1	3·6	0·3	1·5	45·0
1978	−4·2	−3·8	4·0	3·0	−0·5	−1·5	−1·0	43·1
1979	−3·2	−3·2	7·5	3·2	3·1	−1·2	0·9	40·6
1980	−3·5	−1·1	5·7	3·6	3·2	1·1	2·1	37·2
1981	−2·8	1·8	4·8	3·8	5·8	4·8	5·3	36·5
1982	−2·1	3·3	2·6	3·5	5·2	6·1	5·6	35·7

Notes: [a] Cyclically adjusted.
[b] Alternative adjustments from Miller (1985).   I – current adjustment
                                                  II – alternative (permanent income) adjustment

[c] III is derived using current adjustment
    IV is derived using 'alternative' adjustment
    V is average adjustment, as suggested by Begg (1987).
[d] Net Monetary Liabilities of the Public Sector, at Market Values.

Source: Based on data in Miller (1985).

seen, figures for the mid-1970s vary widely – much more than for the 1980s. Though uncertainties remain, some of the issues have been clarified.

One aspect of inflation adjustment is effectively a matter of accounting error. The capital gain or loss to a sector resulting from the effect of inflation on financial assets is not computed in conventional statistics. On the other hand nominal interest flows are included as part of income. This means that even in a *fully adapted economy*, where nominal interest rates fully compensate financial asset holders for inflation, there would be a major accounting error. Personal savings would be distorted upwards, and the public-sector deficit would be overestimated by the extent of the inflation tax. This is roughly the situation in the early 1980s.

In the mid-1970s, with which we are principally concerned, the situation is not so simple. The reason is unanticipated capital losses, or, equivalently, *ex post* real interest rates which are substantially negative. In such circumstances, financial wealth holders suffer capital losses. The question at issue is how these should be treated.

The Bank of England method of inflation adjustment treats these losses as falling fully in the year in which they occur. As seen, this provides very large figures for the required adjustment (e.g. for 1975 the adjustment is 11·2% of GDP). The Miller (1985) method takes the permanent income effect of these losses – producing much smaller, but still highly significant adjustments (2·9% for 1975). Begg (1987) notes that both are extreme behavioural assumptions, and takes an average. (In the 1980s, with anticipated inflation and positive real interest rates, capital losses due to inflation are not nearly so important.)

The presence of large wealth effects in the 1970s means that the true stance of fiscal policy is very hard to assess. This is a general point since capital losses due to inflation were certainly not the only losses to take into account – viz. the enormous capital losses on the stock exchange in 1974. Nevertheless a reasonable assessment of the data hardly suggests an irresponsible fiscal policy over the period, an assessment that accords with the figures for national debt ratios, which – unlike the situation in many industrial countries – declined. Further analysis of the position of the public sector, taking into account such factors as North Sea oil and public investment (on a permanent income basis), as estimated by Begg (1987), confirms this general picture.

There is one argument, familiar in the 1980s, that needs to be addressed. This is that concentration on the real PSBR or public borrowing is quite inappropriate since it involves accommodating inflation. The argument is frequently misapplied. If the question at issue is the stance of fiscal policy, the real figures are the appropriate ones. What is true is that real PSBRs, or for that matter the real money supply or the real exchange rate, are inappropriate as targets or indicators in setting up a policy reaction function against inflationary shocks. Maintenance of a nominal public borrowing target as inflation rises implies a fall in the real PSBR, a sensible if not an optimal reaction. (By the same token, the nominal PSBR is destabilising against real shocks, a problem of the 1980s, see Allsopp (1985).) In fact, as targets were introduced in the later 1970s, they were specified in nominal terms.

It is, nevertheless, true that high nominal borrowing accommodated, at least in part, inflation at high rates. Many, with the hindsight of the 1980s, would argue that fiscal policy should have been tighter (real deficits smaller) to bring down inflation more quickly. This, however, would be to misunderstand the underlying basis of policy: the main thrust was to bring down inflation with incomes restraint, rather than demand management. In the process, the stance of fiscal policy should be restrained and helpful. The evidence suggests that, by and large, it was.

This is an important conclusion. But it leaves unanswered another of a more detailed kind. Given that there was a crisis half-way through the period of office, which led to fiscal tightening and cuts exercises to satisfy the IMF, was there a period around 1976 when fiscal policy was — in an *ex ante* sense — out of control? Was fiscal policy, in part or in whole, to blame for the crisis of 1976? Public expenditure policy is the subject of another chapter of this book. What can be said here is that the projected PSBR for 1977 — at some £10·5 billion — was considerably higher than the out-turn for 1977 due both to the cuts exercises and to a serious misforecast by the Treasury of the underlying situation (see Healey, 1989). The influence of fiscal stance in accounting for the crisis and the return in confidence is further discussed below.

4 Monetary policy

Rather similar considerations apply to monetary policy. Though the conventional wisdom of the 1980s would point to a loose monetary policy as a feature of the 1970s, the evidence is much more equivocal. Table 2.3 shows some indicators (see also Chapter 3). The outstanding feature is that £M3 rose rapidly as a proportion of nominal GDP after Competition and Credit Control (from 32% in 1971 to 40% in 1974) and then declined sharply (to 29%) by the end of the period of office. Imperfect as this indicator is, it does not suggest a particularly loose policy.[4] It is consistent with the view, however, that the monetary overhang that was a legacy of the previous government was dealt with too slowly. £M3 is now out of fashion. Figures for M1, however, do not suggest a lack of control either.

From the standpoint of the early 1990s, an emphasis on the stock of money looks strange. Central banks have moved back to admitting that the main instrument of monetary policy is short-term interest rates. From this point of view, analysis of monetary policy should focus more on what was happening over the period to the costs of borrowing and real interest rates.

Table 2.3 *Indicators of monetary stance*

	£M3/GDP (%)	M1/GDP (%)	Change in £M3 year end (%)	Interest rates Short[a]	Long[b]	Competitiveness[c]
1970	0·32	0·19	9·7	7·1	9·3	71
1971	0·32	0·19	14·2	5·6	8·9	73
1972	0·35	0·19	25·2	5·7	9·0	71
1973	0·38	0·18	27·0	9·8	10·8	63
1974	0·40	0·17	10·4	11·7	14·8	63
1975	0·35	0·15	6·7	10·4	14·4	69
1976	0·32	0·15	9·7	11·5	14·4	63
1977	0·29	0·14	10·2	7·7	12·7	62
1978	0·29	0·15	15·2	8·8	12·5	68
1979	0·28	0·15	12·9	13·6	13·0	81
1980	0·28	0·13	18·9	15·6	13·8	100
1981	0·30	0·13	13·6	13·5	14·7	100
1982	0·30	0·13	9·4	11·7	12·9	94

Notes: [a] Treasury bill average yield
[b] 20 years Gilt average yield
[c] IMF Index of Relative Unit labour costs: Index 1980 = 100.
Sources: *Economic Trends*; *Financial Statistics*.

On the face of it, interest rate policy in the mid-1970s looks extremely loose with negative *ex post* real interest rates of 10−12% in 1974/75. It is clear, however, that this was not true *ex ante* − the inflation seems to have been substantially unanticipated at that time.

Unanticipated inflation has the fiscal effects already described. Inflation losses tended to lower spending. A policy of higher interest rates would have offset these effects in some areas (the losses applying to holders of floating-rate debt would have been eliminated). Much then depends upon whether higher nominal interest rates would have been financed by additional deficits or by higher taxes or further expenditure cuts. The overall effect would also depend upon the effects of the high interest rates themselves on borrowing decisions − and hence on spending.

The observation that nominal interest rates rose, initially, much less than inflation, is thus far from decisive in showing a loose monetary stance. What it does show is the extent of disequilibrium and the general difficulty of assessing monetary stance in any unambiguous way over the earlier part of the period. In particular, monetary stance cannot be evaluated independently of fiscal policy, given the importance of debt interest flows in the UK economy at that time.

Clearly, however, the conduct of interest-rate policy changed over the period. Especially in 1974 and the first half of 1975, the authorities were inhibited by the Secondary Banking crisis. Interest rates were used to initiate the decline in sterling in 1976 and subsequently to support the rate (especially in the final quarter when MLR was raised to 15%). With the revival of confidence in 1977, upward pressure on the pound was fought with falling interest rates (MLR down to 5%) before the pound was uncapped in the autumn. From then on, policy was effectively directed towards domestic considerations, including the financial targets in operation.

The detailed conduct of monetary policy is discussed in Chapter 3. Here, three further interrelated issues of monetary policy need to be sketched. The first is the justification for monetary targets, in formal operation after 1976. The second relates to the counterpoint methodology used in the Bank of England and the interconnection or otherwise between monetary and fiscal policy. The third relates to foreign exchange intervention and, in particular, the decision to uncap the exchange rate for fear of monetary consequences in 1977.

Monetary targets may have many justifications other than those that arise conventionally from monetarist theory − which was not influential in political circles though it was amongst officials. The most important, which emerges relatively early, is the view that in the absence of an exchange-rate target, as operated under the Bretton Woods system, an alternative fulcrum or basis for financial policy is needed. A monetary target may set up a rather similar policy reaction function, and there may be expectational advantages as well − a view put forward strongly by the Bundesbank at this time. Also influential was the developing criticism of Bank of England policy that they were, in the 1960s, 'targeting' nominal interest rates. Though this is not really true (there was an exchange rate to consider) there is much advantage in targeting a nominal quantity rather than a nominal interest rate in a situation of rising and volatile inflation.

The choice of broad money, which continued into the 1980s and caused major problems, owed much to institutional procedures within the Bank. The flow of funds or credit counterpart approach only looks sensible if applied to the whole banking system, implying that the relevant aggregate is £M3. (Though targets were for money, the Bank's procedures in fact focused on credit.) Moreover, research at the time tended to show a good connection between broad money and nominal spending. Another influential argument was that control of M1 (via interest rates) would be largely cosmetic, involving switches from non-interest-bearing to interest-bearing deposits within the banking system.[5]

The counterpart approach is one of the reasons for the view that there is an intimate connection between public borrowing and money. One of the counterparts is the PSBR which enters the identity positively. It is almost irresistible to see the PSBR as causing changes in £M3 − though such an inference from an identity is unwarranted. In fact the government contribution to monetary expansion over the 1970s was small and any connection, let alone a causal relationship, between the PSBR and M3 extremely hard to detect. Broad money rose with Competition and Credit Control, well before the rise in public borrowing, and came under control in 1975 as the PSBR rose. All this is damaging to the view underlying the later Medium Term Financial Strategy (MTFS) that the main importance of public borrowing was its influence on money. It is also damaging to the cruder versions of the IMF's belief in financial programming, which were important in 1976. It is not damaging, however, to the Labour government's formulation of policy, which treated monetary and fiscal commitments as more separate, with monetary and fiscal policy having their conventional effects.

Institutional procedures for forecasting and controlling money are also important, it would appear, in accounting for the uncapping of sterling in the face of capital inflows in late 1977 after the turn-round in confidence. Rises in the exchange rate were countered by interest-rate falls and by heavy intervention. There is a conventional, but false, view that intervention necessarily raises the money supply. That it imposes control problems and leads to information difficulties is not in doubt. But in principle, inter-vention to swap foreign assets for sterling to slow or prevent a rise in the exchange rate can proceed without limit. Neither external sterling nor foreign assets are part of the relevant aggregate. The difficulty is that domestic holders of foreign assets may switch to sterling (though why this should matter is not explained), which does affect the aggregate, and that foreign holdings of sterling may affect banking behaviour and credit flows in the domestic markets. Sterilisation is as easy or difficult as the control of monetary aggregates in the first place. Thus, in principle, intervention could have proceeded further. Whether heavier intervention would have worked to provide more room for manoeuvre (especially in decoupling, to an extent, the exchange rate and domestic interest rates), and whether a lower exchange rate in 1978 and 1979 would have been desirable on wider grounds, are much more difficult questions. The fact is that when there was an apparent conflict between the desire for a competitive exchange rate and monetary rectitude, the decision was taken in favour of monetary rectitude.

5 1976 and all that

If the above arguments are accepted, even in outline, the main puzzle is, as noted, to account for the major speculative attack on sterling and economic crisis of late 1976. Inflation was apparently coming under control after the major turmoil and fears of hyper-inflation a year or so before. The balance of payments position had improved and anyone could see that it was about to improve much further with North Sea oil coming on-stream in 1977. The overall stance of fiscal and monetary policy does not appear, at least with hindsight, to have been out of line. What then accounts for the crisis, and the subsequent problem of strength?

Before indicating various hypotheses, it is necessary to pin down further what it is that appears so difficult to explain. 1976 was a crisis year for the government. Sterling really started to slide on 4 and 5 March when the Bank of England's operations were, it is usually suggested, misinterpreted by the market as implying a desire for a lower exchange rate. (At the same time the Nigerians began shifting out of sterling.) But was this, in fact, a misinterpretation? The UK had lost competitiveness in 1975 and there were certainly those within the Cabinet and in the Treasury and the Bank of England who favoured a 'low' exchange rate policy. With pay-restraint holding, it seemed that a real adjustment could be made. The slide, however, appears to have gone further than intended – reaching a 15% depreciation at the beginning of June. The authorities intervened heavily, especially in March, to slow the fall. In June, a support operation with foreign central banks (to a limit of $5·3 billion) was announced, and was used to drive the rate up to about $1·80 by the beginning of July. Since this facility was limited to six months, later recourse to the IMF became more or less inevitable.

Concern over sterling interacted with domestic uncertainties over policy. The Public Expenditure White Paper of February announced the intention of keeping the volume of spending roughly flat between 1976 and 1980, with cuts of £1 billion for 1977/78 and £2·4 billion for 1978/79 as compared with previous plans. In March, the government was defeated in the debate on the White Paper, but won the confidence motion the following day. Wilson announced his resignation on 16 March; Callaghan became Prime Minister on 5 April. In the Budget of 6 April, Healey announced tax cuts conditional on acceptance of a new pay norm of 3%; cash limits on public spending were strengthened. Concern over public expenditure continued, however, and a further 'cuts exercise' was announced on 22 July of an additional £1 billion (compared with previous plans), together with a rise in National Insurance contributions to start the following April (expected to raise a further £1 billion). These measures were, after bitter fights, ratified in August. A new phase of pay policy was also agreed.

With hindsight, despite the political turmoil, this period, up to the summer of 1976, does not seem to raise major difficulties of interpretation. The exchange rate was regarded as too high in 1975: there was, it seems, a strategy of depreciation, though it is not clear what degree of devaluation was contemplated, or even whether it was formalised. The emphasis of policy was still on pay restraint. Most importantly, the period is marked by politically damaging but economically rather successful attempts to rein in public expenditure and to lower public borrowing. By August, it can be argued, policies were in place which had a degree of coherence.[6]

Despite this, sterling weakness re-emerged in the autumn. Minimum Lending rate was raised to 13% in September and 15% on 7 October. At its lowest point, the pound fell below $1·60 (briefly touching $1·555). The application to the IMF was announced at more or less the last possible moment on 29 September and the delegation arrived on 2 November. Further public-spending cuts were demanded and eventually conceded, along with a target for Domestic Credit Expansion, in the Letter of Intent which accompanied the granting of the standby credit of £2·3 billion.

Given what had already happened up to the summer, and given the problem of sterling strength which emerged in 1977, this politically damaging episode remains extremely difficult to explain. All that can be done is to present some hypotheses: factors which may have been important. The lessons depend on what explanation is adopted.

The first hypothesis is that markets got the idea that a further strategy of devaluation was in train, and that the government and/or the IMF wanted a low exchange rate. An important newspaper article in October by Malcolm Crawford suggested that at least some members of the visiting IMF delegation had in mind a target for the exchange rate of about $1·50. (For a full account, see Crawford, 1983.) If this was the climate of expectation, the fall below $1·60 was hardly surprising.

There clearly was a devaluationist wing of the Cabinet. It is not clear, however, what degree of weight should be given to this strand of policy: the subsequent crisis threw disagreements over strategy into sharp relief – disagreements which, previously, were unresolved. Certainly, major politicians were not prepared for the kind of rapid and major fall that eventually occurred. But this, by itself, is not decisive. It may be that markets got the idea that a low exchange rate would be forced by IMF conditions. Another factor is that it was known that some American officials had been unhappy about the use of the June facility to support sterling: basically they favoured a cleaner float.

A second hypothesis is that policy was, or was perceived to be, in disarray. The autumn weakness started with a threatened seamen's strike, and continued with a difficult Labour Party conference (during which Healey dramatically delayed his departure to the IMF Conference). There was a perception of financial disarray, not helped by over-pessimistic Treasury forecasts for the PSBR. Economists may be sceptical about the meaning of nominal PSBR figures and about some of the purported interconnections between fiscal and monetary policy. But markets react to their own perceptions, justified or not. Nominal public borrowing was clearly a concern of the IMF at that time, as well as of the City. At a deeper level, public spending may still have appeared out of control or excessive: the impact of policy changes already made may have been underestimated. A policy muddle is not conducive to market confidence. On this view, the importance of the IMF Letter of Intent is that it changed and clarified the overall strategy towards coherence.

A third hypothesis is that the exchange-rate fall reflected the irrationality of exchange market behaviour – a speculative run, perhaps triggered by foreign attitudes to a Labour government leading to asset switches, which had little to do with domestic policy. Speculative movements could, of course, be part of most other explanations.

A fourth explanation is that the major capital movements reflected perceived political risk, and in particular the possibility of the adoption of the Alternative Economic Strategy, which might have implied restrictions, giving a strong incentive to get out of sterling in advance.

I would speculate that there is some truth in all of these. From the standpoint of the 1980s, it appears that governments need to have a coherent and credible set of policies towards the exchange rate, involving a commitment to contingent action. That was not the case in 1976. There was too much internal disagreement over strategy.

The change that occurred with the revival of confidence in 1977 was remarkable. It illustrates another difficulty – more familiar from the 1980s. Effectively policy became focused on internal conditions, including financial targets. There was still no exchange-rate strategy – though there were many pious hopes. As was found later in the 1980s, both in the UK and in the USA a concentration on domestic conditions (which is seen as ruling out contingent responses to exchange-rate movements) appears to favour runs of sentiment on the exchanges and speculation.

6   How monetarist?

It is frequently claimed that the Thatcher policies of the 1980s effectively started after the change in policy in 1976. Some of the parallels are clear. The focus on £M3 and the PSBR was carried over to the MTFS. Toleration of a rising exchange rate started in 1977. But the differences are also great.

By far the greatest difference was the emphasis on incomes restraint in a corporatist framework rather than the later emphasis on financial control at all costs. The assignment of instruments was completely different. Nevertheless, demand management policy was effectively set with reference to nominal financial magnitudes, implying a reaction function which was counter-inflationary. The corporatist experiments of Healey, bargaining tax cuts against incomes restraint also fit into this framework – though they did not appear to have much success.

The other main difference is in attitudes to fiscal and monetary policy and their interconnection. In the period of the Labour government, fiscal and monetary policy were seen as alternative ways of controlling spending – in some sort of trade-off relation. There is no hint of the assignment of fiscal policy exclusively to monetary control (with a neglect of direct effects) characteristic of the MTFS. Hindsight suggests that the underlying theory of early versions of the MTFS is the one out-of-line with reality.

Perhaps it is best to summarise this period as marking a gradual diversion of the macroeconomic instruments towards control of inflation rather than output and employment. The process was extremely painful, especially during 1976. The diversion became dramatic, however, only with the change of government in 1979. Large as this change was, it is dwarfed by the changes in attitudes to incomes policy and the supply side.

7 The legacy

One of the most controversial questions of all is the extent to which the policy adopted by the Labour government bequeathed high inflation to its successor. (We have already seen that Labour inherited considerable problems.) Like all counterfactual questions, there is no definitive answer. Some features of the situation are, however, relevant to any assessment.

At the time of the election of the Conservative government, retail price inflation was running at about 10% and wage inflation at about 12%. Incomes restraint had broken down in the Winter of Discontent. There is no doubt that the underlying rate of inflation was on the way up. But by how much?

There are several features of the incoming government's policy in the first year of office that need to be brought out. One is that at the time, the economy had become self-sufficient in oil and energy. Despite this the UK's response to the second oil crisis had marked similarities with that to the first. An important part of the explanation is that the oil price rises were allowed through to affect the non-oil private sector in just the same way as they came through to oil-importing countries. As far as the *non-oil* private sector was concerned there was, therefore, the equivalent of a large indirect tax increase (of the order of 3% of GDP) which was not offset and which raised the price level and cut incomes and spending. This often-neglected factor is one of the principal reasons for the onset of recession (which was earlier than in most other countries). In principle the public sector gained to the extent that the private sector lost − but tax revenues from oil price rises were delayed by several years, and the initial impact was not offset by government action. The price-raising effects were magnified by the ill-judged decision to lower direct taxation and to raise VAT at that time − which accounted for a further substantial rise in measured inflation.

This is not the place to judge the merits or demerits of the policies followed during 1979. What is clear, however, is that potentially avoidable price rises did feed into the labour market at that time, substantially worsening inflation in the short term. These policies had nothing to do with the legacy from previous policy. The one aspect that did was the Clegg awards, which were honoured − providing an interesting parallel between the situation facing the incoming Conservative government and the maintenance of the threshold scheme in the first months of the Labour government.

8 Conclusions

Macroeconomic strategy under the Labour government depended on incomes restraint. When this broke down, the whole basis of the strategy was threatened. Given the centrepiece, examination of the macroeconomic record suggests consistency. Macroeconomic policy *per se* was not the main problem. In particular, the record does not suggest that fiscal or monetary policy was 'irresponsible' in the mid-1970s.

Consistency was only achieved, however, at great political cost. It involved postponing the objective of lower unemployment (which at the time was thought of as almost unthinkably high) and major cuts in public expenditure. It has been argued that these adjustments had largely been made by the summer of 1976. Despite this, the focus of negotiations with the IMF was on the need for further cuts.

Thus, a major difficulty remains in interpreting the exchange market crisis of late 1976. Given the policy changes that had occurred by the summer and the improving macroeconomic climate, it is hard to explain it by appeal to the 'fundamentals'. What is true is that policy was perceived to be in disarray and there was no clear strategy. The hindsight of the 1980s suggests that these are the circumstances when speculative forces may take hold.

But there was more to it than that. There was a strong strand of policy (domestically and within the IMF) which favoured a 'low' exchange rate. A commitment to maintain the competitiveness of manufacturing was even part of the Letter of Intent. Subsequent upward pressure on sterling was fought, by intervention and interest-rate declines, through much of 1977. The decision to 'uncap' sterling at the end of October marked a further important change in the basis of economic policy.

Some elements of policy carried through to the next government, despite the apparent break and the monetarist rhetoric of the early Thatcher years. There were, of course, further large changes in the formulation of macroeconomic policy. These were, however, perhaps less far-reaching than the changes set in train in attitudes to the labour market, to industrial intervention, and to redistribution − the subject matter of other chapters in this book.

Notes

1 This type of strategy was outlined by Kaldor (1971) and a variant of it, with import controls rather than depreciation, was part of the Left's Alternative Economic Strategy.

2 In the UK, the expected longer-run impact of the oil price rise was, on a forward-looking basis, considerably smaller than on other oil-importing countries, due to anticipated oil production at costs not greatly exceeding the costs of importing oil prior to 1973 (Bank of England, 1982). Thus offsetting policies in the short run might seem particularly appropriate. A non-offsetting policy, analogously to any

rise in indirect taxes imposed on the private sector, would be expected to have both demand- and supply-side effects as well as effects on measured rates of inflation. (For a fuller analysis, see Allsopp and Rhys, 1989).

3   As in the 'Hendry type' consumption function used by the Treasury modellers (see Hendry, 1983).

4   The stance of monetary policy is notoriously hard to assess. In an equilibrium framework, such as that of the quantity theory, the rate of growth of the money supply is normally taken as the principal indicator. Disequilibrium may, however, be better indicated by rises or falls in the stock of money relative to some normal level (Allsopp and Mayes, 1985). A fall in the money supply/GDP ratio (or rise in velocity) implies, of course, that monetary growth is less than the growth of nominal GDP, suggesting support for the counter-inflation objectives of the incomes policy.

5   This argument in favour of broad money came to look a bit odd when it later turned out that broad money, much of it interest bearing, was not controllable by the available instruments of interest rates or debt management.

6   On this view, one of the hardest things to explain is intervention policy. The large use of reserves to support sterling in March seems perverse if there was a strategy of lowering the exchange rate: likewise, the use of the standby credit to strengthen sterling in June − however justified a 'bear squeeze' may have appeared − increased vulnerability later in the year.

References

Allsopp, C. J. (1985), 'Monetary and fiscal policy in the 1980s', *Oxford Review of Economic Policy*, I, no. 1.

Allsopp, C. J., and Mayes, D. (1985), 'Demand management: theory and measurement', in D. Morris (ed.), *The Economic System in the UK*, Oxford University Press, Oxford.

Allsopp, C. J., and Rhys, J. (1989), 'The macroeconomic impact of North Sea oil', in D. Helm, J. Kay and D. Thompson, *The Market for Energy*, Oxford University Press, Oxford.

Bank of England (1982), 'North Sea oil and gas: a challenge for the future', *Bank of England Quarterly Bulletin*, XXII, pp. 56−73.

Begg, D. (1987), 'Fiscal policy', in R. Dornbusch and R. Layard (eds), *The Performance of the British Economy*, Oxford University Press, Oxford.

Crawford, M. (1983), 'High-conditionality lending: the United Kingdom', in J. Williamson, *IMF Conditionality*, Institute for International Economics, Washington DC.

Healey, D. (1989), *The Time of My Life*, Michael Joseph, London.

Hendry, D. (1983), 'Econometric modelling: the consumption function in retrospect', *Scottish Journal of Political Economy*, XXX, pp. 193−220.

Kaldor, N. (1971), 'Conflicts in policy objectives', in N. Kaldor (ed.), *Conflicts in Policy Objectives*, Oxford University Press, Oxford.

Miller, M. (1985), 'Measuring the stance of fiscal policy', *Oxford Review of Economic Policy*, I, no. 1, pp. 44−57.

Taylor, C., and Threadgold, A. (1979), 'Real national savings and its sectoral composition', *Bank of England, Discussion Paper 6*, London.

Townend, J. (1976), 'The personal savings ratio', *Bank of England Quarterly Bulletin*, XVI, pp. 53−73.

3 *David Cobham*

Monetary policy

This chapter is designed to focus on matters of monetary control and policy that are, as it were, below the level of overall macroeconomic policy. It proceeds from a basic narrative of monetary policy over the period to an examination of the official view of monetary control and the effectiveness of the various methods of monetary control employed during the period. It then examines the use of monetary targets from 1976–77 onwards and looks briefly at the experience of monetary policy and control since 1979, before drawing out some conclusions.

1 A basic narrative

When the Labour government assumed office in early March 1974 monetary growth as measured by the broad aggregate M3[1] had just begun to turn down from the rates of 25% and more reached in the Heath–Barber expansion of 1972–73. That expansion had finally run into the ground in the summer of 1973, with sterling depreciating, inflation rising and output stagnating. The Heath government, reluctantly recognising the need to change course, raised interest rates sharply and called for Special Deposits in November, and then introduced the Supplementary Special Deposits Scheme (the 'corset') in its deflationary package of December 1973. The secondary banking crisis, and the 'lifeboat' arrangements by the Bank of England and the clearing banks to deal with it, began within a week of that package, providing an important argument in favour of caution and moderation rather than a drastic U-turn in monetary policy.

In his first Budget Statement the new Chancellor, Denis Healey, criticised the previous government for allowing the excessive monetary expansion of the previous year. He himself was aiming for a 'massive reduction' in the public sector borrowing requirement (PSBR) whose level had been 'an important factor' in the monetary growth of the previous year; and he hoped that the corset would 'enable us to keep the growth in money supply at a much lower rate in the next twelve months'.[2] The authorities began to make greater efforts to sell gilt-edged securities, and interest rates (see Fig. 3.1) were allowed to decline only very gradually from their November 1973 peak through 1974 and the first half of 1975; pressure on sterling in the summer of 1975 provoked a renewed rise in July and again in October, when debt sales considerations were also important.

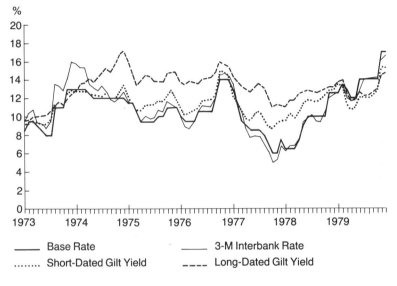

Fig. 3.1

In fact monetary growth in 1974 and in 1975 was well below the levels of the two preceding years, as can be seen from the data in Table 3.1 for £M3, the main measure of broad money used from 1977 (which is very close to M3). The table also gives data for M1, the standard measure of narrow money in this period, which grew more slowly than £M3 in 1972−73 but more quickly over the years 1974−79; and for PSL2, a wider measure including deposits in building societies that was introduced in September 1979 (and renamed M5 in 1987), whose growth was generally closer to that of M3 or £M3.

The data on the counterparts of £M3 in the table show that the PSBR rose in 1974 instead of falling and rose again in 1975, but unprecedented amounts of public sector debt (mainly gilts) were sold and the private sector's demand for bank credit declined very sharply under the influence of the recession; the large sales of foreign exchange undertaken to minimise the depreciation of sterling (which were fairly successful up to the middle of 1975 but less so thereafter) also exerted a significant contractionary effect on the growth of the money supply.

Table 3.1 *Monetary growth 1972–79*

£M3 and its counterparts (% £M3 outstanding)

	PSBR	Net sales of public sector debt to private sector (−)	Sterling lending to private and overseas sectors	DCE	External and foreign currency finance	Net non-deposit liabilities	Change in £M3	Change in M1 (%)	Change in PSL2 (%)
	(1)	(2)	(3)	(4)	(5)	(6)	(7)	(8)	(9)
1972	10·5	− 5·2	28·9	34·3	−5·7	−3·3	25·2	14·2	20·6
1973	16·9	− 9·2	24·8	32·5	−3·5	−2·0	27·0	5·3	19·7
1974	20·3	−10·1	11·9	22·1	−9·5	−2·2	10·4	11·1	9·9
1975	30·4	−16·1	−1·2	13·1	−3·8	−2·5	6·7	14·1	9·7
1976	24·7	−15·6	11·1	20·2	−7·5	−3·1	9·7	11·6	10·8
1977	14·8	−21·0	8·9	2·8	8·5	−1·1	10·2	19·5	11·6
1978	18·7	−13·5	12·9	18·1	−0·9	−2·1	15·2	16·7	15·0
1979	24·5	−21·4	16·7	19·9	−5·4	−1·6	12·9	9·3	13·6

Note: Relationship between columns: (1) + (2) + (3) = (4); (4) + (5) + (6) = (7).
Source: Economic Trends Annual Supplement, 1982 edition.

In the 1976 Budget Statement the Chancellor took credit for this monetary slowdown, with some justification. However, he also noted that 'after two years in which M3 has grown a good deal more slowly than money GDP, I would expect their respective growth rates to come more into line in the coming financial year'.[3] This statement can perhaps be interpreted as some sort of recognition of the unusual fluctuation in the velocity of circulation in the first half of the 1970s that was first discussed by Artis and Lewis (1974). Figure 3.2, which is taken from their 1981 book, shows clearly how velocity declined sharply in 1972 and 1973 but returned to its trend level by 1976. The implication is that, coming after the monetary expansion and velocity decline of 1972–73, the slower monetary growth of 1974–75 was both easier to realise and less deflationary in its impact than a similar rate of growth under more normal circumstances.

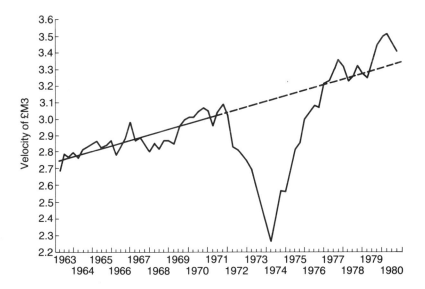

Fig. 3.2

The long-drawn-out sterling crisis of March–November 1976 involved a sharp acceleration of monetary growth in the short run, followed by an absolute contraction in the three months from mid-November to mid-February 1977. The crisis period was characterised by lower debt sales and a resurgence of bank lending to the private sector, both associated with weak confidence in sterling (the PSBR, on the other hand, was now undershooting its forecast in the wake of the introduction of cash limits). For most of the crisis period monetary policy seems to have been almost paralysed by the belief that the lack of confidence was fundamentally unjustified and ought therefore to unwind itself rapidly. Interest rates were increased in line with, rather than ahead of, market sentiment and the authorities made little direct attempt to restrain the acceleration of bank lending or to stimulate debt sales; instead they sought to calm the markets by announcements of support from other monetary authorities and of changes in future policy. In the end, however, the authorities acted more decisively, raising interest rates sharply in September and again in October, and reactivating the corset in November; at the same time they opened negotiations with the International Monetary Fund (IMF) in November which led to an agreement with the Fund in mid-December. From mid-November, and particularly from mid-December, there was a sharp turn-round in both financial market confidence and monetary growth itself: monetary growth was negative for a few months, the reserves were rapidly rebuilt and an appreciation of sterling restored by mid-January about a third of the 22% fall (in effective terms) that had occurred between the end of February and the end of October 1976.[4]

An important by-product of the sterling crisis was the adoption of monetary targets: in July 1976 the Chancellor had said, in a statement designed to improve confidence, that he expected M3 to grow by about 12% in financial year 1976/77, and this was referred to specifically as a 'target' by the Governor of the Bank of England in October 1976.[5] The IMF negotiations produced formal ceilings for domestic credit expansion (DCE) rather than M3,[6] but these were accompanied by an official 'expectation' of 9−13% growth in £M3 in 1977/78. The rapid recovery of the balance of payments and the associated decline in the IMF's influence over UK policy led to the £M3 range rapidly assuming the status of a target, indeed of the main target for monetary policy. That status was endangered for a while in the autumn of 1977, when the authorities resisted the strong speculative inflows that had developed by reducing interest rates. But in the end it became clear that they had to choose between their monetary target and their (implicit) exchange rate target, which involved the maintenance of the competitive advantage generated by the depreciation of 1976; and, apparently after no little agonising,[7] the government chose the former. By January 1978 the effective exchange rate was some 7% higher than in the first half of 1977; but it had returned to the previous level by the end of March.

By the time of the 1978 Budget it was thought that £M3 growth for 1977/78 would be towards, but within, the top of the target range. A slightly lower target range was set for 1978/79 despite the significantly lower growth of prices and money GDP forecast; fiscal policy was also eased at this time. A few months later, however, it became clear that the 1977/78 target had been overshot; the government responded by raising interest rates and reactivating the corset (previously suspended in August 1977). Bank lending to the private sector continued at a high level, but interest rates were raised in November 1978 and February 1979 in (successful) attempts to encourage debt sales, and the target was met. The effective exchange rate appreciated a little in July 1978, and again in December and in March 1979; on the day of the election (3 May 1979) it was some 10% above the level of April 1978.

2 Monetary control

From when they first began to talk in terms of monetary aggregates, the UK monetary authorities had shown a preference for broad money as the best measure of monetary growth, and a tendency to view the methods of monetary control in terms of the credit counterparts to the change in broad money.[8] This 'counterparts methodology' enabled the authorities to relate monetary growth through the counterparts to particular policy instruments: the PSBR was related to fiscal policy, debt sales to interest rates, bank lending to direct and indirect credit controls, and the external counterparts to foreign exchange market intervention. It also enabled the authorities to believe and to claim that they were acting on the money supply from the supply side rather than from the demand side. This general perspective continued to underpin monetary policy through the rest of the 1970s and much of the 1980s, reinforced by the introduction of monetary targets for M3 and later £M3. With hindsight it is open to criticism, particularly for encouraging an unthinking emphasis on cutting the PSBR as the way to reduce monetary growth, but its use in the 1970s was the result of a longer evolution which had an internal logic of its own.

In the 1960s the monetary authorities had relied on direct controls over bank lending as the main method of monetary control, but this was replaced in 1971 by the 'new approach' of Competition and Credit Control, according to which bank lending to the private sector should be rationed by price, rather than quantity. In the event this method of monetary control was unsuccessful, mainly because the demand for bank credit turned out to be much less interest-elastic, particularly in the short run, than expected.[9] Thus in 1972 and 1973 the UK experienced record rates of growth of broad money.

During its term of office the Labour government made use of the corset, the new method of indirect control over bank lending introduced by its predecessor in December 1973. But it also attempted to limit the PSBR for purposes of monetary control, and it used a variety of techniques to improve official control over the level of public sector debt sales.

The corset operated by requiring banks to place with the Bank of England special non-interest-bearing deposits at specified and steeply rising rates, if the growth of their interest-bearing eligible liabilities (IBELs) − essentially the variable element of the sterling resources available to the banks for on-lending − exceeded a norm predetermined by the authorities. Thus the corset worked by raising the marginal cost of deposits to the banks; it was intended to discourage the practice of liability management that had developed rapidly (along with the parallel money markets) since 1971, according to which banks bid for deposits to fund the lending they wish to make, rather than making loans in line with the deposits they find at their disposal, as in the traditional practice of asset management. The scheme was in action from December 1973 to February 1975, from November 1976 to August 1977, and from June 1978 to June 1980.[10]

The evaluation of economic policy measures always comes up against the problem of specifying the appropriate counterfactual. In the case of the corset there are at least four particular difficulties involved (Bank of England, 1982). First, in each of the three episodes in which it was used the introduction of the corset was part of a wider package, and the effects of the corset cannot easily be distinguished from those of other elements of the packages. Secondly, there may have been important indirect effects from the corset on monetary growth: for example, the effect of its announcement on the state of confidence in financial markets and on interest rates may have stimulated sales of gilt-edged securities. Thirdly, the corset may have provoked an artificially high growth of IBELs during 'policy-off' periods, as the banks took action to secure advantageous positions for themselves in the event of its being reactivated. Fourthly, it is now widely agreed that at least some part of the impact of the corset was cosmetic, in the sense that the recorded monetary aggregates may have been affected without underlying monetary growth being affected to the same degree. In other words the corset may have stimulated disintermediation, that is, the re-routing of financial flows outside the banking system without a genuine decline in the availability of credit, notably through an increase in issues and private sector holdings of commercial bills, or through an increase in private sector deposits with and borrowing from offshore banks.

It is clear that the corset had the effect in most periods of raising bank base rates relative to wholesale money market rates, and that where supplementary special deposits (SSDs) had to be paid it raised the marginal cost of funds to the banks.[11] Moreover, despite the difficulties listed above, it seems possible to make a broad evaluation of the contribution the corset made to monetary control during the period of the Labour government.[12] As regards the first episode, it is clear that the demand for bank credit declined sharply from the end of 1973, and even more sharply in late 1974/early 1975: thus while the corset may have 'bitten' in the first few months, and while its introduction may also have had a useful announcement effect, it was not a major influence on the course of monetary growth after that. In the second episode the corset was activated right towards the end of the 1976 sterling crisis. Again it may have contributed to the decline in bank lending to the private sector, and via the announcement effect to the increase in public sector debt sales, in the first few months. But it is clear that the surge in bank lending during 1976 was closely associated with the sterling crisis and the corset was by no means the only measure that led to the unwinding and reversal of that crisis.

In both of these episodes the amount of SSDs actually required under the scheme was very small, and the amount of measurable disintermediation – the 'bill leak', that is the increase in the amount of bills held in the private sector – was also small. The same cannot be said, however, for that part of the third episode of the corset which occurred during the Labour government's period in office. It is true that from when SSDs were first payable, in November 1978, to May 1979 few banks had to pay them; whereas from June 1979, and particularly from January 1980, a large number of banks came to be paying SSDs, many of them in 1980 in the second and third tranches where the rate of SSDs was much higher. However, the amount of bills held outside the banking system rose from £232 million at the end of June 1978 to £1082m. at the end of June 1979, and to a peak of £2664m. in mid-June 1980; it then declined rapidly after the corset was abolished, stabilising at around £400–500m. in 1981.[13] The key difference between the episodes was that during the third the demand for bank credit was high and rising; faced with pressure of that sort the corset seems to have been relatively ineffective.

This suggests that in the first two episodes the corset did not make a major contribution to restraining monetary growth, and did not provoke much disintermediation either. During the third episode, however, including the earlier part of the episode during the Labour government's term of office, there was significant and growing disintermediation via the bill leak (together with some effect, perhaps, in the intended direction on bank lending); after the abolition of exchange controls in the summer and autumn of 1979 disintermediation increased and the (non-cosmetic) effectiveness of the corset probably diminished.[14] In more general terms and with hindsight, however, it can be argued for the period as a whole that the existence of the corset, even though it was not always in operation, served to restrain the expansionary ambitions of the banks, which continued to play only a small role in the mortgage market and did little to respond to the competitive threat posed by the building societies.[15]

From the beginning of his term as Chancellor, Healey had sought to limit the PSBR partly for the purposes of monetary control. This idea became a more accepted part of both public debate and government thinking as time went on; and a limit on the PSBR was an important element in the agreement reached with the IMF in December 1976.

Table 3.2 gives the forecasts, out-turns and intra-year fiscal policy changes for the five financial years of the Labour governments. In 1974/75 the Chancellor had hoped to reduce the PSBR well below the £4·4bn of the previous year, but even after allowing for mid-year fiscal policy changes it overshot by a wide margin both the forecast and the previous year's figure. The main reason for this overshoot seems to have been the higher-than-expected inflation and the very large relative price effect; other factors included the recent reorganisation of health, local and water authorities and

Table 3.2 *PSBR forecasts and out-turns, 1974/75 to 1978/79 (£m)*

	1974/75	1975/76	1976/77	1977/78	1978/79
Budget forecast	2733	9055	11962	8471	8537
Effect of intra-year fiscal policy changes	+1130	–	–50	–1229	+13
Out-turn	7999	10482	8520	5594	9198
Divergence of out-turn from adjusted forecast	+4136	+1527	–3392	–4106	+648
(Divergence as % of GDP at current market prices)	(+4·6)	(+1·4)	(–2·6)	(–2·7)	(+0·4)

Sources: Cobham (1982b), *Economic Trends Annual Supplement*, 1989 edition.

the government's attempts to hold down by subsidies the prices of certain foods, some nationalised industry products, and public sector rents.[16] The following year there was a further, though smaller, overshoot on a much higher forecast of the PSBR; again the evidence suggests that higher-than-expected inflation was the main factor responsible.

In the next two years the PSBR experienced major shortfalls. In 1976/77 the shortfall seems to have been due mainly to precautionary underspending induced by the new system of cash limits; at the same time the public corporations made larger-than-expected surpluses, and the relative price effect was negative, mainly, perhaps, because of the incomes policy which had come into effect in August 1975. In 1977/78 GDP growth and hence tax revenue were above forecast, and expenditure undershot, again partly as the result of cash limits and a negative relative price effect. Finally, in 1978/79 the PSBR as a whole was more or less on target, although a number of individual items of expenditure or revenue were well off-target.

It is clear, then, that despite its intentions the government was unable to use control of the PSBR as a means of controlling monetary growth. At first glance it looks as though the introduction of cash limits (together, perhaps, with the use of incomes policy) brought the problem of PSBR overshoots under control, but there were two years of important undershoot first and it was only in the last year of the period that the PSBR out-turn was near the forecast. Moreover, the succeeding period witnessed a further series of overshoots and undershoots. On the other hand it can be suggested that the government's acceptance, which was at least partly deliberate, of very large PSBRs at a time of high inflation meant that some kind of implicit or unconscious inflation-adjustment of fiscal policy was made, in contrast to the conscious rejection of the inflation-adjustment argument in the 1980s.

The other main domestic counterpart of monetary growth, net sales of public-sector debt to the private sector, includes sales of a number of items such as certificates of tax deposit and Treasury bills whose contribution to the non-bank financing of the public sector is small and not susceptible to close control by the authorities. Before this period the terms on national savings debt were varied only infrequently, and it too was commonly regarded as 'not generally subject to the immediate or precise control of the monetary authorities' (Goodhart, 1973, p.252). In 1975, however, the government issued an index-linked national savings certificate for pensioners, which proved very popular, and throughout the period it made efforts to keep the terms on national savings debt more competitive; the amount of debt sold increased in each financial year from £128m. in 1974/75 to £1618m. in 1978/79.

In the gilt-edged market the authorities abandoned their traditional practice of supporting gilt-edged prices (a practice which had already been considerably diluted since the late 1960s), and showed themselves much more willing to allow sharp movements in gilts prices in order to ensure significant net sales. Their tactics, of forcing sharp rises in interest rates followed by gentle declines, came to be known as the 'Duke of York strategy'; they reflected a compromise between the 'economists' theory' and the 'cashiers' theory' of the demand for bonds.[17] The tactics 'worked' in the sense that they enabled the authorities to exercise much greater control over gilts sales, but as the financial markets came to anticipate them sales of gilts came to be heavily concentrated at the peak of the interest rate cycle. The authorities countered this tendency to some extent by the introduction of payment for gilts by instalment, so that while decisions to buy gilts might be heavily concentrated the stream of payments would be less so. At the same time the authorities took steps to offer to the market a variety of stocks, with different maturities and different coupons, in order to tap the widest possible demand.

Table 3.3 gives the forecasts made at the time of the Budget and the outturns for net sales of gilt-edged securities to the non-bank private sector. Coleby, the source of the forecast figures, comments that 'the Bank was able persistently to exceed the volume of sales which the financial forecasts had suggested would be needed. Overperformance was necessary because other elements of the projections, e.g. the fiscal deficit, departed from their projected path.'[18] No official forecast is available for 1974/75, but sales of gilts were at an unprecedented level, and it seems likely that they exceeded the authorities' original expectations in that year as well.

Overall, then, it seems clear that the authorities' techniques for selling public sector debt to the private sector were both greatly improved and reasonably successful during this period. It can be argued that the structure of sectoral balances through the period (notably the large public sector deficits) made it relatively easy to sell debt, but there is no doubt that the authorities chose to make full use of the opportunity. Over the medium term they were able effectively to control the volume of sales, and to use it as a key instrument in the control of £M3.

Table 3.3   *Net sales of gilt-edged to the non-bank private sector, forecast and out-turn (£m)*

	Forecast	Out-turn
1974/75	n.a.	2290
1975/76	1350	3850
1976/77	3000	5800
1977/78	3900	4900
1978/79	5800	6200

Sources: Coleby (1983), and *Bank of England Quarterly Bulletin*, June 1979, for 1974/75 out-turn.

Finally, there were large swings in the external and foreign currency counterparts over this period, from a large negative contribution to the growth of the domestic money supply in 1974/75 and smaller negative contributions in 1975/76 and in 1976/77, to a large positive contribution in 1977/78 and a small negative contribution in 1978/79. These swings reflected first the government's decision to reduce the balance of payments deficit only gradually, then its attempt to resist the speculative inflows of 1977, and finally the moderately expansionary policies embarked on in 1978.

3   Monetary targeting

In his 1978 Mais lecture the Governor of the Bank of England stated that since 1973

emphasis has continued to be placed on controlling the growth of the monetary aggregates as a specific proximate target for policy. Only since 1976 has this taken the form of publicly declared quantitative targets. Before that it constituted an internal aim: I think it is not therefore entirely accidental that during each of the three years 1974–76 the growth of sterling M3 was about 10%, well below the rate of expansion of national income in current prices.[19]

However, the continuity of policy should not be exaggerated: the 1975 growth of £M3 (Table 3.1) was well below 10%, and in the summer of 1976 the authorities allowed monetary growth well above the quasi-target of 12% for some months without taking any action. The introduction of publicly announced targets did mark a significant turning-point in the evolution of monetary policy, and the formal targets for 1977/78 and 1978/79 deserve more detailed attention than their less formal (and, before 1976, unpublished) predecessors.

There seem to have been a number of reasons behind the decision to introduce publicly announced monetary targets. First, once the authorities had begun to focus on the growth of monetary aggregates rather than interest rates (essentially because of the difficulties in designing and operating a policy for interest rates in a period of high and variable inflation, both actual and expected), it seemed that the process of setting, and then trying to fulfil, a quantitative target would usefully concentrate their mind: in Dow's words, 'in face of an evident tendency by the Bank simply to accommodate to events, it would lead the monetary authorities to define their aim and thus have a policy' (Dow and Saville, 1988, p. v). Second, it was thought that the publication of such targets would provide the private sector with a point of stability that would enable it to make more accurate and certain forecasts of the economy. Third, they might have an independent effect on expectations of inflation and thereby lower the unemployment cost of reducing inflation. And fourth, they might improve the credibility of the authorities since they represented such a public acceptance by them of the need for discipline and constraint. More broadly the adoption of targets in the UK and in many other countries during the years 1974−76 can be regarded, in the Governor's words, as a substitute 'guarantee of stability' to that provided in earlier years by 'fixed exchange rates or Gladstonian budgetary principles'.[20]

It must be emphasised that many of the certainties on which conventional Keynesian demand-management policies in the 1950s and 1960s had been based were dissolving during this period, under the impact of events as much as of the critique provided by monetarism: the Bretton Woods system of fixed exchange rates had broken down and the long boom of the 1950s and 1960s had been replaced by stagnation and turbulence, while the dash-for-growth experience of 1972−73 had put a major question mark against conventional Keynesian policy prescriptions. Indeed the difficulties facing policy are well illustrated by the paralysis of decision making in 1976 and the lack of developed alternatives from economic advisers or politicians. Fforde (1983, p. 203) relates the decision to introduce publicly announced monetary targets precisely to the low and falling level of confidence in financial markets, and characterises the 1976−79 period in terms of the 'use of a published M3 target as an "overriding constraint" upon other aspects of policy, which then continued to be conducted broadly along Keynesian lines'. Thus the introduction of targets should be regarded as a move towards the centre of the macroeconomic spectrum rather than a radical shift towards the monetarist pole.

At a quantitative level it is often difficult to see the reasons for the precise target number or range chosen in different years, since the authorities have rarely given any indication of their thinking. However, these matters have been examined elsewhere in a study (Cobham, 1989a) which compares the target ranges with official views at the time both of the likely development of the economy and of the likely trends of monetary growth. Tables 3.4 and 3.5 present the key data for the two years 1977/78 and 1978/79 (the target

Table 3.4   *£M3 targets and economic forecasts, 1977/78 and 1978/79 (%)*

	1977/78	1978/79
Forecasts		
Real GDP	1½	3
Retail prices	11¼	7½
Money GDP (implicit)	12¾	10½
£M3 target	9–13	8–12
£M3 target midpoint less money GDP forecast	−1¾	−½
£M3 out-turn	16·0	10·5

Source (and further details): Cobham (1989a).

Table 3.5   *£M3 targets and counterpart forecasts, 1977/78 and 1978/79 (£bn)*

	1977/78	1978/79
Change in £M3:		
Target (target midpoint times previous period outstanding stock)	4·4	4·6
Out-turn	6·2	5·3
PSBR:		
Official forecast	8·5	8·5
Out-turn	5·6	9·2
Net sales of public sector debt to private sector (−):		
Estimated forecast[a]	−5·5	−7·0
Out-turn	−6·7	−8·5
Sterling lending to private sector:		
Estimated forecast[a]	3·0	4·0
Out-turn	3·7	6·3
External and foreign currency counterparts:		
Estimated forecast[a]	−0·5	0
Out-turn	+4·0	−0·6
Net non-deposit liabilities:		
Estimated forecast[a]	−0·8	−0·8
Out-turn	−0·4	−1·0
Residual (target change in £M3 less sum of counterpart forecasts)	−0·3	−0·1

Note: [a] These figures are estimates of the likely forecasts made (but not published) by the authorities.
Source (and further details): Cobham (1989a).

for 1976/77 was more ad hoc and less formal, and it does not seem appropriate to attempt to evaluate it in the same way). The figures in Table 3.4 for the target growth of £M3 minus the (implicit) forecast for money GDP can be interpreted (with the sign reversed) as the growth in velocity which would occur if the forecasts were fulfilled and £M3 grew at the midpoint of the target range: during this period it is thought that the authorities expected a trend growth of velocity of about 2% a year, so that the 1977/78 target 'makes sense' while that for 1978/79 is, if anything, a little generous.[21] In Table 3.5 the residual indicates the difference between the implied target change in £M3 and the sum of the (separately derived) counterpart forecasts – the latter consisting of the official forecasts for the PSBR and estimates of the unpublished forecasts for the other counterparts. The small size of the residual in both cases indicates that the target was consistent with the monetary growth the authorities believed was likely to occur. Thus the quantitative targets for these years seem to have been set on a realistic basis (in contrast to some of the targets in the 1980s).

The 1977/78 target was overshot by some 3%, essentially because the authorities did not act decisively enough after they had opted for the monetary target over their implicit exchange rate target in the autumn of 1977. The 1978/79 target was met, with higher-than-expected bank lending being offset by higher debt sales. Whether the targets fulfilled any of the objectives outlined above is another matter. It is obviously difficult to identify any effects either on the accuracy and certainty of private sector economic forecasts or on expectations of inflation. On the other hand it seems likely that the existence of publicly announced targets encouraged a more prompt and vigorous response by the monetary authorities to any signs of monetary growth diverging from the desired course; and that without them the financial markets would have reacted more violently to some developments such as those on the industrial front in the winter of 1978–79.

4   Experience since 1979

The decade following the Labour government witnessed a large number of changes in monetary policy. Monetary targets were elevated to the status of the primary instrument of macro policy with the introduction of the Medium Term Financial Strategy (MTFS) in the 1980 Budget. This involved the announcement of monetary targets for several years in advance, together with projections for the PSBR that entailed a gradual decline in tandem with the declining target ranges for £M3. Thus the MTFS embodied a stronger, and more controversial, subordination of fiscal to monetary policy than that which existed under the Labour government, together with much larger public sector surpluses (adjusted for inflation and the cycle).[22]

The corset was abolished in June 1980 (it had already been rendered impotent by the abolition of exchange controls in 1979, which made offshore evasion and disintermediation cheap and simple). Between October 1980 and August 1981 there was several changes to the authorities' operating techniques in the money market, and in August 1981 the 12½% reserve assets ratio for banks was abolished. The continuing evolution of techniques for selling public sector debt included the introduction of index-linked gilts in 1981.

The rationale for medium-term (several-year) targets is presumably the argument that they should provide the same benefits as one-year targets but in larger measure. At the same time, of course, medium-term targets carry a greater disadvantage in so far as they reduce the flexibility with which the authorities can respond to unforeseen events. As it turned out, monetary targeting in this period experienced major problems in the form of overshoots of the £M3 and PSBR targets. Eventually, despite repeated modifications of the MTFS until it had become a shadow of its former self, targets for broad money were abandoned entirely in 1987, leaving only the fig-leaf of a target for M0. Some of these difficulties were without doubt caused by unanticipated financial innovation, and the latter was used as the excuse for the abandonment of targeting. But the government had contributed to the failure of targeting itself, by setting quantitative targets in a number of years which were inconsistent with its own forecasts for the development of the economy (and its expectations about velocity) and/or with its own expectations about the counterparts of monetary growth (Cobham 1989a, 1989b). At the same time the authorities found themselves without effective means of controlling monetary growth, particularly after the abandonment in 1985 of the practice of overfunding, which had led to a marked distortion of financial flows and probably also of interest rates.

5 Conclusions

The first conclusion that emerges from the preceding analysis is that, over the medium term at least, monetary control seems to have been adequate during this period: the authorities succeeded in bringing about roughly the rate of monetary growth they had wanted. No doubt there were elements of endogeneity involved in the processes which determined monetary growth, notably effects from the development of the 'real economy' on the demand for bank credit. And for much of 1976 in particular it is clear that the authorities had lost (short-term) control, and could not decide how to deal with the continuing crisis. Nevertheless monetary growth over the medium term was consistently around the levels intended, and no runaway explosion such as that of 1972–73 was experienced.

Secondly, this relative success in monetary control occurred despite the enormous and repeated difficulties in controlling and forecasting the PSBR, largely because the successful evolution of techniques for selling debt gave the authorities far more control over debt sales than they had had before.

It also owed little to the corset, which was becoming less effective even before the abolition of exchange controls in 1979 and would probably have had to be restructured or phased out before long anyway. It is also worth noting that the government resisted any temptation to reintroduce direct credit controls of the kind used in the 1960s.

Thirdly, the introduction of one-year monetary targets as they were operated during this period can be defended as a sensible, pragmatic adaptation of policy to the new environment which economic policy making faced in this period. Such targets, if the authorities are expected to observe them properly, can contribute to the government's control over aggregate demand and, most importantly, over the exchange rate; and they can reduce the pressures that may be exerted on policy by the financial markets.

Finally, however, it has to be said that the introduction of targets for broad money and the associated emphasis on control of the PSBR for monetary purposes created hostages to political fortune: political debates in the years after the Labour government were littered with claims by the new government that it was simply continuing what its predecessor had done. That this was not true should be obvious from the previous section, but the problem for the Labour government and the Labour Party later in opposition was that it could not find a positive way of defending its policies: the reasons for this, however, lie well outside the scope of this chapter.

Notes

1 M3, which included demand and time bank deposits of residents, in both sterling and foreign currency, was the standard measure of broad money at this time.

2 *House of Commons Report*, vol. 871, cols 294, 284.

3 *House of Commons Report*, vol. 909, col. 237.

4 See Cobham (1982a) for a detailed discussion of monetary policy over the period, Fay and Young (1978) for a more political account, and Browning (1986, pp. 71–100, especially pp. 94–100) for an overall appraisal, in addition to Chapter 2 above.

5 *Bank of England Quarterly Bulletin*, December 1976, p. 454.

6 At the same time the definition of DCE was changed to exclude bank lending in foreign currency, and emphasis was from now on to be put on the sterling M3 measure of the money supply. Sterling M3 and M3 became, respectively, M3 and M3c in 1987, and both were abandoned in 1989, when the Abbey National Building Society was converted into a public limited company and hence into a bank, in favour of M4 and M4c.

7 See Browning (1986, pp. 104–8).

8 The preference for broad money had survived a minor flirtation with M1 during the years 1972–73, when it grew more slowly than M3. On the general perspective see, for example, Bank of England (1978), Fforde (1983) and Goodhart (1973; 1984, ch. III).

9 See, for example, Gowland (1982, especially chs 5–7), Goodhart (1984, ch. III).

10 See Bank of England (1982) for a clear account of the scheme and its operations.

11 See Spencer (1986, chs 5 and 6).

12 The following remarks draw both on contemporary official impressions as recorded in the *Bank of England Quarterly Bulletin* and on the analysis of Spencer (1986).

13 It is also worth noting that on the estimate given in Cobham (1989a) of the official Budget-time forecast, sterling lending to the private sector in 1978/79 was well above forecast despite the activation of the corset in June 1978.

14 Spencer assesses the scheme as 'particularly effective during 1979 and the first half of 1980' (1986, p. 104), because his concept of 'effects' includes cosmetic ones.

15 See Dow and Saville (1988, pp. 156–7). The banks began to compete much more vigorously with the building societies after the abolition of the corset in 1980.

16 GDP growth was less than expected, but this does not seem to have been responsible for the PSBR overshoot. The discussion of the PSBR in this and the following years is based on that in Cobham (1982b, pp. 341–61), which includes a detailed comparison of forecast and out-turn for all revenue and expenditure items, and on material in Neild and Ward (1978), Justsum and Walker (1979), Imber (1980), Bevan (1980) and Hepworth (1980).

17 See Gowland (1982, pp. 90–93, 148–52) for further discussion of this point, and Bank of England (1979) on the changes in official techniques over the period.

18 Coleby (1983, p. 211). Coleby's table excluded 1974/75 but included 1979/80, 1980/81 and 1981/82.

19 Bank of England (1978, p. 33).

20 Bank of England (1978, p. 34). See also Foot (1981) and Sumner (1980) on the general adoption of monetary targets, and Lane (1985) for a review of the academic, rather than central bank, rationale for targets.

21 On a similar basis, the 12% figure given as a target for 1976/77 can be considered as broadly consistent with the Budget forecasts of 4% growth for GDP and inflation 'under 10% by next winter' (*House of Commons Report*, vol. 909, col. 281), given an expected trend rise in velocity of about 2%.

22 See Chapter 2.

References

Artis, M. J., and Lewis, M. K. (1974), 'The demand for money: stable or unstable?', *The Banker*, CXXIV, pp. 239–47.

Artis, M. J., and Lewis, M. K. (1981), *Monetary Control in the United Kingdom*, Philip Allan, Deddington.

Bank of England (1978), 'Reflections on the conduct of monetary policy', *Bank of England Quarterly Bulletin*, XVIII, pp. 31–7.

Bank of England (1979), 'The gilt-edged market', *Bank of England Quarterly Bulletin*, XIX, pp. 137–48.

Bank of England (1982), 'The supplementary special deposits scheme', *Bank of England Quarterly Bulletin*, XXII, pp. 74–85.

Bevan, R. G. (1980), 'Cash limits', *Fiscal Studies*, I, no. 4, pp. 26–43.

Browning, P. (1986), *The Treasury and Economic Policy, 1964–1985*, Longman, London.

Cobham, D. (1982a), 'Domestic credit expansion, confidence and the foreign exchange market: sterling in 1976', *Kredit und Kapital*, XV, pp. 434–56.

Cobham, D. (1982b), 'Domestic credit expansion, the balance of payments and exchange rate, and inflation: some aspects of UK monetary policy 1963–78', Ph.D. thesis, University of Manchester.

Cobham, D. (1989a), 'UK monetary targets 1977–86: picking the numbers', in D. Cobham, R. Harrington and G. Zis (eds), *Money, Trade and Payments*, Manchester University Press.

Cobham, D. (1989b), 'Financial innovation and the abandonment of monetary targets: the UK case', in R. O'Brien and T. Datta (eds), *International Economics and Financial Markets*, Oxford University Press.

Coleby, A. L. (1983), 'The Bank's operational procedures for meeting monetary objectives', *Bank of England Quarterly Bulletin*, XXIII, pp. 209–15.

Dow, J. C. R., and Saville, I. D. (1988), *A Critique of Monetary Policy: Theory and British Experience*, Oxford University Press, Oxford.

Fay, S. and Young, H. (1978), 'The day the £ nearly died', *Sunday Times*, 14, 21 and 28 May.

Fforde, J. S. (1983), 'Setting monetary objectives', *Bank of England Quarterly Bulletin*, XXIII, pp. 200–208.

Foot, M. D. K. W. (1981), 'Monetary targets: their nature and record in the major economies', in B. Griffiths and G. Wood (eds), *Monetary Targets*, Macmillan, London.

Goodhart, C., (1973), 'Analysis of the determination of the stock of money', in J. M. Parkin and A. R. Nobay (eds), *Essays in Modern Economics*, Longman, London.

Goodhart, C. (1984), *Monetary Theory and Practice*, Macmillan, London.

Gowland, D. (1982), *Controlling the Money Supply*, Croom Helm, London.

Hepworth, N. P. (1980), 'Local authority expenditure', *Three Banks Review*, September, pp. 3–24.

Imber, V. (1980), 'Public expenditure 1978–79: outturn compared with plan', Government Economic Service Working Paper no. 31.

Justsum, C. and Walker, G. (1979), 'Public expenditure 1977–78: outturn compared with plan', Government Economic Service Working Paper no. 28.

Lane, T. D. (1985), 'The rationale for money-supply targets: a survey', *Manchester School*, LIII, pp. 179–207.

Neild, R. and Ward, T. (1978), *The Measurement and Reform of Budgetary Policy*, Heinemann, London.

Spencer, P. D. (1986), *Financial Innovation, Efficiency and Disequilibrium*, Oxford University Press.

Sumner, M. T. (1980), 'The operation of monetary targets', *Carnegie-Rochester Conference on Public Policy*, XIII, pp. 91–130.

Incomes policy

1 Introduction

Incomes policies played an important role in the political economy of the 1974–79 Labour government. During the whole lifetime of the government, hardly a week went by without the media featuring a story on pay norms being agreed, pay norms being breached, disputes about wage increases, arbitration on pay increases, and so on. The reaction of politicians to this was an obligatory part of the story. The contrast with the years of the Thatcher governments could not be sharper. Under Wilson and Callaghan it was expected that politicians would be actively involved in issues connected with wages, in both the public and private sectors. Under Thatcher, far less direct intervention in pay settlements has become the accepted norm.

Of course, even since 1979 the government has of necessity been involved in decisions on pay in large parts of the public sector. Pay was also determined politically in the non-trading public sector during the 1974–79 government as well, and it is here that incomes policies had their most direct effect.

The usual perception is that incomes policies eventually effected a successful reduction of wage increases in the private sector and thus helped bring the inflationary spiral to an end. However, at crucial times when an incomes policy, or lack of one, had an apparent effect on earnings growth, the overall economic circumstances were conducive to generating the same effect. This issue is discussed below, and we argue in particular that much of the 1975–77 slow-down of earnings growth in the private sector would have happened even if incomes policies had not existed.

Incomes policies did, however, exercise important influences on aspects of the economy other than the immediate increase in nominal wages. Their impact was most clearly felt on public sector finances and on demand management, and, because these policies impacted on profits, there was also a direct impact on employment.

In many ways, a rise in unemployment was inevitable given the wage behaviour of the time. Real wages needed to fall following the oil price shock. The increase in the real price of imported raw materials meant that the warranted level of the real wage was reduced. The failure of the real wage to adjust caused a consequential reduction in the profit share, which in turn itself led to an increase in unemployment.

It is a conjecture of Malinvaud (1980) that attempts at restoring the appropriate income distribution are more successful than pure demand-management policies in the medium term for curing unemployment. Despite the fact that Malinvaud's book is a decade old, his ideas have not had a wide enough circulation in the UK. The decision to honour the threshold payments under the Heath policy in November 1973 was from this — and other — points of view a complete disaster, and was easily the single most damaging policy decision of the entire lifetime of that government. The 1975 and 1976 policies helped to create the preconditions in which the profit share could rise, and the level of unemployment fall in a potentially sustainable way in the medium term.

2 The background

It is perhaps helpful to begin with a summary of incomes policies in the period (see Table 4.1), beginning with the threshold agreements negotiated in the months before February 1974 by the Conservative government of Mr Heath.

Table 4.1 *Summary of incomes policies 1974–79*

Date	Policy	Target	Exceptions/Guides
Nov. 1973–Feb. 1974	Stage III	Larger of 7% or £2·25	Various, but principally threshold payments
July 1974–July 1975	Social Contract	Cost of living (informal)	Low-paid, women
July 1975–July 1976	Stage One	£6 per week; zero for above £8500 p.a.	
Aug. 1976–July 1977	Stage Two	5% with min. = £2·50 and max. = £4·00	
Aug. 1977–July 1978	Stage Three	10%	Productivity
Aug. 1978–Feb. 1979	Stage Four	5%	Productivity, 'special cases'

Source: Fallick and Elliott (1981).

What was in many ways the key decision of the whole 1974–79 government was taken shortly after assuming office in March 1974. This was the agreement to honour the system of threshold payments which Labour inherited from the incomes policy of the Heath administration.

By the spring of 1974, the UK was facing serious external inflationary threats. The prices of basic commodities other than oil had been rising very rapidly during 1973, both in dollar and sterling terms. Between the end of 1972 and the end of 1973, for example, the price of food exports of the primary producing countries rose by 49%, non-food agricultural products by 73%, and minerals and metals by 66%.

The inflationary consequences of the rise in the price of basic materials and fuel were exacerbated by the Heath system of thresholds. Introduced in November 1973, before the bulk of the oil price rise took place, the threshold system involved an automatic increase of 1% of the average wage (40p a week) for every 1% increase in the retail price index once it had risen 9% above its November 1973 level. In other words, the usual lag between price increases and wage increases was eliminated by the threshold agreement. The additional wage increases were in turn transmitted into further price increases. Eleven threshold payments were made before the agreements expired in November 1974, and they played a major part in the acceleration of the annual rate of increase of earnings from 12·5% in the fourth quarter of 1973 to 25·5% in the fourth quarter of 1974.

During 1974, because of the domestic political situation, the government felt obliged to pursue mildly expansionary demand policies. The March 1974 Budget was broadly neutral in its impact, and was supplemented during the year by various subsidy measures designed to help control inflation, and principally by the mini-budget of July 1974.

At the time of the initial oil price shock in 1973/74, the UK was by no means self-sufficient in oil. A redistribution of income from the UK to OPEC members was therefore required. During 1974, however, the threshold agreements prevented the real wage from falling even on a temporary basis. If the normal practice of annual wage settlements had obtained instead of the immediate indexation under the thresholds, some temporary erosion of real wages could have taken place as the increased raw material costs were passed through in the form of higher prices. Further, a more sustained fall in the real wage could have been achieved by a deflationary fiscal policy leading to higher unemployment and a reduction in wage increases.

The economic situation in 1974 can therefore be characterised as follows:

(i)   an over-ambitious level of the real wage was maintained;

(ii)   the threshold agreements allowed workers to obtain almost instant wage increases following price increases, effectively eliminating the normal annual period between the wage increase of any individual group of workers;

(iii) in the circumstances, companies passed on cost increases very rapidly.

In his taxonomic analysis of various wage–price models, Meade (1982, see especially pp. 159–81) identifies the above set of conditions as being such as, if they were satisfied absolutely, would lead the price level to explode immediately to infinity. Of course, the theoretical conditions did not exist in their purest form in practice, but when one considers that in early 1975 the National Union of Railwaymen turned down a 27·5% pay award from an arbitration tribunal on the grounds that it was wholly inadequate, it was clearly a close-run thing.

Perhaps the most important political effect in the longer run of the impact of the Heath threshold incomes policy was to help prepare the ground for the election of Mrs Thatcher in 1979. Inflation is disliked by the electorate, and the high and accelerating rates experienced during 1974–75 were a principal cause of the decline in Labour's popularity with the electorate at an early stage in the lifetime of the majority government elected in October 1974. Sustained unpopularity erodes the confidence of politicians and damages their ability to take decisive actions. So, when a dangerous challenge to the government emerged during 1978/79 with public sector pay disputes and the Winter of Discontent, the exhausted members of the government did not have the will to deal with the issue. For most of the life of the government, Labour had been unpopular electorally, beginning with the high-inflation period at the outset of the period of office.

In terms of the political economy effects of thresholds, perhaps a more subtle point emerges from the effects on public sector finances. Mainly because of high wage awards – average pay in central government increased by 40% between the second quarters of 1974 and 1975 – the public sector deficit rose to enormous levels. In the financial year 1973/74, the PSBR was well under 7% of GDP, rising to almost 10% in 1974/75 and 11% in 1975/76. Translated into 1989/90 prices, this amounts to a PSBR in the range of £40–50 billion a year. The impact on political attitudes arises from the fact that much of the deficit arose not to finance the provision of actual services, but to finance the private consumption of those employed in the public sector. The theme of the public sector being run in the interests of its producers rather than the interests of its consumers has been a strong and persistent one in Conservative arguments since Mrs Thatcher became leader of the party. The evidence of 1974–75 could only have given credibility to this view amongst the electorate.

The political symbolism and imagery provided by the 1974–75 experience was a very powerful weapon for the Conservatives. Labour was seen as the party of high inflation. And the public sector began to be regarded as being in the grip of producer interests. In these key ways, the seeds of electoral defeat were sown for Labour in 1974/75, arising from the threshold agreements in the incomes policy then in force.

In summary, the consequences of the threshold agreements were very damaging to the British economy. This judgement does not of course dismiss the political constraints under which the government was operating. The February 1974 election produced an inconclusive result, and Labour had to wait until October of that year to obtain an overall majority, albeit an extremely small one. In the circumstances, it is perfectly understandable that the government chose not to offend substantial sections of the electorate by reneging on existing agreements. Further, it is entirely plausible that in the counterfactual scenario of reneging on the thresholds, the cost would have been to bring forward the Winter of Discontent. It was certainly politically expedient to implement the threshold agreements. And it is almost certainly true that at the time, given the then entrenched position of trade unions in the political and economic process, political imagination as to what was feasible did not extend to reneging on agreements despite the *force majeure* of radically altered circumstances. Nevertheless, the economic logic of the situation facing the British economy in 1974 required real wages to fall. The thresholds secured only temporary protection from this, at the cost of both exceptionally high inflation and of future rises in unemployment.

3   Stages One and Two: the impact on inflation

Labour did succeed in reducing inflation from an annual rate of 26% in the summer of 1975 to 8% in the winter of 1978/79. Casual empiricism would suggest that this success was due to the two very tight incomes policies in force from August 1975 to July 1977. Stage One of the policy allowed a maximum increase of £6 per week, with a cut-off point at £8500 per year. Stage Two allowed increases of only 5%, tighter than Stage One, with a maximum of £4 a week.

In terms of evaluating the impact of these policies, it is important to distinguish between the private and public sectors. The definition of what constitutes the public sector has of course changed in recent years with the privatisation of trading companies in the public sector. An initial feel for the experience of wage increases in the two sectors during the 1974–79 government can, however, be obtained from Figure 4.1. This plots annual increases in average earnings per head in the private and central government sectors (the movement of local authority sector earnings is very similar to that of central government). The data are taken from the Treasury model database maintained by the Macro-Economic Modelling Bureau at the University of Warwick.

As is usual with such series, there are occasional blips in behaviour, but the pattern is clear. During the initial phase of threshold agreements, public sector earnings accelerated more rapidly than those in the private sector,

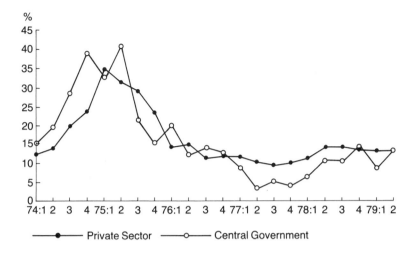

Fig. 4.1

but Stage One of the incomes policy led to a sharp slow-down in public sector pay increases, while private sector increases gradually decelerated during 1976 towards the rate of growth of public sector pay. During Stage Two (1976–77), there was a further sharp slow-down in public pay increases, not matched in the private sector, but during the last eighteen months of the government, public pay increases gradually accelerated back up to the rate prevailing in the private sector.

A powerful way of illustrating the difference in behaviour between the private and central government sectors in terms of wage increases is to examine the movement in real wages during the 1974–79 period. Both sectors were essentially affected equally by tax changes, so we consider the gap between the annual increase in money earnings and in the consumer price index (CPI). Table 4.2 sets out the average difference, in percentage points, between the increase in the CPI and the earnings of the two sectors over different time periods.

The table reinforces the impression of Figure 4.1, namely that the respective behaviour of public and private sector earnings were quite different during the 1974–79 government. The period 1974:2–1975:2 covers the period of the threshold payments and the immediate aftermath, 1975:3–1976:2 covers Stage One, 1976:3–1977:2 Stage Two, and 1977:3–1978:2 Stage Three. Real wages exploded in the public sector in the first year of the government, and then experienced three consecutive years of sharp reductions. In contrast, the fluctuations in real wages in the private sector were far less violent.

Earnings in the public sector were effectively determined politically by the incomes policies during the 1974–79 government. In any event,

Table 4.2   *Average percentage difference between annual increases in earnings and the consumer price index*

	Central government	Private sector
1974:2–1975:2	11·9	4·6
1975:3–1976:2	−3·8	−0·6
1976:3–1977:2	−5·2	−3·6
1977:3–1978:2	−5·0	−0·3
1978:3–1979:2	1·8	3·8

Source: Calculated from the Treasury model database.

an explanation in terms of economic variables alone seems infeasible. Capella and Ormerod (1982) attempted to construct an econometric wage equation for earnings in the non-trading public sector, using Treasury model data over the period 1971–80. The wage equation was an eclectic one of a form widely used in empirical work in the UK. Wage increases were related to expected inflation, unemployment, the lagged real wage, a time trend, and the proportion of earnings retained after tax and other deductions. A variety of variables was used to proxy expectations, such as a fourth-order autoregressive process on inflation, and the fitted values of the consumer price equation in the Treasury model, but the results were not sensitive to this particular choice.

There is strong evidence, therefore, that incomes policies succeeded in reducing sharply the rate of increase of wages in the public sector. Can the slow-down in private sector pay increases during Stages One and Two also be attributed to the policies? Examination of the data leads to the suspicion that the overall economic circumstances were conducive to obtaining the objective sought by the policies, irrespective of their existence.

In the year immediately prior to the introduction of Stage One in July 1975, private sector earnings increased by just over 31% (taking the second quarter of 1975 on the same period in 1974). One year later, this had fallen to 15%, and by mid-1977 to only 10%. But private sector earnings growth had already begun to slow from its 35% peak in the first quarter of 1975 before the incomes policy started. Unemployment had in fact begun to rise quickly from the beginning of 1975, and the quarterly average of 650,000 in the final quarter of 1974 had almost doubled to 1·125 million by the final quarter of 1975.

It is this rapid rate of change of unemployment which was the key determinant in slowing down wages growth in the private sector during Stage One of the incomes policies. A similar conjunction of circumstances is to be found in the 1980/81 pay round, when no incomes policy was in operation, at least as far as the private sector was concerned. Between the middle of 1979 and the middle of 1980, private sector earnings rose by some 20%, a rate which slowed to only 11% by the middle of 1981, a figure which no commentator had thought possible a year earlier. But from mid-1980 to mid-1981, unemployment rose by 1 million, an increase which constitutes further prima-facie evidence that the rate of change of unemployment can play a key role in slowing down the rate of increase of money earnings in the UK.

Capella and Ormerod (1982) also constructed a model of private sector pay increases using quarterly data from the end of 1971 to the end of 1979, a data period not too different from the lifetime of the Labour government. A typical equation that they report, which was stable when the data period was extended to the middle of 1981, is as follows:

$$
\begin{aligned}
DW = \ & \text{constant} \\
& + \underset{(4\cdot11)}{0\cdot599DPE} + \underset{(\text{imposed})}{0\cdot401DW(-1)} - \underset{(2\cdot72)}{0\cdot150DDU(-1)} + \underset{(2\cdot00)}{0\cdot273DRR} \\
& - \underset{(3\cdot80)}{0\cdot063U(-1)} + \underset{(2\cdot62)}{0\cdot329RR(-1)} - \underset{(3\cdot40)}{0\cdot375(RW)(-1)} + \underset{(1\cdot86)}{0\cdot0015T}
\end{aligned}
$$

$RSSQ = 0\cdot0066$; $R^2 = 0\cdot516$; $DW = 2\cdot57$; $LM(4) = 9\cdot30$; $PPS(4) = 2\cdot93$

The figures in brackets are t-statistics, $RSSQ$ is the residual sum of squares, LM is the Lagrange multiplier test for random residuals, and PPS is a post-sample parameter stability test with a chi-square distribution. DW is the rate of change of earnings in the private sector (all variables are in natural logs); DPE is the expected rate of price inflation; DDU is the difference in the rate of change of unemployment; DRR is the rate of change of the retentions ratio, RR. defined to be equal to $(1 - DED/WS)$ where WS is total wages and salaries and DED is total deductions from WS; RW is the real wage, and T is a time trend. The coefficient on $DW(-1)$ is imposed (a restriction not rejected by the data) to ensure that the long-run coefficent on inflationary expectations is equal to unity.

The equation has the property that a doubling of the level of unemployment eventually leads to earnings being 16·8% below what they would otherwise have been. Of course, this is the first-round effect, as it were, since lower pay increases would lead to lower price increases, and hence to reductions in inflationary expectations and to a further slowdown in earnings growth. Notice, however, that there is a particularly strong shorter-run effect of unemployment associated with the movement in the rate of change. Without placing too much emphasis on the parameters, it is clear that if an equation such as this is a reasonably realistic representation of pay behaviour in the private sector for 1974–79, the rate of increase of unemployment during 1975 would itself have been sufficient to slow down pay increases irrespective of whether an incomes policy had existed or not.

The above model thus enables a powerful explanation of wage behaviour from 1974 to 1979 to be obtained without recourse to incomes-policy dummy variables. Although their data period only covered the start of this period, Henry and Ormerod (1978) found that whilst some incomes policies in the 1960s and early 1970s had had some impact in reducing wage increases, catch-up periods followed which dissipated the gains of lower inflation. More recently, Artis and Ormerod (1990) tested explicitly for incomes-policy effects in the context of a wage equation specified in a very similar manner to the one discussed above. They could find no effect of Stage One of the policy. Wage increases were reduced by the sharp rise in unemployment. There was some evidence that Stage Two did lead to wage increases being somewhat lower than would otherwise have been the case. The most striking finding was the dramatic increase in wages attributable to the threshold agreements.

Both examination of the data and more formal econometric work suggest that the change in unemployment (with a lag) was a key determinant of the reduction in private sector pay increases during Stage One. In Stage Two, there was a further deceleration. In the year to the second quarter of 1976, private sector earnings rose by 15%, and in the year to the second quarter of 1977 by only 10%. The comparable figures for inflation were, respectively, 15·4% and 16·3%. The latter figure was something of a small blip upwards, but there was no slow-down in inflation during the whole of Stage Two. During the calendar year 1976, however, unemployment rose by around one-sixth. The calendar year is a more appropriate period for which to calculate the change in unemployment in this context, because of the lags between unemployment changes and subsequent effects on pay behaviour. It should be noted also that from the second quarter of 1975 to the second quarter of 1976, inflation did fall from 24·5% to 15·4%, but this fall was by no means as rapid as the fall from 31% to 15% in the annual rate of increase of pay in the private sector.

4   The unemployment consequences of the 1974−77 policies

As far as inflation was concerned, the implementation of the threshold agreements during 1974 was a complete disaster. In terms of the private sector level of pay settlements, Stages One and Two were largely irrelevant.

Both the threshold period and Stages One and Two, however, had the same impact on unemployment in the shorter term. They both served to increase the level of unemployment.

The effect of the threshold agreements was the more marked, compared to the combined influence of Stages One and Two. The main channel of influence on unemployment was by the supply side, and the profitability of production. As noted above, during 1974 and early 1975 the economy in practice bore a close resemblance to theoretical models in which the price level explodes to infinity. An important reason why this did not happen is that companies were either unable or unwilling to pass on cost increases into price increases with as short a lag as price increases were passed on to wage increases by the threshold agreements. Real wages rose much faster than output in consequence, and the profit share in national income fell sharply. Table 4.3 shows the profit share of non-oil industrial and commercial companies net of stock appreciation over the 1973–79 period.

Table 4.3 *Non-oil profits (net of stock appreciation) as a percentage of GDP*

1973	13·5	1977	12·0
1974	10·5	1978	12·5
1975	9·1	1979	10·6
1976	9·3		

Source: Calculated from CSO Blue Book data.

The profit share defined in this way is a more accurate measure of the profit prospects facing industrial and commercial companies than the unadjusted aggregate figure for profits. Increases in recorded profits due to stock appreciation are purely notional profits, and are unrelated to the underlying level of real profitability which affects output and employment decisions. Further, the North Sea oil sector, of growing importance over this period, is also largely irrelevant in terms of its profits to the profitability of ordinary industrial and commercial companies. It should be noted that these adjustments mean that the profit share is no longer simply equal to unity minus the share of wages in national income, and indeed there is only a relatively weak correlation between these two variables in the 1970s.

Our interest in the profit share arises from Malinvaud's theoretical work (see, for example, his 1980 book). Three types of unemployment are distinguished: first, that arising from a lack of profitability of production; second, that due to deficient aggregate demand; third, that due to the fact that the capital stock is insufficient to employ everyone who wishes to work. In practice, of course, all three types could exist at an aggregate level, with individual sectors of the economy each facing different types of unemployment. In practice, also, the three are interrelated. For example, low aggregate demand tends to depress the profit share, as companies do not have the same power to pass on cost increases as during a boom. Low profitability will affect investment plans adversely, leading to potential shortages of capital stock.

The concept of the capital stock being inadequate to sustain full employment in the UK is not one which is widely shared amongst economists, although strong non-econometric evidence in its favour comes from the fact that reported capacity utilisation rates of the CBI have shown no visible trend despite the persistence of very high levels of unemployment, particularly in the 1980s. Artis (1983) found support for the view, discussing various data from the CBI at some length.

The presumption from the facts must be that during the 1950–73 period, profits in the UK were sufficiently high not to act as a deterrent either to current production decisions or to investment decisions. The level of profits and the size of the capital stock were sufficient to sustain full employment in the UK. Unemployment in this period was essentially caused by temporary fluctuations in aggregate demand.

During the 1950–73 period, the share of profits in GDP was in the 12–16% range, and mainly above 13%. The sharp fall in 1974 was to an extremely low level. The proximate cause of this was the high wage settlements under the threshold agreements.

A well-specified relationship between unemployment, profits, capital stock deficiencies and external competitiveness was reported for the 1966–87 period by Ormerod (1988). The preferred equation in the paper was as follows:

$$U = \text{constant}$$
$$+ 0\cdot282U(-1) - 0\cdot342P(-1) + 0\cdot00156COMPET(-1)$$
$$\quad (3\cdot62) \qquad\qquad (10\cdot06) \qquad\qquad (4\cdot42)$$
$$- 0\cdot000431GAP$$
$$(5\cdot67)$$

$RSSQ = 0\cdot000139$; s.e. $= 0\cdot0029$; $\bar{R}^2 = 0\cdot995$; $DW = 2\cdot487$; $h = -1\cdot49$; $LM(3) = 5\cdot21$; $RSE3 = 0\cdot47$; $RSE4 = 5\cdot11$; $ARCH(3) = 3\cdot53$; $RESET = 0\cdot91$.

The figures in brackets are t-statistics; h is the Durbin h-statistic; $RSE3$ and $RSE4$ are tests for skewness and kurtosis, with chi-square distributions with five degrees of freedom; $ARCH$ is the test statistic for autoregressive conditional heteroscedasticity with a chi-square distribution with three degrees of freedom; $RESET$ is the Ramsey specification test for functional form, which has an F-distribution with $(2,15)$ degrees of freedom. U is the unemployment rate; P is the profit share in GDP as defined above; $COMPET$ is a measure of external competitiveness; and GAP is a measure of the discrepancy between the actual net capital stock and the trend level implied by pre-1975 data. It is worth noting that a non-nested test for model selection decisively rejected the real product wage hypothesis and accepted the profit-share one.

The equation does not rule out the existence of temporary fluctuations in unemployment due to demand deficiency. Such fluctuations influence the profit share, which in turn will affect unemployment. The economic cycle will also influence investment, and hence the discrepancy between the actual capital stock and the level required to sustain full employment. But no matter how the changes arise, the direct effect of the profit share on unemployment is strong. Companies in the UK are influenced in their short-run output and employment decisions by the level of profits, and may choose not to produce if profit levels are inadequate.

We can use the above model to calculate the subsequent effect on unemployment of the decline in the profit share in 1974. On an annual average basis, the unemployment rate rose from 2·6% in 1974 to 3·9% in 1975, and to 5·3% in 1976. The fall in the profit share which arose from wage-bargaining behaviour in 1974 was responsible for no less than one full percentage point increase in 1975, out of a total rise of 1·3 percentage points. The cumulative effect on unemployment in 1976 of the profit-share reductions in 1974 and 1975 was to increase the rate by 1·8 percentage points above what it would otherwise have been. The actual increase between 1974 and 1976 was 2·7 percentage points, so around two-thirds of the actual increase was directly due to profitability being too low.

Because of rising unemployment, wage-bargaining behaviour was much more responsible during 1975 and 1976 in the private sector, and was restrained severely in the public sector by Stages One and Two. The erosion of the profit share in 1975 was due mainly to lack of demand in the economy rather than to aggressive wage bargaining.

Stages One and Two of the incomes policies intensified the deflation by squeezing the real earnings of those employed in the non-trading public sector. At the time, just over 20% of the labour force was employed in this sector, so real wage reductions of the order of 4–5% a year obviously affected the overall level of aggregate demand. Given that income from employment is around two-thirds of the total income of the personal sector, these real wage cuts reduced real personal disposable income growth by around three-quarters of a percentage point during the years covering Stages One and Two of the policies. This was a decidedly non-trivial reinforcement of the more orthodox measures taken to curb demand in the economy in 1975 and 1976.

The reduction in overall demand via the real incomes of public sector workers was reinforced by the deflationary stance belatedly adopted in 1975 and 1976. Together, these had the short-run effect of increasing unemployment. Such an increase was essential, given wage behaviour in the private sector, in order to restore the profit share towards a level compatible with the maintenance of full employment in the longer term. Stages One and Two of the incomes policies, by cutting real wages in the public sector, helped to curb demand and to increase unemployment. This in turn restrained wage increases in the private sector, enabling the share of profits to be restored.

The damage created by the threshold agreements, however, can hardly be overstated. The massive exogenous shift away from profits to wages had severe longer-term consequences for the economy, apart from the rise in unemployment caused directly by profits being too low and thus constraining output.

Econometricians have had great difficulty in establishing strong links between profits and investment. Ormerod (1988) does report such an equation, although it does not perform better than a more orthodox accelerator model in which profit and liquidity factors are dominated by output terms. However, the feeling persists amongst economists, and certainly amongst businessmen, that high profits are conducive to investment and that low profits deter investment.

The slow-down in economic activity in the mid-1970s was obviously of itself a deterrent to investment. Although it is difficult to quantify, the exogenous shift from profits to wages caused by the threshold agreements must have contributed to the investment slump of the time. For the first time since the war, the capital stock of the country began to be inadequate to sustain full employment. Table 4.4 shows the real net capital stock of UK industrial and commercial companies, the level implied if the growth trend of the 1960s and early 1970s had continued, and the difference between them. In addition, the annual growth in net capital stock and the profit share are shown.

Table 4.4 *Real net capital stock of UK industrial and commercial companies*

	Real stock	Trend stock	Gap	Growth in stock	Profit share
1973	168·3	165·1	3·2	14·7	13·5
1974	180·5	174·6	5·9	12·2	10·5
1975	181·3	184·9	−3·4	0·7	9·1
1976	184·2	195·3	−11·1	2·9	9·3
1977	185·6	206·6	−21·0	1·4	12·0
1978	193·6	218·5	−24·8	8·0	12·5
1979	201·3	231·0	−29·7	7·7	10·6

Source: Calculated from Central Statistical Office Blue Book data.
Notes: (a) Real stock, trend stock and gap are measured in £m at 1985 prices.
         (b) The growth in stock is the percentage change in the real net stock.
         (c) Trend stock is stock on the trend over the period 1963–87.

As can be seen, a gap began to open in 1975 between the actual real net capital stock and the level required to sustain full employment. The restoration of the profit share in 1977 and 1978 appears to have encouraged faster growth in investment, but not sufficient to close the gap, or indeed to prevent it from widening. Profits needed not just to be brought back towards their average GDP share of the 1950s and 1960s, but above that in order to stimulate sufficient investment to fill the gap between the actual and required levels of the industrial capital stock. Obviously, the quality of the CSO data may have been affected in this period by premature economic obsolescence of equipment, so that the true gap is bigger than reported. Ormerod (1988) discusses this issue, and finds that the qualitative results are not affected by a range of different assumptions on this issue.

Although it would have been difficult to sustain business confidence and hence investment, what was required in 1974 and 1975 was a set of policies which would have protected the profit share at the expense of real wages. Whether such a set of policies could have been constructed is a matter for conjecture, but the actual policy stance was disastrous. By the middle of 1977 at the end of Stage Two, a certain amount of stability had been restored to the economy. Inflation, although still high, had been brought down substantially from its peak levels in 1975. The profit share had stabilised and, given the relative weakness of wage bargainers in the face of high and rising unemployment, was set to rise. But the longer-term damage caused by the threshold policy remained.

5 Stages Three and Four

From a purely economic perspective, Stages Three and Four were relatively uneventful. As noted above, by the middle of 1977 the economic situation had stabilised. The government was helped by a huge expansion of world trade of manufactures, which grew no less than 12% in volume terms in 1976 and by 17% over 1975–77. In addition, North Sea oil was beginning to come onstream in significant amounts, resulting in a move back towards a surplus on the current account balance of payments, as was in fact achieved in 1978.

Against this background, the government felt able to introduce expansionary Budgets in March and October 1977 and again in April 1978. These were partly designed to improve take-home pay through tax reductions. As well as the electoral desirability of increasing living standards as the general election approached, it was hoped that the tax cuts would help to contain demands for money wage increases. The evidence from the wage equation noted above, however, is that such tax cuts might well have had a perverse effect. The coefficients on the retentions ratio terms are 'incorrectly' signed – an increase in the tax burden leads to a reduction in the rate of increase of money wage settlements. This is a finding which researchers into econometric wage equations encounter frequently, although not all the results find their way into the literature. The sign on the coefficients could in fact be a function of the overall perception by both workers and employers of the policy regime in force. In other words, increases in tax tend to be associated with a tightening of government policy, and a reduction with a relaxation. Both employers and workers could perceive this, and adapt their behaviour accordingly to the prevailing policy regime.

Stages Three and Four themselves were relatively loose, indeed Stage

Four was so loose as to be almost non-existent. Stage Three was designed to permit pay increases of up to 10%, although during its existence the annual rate of increase of private sector earnings rose from around 10% to some 14%.

The government did hope to be able to introduce a tight Stage Four in the autumn of 1978, limiting pay increases to a maximum of 5%. This was against a background of annual increases in the retail price index of just under 8% since April 1978. In terms of the private sector, this putative policy was irrelevant. In the public sector, however, determined attempts were made to destroy the policy in the winter of 1978/79 by public sector workers. In this they were largely successful.

The main consequence of Stage Four was not purely economic, but was one of political economy. During 1978, Labour's standing in the opinion polls had recovered, and there was much speculation as to whether an election would be called in the autumn of that year. In the event, the Prime Minister decided not to dissolve Parliament. The impact on the image of the Labour Party of the public sector industrial disputes in the subsequent winter was devastating. It was such a valuable weapon to the Conservatives that not only was it a feature of the 1979 General Election campaign, it has even resurfaced following the decisions of the TUC conference on industrial law in September 1989.

6 Conclusion

The most important aspect of incomes policies in the 1974–79 government was the decision to honour the threshold agreements of the Heath incomes policy initiated in November 1973. This proved to be a very serious mistake whose economic consequences affected the government's whole period of office, and whose consequences in terms of political economy are still with us today. Given both the external inflationary pressures external to the UK and the mildly reflationary fiscal stance adopted in 1974 and early 1975, the implementation of the thresholds ensured that a very rapid acceleration of inflation would take place during that period. The wage–price relationships in the UK approximated those of a stylised model in which the price level explodes very quickly to infinity.

The reason inflation was not even more rapid was the inability or unwillingness of companies to raise prices as frequently as wages were being increased by the thresholds. An exogenous shift in income distribution took place from profits to wages, resulting in the profit share in 1974 falling to a record low. This lack of profitability caused a substantial proportion of the rise in unemployment which took place during 1975. In addition, via its adverse effect on investment, it helped to reduce the real capital stock below the level required to maintain full employment.

Wage increases and inflation did slow down markedly during Stages One and Two of the incomes policies from mid-1975 and mid-1977. But conditions in the private sector were conducive to such a slow-down irrespective of the existence of the policies. The rapid increase in unemployment constrained wage bargainers. In the public sector, the sharp falls in real wages caused by the policies were an important component of the overall deflationary policy stance adopted by the government during this period.

Stages Three and Four of the incomes policies were quite inconsequential as far as their pure economic impact is concerned.

The defeat by public sector workers of the attempted introduction of a tight Stage Four in the winter of 1978/79 did, however, have very important consequences for political economy. It did enormous damage to Labour's political image, primarily in the 1979 election but also throughout the 1980s. Many of the leading figures in the government appeared to have lost the will to conduct a successful struggle. The circumstances of the government had of course been exceptionally difficult, but the early decision to implement the threshold agreements was a serious mistake from which the government never really recovered.

The 1974–75 experience itself had longer-term consequences for the political economy of the UK. Labour began to incur electoral unpopularity soon after being elected with a majority in October 1974, with inflation a major reason for this. Prolonged unpopularity erodes the confidence of politicians, and must have been a handicap to the government during its period of office. More directly, the very high rates of inflation experienced during 1974 and 1975 damaged Labour's image and have allowed its opponents to characterise it as the party of high inflation not just in the 1970s but into the 1980s as well. Further, the large wage increases in the public sector led not only to a PSBR well in excess of 10% of GDP, but to the perception of public expenditure being used to support the private consumption of workers in the sector rather than in the provision of services. The concept of public expenditure as inherently wasteful, an important component of Thatcherism, received strong empirical support from this period of the Labour government.

Overall, the experience with incomes policies in 1974–79 was not one which governments are likely to wish to repeat. The 1974–75 policy was perhaps the biggest single mistake in the whole of post-war economic policy. Subsequent policies were largely irrelevant to wage behaviour in the private sector, and the attempt to impose a strict policy on the public sector at the end of Labour's period of office proved very damaging electorally to the government of the day.

References

Artis, M. J., (1983), 'The capital constraint', in S. Frowen (ed.), *Controlling Industrial Economies*, Macmillan, London.

Artis, M. J., and Ormerod, P. (1990), 'Variable parameter wage equations', *mimeo*, University of Manchester.

Capella, P., and Ormerod, P. (1982), 'Earnings and the pressure of demand in the UK', mimeo, paper presented to the Centre for Labour Economics, London School of Economics, and to HM Treasury Academic Panel.

Fallick, J. L. and Elliott, R. F. (eds.) (1981), *Incomes Policies, Inflation and Relative Pay*, Allen & Unwin, London.

Henry, S. G. B. and Ormerod, P. (1978), 'Incomes Policies and Wage Inflation', *National Institute Economic Review*, no. 85, pp. 31–9.

Malinvaud, E. (1980), *Profitability and Unemployment*, Cambridge University Press, Cambridge.

Meade, J. E. (1982), *Stagflation: Vol. 1: Wage Fixing*, Allen & Unwin, London.

Ormerod, P. (1988), 'Unemployment and profitability in the UK', *mimeo*, paper presented to the Money Study Group Conference, Oxford.

5 *Peter M. Jackson*

Public expenditure

1 Introduction

Public expenditure played a significant role in the life of the 1974–79 Labour government. Not only did the government have to battle both inside and outside Cabinet with public expenditure cuts, a process which was both gruelling and exhausting to all concerned, but it also had to manage public expenditure within a system that was more accustomed to planning for growth than controlling to effect cutbacks. It might even be argued that the inherent weaknesses of the public expenditure planning system failed to provide the 1974–79 government with adequate information for the 'political management' of public expenditure and that this contributed to inappropriate policy decisions, which weakened the government's standing in the polls when it went to the country in 1979.

Despite these difficulties the Labour government of 1974–79 managed to achieve a great deal in the sphere of public expenditure management. It presided over the largest cuts in real public expenditure that have occurred in the last fifty years. These cuts were on a scale similar to the famous Geddes axe of 1922. Furthermore, it was during 1974–79 that significant and long-lasting changes were made to the system of public expenditure planning that lay behind the annual Public Expenditure White Papers. During Joel Barnett's term as Chief Financial Secretary to the Treasury public expenditure was cash limited and planned in cash terms rather than in real terms as had hitherto been the case.[1] Also, a new system of monitoring and cash-managing public expenditure was introduced. Unfortunately it was to be the subsequent Conservative government that was to enjoy the benefits of these reforms. Changes also took place during 1974–79 to public expenditure's macroeconomic role. Until the early 1970s public expenditure had contributed to policies designed to achieve the full-employment objectives of the 1944 Employment White Paper. Fiscal policy was dominant and monetary policy was, in varying degrees, accommodative. Callaghan's famous speech to the 1976 Labour Party annual conference signalled an end to this state of affairs. Public expenditure was to be controlled in order to meet the government's public sector borrowing requirement targets and hence its monetary targets. Monetary policy was to be dominant and fiscal policy was henceforth to be accommodative. At the same time aggregate demand management slowly began to give way to a greater emphasis on supply-side policies.

These changes reflected a counter-revolution to the earlier Keynesian revolution. This policy debate, which was carried out amongst academics and influential 'think tanks', questioned the effectiveness of fiscal policy in the medium-to-long term. Were the short-run output and employment gains of fiscal policy lost in the medium term through a crowding out of private sector expenditures brought about by the higher interest rates caused by public sector borrowing (Anderson and Jordan, 1968)? Did high marginal rates of taxation destroy incentives and weaken the supply side of the economy? Did public expenditure and public sector borrowing promote inflation? Bacon and Eltis in a series of commentaries, first published (1975) in the *Sunday Times* and later in book form (1976) asserted that Britain's economic problems had been caused by the public sector's expansion. Milton Friedman (1976, 1977) and other libertarians drew attention to the UK's ratio of public expenditure to GDP which in 1975/76 came close to 60% and in Friedman's mind signalled that Britain was on the edge of destroying the liberties and freedoms of a pluralistic democracy.[2] Others believed that Britain as a nation was on the very edge of bankruptcy (Rose and Peters, 1978).

Many of the sentiments of the time can be summed up in a statement made at the first CBI annual conference in 1977, according to which 'Between 1964 and 1975 public expenditure had risen by two thirds in cost terms ... The government and the nation were living beyond their means ... Enterprise was being strangled by bureaucracy. It had become vital to shift the balance back in favour of the wealth producing sectors.'

This statement is not too dissimilar to one which was made earlier by James Callaghan: 'it is important that productive jobs should be created that rely upon investments on which a sensible rate of return can be expected. That is the way we shall get full employment – not by transferring more and more jobs to the public sector' (House of Commons speech, April 1976).

Public expenditure's management and control, along with its economic role, was being reforged in the crucible of heated academic and political debate. The sections that follow trace out some of the more significant events that took place in this reforging from 1974 to 1979.

2   The time pattern of public spending

The data contained in Figure 5.1 show that for most of the post-war period public expenditure has grown faster than GDP as reflected in the rising ratio of government expenditure to GDP. This rising trend in the relative size

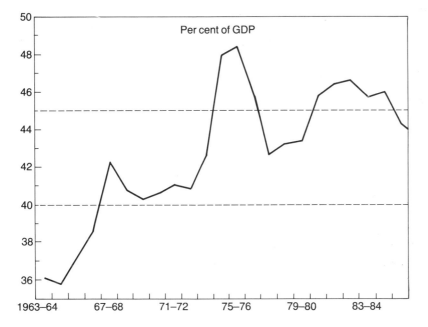

Fig. 5.1

of the public sector is due to the interaction of a number of complex factors. In part it is accounted for by real income growth and the fact that the demand for many of the public services provided is income-elastic; another reason is that the prices of public sector inputs rise faster than the prices at which GDP is valued; but it is also due to the growing importance of public sector transfer payments, especially pensions, which are not part of GDP and, therefore, make the interpretation of the ratio somewhat tricky (Brown and Jackson, 1990).

During the years of the Heath–Barber boom (1970–74) public expenditure in real terms increased at an annual average rate of 4·8% compared to a 2·5% annual increase in GDP. The incoming Labour government of 1974 inherited a set of public expenditure plans which would have maintained these rates of growth. As is well known, controlling public expenditure in the short run is difficult. This reduced the amount of discretion available to the new Labour government when it came to formulate its plans for public spending. Furthermore, the Heath Conservative government had awarded substantial pay increases to nurses and teachers (under the Halsbury and Houghton Committees respectively) which came due for payment in the first year of the Labour government's term in office.

This inheritance contributed to the 'public expenditure crisis' of 1975/76 which caused the Chancellor of the Exchequer, Denis Healey, to demand real public spending cuts on a scale never seen before. It fell to Joel Barnett, the Chief Financial Secretary to the Treasury, to negotiate these cuts (Barnett, 1982). Figure 5.1 also shows a massive rise in the relative size of the public sector between 1974 and 1976. Many commentators at the time interpreted this to indicate that public spending was out of control. Further examination, however, leads to an alternative view.

Two major factors influenced the increase in the government expenditure-to-GDP ratio between 1974 and 1976. The first was that the rate of growth in real GDP was negative in 1974 and 1975. Between 1974 and 1976 real GDP fell by 2·46%. A ratio will rise if the numerator rises (in this case public spending) but it will also rise if the denominator falls (in this case GDP). The second reason for the large increase in the ratio is due to the relative price effect: the fact that the prices at which public expenditures are valued tend to rise faster than the prices at which GDP is valued. Table 1 of Appendix B to this volume shows that real government consumption rose by 5·58% between 1974 and 1975. This, however, overstates the real growth in government consumption because it does not take into account the relative price effect. In order to obtain some idea of the size of the relative price effect for 1974/75 it is instructive to examine what was happening to wages in the public sector: see Table 5.1.

Table 5.1   *Annual rate of increase in public sector pay (%)*

	1973/74	1974/75	1975/76	1976/77
Teachers	5·5	31·0	26·0	7·5
Nurses	12·0	39·5	28·0	13·5
Police	10·0	12·5	26·5	14·5
Civil servants	16·5	11·5	33·0	16·0
Armed forces	6·0	12·5	28·0	14·0
Average public sector pay	9·2	22·4	27·7	12·3
Average pay Whole Economy	12·5	23·1	23·8	13·4
Retail price index	18·0	24·5	15·0	14·0

Source: Bailey and Trinder (1989), Table 3.3.

The information contained in Table 5.1 shows a strong relative price effect for the years 1974−76 due to the increases in public sector pay, since most public sector services are highly labour-intensive. Public sector pay increases, as the table also shows, were not out of line with those in the rest of the economy or the changes in the retail price index. Much of the increase in public spending, therefore, went into the increase in public sector wages to maintain the consumption of public sector employees rather than into an expansion in the level of services.

Another source of increase in public spending was the growth of transfer payments. In an attempt to keep the rate of inflation below 30% the Chancellor of the Exchequer in July 1974 increased subsidies on food, housing, local authority rates, and fuel. At the same time the rising level of unemployment meant that public expenditure on unemployment benefits rose. Between 1974 and 1979 current grants and subsidies increased by an average of 29% p.a. (in money terms) compared to 18% p.a. under the previous Conservative government. In real terms, between 1974 and 1979 current grants and subsidies rose by 3·8% p.a. (1975 prices).

Taking these points together it is seen that public expenditure between 1974 and 1976 rose in part as a countercyclical response to the negative growth in GDP and as a result of the large relative price effects caused by inflation.

3   Cutting public expenditure

Denis Healey's first set of budgetary measures introduced in March 1974 was essentially a holding tactic until a full assessment of the nature and scale of the economic and corresponding budgetary problem could be made. Subsidies to the nationalised industries were cut from £1400 million to £500 million. Value Added Tax was cut from 10% to 8% in July 1974, and subsidies on food and housing were increased. These measures were aimed at holding down the rate of inflation.[3]

The first major changes in public expenditure came in the January 1975 Public Expenditure White Paper (PEWP) (Cmnd. 5879). This contained cuts in *planned* public spending of £1 billion (i.e. 2% of total public spending) for 1976/77, building up to a £3·75 billion cut for 1978/79. These cuts fell mainly on programmes for defence; food subsidies; nationalised industry capital spending; and capital programmes in transport, housing and education. These cuts arose because it was feared that unless they were made the standard marginal rate of income tax would rise to 50% and the PSBR would reach such a high level that financing it would be damaging to the rest of the economy.

In the February 1976 PEWP (Cmnd. 6393) public spending was planned to stabilise at its 1976/77 level and, thereafter, to fall as a proportion of GDP as the economy recovered. This PEWP was both controversial and significant. It broke the post-war expectation of a continuous rise in public spending. Furthermore, it announced cuts in the real level of social services. To many this signalled the abandonment of socialist policies and gave rise to the formulation of alternative economic and social policy strategies within the Labour Party.[4] These problems were exacerbated because the provision for the payment of debt interest within the public expenditure total was increased, indicating a transfer of expenditures (and hence benefits) from the consumers of social services to the holders of gilts. Furthermore, greater emphasis in public spending programmes was given to industry and employment support (e.g. subsidies to British Leyland and financing of the National Enterprise Board).

During 1976, two further announced cuts in public spending were made. The first, in July, cut £1012 million from the planning total for 1977/78. Barnett (1982) points out that it took six meetings of the Cabinet to agree these changes. The second round of cuts was the more substantial and amounted to £3 billion. They were required by the IMF as a condition for its loan and were set out in the Letter of Intent sent on 15 December.

When deciding upon the 1977 PEWP the problem which faced the Cabinet was to ensure that the Social Contract, the industrial strategy, the employment objectives, and the IMF loan conditions were simultaneously satisfied. Obviously this would prove to be difficult both technically and politically. The December 1976 public expenditure cuts, required by the IMF, were an integral part of the January 1977 PEWP (Cmnd. 6721). This White Paper represented a sea change. It was the first time that a PEWP was published without containing a medium-term economic assessment. Secondly, and more important, the government was now committed to reducing (not just stabilising) the programmed expenditure for 1977/78 and 1978/79. That is, the *level* of public expenditure for those years was to be reduced from the levels of 1975/76 and 1976/77 (see p. 1 of Cmnd. 6721:I). Cuts were being made in real service levels. It was no longer an exercise in cutting the fairy gold of some planning total. There was, however, a commitment to increase public spending again once real growth in GDP was re-established.

In January 1978 a further PEWP (Cmnd. 7049) was published, allowing public expenditure to increase by 2·2% between 1977/78 and 1978/79 whilst indicating £1 billion of cuts in public spending for 1978/79. The Labour government's final PEWP (Cmnd. 7439) was published on 17 January 1979. By this time public expenditure estimates were no longer based upon projections of the availability of real resources (i.e. real GDP). It was now recognised that such forecasts were unreliable and would lead to fragile public expenditure plans based upon over-optimistic assumptions about growth.

Between 1974 and November 1978 there were fourteen public expenditure packages presented for Cabinet approval. Were these real cuts or were they simply cuts in a planning total? How did the various programmes fare? Which were cut more than others? Where did the axe fall? To answer these questions we now look at what happened to public spending rather than what happened to the plans.

4 Public expenditure changes 1974–77

Without making adjustments for the relative price effect, Table 5.2 shows what happened to real public spending on goods and services (current and capital) at 1985 prices expressed as a proportion of GDP. The government was successful in stabilising public spending as a proportion of GDP and ended its period of office in 1979 with public spending absorbing a smaller proportion of the economy's resources than when it took office in 1974.

Table 5.2 *Public expenditure as a proportion of GDP (market prices) (1985 prices)*

	1970	*1974*	*1975*	*1976*	*1977*	*1978*	*1979*	*1985*
Final consumption								
(i) Central government	13·1	13·1	13·9	13·8	13·4	13·1	12·9	13·0
(ii) Local government	7·8	8·4	8·9	8·7	8·3	8·3	8·3	7·9
Total final consumption	20·9	21·5	22·8	22·5	21·7	21·4	21·1	20·9
Capital	4·9	4·6	4·3	4·0	3·1	2·6	2·4	2·0
Total expenditure on goods and services	25·8	26·1	27·1	26·5	24·8	24·0	23·5	22·9
Transfer payments								
Current transfers and grants	10·4	13·4	13·5	13·5	13·4	13·8	14·0	16·2
Other transfers	5·5	5·4	5·0	5·3	5·4	5·4	5·3	5·9
Total expenditure on transfer payments	15·9	18·8	18·5	18·8	18·8	19·2	19·3	22·1
Total public spending	41·7	44·9	45·6	45·3	43·6	43·2	42·8	45·0

Source: *Economic Trends*, 1989 Supplement.

Most of this achievement was through reductions in capital spending. The rises in the ratio for 1975 and 1976 are again due to negative rates of economic growth in these years and an inadequate account being made (in the 1985 deflator) for the relative price effect. The restoration of economic growth in 1977 and a slowing down in the rate of inflation helped to bring down the ratio of real public spending to GDP.

Transfer payments to the personal sector (at 1985 prices) as a proportion of GDP increased from 13·4% in 1974 to 14·0% in 1979.

What happened to individual programmes? These are shown in Table 5.3. Crude allowances have been made for the relative price effect when

Table 5.3   *Changes in public expenditure programmes 1974–79 (1985 prices)*

Programme	Average annual % change 1974–79
Defence (11·0)	1·5
Roads/lighting (2·5)	−3·9
Transport and communication (1·6)	0·7
Research (10·8)	−1·4
Agriculture, forestry, food (1·6)	−0·7
Housing (8·2)	−9·6
Water, sewage, refuse (0·9)	−5·0
Public heath (0·3)	3·7
Parks (0·7)	0·1
Libraries, museums (0·5)	0·8
Police (2·0)	3·5
Prisons (0·5)	2·3
Fire (0·4)	2·4
Education (12·6)	0·1
NHS (10·9)	2·3
Personal social services (2·0)	4·3
Subsidies and grants	
Social security (24·0)	7·0
Housing (2·3)	23·0
Education (2·2)	2·3

Notes: (a) Definitions of public spending programmes were changed in 1985. We have used the definitions which were in place in 1974–79.

(b) The figures in parentheses show each item of public expenditure as a percentage of total public spending.

Source: *National Income and Expenditure*, 1980.

constructing this table. It is readily seen that there is an unevenness in experiences between programmes. The rate of growth of expenditures on personal social services, the NHS, the protective services (police, prisons and fire), and public health were maintained. Those for education, defence, and libraries and museums were stabilised. The main cuts came on capital spending programmes such as housing and roads. The increase in the real absolute value of social security payments reflects the growing number of unemployed.

It was generally believed that local authority expenditure was difficult to control and would cause the Treasury problems in meeting its spending targets.[5] A senior Treasury official, when giving evidence to the Layfield Committee in 1976, described local government as the 'Achilles' heel' of the

Treasury's control over public spending. Local authorities had recourse to their locally generated rate income to finance any expenditure over-runs. The problem of financing local government in the UK was the subject of an inquiry (see the Layfield Committee Report, Cmnd. 6453, 1976) and evidence given to it confirmed some of these concerns. Whilst the Treasury could limit the value of grants-in-aid paid to local authorities and could tighten loan sanctions for capital spending, the success of central government's ability to control local government spending nevertheless essentially rested upon moral suasion. How successful was this between 1974 and 1979?

Guidelines were issued to local authorities on the appropriate level of public spending by local authorities generally. No specific guidelines were issued, in England and Wales, to individual local authorities (the practice differed in Scotland). Table 5.4 shows local authority current expenditure targets and out-turns. It would seem that the overall policy was successful – this of course ignores redistributions between individual local authorities within the total. The majority of local authorities lost non-specific Rate Support Grant income between 1975/76 and 1979/80. The 1979/80 Rate Support Grant was 92% of its 1975/76 level. The 1976 Rate Support Grant was cash-limited and housing starts were controlled in July 1976 for the first time since 1966.

During this period of fiscal restraint the relationships between central and local governments, which are by nature tense, became full of conflict. The larger Labour-controlled inner-city areas, which contained serious social problems, unemployment, deprivation and severe infrastructure needs (Greenwood *et al.*, 1977), required more to be spent on them relative to the

Table 5.4 *Local authority grant expenditure target and out-turn (£m at November price base)*

	Expenditure target	Out-turn	Deviation (%)
1975/76 (Nov. 1975 prices)	8,610·4	8,754·5	+1·7
1976/77 (Nov. 1976 prices)	9,818·5	8,741·9	−0·8
1977/78 (Nov. 1977 prices)	10,709·8	10,423·4	−2·6
1978/79 (Nov. 1978 prices)	11,923·4	11,738·4	−1·5
1979/80 (Nov. 1979 prices)	13,853·6	13,748·9	−0·7

Source: Annual Rate Support Grant 1975/76 to 1979/80, Local Authority Association.

rest. To an extent this was helped by central government bending some of the main spending programmes towards the inner cities. But there was also a resentment from local politicians that public expenditure control by the Treasury implied more centralisation and the replacement of democratic control over public spending via the ballot box by bureaucratic procedures and administrative fiat.

Because the interpretation of data on real public expenditure depends crucially upon the appropriate choice of price deflator it is also instructive to examine what happened to public sector employment over the period (see Table 5.5). Once again the picture that emerges is that real improvements in public services were achieved between 1974 and 1979. These public employment data must, however, be treated with care. At best they only give indications of real service improvement. The problem is that much of the growth in public sector employment has come via part-time employment and, unless this is adjusted for when calculating full-time equivalents, the figures will overstate the improvement.[6]

Table 5.5   *Public sector employment*

	1970	1974	1979	% change 1974–79	Annual average %
Central government					
HM forces	372	319	314	−1·6	−0·3
NHS	741	911	1152	26·0	5·2
Other	818	884	921	4·2	0·8
Total	1931	2140	2387	11·5	2·3
Local authorities					
Education	1241	1453	1539	5·9	1·2
Health and social services	265	272	344	26·0	5·0
Construction	128	135	156	15·0	3·0
Police	145	160	176	10·0	2·0
Other	781	762	782	2·6	0·5
Total	2559	2782	2997	7·7	1·5

Source: Annual Abstract of Statistics, 1989 Supplement.

5 The crisis of control

Public expenditure decisions are made by Cabinet. These decisions are informed by the output of the Public Expenditure Survey Committee (PESC). The philosophy which had guided PESC since the early 1960s was that public spending should be planned over the medium term in real terms with regard to forecasts of the supply of real resources (GDP). Whilst this was a rational system for making decisions when rates of growth were always positive and predictable and rates of inflation were low it was not suitable for the 'stagflationary' conditions of the mid-1970s. Negative rates of growth and rapid inflation placed great stress on the PESC system and found its weaknesses. One problem was that there was no provision made for a financial plan to back up the real resource plan. How was public spending at current prices to be financed?[7] The real plan was simply financed at the prices ruling on the day and increases in public spending were approved through issuing a series of supplementary estimates. In other words, public spending was to all intents and purposes fully index-linked. Since the tax structure was not fully index-linked then in order to meet the real spending levels of the public expenditure plan and the PSBR targets marginal rates of income tax would have needed to be raised to ridiculously high and politically unacceptable levels.

This issue of the planning and control of public spending was highlighted when Wynne Godley, himself a former senior adviser to the Treasury, gave evidence to the House of Commons Treasury Select Committee. Godley pointed out that the public expenditure out-turn for 1974/75 was £5·8 billion greater than the forecast for 1974/75 made in 1971. He argued that a large proportion of this overspend was due to increases in real public spending which had never been approved by Parliament. In other words, 'we do not have a proper planning system and we have not got a proper control system' (Godley, 1975).

These issues moved the government to action, and in 1976 a number of significant changes were made: (a) a system of cash limits on about 60% of public expenditure was introduced; (b) a financial information system (FIS) was established in each central government department to monitor cash flow (local authorities had been doing this for years); and (c) the contingency reserve was increased in size and was to be used as a buffer in the system. After 1976, departments found it more difficult to make a claim on the contingency reserve since all such competing claims had to be argued out in Cabinet.

Increasing the size of the contingency reserve meant that at the time the PEWP was published a greater proportion of public expenditure remained unallocated. For example, the contingency reserve was substantially increased from £750 million in 1978/79 to £1500 million in 1979/80. Whilst this change was intended to give greater stability to the public expenditure plans it also had the consequence that it gave the Treasury greater control over allocating public spending. This amounted to a shift in power from Parliament to the Treasury because Parliament was being asked to approve a PEWP which included a significant proportion of spending which was as yet unallocated to specific programmes.

Cash limits provided the basis of the financial plan which had been missing from previous discussions of public spending. Some regarded the cash-limit squeeze on public spending as the counterpart of the money-supply squeeze on the private sector (Pliatzky, 1980).

The introduction of cash limits did, however, have an unintended consequence on the course of public spending. They resulted in a substantial 'shortfall' or underspending of public expenditure plans in the first two years of their operation. This shortfall was in *real* public spending and amounted to 3½% of total planned spending in 1976 and 4½% in 1977.

Shortfall came about in part because of inaccurate forecasts of the inflation in public sector input prices. These had been projected in the 1976 PEWP to rise by 9%, and this assumption was used when setting cash limits. In the event, public sector input prices rose by 17% during 1976/77. To stay within cash limits departments had, therefore, to cut into real public spending which meant that the cuts in real public spending were greater than had been planned. Another reason for shortfall was that departmental managers had to learn how to manage their programmes in cash terms and many were over-cautious and squeezed too much too early in order to stay within their limits. An analysis of shortfall shows that it tended to be concentrated in capital programmes (see Justsum and Walker, 1979).

The size of the shortfall for the fiscal year 1977/78 was about £750 million, that is, 5% of public spending. Leaving out nationalised industry debt interest, a shortfall of £1600 million remained, which was about equal in size to the public spending cuts announced in December 1976. Whilst the December 1976 cuts were discussed in Cabinet and by Parliament cuts due to shortfall were not.

Shortfall has implications for economic and political decisions. First, it impacts on decisions relating to the design of fiscal policy. The February 1976 PEWP was an input to decisions made about fiscal policy for the year 1976/77. That White Paper had forecast that public expenditure would rise by 2½% in real terms in 1976/77, but in fact it declined by 2%. Fiscal policy turned out to be more restrictive than had been planned: the shortfall could have been used to reduce taxes and/or borrowing. Hughes (1978) estimated that the 1976/77 and 1977/78 combined shortfall was equivalent to 2% of GDP and could have added 250,000 to the number of unemployed in 1976/77, possibly rising to 300,000 in 1977/78.

The shortfall in public spending meant that actual spending cuts were larger than those which had been negotiated with the IMF. If, during the year 1976/77 when negotiations with the IMF were proceeding, it had been realised that there would be a public expenditure shortfall on the scale that did emerge, then the externally imposed cuts in public spending, upon which the IMF loan was in part conditional, would not have been necessary.

To implement the IMF cuts in the absence of knowledge about the size of the shortfall required that the cash limits for 1979/80 be set at a level which assumed a 5% increase in public sector staff costs and an 8½% inflation of goods and services. It was these stringent measures on public sector pay, in order to deliver the IMF cuts, coupled with the existing incomes policy, that so aggravated public sector unions and which caused the government so much political embarrassment. The incomes policy which was in place would have caused the government problems with the public sector unions. These problems could, however, have been reduced if only the government had known how much room it had to manoeuvre on public spending. It could, for example, have relaxed the cash limits for 1979/80 and bought itself more space in which to negotiate with the public sector unions by expanding employment in the public sector instead of presiding over job losses and by expanding non-employment items of public spending such as on capital and maintenance, which would have created employment in the private sector.

Clearly the system of public expenditure planning and control failed the 1974−79 Labour government in the sense that it failed to provide it with adequate information upon which to make strategic political decisions. Following this episode the Treasury introduced a more sophisticated information system which allowed it to monitor cash flows in greater detail and to forecast shortfall. But these changes were too late for the Labour government of 1974−79.

6 Conclusion

The Labour Government of 1974−79 faced the toughest set of public expenditure decisions that had been confronted by any government since 1922. It implemented large real cuts in programmes rather than cosmetic cuts in planning totals. This helped to stabilise the economy, but failure to realise the size of shortfall probably meant that overall fiscal policy was more restrictive than was necessary.

Important changes were made to the system of planning, controlling and managing public expenditure: especially the introduction of financial planning via cash limits and the financial information system.

An examination of Figure 5.1 shows that the incoming Conservative government of 1979, despite its political rhetoric about rolling back the frontiers of the state, faced similar problems as the 1974 Labour government. From 1979 to 1987 the ratio of government spending to GDP was higher than when the Labour government left office.

Would the course of political history have been different if when setting the cash limits for 1979/80 the Cabinet had realised the size of the public expenditure shortfall? That is left for speculators to muse upon.

Notes

1 Whilst some items of public expenditure had been previously limited in cash terms it was not until 1976 that cash limits were set for 60% of total public spending. Cash limits were simply a monetary value (cash amount) allocated to each item of public spending covered by the scheme. Public sector managers could not exceed these limits. Prior to 1976 public expenditure had been set over the medium term in real terms, i.e. at the (constant) prices ruling in the year the plan was made. After 1976 plans had to be made in cash on nominal terms. These cash limits differ from the system of cash planning introduced by the 1979 Conservative government, which incorporated assumptions about inflation that were not genuine forecasts (see Pliatzky, 1984).

2 This ratio is based upon the old (and misleading) definition of public expenditure which was in use prior to the change in definition which was introduced in 1976. Throughout this chapter figures are based upon the new definition.

3 As part of its counter-inflation policy introduced on 22 July 1974 the government entered into a social contract with the trade unions. Under this arrangement the government would maintain public sector subsidies that would moderate rises in the cost of living and in return the unions would keep down the size of their wage rises. This public spending was dubbed the 'social wage' and was valued at £1000 for each member of the working population in 1975.

4 Many of these debates are subsequently developed in Currie and Smith (1981), Currie and Sawyer (1982) and Sawyer and Schott (1983).

5 See Jackson (1976a).

6 Jackson (1976a) has shown that insufficient allowance has been made for the growth of part-time employment. The public employment data, therefore, tend to overstate the growth of public employment on a full-time basis.

7 Plans of public expenditure at constant prices were somewhat disparagingly referred to as 'funny money' by Sam Brittan in many of his *Financial Times* articles throughout the 1970s. This idea of 'funny money' entered the mythology of public expenditure planning and has tended to obscure the important problems of how real resource plans and financial plans should be reconciled.

References

Anderson, L.C., and Jordan J.L. (1968), 'Monetary and fiscal actions: a test of their relative importance in economic stabilization', *Federal Reserve Bank of St Louis Review*, November.

Bacon, R., and Eltis, W. (1975), 'Too few producers: the drift Healey must stop', *Sunday Times*, 14 November, p. 16.

Bacon, R., and Eltis, W. (1976), *Britain's Economic Problem: Too Few Producers*, Macmillan, London.

Bailey, R., and Trinder, C. (1989), *Under Attack? Public Sector Pay after Two Decades*, Public Finance Foundation, London.

Barnett, J. (1982), *Inside the Treasury*, Andre Deutsch, London.

Brown, C.V., and Jackson, P.M. (1990), *Public Sector Economics*, 4th edn, Basil Blackwell, Oxford.

Currie, D., and Sawyer, M. (eds) (1982), *Socialist Economic Review 1982*, Merlin, London.

Currie, D., and Smith, R. (eds) (1981), *Socialist Economic Review 1981*, Merlin, London.

Friedman, M. (1976), 'The line we dare not cross: the fragility of freedom at 60%', *Encounter*, November.

Friedman, M. (1977), 'From Galbraith to economic freedom', Institute of Economic Affairs, Occasional Paper no. 49.

Godley, W.A.H. (1975), Evidence Given to the Select Committee on Expenditure, 1st Report from the Expenditure Committee 1975/76, *The Financing of Public Expenditure*, V: II.

Greenwood, R., Hinings, C.R., and Ramson, S. (1977), 'The politics of the budgetary process in English local government', *Political Studies*, XXV, March.

Heclo, H., and Wildavsky, A. (1974), *The Private Government of Public Money*, Macmillan, London.

Hughes, J. (1978), 'Public expenditure: the strategic arithmetic', *Economic Appraisal*, no. 22, Trade Union Research Unit, Ruskin College, Oxford.

Jackson, P.M. (1976a), 'The growth of public sector employment: the case of the UK', in *Fiscal Policy and Labour Supply*, Institute for Fiscal Studies Conference Series, no. 4.

Jackson, P.M. (1976b), 'Trends in local government expenditure and the prospects for the future', in *Growth and Control of Public Expenditure*, Institute for Fiscal Studies.

Justsum, C., and Walker, G. (1979), 'Public expenditure 1977/78: outturn compared with plan', Government Economic Service Working Paper no. 28, July.

Middleton, P. (1985), 'Managing public expenditure', in *Public Expenditure and Management*, Public Finance Foundation Discussion Paper no. 5.

Pliatzky, L. (1980), 'Crisis in public expenditure planning', *Scottish Journal of Political Economy*, November.

Pliatzky, L. (1984), *Getting and Spending*, Basil Blackwell, Oxford.

Rose, R. and Peters, G. (1978), *Can Government Go Bankrupt?* Basic Books, New York.

Sawyer, M. and Schott, K. (eds) (1983), *Socialist Economic Review 1983*, Merlin, London.

A model-based analysis

1 Introduction

This chapter provides measures of the effect of fiscal and monetary policy for the period 1974–79, derived from simulations conducted on a macro-econometric model, the National Institute's model (version 11). We take the macroeconometric model to represent a coherent summary of the major behavioural and accounting relationships within the economy and use counterfactual simulations as a tool for unravelling the effects of policy actions undertaken at various times.

The remainder of the chapter is divided into three sections. In Section 2 we outline the basis of the policy measures utilised in the study and discuss some of the problems that arise in implementation. In particular the question of model choice is considered and we indicate the main advantages derived from adopting version 11 of the National Institute model for our purpose. The range of potential policy instruments available for examination is effectively determined by the structure of the model and for this reason we also include in Section 2 a brief outline of the major structural characteristics of the National Institute model.

The principal results of the paper are contained in Section 3 and these provide a basis for the discussion of the effects of fiscal and monetary policy over the period for GDP, inflation and the balance of payments. One notable feature of these results is the role played by the exchange rate and for this reason we have chosen, in presenting the results, to isolate its effect in the overall transmission mechanism. Accordingly, the discussion is focused initially on the effects of fiscal and monetary policy over the period under the assumption that the authorities intervene continuously in the foreign exchange market so as to maintain the exchange rate at its historic value. This assumption is subsequently relaxed and the implication of exchange rate movements for policy appraisal is then reported. Here a significant finding of the study is that the policy actions undertaken during the early part of the Labour administration do imply a substantial depreciation of sterling by 1976, a year in which there was a severe foreign exchange crisis.

Finally, it is useful to compare the effects of policy with the effects of disturbances impacting on the British economy from outside. The final set of results presented in Section 4 pertains, therefore, to the effect of disturbances in world trade on the UK.

A feature of the model we are using is that it can be solved under one of two alternative assumptions about the way in which expectations are formed – either as adaptive and 'backward-looking' or as model-consistent and 'forward-looking'. General considerations do not dictate a clear preference for one or the other to be made in the case with which we are concerned, and for reasons of economy and expediency we concentrate in this chapter on results obtained using the adaptive expectations assumption. With this assumption, a well-established framework of analysis is available and readers may make comparisons between the results reported here and earlier results obtained for this and other episodes (e.g. Artis and Green, 1982; Artis *et al.*, 1984; Saville and Gardiner, 1986; Artis and Bladen-Hovell, 1987). Interested readers may pursue the analysis of policy under the alternative assumption of consistent expectations in Artis and Bladen-Hovell (1990) and Artis *et al.* (1990).[1]

2 Method

The measure of policy provided here is based on the counterfactual simulation of an econometric model and follows from work originally conducted by Blinder and Goldfeld (1976). In the context of policy appraisal for the United Kingdom, the measure has been successfully applied by a number of authors, notably Artis and Green (1982) who apply the method to an early version of H.M. Treasury model to obtain an appraisal of fiscal policy for the Labour government 1974–79 and Artis and Bladen-Hovell (1987) where the conduct of policy undertaken by the subsequent Conservative government is examined.

Implementing the method involves two main steps. The first requires a definition of a 'neutral' trajectory for policy instruments in the model over the period. Differences between the 'neutral' path and the actual instrument trajectory are then taken as a measure of the amount of policy activism in the period and all that is required in order to complete the exercise is to translate these movements in the instruments of policy into changes in the output variables of the model such as GDP, inflation, unemployment and the balance of payments. In the analysis that follows we achieve this by adopting the incremental approach described in Artis *et al.* (1984). Under this approach each successive change in policy (defined as the period-by-period change in the difference between the neutral and the actual instrument trajectory) is taken as a permanent change and its effects are simulated through the econometric model for all future periods. This means that, for any given quarter, the total policy effect can be decomposed into the effects of policy undertaken in that quarter and in each of the preceding quarters. In this way the policy 'overhang' (the effects of previous policies impinging on the current quarter) can be identified separately from the contribution of the current quarter's policies.

Expressing these ideas more formally, denote $\Delta(I_A - I_N)$, the vector of first differenced measures of policy activism by I'; then the effects on the hth output variable by any quarter j, Z_{hj}, may be written as:

$$Z_{hj} = \sum_{k=1}^{j} \Omega_{hk} I'_{j+1-k}$$

where Ω_{hk} is the dynamic multiplier for the hth output variable in period j.

Implementing the policy measure in this manner assumes that the initial date of impact for any policy change can be successfully identified with the period in which the actual change in policy activism took place, and precludes the possibility that agents may change their behaviour *in response to* an expected policy change. This restriction would be avoided by the assumption of consistent expectations, but at the cost of additional complications. Under this alternative assumption it becomes necessary to spell out whether a policy change was expected or not and, if it was antici- pated, how far ahead in time such an expectation was formed. A technical problem arises in the need to specify the value of expectational variables beyond the period over which the model is solved (the 'terminal condition'). These puzzles do not arise under the assumption that expectations are formed exclusively as a function of past developments. But whilst our choice of this assumption for solving the model is thus expedient it is also not unreasonable to assume as we are doing, that agents are cautious in changing their views of the future and require evidence of a sustained change to convince them that a transformation has occurred.

2.1 *Model structure*

From a practical point of view the main constraint on the choice of model for conducting the exercise is the question of availability. In this respect we gratefully acknowledge the assistance of the National Institute in making its model available to us. In addition to being one of the main UK forecasting models, the recently released version, model 11, provides the distinct advantage of covering the historical data period, 1970–88, and can be simulated from 1974 onwards.

As with most of the large-scale forecasting models for the United Kingdom, the National Institute model developed within the mainstream of Keynesian macro theory which treated output as demand-determined and gave little emphasis to the determinants of aggregate supply. However, the supply side has received far greater attention in recent versions of the model and in the current release determinants of supply are specific in detail.[2]

Simulations of the model suggest that it is broadly representative of (or at least, not an outlier to) the principal UK macroeconometric models. Government expenditure simulations (in consistent-expectations mode at least) are notably cautious in their output implications, leading *Wallis et al.* (1989) to remark on the model's recent 'movement away from the simple Keynesian position' (p. 84); on the other hand, the model shows comparatively lively output responses to tax reductions, especially those in indirect and employment taxes. Its output response to interest rate changes is somewhat on the low side, but its inflation responses − reflecting the sensitivity of the exchange rate − are rather bigger than those to be found in competing macro models.

Whilst the results of the exercise reported below are certainly model-dependent, the evidence suggests that the results obtained using NI Model 11 would, broadly, be replicated were we to have used any other of the principal models available.

2.2 *Policy definition*

The overall structure of the National Institute model is sufficiently disaggregated to identify a wide range of policy instruments. For fiscal policy these include the major components of government expenditure expressed in constant price terms, the main indirect tax instruments and the standard rate of income tax and personal allowances. The model also contains an automatic facility for indexing tax allowances and specific duties in the second quarter of each year to the annual rate of inflation, lagged two quarters. For monetary policy the main policy instrument is the Treasury bill rate. In version 11 this is determined by means of a reaction function that relates changes in the Treasury bill rate to movements in the exchange rate, output and the rate of inflation. For the purpose of the current exercise, however, we suppress this mechanism and treat the Treasury bill rate as an exogenously determined instrument of policy.

With the exception of personal allowances, we define the neutral trajectory for each of the policy instruments on the basis of unchanged policy. For government expenditure, direct taxation, VAT and the Treasury bill rate, unchanged policy corresponds to the continuation of the previous quarter's value. For personal allowances, however, the presumption underlying the notion of unchanged policy is that the authorities will index tax allowances each year to the preceding rate of inflation.

3 An appraisal of policy

To implement the measure of policy effectiveness outlined above, simulations were conducted on the National Institute model to remove, on a quarter-by-quarter basis, changes in the various monetary and fiscal policy instruments contained within the model.[3] For fiscal policy this amounts to the removal of all quarterly changes in direct and indirect tax rates, tax allowances and real government spending. For monetary policy the simulation exercise involves the removal on a quarter-by-quarter basis of changes in the Treasury bill rate. The results, expressed in terms of deviations from the historical base path for GDP, inflation and the current account of the balance of payments are given below in Tables 6.1 and 6.2 on the assumption that the exchange rate remains at its historical value throughout the period. In both tables the results for each variable are presented on the basis of the cumulative effect, measured at the end of each fiscal year 1974/75 – 1978/79, of policy actions undertaken within that particular year and in each of the preceding years of the Labour government. The total effect of policy, including the effect of any policy overhang associated with the lagged response of the economy to policy actions undertaken in previous years can be found by summing each column vertically. The first difference of this total effect, given at the foot of each table, then represents the change in policy stance on a fiscal year basis.

Consider first the effect of fiscal policy on the level of output in the economy. Here the most noticeable feature of the results is the sharp turnabout in GDP which occurs in the fiscal years 1977/78 and 1978/79. Given the construction of the table it is clear that most of this deflationary swing can be traced to policy actions undertaken during 1976/77. Indeed the force of the deflationary package initially administered in that year and continued in a somewhat more relaxed form the next was sufficiently strong to produce a cumulative turn-around of GDP amounting to 3½% in fiscal years 1976/7 and 1977/78. The unemployment effects that flow from this sharp decline in output are not reported in the table, but, as might be expected, are highly correlated with it with a lag. By 1978:1, for example, unemployment is estimated to have fallen by just over 750,000 as a result of the policy actions undertaken over the previous four years. However, by this stage, the incremental effect of the deflationary policy was beginning to become increasingly apparent. One year later, the deflationary consequences have reached the point where they partially offset the expansionary effects of the earlier policy actions and unemployment ends the period only 500,000 lower than would otherwise have been the case.

The effects of fiscal policy for both the rate of inflation and the current account are given in the final two sections of Table 6.1. For inflation these effects indicate that policy actions undertaken over the first three years of the administration were initially disinflationary in nature, reversing in the final year to become inflationary. In contrast, policy actions in the final two years tend to add to inflation within the economy. For the balance of payments, the mildly expansionary mix of tax and expenditure policy undertaken during the years 1974/75 and 1975/76 served to worsen the current account. Whilst a sharp reversal of this position was produced by the deflationary package of 1976/77 the overall effect on the current account was to produce a surplus on the current account of almost £390 million in

Table 6.1 *Fiscal policy effects 1974:2–1979:1 (exchange rate fixed)*

A: *Effects on GDP*

| | | | | | *(% difference base)* |
| | | | *Cumulative effect by:* | | |
Policy actions taken during:	*1975:1*	*1976:1*	*1977:1*	*1978:1*	*1979:1*
FY1974/75	1·5	2·4	2·8	2·3	2·7
FY1975/76	–	1·0	1·1	0·3	0·6
FY1976/77	–	–	– 1·7	– 2·3	– 1·5
FY1977/78	–	–	–	– 0·5	– 0·4
FY1978/79	–	–	–	–	0·0
Total effect	1·5	3·4	2·2	– 0·2	1·4
First difference	1·5	1·9	– 1·2	– 2·4	1·6

B: *Effects on inflation*

| | | | | | *(% point difference)* |
| | | | *Cumulative effect by:* | | |
Policy actions taken during:	*1975:1*	*1976:1*	*1977:1*	*1978:1*	*1979:1*
FY1974/75	– 1·02	– 0·05	– 1·25	– 2·64	2·87
FY1975/76	–	0·42	– 0·05	– 1·98	3·01
FY1976/77	–	–	– 1·04	– 2·75	0·21
FY1977/78	–	–	–	0·60	0·90
FY1978/79	–	–	–	–	0·82
Total effect	– 1·02	0·37	– 2·34	– 6·77	7·81
First difference	– 1·02	1·39	– 2·72	– 4·43	14·59

C: *Effects on current account surplus*

| | | | | | *(£m)* |
| | | | *Cumulative effect by:* | | |
Policy actions taken during:	*1975:1*	*1976:1*	*1977:1*	*1978:1*	*1979:1*
FY1974/75	6·5	– 202·3	– 458·6	– 172·8	– 337·4
FY1975/76	–	– 213·8	– 426·1	– 87·6	– 204·1
FY1976/77	–	–	166·6	486·6	463·1
FY1977/78	–	–	–	160·0	87·3
FY1978/79	–	–	–	–	– 38·2
Total effect	6·5	– 416·1	– 717·1	386·2	– 29·2
First difference	6·5	– 422·6	– 301·0	1103·2	– 415·5

Table 6.2   *Monetary policy effects 1974:2–1979:1 (exchange rate fixed)*

A: Effect on GDP

| | | | | | (% difference base) |
| | | | Cumulative effect by: | | |
Policy actions taken during:	1975:1	1976:1	1977:1	1978:1	1979:1
FY1974/75	−0·1	0·6	1·0	0·5	0·8
FY1975/76	−	0·4	0·5	−0·2	0·4
FY1976/77	−	−	0·0	−0·6	−0·1
FY1977/78	−	−	−	0·2	0·8
FY1978/79	−	−	−	−	−0·3
Total effect	−0·1	1·0	1·5	−0·1	1·6
First difference	−0·1	1·1	0·5	−1·6	1·7

B: Effect on inflation

| | | | | | (% point difference) |
| | | | Cumulative effect by: | | |
Policy actions taken during:	1975:1	1976:1	1977:1	1978:1	1979:1
FY1974/75	0·0	−1·04	−1·26	−1·47	1·72
FY1975/76	−	0·0	−0·34	−2·68	2·89
FY1976/77	−	−	0·0	−0·90	0·36
FY1977/78	−	−	−	−0·15	−0·13
FY1978/79	−	−	−	−	0·0
Total effect	0·0	−1·04	−1·60	−5·20	4·84
First difference	0·0	−1·04	−0·56	−3·60	10·04

C: Effect on current account surplus

| | | | | | (£m) |
| | | | Cumulative effect by: | | |
Policy actions taken during:	1975:1	1976:1	1977:1	1978:1	1979:1
FY1974/75	77·8	−95·9	−306·9	22·3	−60·7
FY1975/76	−	−132·5	−301·7	25·8	−66·3
FY1976/77	−	−	−56·4	162·4	94·3
FY1977/78	−	−	−	−0·5	−203·7
FY1978/79	−	−	−	−	77·7
Total effect	77·8	−228·4	−665·0	210·0	−158·7
First difference	77·8	−306·2	−436·6	875·0	−368·7

1978:1. However, this improvement is relatively short-lived and by the end of the following year the combination of previous expansionary pressures and the easing of the contractionary package is sufficient to push the current account back into a modest deficit position.

Turning now to consider the effects of monetary policy over the period we find (Table 6.2) that, with the exchange rate maintained at its historical value, movements in the Treasury bill rate produced a general stimulus to the level of economic activity. Once again, however, there is some evidence of a downturn in GDP towards the middle of the period though the contribution to this of policies undertaken in the fiscal year 1976/77 appears rather modest. We can also read off from Table 6.2 the effects of monetary policy for inflation and the balance of payments. For the latter, policy effects contributed at first a marked deterioration, then a sharp recovery, with a milder easing toward the end of the period. Inflation tends to fall throughout the period until mid-1977 and to rise from then on, ending the period almost 5 percentage points above its historical value.

At this point it is perhaps worth noting that monetary and fiscal policy induced movements in inflation over the period have a great deal in common. In particular, the figures reported in both Tables 6.1 and 6.2 indicate that each policy is associated with a sharp upturn in the inflation rate in the final year of the simulation. To clarify this picture, we reproduce in Figure 6.1 a comparison of the actual inflation experienced over the period together with the rates implied by fiscal (p_f) and monetary (p_m) policies. In each case we find that the actual and simulated paths begin to diverge

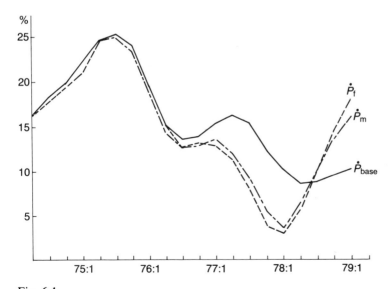

Fig. 6.1

in the early part of 1976 and that, from then on, the simulated rate of
inflation remains below the actual rate until the end of 1977, then increases
in the final year of the simulation. Whilst it is true that a number of factors
contribute to these price movements, by far the largest effect is derived from
the impact of changes in the state of the labour market feeding back on to
average earnings and thence on to prices in the model.

The policy effects discussed so far are those that can be computed on the
assumption that the exchange rate is isolated from any policy impact. Whilst
this is of course unrealistic, it is a helpful device not simply for convenience
of comparison with earlier studies making the same assumption (cf. Artis
and Green, 1982) but as a means of focusing on the role of the exchange rate
in the policy transmission mechanism, a role which a number of research
studies have claimed to be highly important.[4] In order to do this, the results
presented so far should be compared with those given in Tables 6.3 and 6.4.

These tables report the results of simulating the effect of changes in policy
activism which took place over the period but with the exchange rate
determined freely within the model. As before, we concentrate on the
behaviour of three main variables, namely GDP, inflation and the current
account. In addition, we report separately, in Table 6.5, upon the effect of
the monetary and fiscal actions on the exchange rate itself.

Summarising these results briefly we may note the following. First, for
GDP, the broad pattern of response is much the same in the free exchange
rate run as for the fixed exchange rate case, though the precise magnitude of
the individual policy effects is subject to some modification. This is particularly noticeable for the deflationary package administered during the
fiscal year 1976/77 where, for both monetary and fiscal policy, the tables
report a tighter policy being pursued than was recorded in the fixed exchange
rate stimulation. However, the flexible exchange rate simulations cast a
different light on the inflation and balance-of-payments impacts of policy.
As regards inflation, we find that fiscal policy becomes more disinflationary
under the flexible exchange rate regime whilst, for monetary policy, the con-
verse is true. Likewise, policy effects upon the current account are also
enhanced in the flexible exchange rate runs with the turn-round in the
surplus reported between 1977:1 and 1978:1 being almost double the fixed
exchange rate value previously reported for each policy.

Accordingly in Table 6.5 we present results showing the policy-induced
movements in the effective exchange rate itself calculated, as before, on an
end-of-fiscal-year basis. These reveal that although by the end of the period
the cumulative fiscal policy impact on the exchange rate was mildly positive
in contrast to the depreciation impact of monetary policy, both policies are
attributed a sizeable and simultaneous depreciation effect by the end of
1976/77.

The second point to note from Table 6.5 is that, for monetary policy, the
main depreciaton does not occur until 1977:1 at which point the year-on-year

Table 6.3   *Fiscal policy effects 1974:2 – 1979:1 (exchange rate flexible)*

A: *Effects on GDP*

| | | | | | *(% difference base)* |
| | | | *Cumulative effects by:* | | |
Policy actions taken during:	1975:1	1976:1	1977:1	1978:1	1979:1
FY1974/75	1·3	2·2	2·8	2·5	2·2
FY1975/76	–	1·0	2·0	1·4	1·0
FY1976/77	–	–	−1·9	−2·9	−3·1
FY1977/78	–	–	–	−0·6	−0·5
FY1978/79	–	–	–	–	0·3
Total effect	1·3	3·2	2·9	0·4	−0·1
First difference	1·3	1·9	−0·3	−2·5	−0·5

B: *Effects on inflation*

| | | | | | *(% point difference)* |
| | | | *Cumulative effect by:* | | |
Policy actions taken during:	1975:1	1976:1	1977:1	1978:1	1979:1
FY1974/75	−1·53	−0·62	−1·95	−2·33	−2·1
FY1975/76	–	0·42	3·75	0·77	6·27
FY1976/77	–	–	−2·99	−5·90	−7·25
FY1977/78	–	–	–	0·15	0·40
FY1978/79	–	–	–	–	0·95
Total effect	−1·53	−0·20	−1·19	−7·31	−1·73
First difference	−1·53	1·33	−0·99	−6·12	5·58

C: *Effects on the balance of payments (current account)*

| | | | | | *(£m)* |
| | | | *Cumulative effect by:* | | |
Policy actions taken during:	1975:1	1976:1	1977:1	1978:1	1979:1
FY1974/75	−4·0	−176·8	−476·9	88·1	9·1
FY1975/76	–	−298·7	561·1	186·9	3·3
FY1976/77	–	–	−221·9	653·9	533·9
FY1977/78	–	–	–	206·3	38·3
FY1978/79	–	–	–	–	−64·1
Total effect	−4·0	−475·5	−816·1	1135·2	513·9
First difference	−4·0	−471·5	−340·6	1951·3	−621·3

Table 6.4   *Monetary policy effects 1974:2–1979:1 (exchange rate flexible)*

A: Effects on GDP

| | | | | | *(% difference base)* |
| | | | Cumulative effect by: | | |
Policy actions taken during:	1975:1	1976:1	1977:1	1978:1	1979:1
FY1974/75	−0·3	0·6	1·8	1·5	1·7
FY1975/76	−	0·3	1·1	0·7	0·4
FY1976/77	−	−	−0·3	−1·4	−2·6
FY1977/78	−	−	−	0·4	1·7
FY1978/79	−	−	−	−	−0·7
Total effect	−0·3	0·9	2·6	1·2	0·5
First difference	−0·3	1·2	1·7	−1·4	−0·7

B: Effects on inflation

| | | | | | *(% point difference)* |
| | | | Cumulative effects by: | | |
Policy actions taken during:	1975:1	1976:1	1977:1	1978:1	1979:1
FY1974/75	0·0	−0·83	2·53	1·63	8·32
FY1975/76	−	−0·21	3·14	0·76	4·12
FY1976/77	−	−	−1·39	−3·51	−7·65
FY1977/78	−	−	−	1·05	3·56
FY1978/79	−	−	−	−	−1·63
Total effect	0·0	−1·04	4·28	−0·07	6·72
First difference	0·0	−1·04	5·32	−4·35	6·79

C: Effects on the balance of payments (current account)

| | | | | | *(£m)* |
| | | | Cumulative effect by: | | |
Policy actions taken during:	1975:1	1976:1	1977:1	1978:1	1979:1
FY1974/75	51·7	−146·0	−466·6	242·8	65·1
FY1975/76	−	−168·5	−439·3	299·0	140·8
FY1976/77	−	−	41·0	271·7	234·8
FY1977/78	−	−	−	79·0	−276·6
FY1978/79	−	−	−	−	255·0
Total effect	51·7	−314·5	−864·9	734·5	419·1
First difference	51·7	−366·2	−550·4	1599·5	−315·4

Table 6.5   *Exchange rate effects 1974:2 – 1979:1*

A: Fiscal policy

					(% change)
			Cumulative effects by:		
Policy actions taken during:	*1975:1*	*1976:1*	*1977:1*	*1978:1*	*1979:1*
FY1974/75	0·5	1·7	− 6·6	− 2·6	− 4·9
FY1975/76	–	− 2·5	− 14·9	− 10·7	− 17·5
FY1976/77	–	–	2·7	13·8	27·1
FY1977/78	–	–	–	2·6	1·2
FY1978/79	–	–	–	–	− 1·3
Total effect	0·5	− 0·8	− 18·8	3·1	4·6
First difference	0·5	− 1·3	− 18·0	21·9	1·5

B: Monetary policy

					(% change)
			Cumulative effects by:		
Policy actions taken during:	*1975:1*	*1976:1*	*1977:1*	*1978:1*	*1979:1*
FY1974/75	− 0·8	− 1·9	− 14·6	− 12·8	− 24·3
FY1975/76	–	− 1·0	− 13·1	− 8·0	− 13·1
FY1976/77	–	–	5·1	12·7	24·6
FY1977/78	–	–	–	− 5·8	− 16·8
FY1978/79	–	–	–	–	9·1
Total effect	− 0·8	− 2·9	− 22·6	− 13·9	− 20·5
First difference	− 0·8	− 2·1	− 19·7	8·7	− 6·6

change in the currency value amounted to almost 20%.[5] In subsequent years the exchange rate never managed to fully recover from this depreciation. Of far greater interest, however, is the finding that this episode coincides with an equally substantial swing in the exchange rate induced by fiscal policy. This latter movement amounted to an 18% depreciation in the fiscal year 1976/77 with most of the change being associated with policy actions undertaken in the previous year. However, unlike the monetary-policy-induced fall in the currency value, the depreciation of sterling arising from fiscal policy was completely reversed one year later by the effect of the restrictive fiscal policy administered in 1976/77.

   These predicted falls in the currency value roughly coincide in timing with the actual period of the sterling crisis and thus support the view that the 1976 sterling crisis developed as a consequence of inappropriate policy action.

Rather than reflecting a simple lack of confidence, the current exercise suggests that the sterling crisis had its root cause in a misalignment of policy in the early years of the administration, with the tightening of policy that occurred in 1976/77 constituting an appropriate adjustment. Of course, the result depends, *inter alia*, on the behavioural equation governing the determination of the exchange rate in the model. With expectations formed adaptively, changes in the effective exchange rate are determined by the real interest differential between the UK and the rest of the world and by movements in the real value of the balance of payments on goods and services account. Movements in the domestic interest rate therefore impinge directly upon the level of the exchange rate whilst fiscal policy, Treasury bill rate unchanged, impacts only indirectly through its effect on the balance of payments and the rate of inflation.

4 Domestic policy and developments in world trade

In addition to providing information about the effects of domestic policy actions, the methodology employed above may also be used to examine the impact for the United Kingdom of changes in other, non-policy, variables. Here the focus is deliberately kept narrow, a complete investigation of all potential sources of change being beyond the scope of the current paper. Instead we limit ourselves to comparing the effect of developments in world trade upon the level of output and the balance of payments for the United Kingdom with the corresponding effects produced by domestic demand management policies.

Following the oil price increase of 1973, an absolute contraction in world trade occurred in the final quarter of 1974 and the beginning of 1975. This decline was subsequently reversed from the third quarter of 1975 onwards with the balance of world trade continuing to grow over the remainder of the period. Interestingly enough the results suggest that the main deflationary impact of the 1974/75 contraction was not felt in the United Kingdom until the fiscal year 1977/78, at which point it coincided with the effects of the deflationary action undertaken by the Labour government. Similarly, the worsening world trade situation at the beginning of the period is associated with a deteriorating current account position through 1975/76 and 1976/77 only to be replaced in the final two years of the period by a strong recovery.

A comparison of these effects and a corresponding measure of the effect of domestic policy is presented in Figure 6.2. In part (a) of the diagram we plot the first difference of the cumulative effect on GDP of the combined monetary and fiscal policy on the horizontal axis whilst, on the vertical axis, we plot the output effects of movements in world trade similarly expressed. In part (b) we compare the corresponding developments in terms of the current account of the balance of payments expressed as a proportion of historical GDP. By construction, then, the 45-degree line shown in the

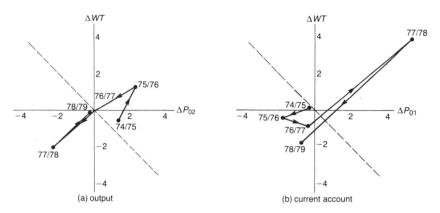

Fig. 6.2

diagrams may be thought of as representing a locus of perfectly offsetting policy and world trade movements. A cursory inspection of both diagrams shows, however, that the observations tend to fall on the opposing diagonal, domestic policy effects reinforcing those of movements in world trade. For the balance of payments, this is particularly noticeable in the case of the turn-round produced in the fiscal year 1977/78, where the post-1975 recovery in world trade combines with the effect of the deflationary package introduced in 1977 to produce a substantial improvement on the current account.

5 Conclusions

According to this analysis the effects of macroeconomic policies undertaken by the Labour government, 1974–79, were dominated by two main features. The first relates to the sharp turn-round in policy that was administered through the deflationary budget and high interest rates in 1976/77: this appears to have cut GDP by 2–3% of GDP. This sharp turn-round occurs independently of exchange rate effects, though the latter are significant for the course of inflation and the balance of payments. The second feature is that, under the assumption of adaptive expectations and with the exchange rate depending on real interest differentials and the current account, the results show policy giving rise to strong depreciation effects by 1976, the period of sterling crisis. Whether the currency situation was the proximate cause of the reversal of macroeconomic policy in that year is not under examination here, but certainly the evidence from the counterfactual simulations is that sterling underwent a significant improvement in value following the tightening of macro policy.

Appendix A Simulation assumptions

The assumptions underlying the various counterfactual simulations are as follows:

I *Neutral fiscal policy*
1 Public authority expenditure in any quarter is held constant at the previous quarter's value;
2 The tax system is fully indexed in the second quarter of each year by the annual rate of inflation lagged two quarters;
3 Tax rates other than specific duties are held constant at the previous quarter's value.

II *Neutral monetary policy*
1 Treasury bill rate is held constant at the previous quarter's value.

III *World trade*
1 Total world trade, world trade in manufacturing and world industrial production held constant at the previous quarter's value.

Notes

1 Model-based policy analysis using consistent expectations is comparatively new. Matthews and Minford (1987) afford an innovative example.

2 Details of the modifications incorporated in Model 11 are given in Wren-Lewis (1988).

3 A complete list of the policy instruments together with details of the changes made is given in the Appendix to this chapter.

4 See, for example, Bladen-Hovell *et al.* (1982) for a model based on study of the transmission mechanism for monetary policy which emphasises the role of the exchange rate.

5 The reader should of course recall that the figures recorded in Table 6.5 are simply the partial effects of *policy* on the exchange rate; in the historical record the actual exchange rate had substantially recovered from its earlier decline by the end of March 1977, though it still stood some 25% below its 1974:1 value.

References

Artis, M. J., and Bladen-Hovell, R. C. (1987), 'The UK's monetarist experiment, 1979–84', *International Review of Applied Economics*, I, no. 1, pp. 23–47.

Artis, M. J., and Bladen-Hovell, R. C. (1990), 'The Labour government's economic record: 1974–79. An appraisal of the macroeconomic policy.' University of Manchester Discussion Papers in Economics, no. 67.

Artis, M. J., and Green, C. J. (1982), 'Using the Treasury model to measure the impact of fiscal policy' in M. J. Artis, C. J. Green, G. W. Smith and D. G. Leslie (eds), *Demand Management, Supply Constraints and Inflation*, Manchester University Press, Manchester.

Artis, M. J., Bladen-Hovell, R. C., and Ma, Y. (1990), 'The measurement of policy effects in a non-causal model: an application to economic policy in the UK, 1974–79', University of Manchester Discussion Papers in Economics.

Artis, M. J., Bladen-Hovell, R., Karakitsos, E., and Dwolatsky, B. (1984), 'The effects of economic policy: 1979–82', *National Institute Economic Review*, May, no. 108, pp. 54–67.

Bladen-Hovell, R. C., Green, C. J. and Savage, D. (1982), 'The transmission of monetary policy in two large-scale models of the UK economy', *Oxford Bulletin of Economics and Statistics*, XLIV, no. 1, pp. 15–30.

Blinder, A. S., and Goldfeld, S. M. (1976), 'New measures of fiscal and monetary policy, 1958–73', *American Economic Review*, LXVI, December, pp. 780–96.

Hall, S. G., and Henry, S. G. B. (1985), 'Rational expectations in an econometric model: NIESR model 8', *National Institute Economic Review*, November, 114, pp. 58–68.

Matthews, K., and Minford, P. (1987), 'Mrs Thatcher's Economic Policies 1979–1987', *Economic Policy*, October, 5, pp. 57–101.

Saville, I. D., and Gardiner, K. L. (1986), 'Stagflation in the UK since 1970: a model based explanation', *National Institute Economic Review*, August, pp. 52–69.

Wallis, K. F., Fisher, P. G., Tanna, S. K., and Whitley, J. D. (1989), 'Comparative properties of models of the UK economy', *National Institute Economic Review*, 129, August, pp. 69–87.

Wren-Lewis, S. (1988), 'Model 11: a new version of the Institute's domestic econometric model', *National Institute Economic Review*, 126.

The international status of sterling

1 Introduction

The election of the Labour government in February 1974 coincided with a period of extreme turbulence in international economic relations. Exchange rate flexibility was forced on, rather than chosen by, the world economy following the collapse of the Bretton Woods system in March 1973. There was an expectation that a new international monetary order would emerge. This was not to occur. The 1973–74 oil price shock intensified prevailing tensions in international monetary relations. To this day the world economy has made no progress towards the creation of an international monetary system to replace that established at Bretton Woods. But the Labour government had to operate not only against an uncertain international economic background. Its period in office coincided with the time when the United States was attempting to come to terms with its defeat in Vietnam and the Watergate scandal. America became increasingly inward-looking. A leadership vacuum developed which made impossible the adoption of an effective collective response to the problems facing the international economy. What measures were introduced were inadequate and were perceived to be so at the time. However, this is hardly surprising, given the divergence in the diagnoses of the ills facing the world economy and, therefore, of the prescribed policies.

The Labour government, then, was confronted with three interrelated sets of issues. First, it had to respond to the problems relating to the world economy. Second, it had to react to the impact of a disintegrating international monetary order on the international status of sterling. Third, it had to deal with a series of domestic economic problems with its ability to choose between alternative policy mixes severely restricted by external developments beyond its control. This chapter concentrates on two issues relating to the international status of sterling. First, it considers how the Labour administration sought to deal with the problems associated with the volatility of sterling balances. Healey (1989) comments that James Callaghan 'had come to believe that our only real problem was the sterling balances' (p. 430).

Second, it discusses the background to the 1978 decision by the UK not to become a full member of the European Monetary System. The choice of this focus rests on the judgement that these two issues presented the Labour government with the opportunity to effect a radical reorientation in its international economic relations by providing a European solution to the sterling balances problem and by joining a new monetary arrangement which would have safeguarded sterling as well as allowing Britain to play a significant role in EEC developments. It will be argued that the Labour government was not alone responsible for the fact that this opportunity was missed. With the departure of Heath from the leadership of the Conservative Party and despite the result of the 1975 referendum, attitudes towards Europe became increasingly lukewarm in both major parties. Be that as it may, it will be suggested that Callaghan's leadership, for a variety of reasons, was not sufficiently effective. The decisions reached in relation to the international status of sterling could have been more innovative.

Section 2 discusses the Labour government's reactions to the problems which faced the world economy. These reactions partly determined the government's responses to the issue of sterling balances, considered in Section 3, and its attitude to the creation of the European Monetary System which is assessed in Section 4. Finally, some conclusions are presented.

2 The world economy

The collapse of the Bretton Woods system was inevitable. Robert Triffin had drawn attention to its inherent instability since the late 1950s. However, the timing of its final breakdown can ultimately be traced to the decision of the USA to finance the escalation of its war in Vietnam and its domestic social programmes, introduced in the mid-1960s, by expansionary monetary policies rather than by raising taxes. As a result, the American balance of payments deficit steadily increased and world inflation accelerated. The rest of the world, particularly Europe, became increasingly unwilling to accumulate dollar balances and import inflation from the USA. There thus emerged a divergence of attitudes which eventually led to the breakdown of the Bretton Woods system in March 1973. The economic nationalism characteristic of US international monetary policies prevented the adoption of commonly agreed responses to the effects of the 1973–74 oil price rise. Healey (1989) observes that 'no change could be made in the structure of world finance without the consent of the United States; and the United States would see no interest but its own, though its view of its interest might differ from person to person, or from administration to administration' (p. 416). In January 1974 the IMF Managing Director, H. J. Witteveen, presented a note to the Committee of Twenty arguing against oil-importing countries introducing deflationary measures in response to the inevitable deterioration in their balance of payments. He warned that such a course would damage international trade and could cause a severe world recession. His thesis was agreed but only Britain and Italy, among the major economies, did not proceed to introduce deflationary policies. The UK was able to finance its deficit by borrowing from the commercial banks and from Iran and Saudi Arabia. However, it felt that there was need for an international scheme which would address the problem of imbalances at an international level. Thus Healey advanced a proposal involving an official mechanism through the IMF which would recycle at least $25 billion of the oil-exporting countries' surpluses to countries whose balance of payments deficits had particularly suffered from the oil price rise. He presented his plan at the IMF annual meeting in October 1974. The United States strongly opposed the UK proposal and argued that the recycling function should be undertaken by commercial banks. It was only after the Labour government secured the support of its EEC partners that it was able to force the USA to agree to the second Witteveen Oil Facility which, however, made available to oil-deficit countries only $6 billion. On the other hand, America's intransigence resulted in the rapid accumulation of commercial bank debt with devastating effects on many Third World countries. It is interesting to note, however, that this episode allowed Healey to conclude 'that it may be possible for the Europeans to secure a change in a fixed American position, providing they are united, determined and well briefed' (1989, p. 426).

Consistent with his views on the need for a comprehensive recycling scheme, Healey was able, when elected Chairman of the IMF's Interim Committee in the autumn of 1977, to secure IMF interest rate subsidies for Third World countries as well as increase their allocation of Special Drawing Rights (SDRs).

The major economic powers were also unable to agree on how to limit the sharp fluctuations in exchange rates. Their principal preoccupation, quite amazingly, was whether or not gold should be demonetised. The United States argued for a system resting exclusively on the dollar but the French and the Italians favoured a continuing role for gold. The compromise which was reached allowed the countries to trade gold among themselves so long as the total official gold holdings did not increase. Of course this did nothing to reduce exchange rate volatility. The same was true of the deliberations of the various annual economic summits, the first of which was held in 1975. However, in the Bonn Summit in 1978, Callaghan was successful in persuading the USA to agree to a reduction in its oil imports and West Germany to adopt reflationary measures.

In summary, the UK's attitudes to the problems facing the world economy were dictated by a desire to protect employment and growth. It failed to secure the consistent support of either the USA or its European partners. Thus it effectively isolated itself and was unable, as a consequence, to introduce domestic policies compatible with those in either of its two main economic partners. Further, it was not possible to develop alliances which could facilitate the transition of sterling from being a major to becoming a relatively minor international currency. The ambiguity of Britain's postion in the world economy has yet to be resolved. Ten years after Labour's electoral defeat, Britain continues to be reluctant to accept the implications that it possesses little, if any, economic sovereignty.

3 Sterling balances

A feature of 1976 was the steep decline in official holdings of sterling balances. Oil-exporting countries halved their holdings from £2839m. in December 1975 to £1421m. in December 1976. Less dramatically, other countries' holdings declined during the same period from £1262m. to £1218m. The main fall in official sterling balances occurred between March and June when oil producers reduced their holdings by almost £700m., that is, 70% of the reduction in aggregate sterling balances for that quarter. Nigeria, motivated by purely political considerations, accounted for well over 50% of the fall in the oil-exporting countries' sterling holdings. In contrast, private sterling holdings in EEC, oil-exporting and other countries rose gently throughout 1976 resulting in an aggregate increase of £250m., which contradicts the view that there was a general collapse of confidence in sterling during the year. The volatility of sterling balances, particularly of the official holdings, prompted the UK to seek and reach a new Basle Agreement in January 1977 as part of the IMF package of measures. The rationale for the 1977 Basle Agreement can be traced back to the 1968 Basle Agreement which, whatever its intentions may have been, led to an increase in the aggregate volume of sterling balances. It will shortly be argued that had the Conservative government of 1970−74 not pursued rather puzzling policies *vis-à-vis* the sterling balances, the problems confronting its successor Labour government would have been significantly less severe.

With the disintegration of the Empire the former colonies sought to loosen their economic ties with the UK by diversifying their trade and other economic links. One dimension of this process was their decision to reduce the sterling component of their reserves. Of course the persistent weakness of sterling during the 1960s was an important factor in the sterling area countries' attempts to reduce their sterling balances, especially after 1964. Table 7.1 presents data for the period 1963−73. The total volume of official sterling balances peaked in June 1964 at £2549m. which also coincided with the peak for overseas sterling area (OSA) at £2026m. Other countries' sterling holdings reached a maximum in March 1964 when they amounted to £474m. On the other hand, private holdings of sterling, in aggregate and for OSA, peaked in June 1966. The respective figures were £1878m. and £1134m. Private holdings for other countries rose to their maximum of £907m. in September 1964. The Labour government of 1964 inherited severe balance of payments problems. Its failure to take decisive measures,

Table 7.1 Changes in sterling balances (£ million)

	Overseas sterling countries		Non-sterling countries		International organisations excluding IMF	Total
	Exchange reserves	Other holders	Exchange reserves	Other holders		
Dec. 1962 to Sept. 1964	246	190	– 25	179	8	598
Sept. 1964 to Sept. 1968	– 512	10	–218	–373	11	–1082
Sept. 1968 to May 1972	1584	473	160	392	116	2725
May 1972 to Dec. 1973	– 49	–344	– 40	177	86	– 170
Total change	1269	329	–123	375	221	2071

Source: Bank of England Quarterly Bulletin, XIV, no. 2, June 1974, p. 171.

particularly to devalue, was largely due to its minute majority. However, even when it acquired a comfortable majority following the 1966 elections it was unable to instil confidence in sterling. The flight from sterling gradually gathered momentum. In the summer of 1966 the UK concluded the first Basle Agreement, which provided for a facility of $1000m. to be made available to the UK by other major countries in the event of its reserves declining in response to fluctuations in countries' sterling reserves. Sterling was finally devalued in November 1967. This did not restore confidence in sterling. Pressures persisted. Thus in the second quarter of 1968 the largest quarterly fall in official holdings, £285m., was registered. The UK entered into negotiations with major countries, except France which declined to participate, and with the Bank for International Settlements (BIS). These negotiations led to the second Basle Agreement of 1968. This involved a facility of $2000m. BIS would be able to draw on deposits with it by central banks, specially those of OSA countries, and the resources made available by the twelve leading countries, and would also be able to borrow in international markets. The Agreement was to last for three years.

The Agreement enabled the UK to draw dollars or other foreign currencies in the event of sterling balances, both official and private, falling below an agreed starting level which was set at £3080m. As the level of the total volume of sterling holdings was in September 1968 already below the 'trigger' point, the UK began making use of the facility immediately. By the end of October $600m. were drawn. By the end of September 1969, however, the Labour government had repaid all that it had drawn and the facility was not used again.

The more significant aspect of the 1968 Basle Agreement was the UK's undertaking to guarantee the dollar value of the OSA countries' sterling balances. More specifically, the UK agreed that in the event of the sterling/dollar exchange rate falling, and remaining for thirty consecutive days, below $2·376, it would make a payment in sterling to restore the dollar value of official sterling balances in excess of 10% of each country's total external reserves. In return for the dollar guarantee OSA countries agreed to maintain a minimum percentage of their total reserves in sterling.

The Basle Agreement was welcomed as providing an opportunity for the orderly phasing out of the reserve role of sterling. This reaction was somewhat puzzling. The dollar guarantee was an incentive for OSA countries to increase their sterling balances and by generating expectations regarding the exchange rate commitment of the UK government to encourage also the rise of private sterling balances. It is, therefore, not surprising that official sterling balances held by OSA countries rose by £1254m. during the three-year period September 1968 to September 1971. Other countries' sterling holdings declined during 1969 and 1970 but by September 1971 they were back at their September 1968 level. At the same time, total private sterling balances increased from £1558m. to £1970m., the rise being accounted for by broadly equal increases in OSA and other countries' private sterling holdings.

The dollar guarantee was renewed for a further period of two years in September 1971 by the Conservative government. This was somewhat surprising in view of developments in the international monetary system. But even more puzzling was the government's decision to extend the dollar guarantee in September 1973 for the period to end March 1974. Given the decision to allow sterling to float in June 1972 it is very difficult to comprehend why the Conservative government chose to extend the dollar guarantee for a further period.

Sterling balances continued to increase, not unexpectedly, throughout 1972, and by June 1973 OSA official holdings had climbed to a new peak of £3083m. while those of other countries had nearly doubled to £571m. On the other hand total private sterling holdings were reasonably stable during 1972 and 1973.

The continual increase in sterling balances after September 1968 was largely due to the dollar guarantee. It is true that the increasing weakness of the dollar did contribute to this increase. Be that as it may, it is difficult to justify the decision to persist with the dollar guarantee after 1971, even allowing for the fact that the volatility of sterling balances was dramatically reduced as a result of the guarantee. Whatever the benefits yielded up to the election of Labour in 1974 it was inevitable that the magnitude of the problem eventually to face the new government would be greater than if the Conservative government had pursued more consistent policies. Neither was the Labour government helped by international political developments. The aftermath of the Arab–Israeli war and the first oil price rise reinforced the effects of the dollar guarantee. The intense hostility of Arab countries towards the USA and their large balance of payments surpluses combined to produce a sharp increase in sterling balances during 1974. Oil-exporting countries' official sterling balances increased from £719m. to £3183m. between September 1973 and December 1974. This increase was only partially offset by the decrease of other countries' official holdings. Again the benefits of this development could not be but short run. As the dollar guarantee was removed at the end of 1974 and Arab–American relations improved, sterling balances started to decline. The fall was gentle during 1975 but, as already mentioned, accelerated during 1976, persuading the government to conclude a new Basle Agreement in January 1977. Table 7.2 presents data for the period 1974–79.

In explaining the purpose of the new Agreement Denis Healey told the House of Commons on 11 January 1977 that its aim

is not only to achieve greater international monetary stability and to ensure that sterling and the exchange markets cease to be affected by pressures associated with any rundown of the official sterling holdings, but also to enable the British Government to achieve an orderly reduction in the role of sterling as a reserve currency.

Table 7.2 *Exchange reserves in sterling and banking and money market liabilities in sterling to holders other than central monetary institutions (£ millions)*

	Central monetary institutions			Other holders		
	Total	Oil exporters	Other	Total	Oil exporters	Other
1974 March	3655	1282	2373	2231	262	1969
June	3856	1868	1988	2386	270	2116
September	4420	2763	1657	2447	299	2148
December	4634	3101	1533	2500	344	2156
1975 March	4862	3449	1413	2519	324	2195
June	4559	3239	1320	2984	367	2617
September	4179	2943	1236	2985	408	2577
December	4100	2838	1262	3229	466	2763
1976 March	4020	2623	1397	3234	473	2761
June	3099	1964	1135	3223	444	2779
September	2750	1541	1209	3435	449	2986
December	2639	1421	1218	3484	497	2987
1977 March	2829	1443	1386	3683	532	3151
December	2835	1360	1475	4965	747	4218
1978 December	2610	1006	1604	5266	984	4282
1979 June	2843	1141	1702	6087	1235	4852

Source: *Bank of England Quarterly Bulletin*, various issues.

How the 1977 Basle Agreement was to contribute to the above objectives is not clear. It involved the governments of Belgium, Canada, West Germany, Japan, the Netherlands, Sweden, Switzerland and the United States agreeing to support a medium-term facility of $3 billion. The UK could draw on this facility if official sterling balances fell below their December 1976 levels. The Agreement was for a period of two years and also provided that the UK could offer official holders the option to convert any part of their sterling balances into negotiable medium-term foreign currency bonds. Contrary to Healey's statement it is difficult to comprehend the rationalisation of the Agreement. It was, just like its predecessors, of only limited duration. It did not involve the OSA countries. It was based on the Group of Ten which, effectively with the collapse of the Bretton Woods system, had ceased to have a clearly defined role in international monetary relations. It ignored the fact that the UK had become an EEC member. In brief, the 1977 Basle Agreement reflected an instinctive defensive reaction by a government that lacked a clear view of how to deal with the sterling crisis. It is not obvious that this agreement was necessary. As already noted, according to Healey the sterling balances problem was perceived by Callaghan to be of major

significance. It may be argued that Callaghan was led to this rather exaggerated judgement because he was Chancellor of the Exchequer at the time the
1968 Basle Agreement was concluded. However, to the extent that there was
a problem, the government could have sought a European solution. But it
proved unable to exploit the crisis to chart a new policy direction which would
have involved the UK collaborating more closely with its EEC partners. This
was politically feasible given the results of the 1975 referendum. Instead, the
UK persisted with alliances and arrangements which had outlived their
usefulness. As will be argued in the next section the Labour government was
consistently unable to overcome its antipathy towards European solutions to
international economic problems.

As the data in Table 7.2 indicate, official holdings of sterling did not
fluctuate to any significant degree between December 1976 and June 1979.
In contrast, private holdings of sterling registered a sharp rise during this
period.

4   The European Monetary System

It may be argued that the 1977 Basle Agreement is one of many examples of
Britain's reluctance to develop closer links with its partners in the European
Community. A European solution to the sterling balances problem could
have been explored. But Britain chose not to press for such a solution and,
instead, opted for an agreement within a framework which was rapidly
becoming out of date. Distaste for European-inspired economic initiatives
was also characteristic of British attitudes immediately before and during the
discussions which eventually led to the creation of the European Monetary
System. Critics of the Labour government's decision not to join the system's
exchange rate mechanism sometimes appear to ignore the fact that in 1978
there was little support for full membership inside or outside Parliament.
The decision was certainly politically convenient for Labour. However,
other considerations and calculations resulted in the Conservative opposition, industry, trade unions, and a variety of other institutions and
observers, coming to share the government's hostility towards the system.
Further, there was widespread scepticism across Europe as to whether the
system would survive for any length of time, especially as the Bundesbank
did not attempt to conceal its doubts and reservations. The general reaction
to the Franco-German initiative facilitated the government's decision. This,
of course, does not imply that the Labour government had no real alternative but to opt against full membership. Errors of judgement, the Labour
Party's stubborn hostility towards the EC, a naive belief in the 'special'
relationship with the USA, and a lack of political will to take a major
decision on the eve of a General Election combined to prevent the Callaghan
government from adopting an unambiguous position towards the EMS.
Thus, the Labour government chose to 'join' the system but not its exchange

rate mechanism. However, it is clear that it did not regard that decision as final. In domestic terms it was a politically 'safe' decision while, by not excluding full membership at some future date, it did not subvert the relations between the UK and its European partners. On the other hand, it was not the decision of a government with clear vision and a sense of purpose.

That the Labour government was drifting with no direction or well-defined objective is perhaps exemplified by Healey's evidence to the House of Commons (1978) Expenditure Committee proceedings on the EMS in November 1978. He summarised the government's position as follows:

If I could put fairly shortly my own and the Government's approach to the matter, we think it would make sense for Britain to join a European monetary system whose objective was to create a zone of greater monetary stability in Europe, providing it satisfied the general principles which were agreed by the Council of Finance Ministers of the Community at its meeting in June, largely as a result of suggestions I made myself. There are broadly eight principles which we then thought the system should embody. First of all, it should be durable. Secondly, it should contain all members of the Community. Thirdly, it should favour higher growth in the Community, rather than constrain growth. For that reason, fourthly, it should impose obligations on the strong, which were symmetrical with the obligations falling on the weaker members. Fifthly, it should dispose of adequate funds for intervention, and credit to support intervention. Sixthly, it should provide for realignments of parities within the system, by agreement. Seventhly, it should not operate to the detriment either of currencies outside [like the dollar or the yen], or to the detriment of the international monetary organisation to which the Third World and Commonwealth countries belong [the IMF]. Finally, it should be accompanied by a movement to produce a less perverse transfer of resources inside the Community than arises out of the existing Community mechanisms like the common budget and the Common Agricultural Policy.

The above statement of the government's attitude towards the proposed system was quite remarkable. Just a month before the meeting of the European Council which was to finalise the details of the scheme to be adopted Britain was advancing propositions which were inherently incompatible with the decision taken the previous summer to create the EMS.

Consider the first feature which according to Healey the system should possess, that is, durability. It is just not clear how any system, whatever its features, can be judged to be 'durable' or otherwise before it is established and functioning. Similarly, it is difficult to comprehend the Labour government's suggestion that all EC countries must be members of the system. By November 1978 the UK Government could not have been in any doubt that the majority of the EC countries were determined to proceed with the creation of the system irrespective of whether or not the UK decided to join it. The proposition that the system should promote growth is somewhat surprising. The Labour government must have fully appreciated that such a condition could not but antagonise at least West Germany. Next, in emphasising the desirability of 'adequate' funds and credit to support foreign exchange market intervention the UK government appeared to relegate to secondary importance the objective on which the other countries focused, namely the control of inflation through collectively determined policies. The argument that the system should not operate to the detriment of the dollar or the IMF was puzzling. It ignored the fact that the Franco-German initiative was partly inspired by disenchantment with US policies. It showed little awareness that Europe by itself could not establish monetary relationships which were consistent also with US objectives. There was little evidence that the United States was willing to collaborate with Europe in creating a new international monetary system. It is also quite difficult to comprehend how the EMS could impact on the IMF. With the final collapse of the Bretton Woods system in March 1973, the IMF ceased to have a clearly defined role in international monetary affairs. It became an institution searching for a role. The EMS could not have affected the IMF's position whatever its features. Finally, in linking the creation of the system with the reform of CAP and the Community budget the Labour government could not have expected to be taken seriously by its European partners.

In brief, then, the Labour government set conditions for joining the system which it must have known could not be satisfied even if the other EC member countries were willing to make every concession. And yet Healey dismissed studies submitted to the House of Commons (1978) Expenditure Committee which were critical of the proposed monetary system on the grounds that views contained in them 'are expressed in ignorance of what shape a monetary system will emerge from the negotiations, so that, to a large extent, they are tilting at windmills'. Similarly, in November 1978 the Green Paper on the EMS stated that the government could not 'yet reach their own conclusion on whether it would be in the best interests of the UK to join the exchange rate regime of the EMS as it finally emerges from the negotiations'. Healey's statement to the House of Commons Expenditure Committee is consistent with the view that the government had already decided against joining the system. That it persisted with the pretence that it was still considering in November 1978 its final decision on membership reflected its growing indecisiveness and the increasing isolation of Britain.

The origins of the EMS can be traced to the fact that the progress towards economic integration achieved in the 1960s was not maintained during the 1970s. Roy Jenkins on becoming President of the Commission in 1977 judged it necessary to introduce new initiatives aimed at reviving the process of integration. He decided that this was most likely to be achieved by renewing interest in the objective of monetary union. Accordingly in the autumn of 1977 he called on EC member countries to proceed with the creation of such a union and the establishment of a European currency. His proposal was too radical. However, Chancellor Schmidt was persuaded that there was need for an initiative in European monetary relations though monetary union was not a politically feasible objective. He decided to explore possibilities with the French President Giscard d'Estaing and secure his support. He was less certain about British reactions. In March 1978 when Callaghan met Schmidt the former presented a plan for world economic recovery. Its principal features were an emphasis on growth and the insistence that it should be implemented through the IMF, thus ensuring the participation of America. Germany was expected to reflate its economy. Schmidt was less than impressed. He considered Callaghan's proposals as highly inflationary and somewhat naive in their aim to involve America and the IMF. He thus decided not to share his thoughts on monetary issues with the British Prime Minister. Instead, he concentrated on reaching an understanding with the French President.

It would appear that the Labour government, through its insistent calls for growth and its desire not to offend US sensitivities was in fact building a wall between itself and its EC partners. It showed little understanding of European concerns about inflation while relations between President Carter and Callaghan were such as to result in the latter being more tolerant of US policies. It is interesting to note the immediate reaction of Callaghan's advisers on learning of Schmidt's plans in Copenhagen in April 1978. According to Jenkins (1989), Callaghan was somewhat unclear about these plans. After they were explained to him, he sought the opinion of his advisers. Jenkins recorded their reaction as follows:

But nobody had much to say, certainly not Hunt. Couzens looked rather pole-axed and kept on repeating, 'But it is very bold, Prime Minister. Did the Chancellor really go as far as that? It is very bold. It leaves the dollar on one side. I don't know what the Americans will say about it. It's very bold, Prime Minister'. After twenty-five minutes of this ...

(p. 248)

It is arguable that the decision not to involve Britain in the discussions on the monetary system from their inception did bias British attitudes. By 1978 the Labour government had overcome the sterling crisis and its aftermath and its pact with the Liberal Party guaranteed it a secure parliamentary majority. Callaghan felt sufficiently confident that he hoped to engage in international economic diplomacy. It would appear, however, that he misjudged his European partners while exaggerating the significance of his relationship with President Carter.

At the meeting of the European Council at Copenhagen in April 1978 Schmidt presented a set of proposals for increased monetary co-operation between EC member countries. President Giscard described the German plan as 'a new Bretton Woods for Europe'. The German plan took by surprise the other EC leaders who wanted time to react. However, Callaghan was highly doubtful, expressing his worries about the impact on the dollar and the IMF that the implementation of the scheme would have. French and

German reassurances were not sufficient and it appears that he was alone in his opposition to the Schmidt proposals. But despite his feelings he agreed that the next phase should involve secret discussions between British, German and French officials. Callaghan eventually nominated Kenneth Couzens. Therefore, it was still possible for Britain to play a significant role in shaping the system which was to be agreed upon at the Bremen meeting of the European Council in July 1978. However, Couzens failed to be an effective participant in the secret negotiations. Eventually relations between him and his colleagues from Germany and France collapsed so that the plan which was presented at the Bremen summit was essentially a Franco-German one. Ludlow (1982), in his excellent discussion of the negotiations preceding the establishment of the EMS, suggests that the breakdown of relations between the British negotiator and the other two reflected 'the fact that Mr Couzens and his masters at home did not share and failed to grasp the significance of the determination of the French and Germans to get something done, come what may' (p. 108).

Ludlow's judgements on the reasons which eventually resulted in Couzens being ignored suggest that Callaghan blundered when choosing a Treasury official to represent him in the secret talks. The German and French representatives were chosen because of their personal relationships with Schmidt and Giscard d'Estaing respectively. This reflected their conviction that if the negotiations were entrusted to civil servants or central bank officials, who were likely to articulate the views of their institutions, no progess would be achieved. Thus, according to Ludlow, Schmidt had hoped that Callaghan would nominate Harold Lever. This did not occur and in Ludlow's judgement Couzens 'spoke and acted throughout as a senior Treasury official' (Ludlow, 1982, p. 109). But the Treasury was unambiguously opposed to a European monetary initiative for a variety of reasons. First, it was suspected that any European scheme, if i. .plemented, would imply that the plan for world recovery through the introduction of expansionary measures in countries such as West Germany would no longer be the subject of even serious consideration. Second, the Treasury felt that an international initiative was preferable to a European one because through the involvement of the IMF, America's participation would be ensured and Britain would be able to exercise greater influence. Third, its thinking was affected by the fact that most of Britain's trade continued to be with non-EC member countries. Fourth, the Treasury was unhappy with any initiative that suggested an anti-dollar motivation. But Ludlow (1982) argues that there were additional considerations of a domestic nature which determined the Treasury's attitudes. Principal among them was the fear that if sterling was to be linked with the Deutschmark, as envisaged by the proposed exchange rate scheme, the UK's de-industrialisation would accelerate, leading to a steep rise in Britain's level of unemployment. The Treasury made little effort to conceal its hostility even during periods when the Labour government made attempts to reassess its position. It was a hostility that never wavered. The Report of the House of Comons (1978) Expenditure Committee judged the Treasury 'to be amongst those who fear the results for the United Kingdom of immediate entry to the proposed EMS' while it noted that the Committee had received no written evidence and characterised a Treasury memorandum as 'uninformative'. Couzens was perhaps expressing the Treasury's feelings when he briefed British journalists in July, after the decision to proceed with the system was taken at the Bremen summit. *The Times*, 11 July 1978, reported the following:

Whilst still accepting the goal of greater monetary stability, the Treasury remains sceptical to the point of contempt of most of the detailed content of the Franco-German scheme ... There is considerable anger at the way in which the proposal was 'sprung' on the rest of the Community ... More substantial criticisms revolve around the vague and often confused terms in which the scheme is phrased, coupled with deep suspicion that the system is little more than a means of holding down the mark and imposing restrictive policies on Germany's partners. There is considerable resentment at what is seen as the success of the German government in presenting its national interest as being a move for the greater good of Europe ... The fact that the whole thing is dealt with in just a few hundred words is generally felt to show the danger of allowing enthusiastic amateurs to dream up schemes for monetary reform.

Further, it is arguable that the Treasury's hostility was one reason why the debate in Britain on the relative merits of the proposed system was uninformed and confused as will be argued later. Thus in November 1978 the Commission in its evidence to the House of Commons (1978) observed that:

the British Government had participated in public discussions of EMS in Britain far less than other EEC governments had done in their own countries with the result that such discussion as there had been ... had been mainly restricted to technicalities.

In Bremen the European Council decided to proceed with the creation of the EMS. It set a timetable for the details of the proposed system to be finalised which envisaged January 1979 as the date when the system would come into operation. Callaghan was less than co-operative at the Bremen meeting and sought to delay any final decisions. His tactics can be explained by his antipathy towards the Franco-German plan rather than by any electoral considerations. At that time an October election was likely. That the details of the system were still to be determined implied that the proposed system was not a potential problem for the Labour government. Callaghan, discovering that he was in a minority of one and suddenly realising the depth of the political commitment of France and Germany to the proposed initiative, did not press his opposition but reserved his position. It is arguable that at this stage Callaghan was still undecided on whether the UK would join the system. For example, he publicly criticised Couzens for his views in an interview with the *Financial Times* on 4 July 1978. However, his decision in September against an October election implied that membership of the system would inevitably become an issue that would affect Labour's electoral fortunes given the Bremen timetable. Peter Jenkins of the *Guardian* maintained on 23 October that Callaghan finally decided against membership immediately after the Labour Party conference during which he became aware of the intensity of the hostility against the proposed scheme. But as already noted the British government continued to pretend that it was still considering the issue and as late as November would allege that it had not yet reached a final decision. To have done otherwise would have resulted in difficulties with the pro-European section of the party and would have exposed the government to the charge of making up its mind even before the details of the proposed system had been finalised. Further, it would have led to the embarrassing situation of being internationally isolated given that the United States had declared itself in favour of the system in July 1978 and when President Carter addressed the IMF Annual Meetings the following September.

The decision not to join the system was facilitated by the prevailing mood of hostility. According to Ludlow (1982) in the Cabinet only Williams, Lever and Rodgers were unequivocally in support of membership. Ministers like Dell, Owen and Hattersley were, rather surprisingly, indifferent if not hostile to the UK joining the proposed scheme. There was little enthusiasm in the Parliamentary Labour Party, the National Executive Committee and the TUC. Similarly, the Conservative Party adopted a rather lukewarm position. Biffen naively argued that the Franco-German plan was not compatible with economic liberalism but the Conservative Party refrained from rejecting membership. It did not have to do so. Developments were favourable to it and it was under no pressure to play a prominent role in the debate. Only the Liberal Party came out in favour of membership but its influence by then had been dramatically reduced.

A number of economists, including Pepper, Ward, Blackaby, Burns and Budd, submitted papers to the House of Commons (1978) Expenditure Committee advising against full and immediate membership. Their opposition rested on a variety of arguments. First, it was maintained that membership would undermine the UK's independence in determining its economic policies. Second, in a variant of the economic policy autonomy argument, it was suggested that if Britain were to join the EMS, it would lose the ability to choose the speed at which the domestic rate of inflation could be reduced. Consequently, it was alleged, the transitional rise in unemployment would be higher than if the country stayed out of the system. Third, it was asserted that membership would result in exchange rates which would exert contractionary pressures. Fourth, some predicted that the system was likely to collapse because of the differences in countries' rates of inflation. This particular view was widely held in the UK but also in some European quarters.

It would be wrong, however, to suggest that there was no support for full membership of the system. Robin Leigh-Pemberton, then Chairman of National Westminster Bank, in his memorandum to the House of Commons (1978) Expenditure Committee argued that if the UK stayed out of the system, 'that in itself is no solution to any problem'. Further, he maintained that 'since it would seem undeniably in our interests as far as possible to be within the main power centres of the EEC we should aim over a reasonable period to join the new monetary system'. Christopher Johnson, of Lloyds Bank, in his evidence to the same Committee forcefully argued in favour of immediate membership, while Sir Jeremy Morse expressed support for the UK joining the EMS, an initiative which in his view would reinforce current policy.

It can be argued that criticisms made during 1978 were ill-informed and unfounded. There was sufficient information about the system, even if not readily available in the UK, for nobody to confuse what was being proposed with the question of European monetary union. It is surprising that the belief was generated in this country that what was being advocated was a system of rigidly fixed exchange rates. Nor is it easy to comprehend why UK observers ignored the price dimension of 'monetary stability', the objective of the system. It is rather ironic that the government refuted some of the arguments against membership in its Green Paper on the EMS. For example, it observed that 'the claim that joining the EMS would involve a loss of economic independence is only partially true' and noted that Britain had 'adhered to the Bretton Woods argument for fixed but adjustable exchange rates for a quarter of a century'. Further, it accepted the proposition that 'joining the exchange rate mechanism of the EMS could help our fight against inflation' which was described as a 'top priority'. On the fears expressed by many about the consequences of the UK being locked into the 'wrong' exchange rate the Green Paper stated that 'the Government for its part has made it clear that it does not regard exchange rate depreciation as a solution to the economic problems still facing the UK'.

It can be said that the Labour government never made the economic case against full membership of the system. It began by grossly misjudging the mood in France and Germany and effectively Callaghan lost the confidence of Schmidt. He proceeded to misjudge the political determination of France and Germany to create a system of some kind. He thus made the error of involving the Treasury in the secret negotiations between the Copenhagen and Bremen meetings of the European Council. Only at the latter does he appear to have appreciated the political character of the Franco-German initiative. By then valuable time and opportunities had been missed and it was no longer easy for Callaghan to readjust his position. Having taken the decision against an October election, and given the hostility against the system inside and outside the Labour Party, Callaghan opted for the politically safe route of 'joining' the system but not its exchange rate mechanism. It is, therefore, difficult to accept his assurances to Jenkins

(1989, pp. 333–4) that the decision against membership was not motivated by domestic political calculations. This would be consistent with the view that emerged in 1978 and was implicitly accepted by the government that the UK should join the system when the time is 'right'. At that time only the Centre for Banking and International Finance of the City University was sufficiently hostile to the system to declare in its evidence to the House of Commons (1978) that 'the time to join the EMS is never'.

5 Conclusions

The reserve currency status of sterling has been a source of difficulties for UK economic policy makers at least since the mid-1960s. Successive governments have failed to define a new role for sterling consistent with the country's post-Empire relative politico-economic power. The Labour governments of 1974–79 had the opportunity to break with the past and implement a radical reorientation in the UK's international economic policy outlook. The 1976 sterling crisis could have been exploited to formulate a European solution to the sterling balances problem. Similarly, the creation of the EMS offered the chance to the UK to enter into a new monetary alliance which would have secured a more stable background for the international role of sterling. The Labour government failed to take advantage of either opportunity. It consistently exhibited a high degree of indecisiveness and allowed itself to be led rather than lead. In retrospect it is ironic to observe that the principal objective which motivated the decisions of the 1974–79 period was ultimately undermined by the policies adopted in that period. The government was concerned to defend the employment prospects of the country. It feared the implications of 'wrong' exchange rates. But its politically motivated decision not to join the exchange rate mechanism of the EMS paved the way for the gross misalignment of sterling during 1979–81 which resulted in a sharp contraction of the country's manufacturing base. However, the Labour government's failure to Europeanise its economic policies is a reflection of the general failure of the UK's political leadership to adapt to the new economico-political relations which began to emerge in the early 1960s. The decisions on which this chapter concentrated were not unpopular. They reflected a consensus.

References

Healey, D. (1989), *The Time of My Life*, Michael Joseph, London.
House of Commons (1978), *The European Monetary System*, Expenditure Committee, Session 1978–79, November, HMSO.
Jenkins, R. (1989), *European Diary: 1977–81*, Collins, London.
Ludlow, P. (1982), *The Making of the European Monetary System*, Butterworth Scientific, London.

The Labour government and the
European Communities

1 Introduction

The record of the 1974–79 Labour government in matters relating to the European Communities is generally regarded as poor.[1] Opinion polls in the run-up to the 1979 election were showing that a majority in Britain was unhappy with the Labour government's handling of EC issues. And undoubtedly this was partly a result of the government's failure to honour its commitment, made at the time of the 1975 referendum, to effect reforms to Community policies – especially the CAP – 'from within'. But almost certainly these polls were detecting a general reversal in British attitudes concerning EC membership which went well beyond the specific matter of Labour's competence. A number of factors were responsible for this. The Common Agricultural Policy was increasingly being seen as an expensive and inefficient scheme that both defied common sense and operated to the detriment of British consumers; the Community's financial arrangements, under which Britain had emerged as the 'paymaster of Europe', were considered to be inequitable;[2] and there was a growing conviction – fuelled by the continuing deterioration in our trade balance in manufactured goods – that Community membership was a contributory factor in Britain's worsening industrial situation.[3] And the very public successes achieved subsequently by Mrs Thatcher in her dealings with the Community did much to reinforce the view that the Labour government had been inept over 'Europe'. During the December 1979 European summit Mrs Thatcher opted to play the 'national card'. The fabled 'table-thumping' demand for a reduction in Britain's net contribution to the Community budget was quickly rewarded when, the following May, agreement was reached that Britain should receive a budget rebate for both 1980 and 1981. At the same time the European Commission was mandated to devise proposals to effect a permanent solution to the Community's long-standing budgetary dispute. In the event budgetary reform was only the first in a series of reforms to EC policies that were introduced during the 1980s. By the mid-1980s major changes had been made to the hitherto sacrosanct Common Agricultural

Policy. The British public once again attributed this to the personal determination and resolve of Mrs Thatcher. And when the inevitable comparisons
were drawn between the combative and nationalistic negotiating style
adopted by Mrs Thatcher and the distinctly low-key approach of Labour,
the immediate and apparently sustained dividends which the former had
paid served only to cast further doubts on the performance of the latter.

Here we investigate the reasons for what many now regard as a failure on
the part of the Labour government to protect Britain's national interest in
a Community where decisions were, or more frequently were not, taken on
precisely this basis. The chapter is arranged as follows. In Section 2 we
present the background to UK membership of the European Communities.
Section 3 reviews the principal issues that emerged over the 1974–79 period
and Labour's handling of these. Section 4 focuses on the changing role of the
European Council from the late 1970s and how this facilitated the reforms
from which the Thatcher administration derived considerable popular
acclaim. We conclude with some reflections on the record of the Labour
administration.

2 Background

When Labour returned to office in February 1974, Britain had been a
member of the European Community for just over a year. On 29 October
1971, the House of Commons had voted by a majority of 112 to accept
membership on the terms set out in the Conservative government White
Paper published in July of that year.[4] This was followed by the signing of
the Treaty of Accession in Brussels on 22 January 1972, whereupon the UK
formally joined the three institutions that comprised the European Communities (EEC, ECSC and EURATOM). The European Communities Bill
subsequently passed through the British Parliament, becoming law on 17
October 1972, and on 1 January 1973, Britain, along with Ireland and
Denmark, became full members of the EC. A five-year transition phase was
agreed upon during which national policies would, where relevant, be
brought into line with Community practice.[5]

Despite the fact that the second application for EC membership had
been lodged by the then Labour government in 1967, the Labour movement remained divided over the issue. For the Left, membership of a
Community expressly based on the 'ideology of liberal capitalism'[6] was not
only inimical to the entire philosophy of socialism, but might also prove
subsequently to be incompatible with specific economic measures that a
future Labour government would seek to implement. A second, and more
immediate, source of concern was the likely impact of membership on the
British economy.

The Labour Party had presented an estimate of the economic costs and
benefits of membership in its 1970 White Paper.[7] Whilst acknowledging

that conforming to the Community's agricultural policy (the CAP) would raise the cost of foodstuffs to the British consumer, the White Paper argued persuasively that this cost would be more than offset by the dynamic benefits which would accrue to British industry as a result of gaining access to the larger Community market. These gains, in the form of cost-reducing scale economies and efficiency-inducing competition, would fuel Britain's comparatively poor rate of economic growth, enabling us to catch up with the more prosperous economies of Europe, particularly France and West Germany. However, it was stressed that a comprehensive assessment of the probable economic consequences of membership would only be possible after negotiations over the precise terms of UK entry had been concluded.

Opponents of entry saw the matter quite differently. In a series of papers in the early 1970s, Kaldor insisted that rather than being a panacea for Britain's economic ills, membership would instead add to our problems.[8] He accounted for the comparatively low rate of economic growth recorded by Britain during the 1960s in terms of the poor performance of our export industries. This in turn was explained by the comparatively low rate of growth of labour productivity in Britain. And because manufacturing industry was typically characterised by significant economies of scale in production, the rate of change in labour productivity was determined, in part, by the rate of change of total output – of which exports constituted a significant component. Britain was, therefore, caught in a 'vicious circle' in which an initial deterioration in the competitiveness of exports induced further losses as the consequent decline in the rate of growth of output prevented industry from exploiting productivity-enhancing scale economies. And the process applied in reverse. Economies with a strong export sector, such as Germany's, would enjoy cumulative gains as the growth of total output drove unit costs of production down, further enhancing their competitive position. Unless EC membership increased Britain's rate of growth of exports by more than the rate of growth of imports – implying a major improvement in competitiveness which could only be brought about by a significant reduction in real wages – dynamic losses rather than dynamic gains would result. And should Britain's trade balance deteriorate after entry, further output and employment losses could be expected as the resulting balance of payments crisis forced government to tighten domestic monetary and fiscal policies.[9]

Of course Kaldor was not alone in doubting the bullish predictions made in the 1970 White Paper. Many questioned the economic sense of membership when it was quite clear that where more exact estimates could be made, such as over the impact of CAP and the Communities' financial system on Britain, they unambiguously showed that the costs exceeded the benefits. By the end of the 1970s it seemed to many that these reservations had been wholly justified.

3 Labour's record

3.1 *Renegotiations 1974–75*

For the first year in office, Labour was preoccupied with renegotiating the terms of Britain's entry to the EC. Following the 1970 General Election, the responsibility for taking Britain into the EC had fallen to the Heath government, and in 1971 a White Paper was presented to Parliament outlining the terms of entry that had been agreed upon. The Labour Opposition immediately took the position that the negotiated terms were unacceptable. Their attack focused on four specific issues: the lack of any estimate of the balance of payments and trade effects of membership; the absence of long-term guarantees for Commonwealth sugar imports; the absence of any arrangements for continued preferential access for New Zealand butter and cheese beyond a five-year period; and concern about the implications for sterling of removing UK capital controls implicit in the EC decision to move towards economic and monetary union by 1980.[10] On the final day of the 'great debate' in October 1971, Wilson gave notice that the next Labour government would immediately reopen discussions with the Community with a view to negotiating improved terms of entry. Should this prove impossible then withdrawal would be considered.

In reality, of course, the renegotiation demand enabled the Labour Party to maintain some semblance of unity over the Common Market question. For the anti-marketeers the option of withdrawal had been retained, while for the pro-EC lobby renegotiation held out the prospect of extracting assurances from the Community that membership was not incompatible with Labour's domestic economic programme. There were two areas of Community action that would be particularly unsettling for a future Labour government. The first was the reaffirmation by the Paris summit in December 1972 of the intention to achieve economic and monetary union (EMU) by 1980. By then the first stage in this process, the 'Snake' exchange rate regime, was already in place.[11] Later stages in the transition to EMU involved the progressive approximation of fiscal and monetary policies between all EC member states.[12] Although sterling had joined the 'Snake' at the outset, within six weeks the Conservative government had abandoned the system, being unwilling to adjust domestic economic policy to maintain the declared parity. Many in the Labour Party were implacably opposed to making any commitment, however vague, that bound monetary and fiscal policies to an exchange rate target at the expense of domestic objectives. Secondly there were concerns that Labour's economic strategy would be incompatible with Community membership. In 1971 a Commission directive had restricted state assistance to industries operating in the prosperous 'central regions' of member states to 20% of the total investment. This raised fears that Articles 92–4 of the Rome Treaty might subsequently be used to outlaw key aspects of the industrial and regional programmes of a prospective Labour government.[13]

By the time of the February 1974 election, Labour had identified the six issues on which the renegotiation process would focus: the CAP, with reforms to reduce the balance of payments costs to Britain of this protectionist regime uppermost on the agenda; the introduction of a mechanism to lower total UK contributions to the Community budget; the commitment to EMU by 1980; an assurance that national economic sovereignty would be protected, with Labour insisting that Parliament retain those powers over the British economy needed to pursue effective regional, industrial and fiscal policies; ensuring that the interests of the poorer Commonwealth countries and other less developed countries were comprehensively protected by enhanced EC trade and aid policies; and a guarantee that the current exemption of certain items in the UK from indirect taxation would not be compromised by fiscal harmonisation (i.e. adopting the Community's VAT system). In addition Labour's election manifesto gave a commitment that, following renegotiation, the public would have the opportunity to decide upon the merits of membership through a General Election or a Consultative Referendum.

Immediately after the February 1974 election, Labour began the renegotiation process with the presentation of a White Paper formalising their pre-election demands.[14] On 1 April the Council of Ministers was officially notified of the position and discussions were initiated. By early 1975 agreement between the UK and the other member states had been reached, and the outcome was detailed in a White Paper presented to Parliament in March.[15] The only feature of any real significance in the new terms was the introduction of a budgetary correction mechanism which provided for a member state to qualify for a direct rebate from the Community budget should its gross contribution be significantly out of line with its comparative economic prosperity.[16] Elsewhere, as Swann (1988) records, the renegotiation process had convinced Labour's leadership that many of their other fears were groundless. On the matter of sovereignty it had already become clear that the Rome Treaty provided sufficient latitude for member states to design and implement domestic policies to suit their needs. The European Council, composed as it was of sovereign Heads of State, was hardly going to argue otherwise. Fears that the commitment to EMU would emasculate domestic macroeconomic policy had also been dispelled – the EMU timetable was already hopelessly behind schedule and at the 1974 Paris summit Prime Minister Wilson became convinced that monetary union was, for all practical purposes, a non-issue.[17] Suitable arrangements covering New Zealand produce were agreed, while the less developed countries of the Commonwealth appeared pleased with the provisions of the recently concluded Lomé Convention. In the area of industrial policy there appeared to be little conflict between the Community's position on state assistance to firms in prosperous areas and that of the British government. The agreement to press ahead with setting up a Community regional fund, this idea having been pushed by the British in 1972, was welcomed as providing an opportunity for British receipts from the EC budget to increase. When presenting the result of the renegotiation to Parliament, the government announced that a referendum would be held in June. The subsequent vote registered a majority of 2 to 1 in favour of remaining in the EC on the negotiated terms.

The impressive speed with which renegotiation was completed reflects the significant role that direct discussion between the Community Heads of State could play in resolving issues of major disagreement between member states.[18] However, although Labour had undoubtedly successfully exploited the summit vehicle on this occasion, and had outmanoeuvred the anti-marketeers within its own ranks in the process, they proved much less adept at influencing the direction of specific Community policies where sole authority resided with the Council of Ministers. For, unlike the European Council, where the Heads of State could ensure that a broad balance between competing national interests over the entire range of Community economic and political initiatives could be struck, the Council of Ministers alone was charged with the task of reaching agreement over the details of EC spending policies which each national representative could subsequently be called upon to justify in his or her domestic parliament. And it was in this essentially 'distributive game' where play concentrated on Community spending policies – dominated by the CAP – that the problems of the Labour government proved to be most acute.[19]

3.2   *The CAP*

From the outset it had been acknowledged that the CAP would constitute the major cost of membership for the UK. Prior to 1973, agricultural policy in Britain was based on direct income support. Imported foodstuffs entered the domestic market free of tariffs, with farm incomes being maintained, where necessary, through a system of direct, or 'deficiency' payments.[20] The CAP, on the other hand, supported farm incomes by guaranteeing producers a minimum selling price for their produce on Community markets. These prices, fixed annually by the Council of Agricultural Ministers, were maintained by intervention arrangements whereby the Commission would purchase excess supplies when required in order to stabilise market prices around the guaranteed level. The Community market was protected by a variable levy applied to foodstuffs imported from outside the Community. This ensured that non-EC farm produce would always sell at a price slightly above the intervention price.[21] Receipts collected by member states from this scheme were, from 1978, designated Community 'own resources' and, along with receipts from the operation of the common external tariff and up to 1% of national VAT receipts, transferred to a common budget to finance Community spending – the overwhelming share of which was used to fund the intervention arrangements of the CAP.[22] As Britain remained less than self-sufficient over a range of CAP products,

UK receipts from the Community budget would be confined to a share of the much smaller regional and social policy expenditure. So in addition to raising the cost of foodstuffs to British consumers, it was anticipated that Britain would quickly emerge as a net contributor to the EC budget. Reform of the CAP therefore became an objective of the Labour government. However, rather than include this as an element in the renegotiations, Labour proposed that CAP reform could best be achieved 'from within' the Community. In the event no substantial changes were made to the CAP during Labour's period in office. This might not have mattered had it not been for a combination of events during the late 1970's which focused attention in Britain on the functioning of the CAP.

The first was the increasing divergence between Community prices and world prices. Unlike the initial period of UK membership when world food prices were rising faster than Community prices, by 1978 EC guaranteed prices were approximately double world market prices[23] and substantial surpluses over a range of farm produce were accumulating.[24] In Britain, where food prices had risen by 143·4% between 1972 and 1977,[25] the failure of the Council of Ministers to bring agricultural support prices more into line with prevailing world prices was regarded as blatant mismanagement. Secondly, there was a growing awareness that an ever higher share of the financial costs of the CAP was being borne by Britain. Finally, the government was also coming under attack from the domestic farm lobby. This controversy surrounded the operation of the Community's 'green currency' system. 'Green' money had its origins in the currency upheavals of the early 1970s. CAP support prices, denominated in agricultural units of account (AUA), were translated into domestic currencies at the (fixed) market exchange rate. However, the move to generalised floating in the early 1970s meant that this arrangement would generate instability in the agricultural sector as a consequence of day-to-day currency movements. To avoid this a dual exchange rate system was devised whereby AUA would be converted to national currencies at a fixed, 'green' exchange rate. And to prevent producers from exploiting the difference between the market and the 'green' rate, a system of border taxes and levies known as Monetary Compensatory Amounts (MCAs) was introduced. A consequence of this arrangement was that a member state could influence the domestic effect of agreed changes in CAP prices by devaluing or revaluing its green rate. The addition of another policy instrument undoubtedly contributed to resolving conflicts between member states during the annual price-fixing rounds of the Council of Ministers.[26] But Labour's policy of conceding to CAP price rises whilst insulating the economy from their inflationary effects by revaluing the green rate led them into direct conflict with a domestic farm lobby for whom the costs were borne through lower incomes. Eventually in 1977, under mounting pressure from farmers, the government reluctantly devalued the green pound.

Their refusal to do so the following year provoked a Commons debate which the government lost.

The controversy surrounding the CAP explains, in part, the general shift in British public opinion against the Community during the late 1970s. But it is difficult to criticise the Labour government for its failure to effect CAP reform 'from within'. The real problem lay in the decision-making procedures of the Council of Ministers. The Luxembourg accord of 1966 had effectively given a member state the right to veto any proposal coming before the Council should this threaten its 'vital national interest'. The CAP had been designed in the early 1960s primarily to compensate France for membership of a Community in which West German industry stood to be the principal beneficiary. Therefore it was only to be expected that the French veto would be used to resist proposals which, if implemented, would undermine this negotiated settlement. Moreover France saw no reason to link the debate surrounding the British contribution to the EC budget to the operation of the CAP. The UK had joined the Community with full knowledge of the CAP and should not now try to change it to compensate for its failure to exploit the industrial opportunities of membership. In one sense, therefore, the crisis of the CAP prior to 1980 is a crisis of enlargement deriving from the fact that the agricultural interests of Britain, as a net importer of foodstuffs characterised by a highly efficient domestic farm sector, were at odds with those elsewhere in the Community. This is not to deny that the CAP was, in another sense, in real crisis. Mounting food surpluses and ever higher price support were propelling the Community towards a financial crisis. At the same time the cost of the CAP was severely constraining the development of other EC policy initiatives. But it was not until the early 1980s, when the Community was confronted with what in effect amounted to bankruptcy, that reticent member states were finally forced to accept reforms. It remains true, however, that the Labour government was unwilling to adopt a determined stance on the CAP for much of its period in office. In part this is explained by continuing divisions within the party, which extended to the Cabinet, over the basic question of EC membership. Any attempt to force a crisis in the Community over the CAP by playing the 'national card' would inevitably have re-opened a debate which the referendum result had done much to conclude. But it was also symptomatic of Labour's preoccupation with the immediate question of the financial consequences of membership.

3.3   *The Community budget*
As we have noted, the financial cost of membership to Britain had been a central issue in Labour's renegotiation of the terms of entry during 1974. Their concern to secure a broad balance in UK contributions to, and receipts from, the Community budget (*'juste retour'*) had led to the introduction of the 'financial mechanism' in 1975 intended to prevent the contributions of

a member state moving out of line with its share in Community GDP. In the event, however, the conditions necessary to trigger this mechanism were never met, confirming that Britain's gross contribution to the EC budget in the late 1970s was not significantly out of line with her share in Community GDP. But with the winding down of the transitional arrangements in the late 1970s, it became clear that Britain's *net* contribution to the common fund was unjustifiably high.[27] Although the Labour government was moving to demand reforms which would end the role of Britain as 'paymaster of Europe', including proposing limits on CAP spending and increasing the share of the budget allocated to regional and social policies, the 1979 election transferred this responsibility to the Conservative government.

Taylor (1983) sees this preoccupation with 'balancing the books in the shorter term' as inevitably leading Labour to adopt an essentially myopic view of British interests as members of the Community. A consequence of the importance attached to achieving '*juste retour*' was that Labour failed to promote the development of Community spending policies, such as the Common Regional Policy, that would favour Britain. And in other EC discussions the government similarly distanced itself from Commission initiatives which were likely to lead to an increase in Britain's share of Community spending. As evidence of this Taylor cites Britain's resistance to the introduction of the New Community Instrument (the 'Ortoli facility') in 1977, its opposition to the European Parliament's attempts to secure increases in the size of the regional fund, and its attempt to block the Commission proposal to designate a percentage of European Regional Development Fund moneys as 'non-quota'.[28] Undoubtedly part of the Labour government's opposition to the development of stronger spending Commission policies is explained by its unwillingness to countenance any increase of the supranational element in economic integration. Any extension to the revenue-raising and expenditure functions of the European Commission or the decision-making power of the European Parliament would immediately be linked to the sensitive issue of national sovereignty, and not only would this be unpopular in the Labour Party itself, it was equally unlikely to be welcomed by the British public.

It is difficult to avoid the conclusion that in emphasising its determination to alleviate the immediate financial consequences of the Community's spending arrangements, the Labour government effectively created a hostage to fortune. Plagued by continuing internal opposition to membership and faced with growing public resentment towards the Community the Labour government found itself unable either to support proposals to extend the economic powers of the Commission despite the advantages which would have accrued to Britain, or to play the 'national card' over reform without reopening the membership debate. And it was precisely this dilemma which ultimately determined its attitude over the EMS negotiations.

3.4 *The European Monetary System (EMS)*

Although the idea of re-establishing currency stability in the EC by returning to a regime of fixed exchange rates was first mooted by Roy Jenkins in a speech at Florence in October 1977,[29] the EMS was the product of a joint initiative between Helmut Schmidt and Giscard d'Estaing. Unlike Jenkins, who clearly sought to resurrect the notion of economic and monetary union in Europe, the Franco-German initiative was driven by the immediate consideration of intra-Community exchange rate volatility. This had increased during the course of 1977 to the extent that both France and Germany considered it now posed a threat to the economic cohesion of the Community.[30] Plans to establish a 'zone of monetary stability' within the EC through a fixed exchange rate system at least as restrictive as the 'Snake' were placed before the Heads of State at the Copenhagen summit in April 1978. The subsequent negotiations focused on the operational aspects of the system. First the weaker member states, worried that pegging their currencies to the Deutschmark would serve only to worsen their economic prospects, insisted that in the event of exchange rates moving out of line the burden of adjustment should be equitably shared between the strong- and the weak-currency countries. Secondly there should be an increase in the regional fund to compensate the weaker members for no longer having recourse to exchange rate adjustment as an instrument of economic policy. The first problem was resolved by the inclusion of a 'divergence indicator' as part of the package. This was designed to provide an early warning that the permissible limit to bilateral currency movements was about to be reached. And although there was no requirement to intervene at this point, a triggering of the divergence indicator was supposed to create a presumption that the country concerned would adjust its macroeconomic policies as appropriate. Significantly for the weaker-currency countries, the indicator could identify the country of the strong currency as responsible for remedial measures if that country was out of line with the rest. This, along with concessions over intervention arrangements and a provision for non-Snake currencies to join the exchange rate mechanism (ERM) under a less restrictive band of permissible movement, convinced those countries that adequate safeguards had been incorporated in the EMS without requiring any substantial increases in the redistributive aspect of the Community budget.

Although agreeing to EMS membership, Labour refused to include sterling in the ERM. The British position was spelled out in the Green Paper of December 1978.[31] Whilst acknowledging that a greater degree of exchange rate stability was necessary to foster economic growth, and accepting that the EMS might contribute to this, it was clear that the UK was sceptical of the viability of any currency arrangement that did not incorporate the US dollar. Further, as the new system bore a close resemblance to the discredited Snake, it was felt unlikely that the EMS would be any more successful in achieving a convergence of economic policy – and so long-term currency stability — than the Snake had been. On the specific matter of sterling, three issues were considered. Over the first, independence of economic policy, the Paper maintained that UK policy was not to regard the exchange rate as an effective instrument of policy and that there were no objections in principle to a commitment to greater currency stability. The second involved possible conflicts in the conduct of monetary policy, central to the UK anti-inflation strategy, as a result of EMS participation. The government was clearly reluctant to see monetary policy targeted at maintaining the exchange rate. Finally, there was concern as to the consequences of the UK balance of payments should sterling join the system at the wrong rate. The appreciation of sterling during January 1978 had raised fears over the competitive position of UK exports and it was felt that membership of the EMS, dominated as it would be by the West German Mark, might cause competitiveness to decline.

It is more difficult in this instance to attribute Labour's refusal to incorporate sterling in the ERM to its by now entrenched opposition to the supranational aspirations of the Commission. As the EMS was a distinctly intergovernmental venture in which the Commission had no direct stake, the issue of creeping supranationalism did not appear to be relevant. In another sense, however, progress in the EMS initiative hinged on developments in other areas of Community policy-making. Membership of an exchange rate regime dominated by the D-Mark would inevitably expose the weakness of a comparatively high-inflation British economy unable to devalue its currency freely in response. The proposal to compensate for the loss of this policy instrument by increasing the size of the Community's regional budget not only raised questions of supranationalism, it implicitly required the UK to retreat from its stated position over the financial arrangements of the Community. Instead the government opted to reaffirm its position, insisting that participation in the ERM was conditional on reaching an agreement to reduce the financial burden of membership to Britain.[32] It was the failure to win these concessions that ultimately convinced the government not to include sterling in the ERM. Significantly, both Italy and the Republic of Ireland opted to join the ERM after securing assurances that provision would be made to increase the funds available to assist in the transition to a greater degree of exchange rate fixity, albeit the moneys involved were significantly less than they first sought. Whilst it is beyond the scope of this chapter to assess whether or not the decision to exclude sterling from the ERM was correct from a broad policy standpoint, the EMS debate once again demonstrated Labour's unwillingness to adopt a perspective on British membership that extended beyond immediate difficulties associated with the Community's financial arrangements.

4 The changing role of the European Council

The failure of the Labour government to resolve Britain's budget problem contrasts sharply with the fortunes of the subsequent administration. However, to what extent did changes both to the role of the European Council and in the balance of competing national interests in the EC in the early 1980s facilitate the reforms from which the Thatcher government derived considerable kudos at home? The European Council had been formally established at the Paris meeting of the Community Heads of State in December 1974. Based on a proposal from President Giscard d'Estaing, it was agreed that the hitherto ad hoc summits should become a regular event. Consequently, beginning in 1975, Heads of State met thrice annually to discuss matters relating both to EC economic and political integration and to the broader issue of European foreign policy co-operation. Although each summit would provide an opportunity for Heads of State to settle outstanding problems which could not be resolved in the Council of Ministers, this was not to be its primary function. The smaller member states in particular were concerned that summitry constituted a move to intergovernmentalism in Community decision-making with the result that the Council of Ministers would thereafter be relegated to a subordinate position. Should this happen, the influence of the smaller member states in Community affairs in general would be weakened. Moreover it is clear that in proposing the new arrangement the French President was seeking to fill a void in the international dimension of Community activity that lay outside the remit of the Community's formal institutional structure. By the end of 1974 the international economic and political environment was considerably more unstable than at any other time during the post-war period. A forum at which EC Heads of State could meet and exchange views at regular intervals was seen to be necessary both to develop European political co-operation and to establish a co-ordinated response to the unfolding economic crisis. The conjunction of the post-OPEC recession and the move to generalised floating had produced substantial problems in the area of economic policy co-ordination which threatened the internal cohesion of the European Communities. The increasing divergence of national economic performance within the Community was leading to conflict. The weaker members, bedevilled by rising unemployment and high rates of inflation, were insisting that the stronger partners, and in particular West Germany, should expand their economies to speed up the recovery process elsewhere. Regular meetings of the European Council not only provided an opportunity to monitor economic developments within the Community and elsewhere, in a number of instances it directly led to the development of novel responses and new policy initiatives.[33]

The initial phase of the European Council's existence was therefore dominated by the need to resolve a range of conflicts associated with the international economic crisis. By the end of the 1970s, however, a different situation had come about which resulted in the European Council redirecting its energies to internal matters. On the one hand the international economic situation, whilst far from stable, had undoubtedly improved. Similarly a framework of European monetary stability in the form of the EMS had been established, serving to formalise EC macroeconomic co-operation to an extent that rendered continual high-level exchanges between member states less important. On the other hand it was becoming evident that the entire Community financial system was rapidly approaching a crisis point which could only be resolved by direct action by Heads of State. The stance adopted by Mrs Thatcher convinced the other members that concessions to Britain were essential if the increasingly fragile nature of European economic and political integration was to be protected. In effect Mrs Thatcher's negotiating attitude, including the threat illegally to withhold Britain's VAT contribution to the Community budget, had dramatically raised the potential costs of failure, thereby shifting the balance of Community interests away from support for the French position. British public opinion was strongly supportive of the government's stance and, unlike the situation that confronted the Labour government, there was no risk that playing the 'national card' would expose divisions in the party ranks. Moreover Mrs Thatcher, as a long-time opponent of the supranational element in Community procedures, was determined that Britain's business would only be conducted through the explicitly intergovernmental forum of the European Council. Elsewhere, the action of the European Parliament in rejecting the 1980 budget due to the failure to gain increases in the resources devoted to regional and social policies, as well as the growing likelihood that within a few years the revenue collected as 'own resources' would be insufficient to cover expenditure commitments, greatly intensified the momentum for extensive reforms to both the Community's budgetary arrangements and the CAP. These factors, along with the patent failure of the supranational element in Community decision-making, resulted in the European Council moving into a new phase where deliberations were dominated by internal problem-solving.

The successful resolution to the British crisis over the budget was, therefore, the result of the conjunction of a number of factors in the early 1980s. This is not to deny the important role played by the Conservative government in forcing what it claimed to be 'common sense' on the Common Market, but it is to emphasise that changes in the external and internal environment greatly eased the resistance that it met. For a number of reasons other than internal party problems, the preceding Labour government had operated within a much more tightly constrained 'policy space' in matters pertaining to the European Community.

5 Conclusion

The difficulty with any attempt to assess the Labour government's policy with respect to the European Communities is that for much of the period it simply had no policy. The renegotiation exercise amounted to little more than a statement of what the government considered ought not to be allowed to happen rather than a positive statement of the role it considered Britain should have within the Communities. This lack of a clear policy, owing much to the continued hostility of many at all levels within the party to EC membership, created a situation in which short-term considerations determined Labour's attitude. And whilst the tactic of overcoming internal divisions by a direct appeal to the electorate had been successful in 1975, by 1979 the shift in public opinion on the issue of EC membership meant that this was no longer a viable option. However, the 'policy space' of the government was not only constrained by internal divisions. The international economic crisis dominated discussions between the Community Heads of State for much of the period. At the same time there was a natural reluctance among most member states to discuss internal issues outside the formal Community channels until the imminence of crisis made this unavoidable. Despite what might be construed as mitigating factors, it remains the case that the Labour government failed to take advantage of the opportunities that arose positively to promote the development of other Community policies from which Britain would have benefited. And the cost of this failure is not only to be measured in financial terms. Public opinion in the UK was shaped in part by the image of the EC presented by the government. By continually portraying relations between the Community and Britain as conflictual, and pointing to failings in the former as the culprit, the government not only reinforced the adverse views of many in Britain on the EC question, but also contributed to a new antagonism the legacy of which is evident even yet. As newcomers to an arrangement which had taken over a decade to establish, it was wholly understandable that Britain's insistence that existing policies be fundamentally overhauled should be strongly resisted by the other member states. Rather than forming alliances with other partner countries or with the Commission itself, the attitude adopted by Labour was to confront the Community at a time when domestic political factors should have persuaded them otherwise.

Notes

1   Butler and Kavanagh (1980) note that in May 1978 a Gallup Poll recorded a 9% majority against the proposition that EC membership was a good thing whereas in 1975 a 26% majority was recorded in favour of the same motion. Of course it might well be the case that it was the 1978 response rather than that recorded in 1975 which more accurately reflected long-term British views on the EC.

2 Denton (1983) reproduces the Commission's figures for 1979 on national contributions to and expenditures from the Community budget.

3 By 1979 Britain's visible trade deficit with the rest of the Community, at £2·7 billion, accounted for three-quarters of the total deficit recorded for that year and had doubled since 1973.

4 HMSO (1971).

5 Over a five-year transitional period all UK import duties and quotas applying to partner countries were to be removed, tariffs with non-member states brought into line with the Community's common external tariff, the CAP adopted, the VAT system adopted, and full contributions to the common budget phased in.

6 Holland (1980, p. 4). Holland presents an excellent critique of the European Communities from a socialist perspective.

7 HMSO (1970).

8 The main papers are collected in Kaldor (1978).

9 Fetherston *et al.* (1979), using a model incorporating the balance of payments constraint, argued that the deterioration in Britain's balance of payments as a consequence of EC entry, which they estimated at £1·1 billion over 1973–77, had reduced UK national income by an average of 6% per annum over that period. See also CEPG (1979).

10 The objective to establish EMU by 1980 was stated by the (six) Community Heads of State in December 1969. A committee chaired by the Luxembourg Prime Minister, Pierre Werner, was set up to examine how this might be achieved.

11 The 'Snake' exchange rate regime, launched in March 1972, required member states to constrain intra-EC currency movements to ±2·25% of parity. This was intended to be the first stage on the road to EMU; however, by the mid-1970s the system had collapsed with sterling, the French franc, and the Italian lira all floating against the other EC currencies.

12 For a full discussion of the history of the EMU initiative, see Tsoukalis (1977) and Kruse (1980).

13 These Articles proscribed government assistance to industry should this distort, or threaten to distort, intra-EC competition. Article 90 of the Treaty extended these provisions to cover nationalised industries.

14 For a comprehensive review of Labour's demands see Nicholson and East (1987). A full account of the renegotiation episode is given in Butler and Kitzinger (1976).

15 HMSO (1975).

16 A member country had to meet four criteria before the correction mechanism was triggered: (a) its per capita GNP had to be less than 85% of the Community average; (b) its real rate of growth should be less than 120% of the Community average; (c) it should be contributing a share of 'own resources' greater than 110% of its share of EC GNP; (d) it should be making a positive net contribution to the Community budget. For a full discussion of the Community's financial arrangements see Wallace (1980) and Swann (1988).

17 See Wilson (1979) pp. 94–5.

18 Until 1975 the European Council met only infrequently; however, since then it has met thrice annually as agreed upon at the Paris Summit of 1974. Until 1987 these summits enjoyed no Treaty status in the Community process, but they have evolved as the dominant forum in determining the progress of economic and political integration in the EC. Bulmer and Wessels (1987) provide the only comprehensive analysis of the European Council available.

19 Bulmer (1985) analyses the Community decision-making process using the language of game theory, throwing considerable light on the nature of the difficulties experienced in resolving internal disputes.

20 It has to be stressed that by the end of the 1960s the UK policy of deficiency payments had all but collapsed under the pressure of mounting Exchequer costs. The government had, by then, introduced a 'standard quantity' system for most agricultural produce which imposed a limit on the volume of output for which it was prepared to guarantee minimum prices – a very similar arrangement to that now operated by the Community. For a fuller discussion, see Howarth (1985).

21 For a detailed analysis of the CAP see, for example, Hill (1984), Neville-Rolfe (1984) and Swann (1988).

22 During most of the period under review the CAP accounted for over 75% of all spending from the Community budget, most of which was accounted for by price support. See Neville-Rolfe (1984, p. 324).

23 See Marsh and Swanney (1983).

24 Swann (1988, p. 218).

25 Neville-Rolfe (1984, p. 84).

26 Neville-Rolfe cites the conciliatory attitude adopted by Peart during the 1976 Council of Agricultural Ministers meeting, while Castle (1981) records the mixed feelings in the Cabinet which greeted him after conceding to CAP price rises.

27 Considerable controversy surrounded the measurement of Britain's net payments to the EC budget. However informed estimates placed the figure at over £1 billion by 1979. See Godley (1980).

28 Taylor (1983, pp. 180–84).

29 The text of the Florence speech is reproduced as Jenkins (1978).

30 Kruse (1980, p. 183). For a comprehensive analysis of the EMS see Ludlow (1982).

31 HMSO (1978).

32 Taylor (1983, p. 184).

33 For a full discussion see Bulmer and Wessels (1987, pp. 59–74). Both EC and 'global' summitry are analysed in Merlini (1984) and Putnam and Bayne (1987). See also Taylor (1983, pp. 184–92).

References

Bulmer, S. (1985), 'The European Council's first decade: between interdependence and domestic politics', *Journal of Common Market Studies*, XXIV, no. 2, pp. 89–104.

Bulmer, S., and Wessels, W. (1987), *The European Council*, Macmillan, London.

Butler, D., and Kavanagh, D. (1980), *The British General Election of 1979*, Macmillan, London.

Butler, D., and Kitzinger, U. (1976), *The 1975 Referendum*, Macmillan, London.

Cambridge Economic Policy Group (1979), 'Policies of the EEC', *Economic Policy Review*, no. 5, pp. 23–30.

Castle, B. (1981), *The Castle Diaries*, Holmes & Meier, London.

Denton, G. (1983), 'Taxation and the Community budget', in C. D. Cohen (ed.), *The Common Market: 10 Years After*, Philip Allan, Oxford, pp. 128–55.

Fetherston, M., Moore, B., and Rhodes, J. (1979), 'EC membership and UK trade in manufactures', *Cambridge Journal of Economics*, III, pp. 399–407.

Godley, W. (1980), 'The United Kingdom and the Community budget' in W. Wallace (ed.), *Britain in Europe*, Heinemann, London, pp. 72–85.

Hill, B. (1984), *The Common Agricultural Policy: Past, Present and Future*, Methuen, London.

HMSO (1970), *Britain and the European Communities; An Economic Assessment*, Cmnd. 4289, HMSO, London.

HMSO (1971), *The United Kingdom and the European Communities*, Cmnd. 4715, HMSO, London.

HMSO (1975), *Membership of the European Community: Report on Renegotiation*, Cmnd. 6003, HMSO, London.

HMSO (1978), *The European Monetary System*, Cmnd. 7405, HMSO, London.

Holland, S. (1980), *UnCommon Market*, Macmillan, London.

Howarth, R. (1985), *Farming for Farmers*, Institute for Economic Affairs, London.

Jenkins, R. (1978), 'European monetary union', *Lloyds Bank Review*, January.

Kaldor, N. (1978), *Further Essays on Applied Economics*, Duckworth, London.

Kruse, D. C. (1980), *Monetary Integration in Western Europe: EMU, EMS and Beyond*, Butterworth, London.

Ludlow, P. (1982), *The Making of the European Monetary System*, Butterworth, London.

Marsh, J., and Swanney, P. (1983), 'Agriculture: how significant a burden?' in C. D. Cohen (ed.), *The Common Market: 10 Years After*, Philip Allan, London, pp. 92–127.

Merlini, C. (ed.) (1984), *Economic Summits and Western Decision Making*, Croom Helm, London.

Neville-Rolfe, E. (1984), *Politics of Agriculture in the European Communities*, Policy Studies Institute, London.

Nicholson, F., and East, R. (1987), *From the Six to the Twelve: The Enlargement of the EC*, Longman, London.

Putnam, R., and Bayne, N. (1987), *Hanging Together; Cooperation and Conflict in the Seven-Power Summits*, Sage, London.

Swann, D. (1988), *The Economics of the Common Market*, Penguin, London.

Taylor, P. (1983), *The Limits of European Integration*, Croom Helm, London.

Tsoukalis, L. (1977), *The Politics and Economics of European Monetary Integration*, Allen & Unwin, London.

Wallace, H. (1980), *Budgetary Politics: the Finances of the European Communities*, Allen & Unwin, London.

Wallace, H., Wallace, W., and Webb, C. (1983), *Policy Making in the European Communities*, Wiley, Chichester.

Wilson, Sir H. (1979), *Final Term: Labour Government 1974–76*, Weidenfeld & Nicolson, London.

The nationalised industries

1 Introduction

In evaluating the government's policy towards the nationalised industries, it is clearly relevant to have before us an outline of the industries' main problems and of their own record in this period. There is, however, something to be said for setting out the record of the industries' performance in some detail − in certain key areas at least − and putting it into the perspective of the whole period from the nationalisations of the 1940s. First, this is because of the complete collapse of this part of the public sector under the privatisations of the 1980s. Secondly, there are certain myths about the industries' performance, especially about internal efficiency and the level of prices − myths which emerged strongly in the 1970s. The proposition that their performance is poor in terms of productive efficiency, that their record is worse than other parts of the British economy, and that this manifested itself in the 1970s in the form of huge increases in prices, is actually lacking substantive support, as this chapter will demonstrate. Thirdly, the nationalised industry sector is a child of the Labour Party which cannot distance itself from the industries' image and performance. The distinctive legal form of the Morrisonian public corporation with its provision for arm's-length control and for promotion of a basically commercial ambience dominates the public enterprise sector in Britain. Indeed, it will be a theme in the conclusions to the chapter that, like the Labour Party itself, the Boards and the government paid inadequate attention to the public image of the nationalised industries, their corporate identity and their achievements. Specifically in the area of prices and finances, they did inherit severe problems from the Heath government and the 1974 surge in fuel and raw material prices, but an inattention to the promotion of corporate identity, together with some complacency about the need for closer financial monitoring, made them very vulnerable by the end of the 1970s.

The focus of the chapter will not be detailed questions of transport and fuel policy, but rather the broad characteristics of the industries as nationalised entities in terms of price levels, internal efficiency and financial viability. The broad significance of these issues is discussed in Section 2, which also sets out briefly the main features of the government's policy. Section 3 then examines measures of the industries' productivity in their use of resources, including comparisons with other sectors of the British economy and other countries. It demonstrates that the good productivity growth trends of the 1974–79 period are consistent with the longer-term trends of 1950–85. Section 4 sets out the movement in prices and unit costs in the 1970s and considers the attempt to restore the industries' finances from 1974 following the discriminatory price restraint of the Heath government. Section 5 provides an assessment of policy and some conclusions.

2 The main features of policy 1974–79

The analysis by economists of the problems of nationalised industries concentrated, in the 1960s and 1970s, mainly on questions of allocative efficiency in the use of resources. As is clear from Heald's 1980 review of economic and financial controls, economists have had little obvious effect on their main target areas. The marginal cost pricing policy associated with the 1967 White Paper (Cmnd 1337) hardly got off the ground. The Test Discount Rate and associated rules for investment appraisal were never fully implemented. The return in the 1978 White Paper (Cmnd 7131) to questions of financial targets revived, amongst other things, the economists' standard criticism that such targets are no guide to allocative efficiency.[1]

We shall not here be concerned with this debate – which continues – but rather with three interrelated issues which seem to have been rather more important in the industries' dealings with politicians and the general public, namely, the general level of fares and tariffs, internal efficiency and the size of financial profits. Prices are a central issue because of the tightrope which the industries have to walk between accusations of on the one hand exploiting monopoly power and on the other hand running deficits and managerial incompetence. In the period 1974–76 the industries attracted much unfavourable publicity from price rises of some 30% p.a. Jones (1979) has argued that nationalised industry prices in any case had a 'magnified image' in consumer consciousness. This was despite having a weight of less than 10% in the retail price index and accounting for only 7·5% of total final goods expenditure and despite the fact that in 1976 the retail sales of each individual industry never accounted for more than 5% of the total spending of any given household income band. The 'magnified image' stemmed, he argued, from the infrequent and lump-sum nature of rail season tickets, fuel and telephone bills, from low income elasticities of demand for fuel, and from the absence in some cases of ready short-run substitutes.

The finances of the industry are important for two main reasons. First, losses raise the question – however unsubstantiated – of inefficiency and incompetence in the minds of public and politicians and X-efficiency in the minds of economists. The second reason relates to the simple tenet of accountability. A major statutory requirement of the industries is to break even. Weak though this benchmark can be, it is the nearest definition of 'failure' which exists. Of course the level of prices and, given costs, the level of profits, also affect resource allocative efficiency, but it was less important for the industries in the 1970s than the above two factors.

What were the main features of policy in these areas in the 1974–79 period? The government's thinking may be found in the 1978 White Paper but in so far as that came rather late in the period of office, and in any case did not propose any major changes, the 1967 White Paper is also a relevant benchmark. This has to be supplemented first by a consideration of the implications of the government's general inflation policy for this sector. Secondly, Labour's programmes and manifestos were, in part, concerned with the size of the public enterprise sector but the specific implications – including those for British Leyland, British Steel and the National Enterprise Board – were developed in the context of industrial policy, which is considered in Chapter 10 of this book.

The main features of official policy were:

(a) Major structural changes in the industries, it was implied, were not needed. The problems identified in the 1976 National Economic Development Office report could be dealt with largely by existing instruments, specifically by reversing the control on public sector prices. The need for clear specification of business objectives and accountability in terms of objectives was to be achieved by placing a corporate plan at the centre of industry–government discussions, by the introduction of performance indicators, and by linking pricing and investment policy more closely to financial targets.

(b) The damage caused to the industries by their use in the 1970–73 period as an instrument of counter-inflation policy was recognised. It undermined accountability and distorted resource allocation. This required selective price increases above the general level and the reduction of subsidies and deficits.

(c) Supply-side structural weaknesses of the British economy included lack of investment, restrictive practices and dominance by multinationals. Planning agreements and an extension of public ownership were to be, according to the programmes, manifestos and White Papers of 1974, important elements of policy in this area. This was to include public ownership of loss-making enterprises in areas such as shipbuilding, whilst planning and extended public ownership were to characterise pharmaceutical, road haulage, construction and machine tools. Specific instances came to be gradually eliminated from policy statements, leading to somewhat weaker statements in the November 1975 White Paper on Industrial Strategy.

3   Productive efficiency: as good as the private sector?

There is now a large body of studies (largely relating to North America) of the performance, in the 1970s, of public enterprise and private firms in the same industry — electricity, railways, airways, water supply[2] — measured through production and cost functions. The results support those who argue that more competition improves managerial efficiency. They cast doubt on those who argue that public ownership is less efficient than private. Ownership *per se*, in the Western industrialised nations, does not seem to have had a decisive effect on cost-effectiveness, though it does affect the range of services offered and the alignment of prices to private costs.

Assessing the productive efficiency of the UK nationalised industries is difficult in the absence of a significant private sector in the same product groupings. No one, moreover, has yet estimated international production or cost functions for these products. One is left then with measures of output per head or total factor productivity in the form of comparisons across countries or over time. The critique of the nationalised industries then takes the form that their productivity growth compares unfavourably with other parts of the British economy, and that their productivity level, *vis-à-vis* other countries, is worse than other parts of the British economy. These points will be disputed. Of course the measures are far from satisfactory and take no account of qualitative differences in products and the differing environments in which production takes place, but they are the ones that underlie the critique.

To this end a sector, 'public enterprise', is defined which embraces in official UK statistics pre-1975 the industries of gas, electricity, water, mining and quarrying, transport and communication. For 1975 and subsequently, it covers transport, communication and 'all other energy and water supply' which explicitly excludes oil and gas extraction and processing. For the whole of the post-war period up to 1985, this sector in the UK was populated largely by publicly owned enterprises. It does include shipping and road transport which were privately owned but accounted for only some 10% of the capital stock of the public enterprise sector.[3]

From the mid-1970s onwards, there have been increasing criticisms of the productivity performance of public enterprises. It now seems part of British folklore that 'nationalised industry, as we know to our cost, is far from efficient'. (This, from a cricket journalist — Edmonds, 1987, p. 30!) The substantive academic criticisms are of two kinds. One relates to productivity growth over time. Now as Table 9.1 shows, for the six-year period 1973–79 total factor productivity was growing on average at more than 1% p.a. faster than the private manufacturing sector. For a longer period embracing the 1960s and much of the 1970s, neither the 1976 NEDO report nor Pryke in his 1981 book could find productivity growing faster in manufacturing than the public enterprise sector as a whole. Rather the argument was first that the

Table 9.1 *Output and resources 1973–79: manufacturing and public enterprise*

	Output GDP at constant factor cost 1975 = 100		Labour Employees in employment (000s)		Capital Gross capital stock at 1975 replacement cost = 100		Labour's share		Total factor productivity	
	Manu-facturing	*Public enterprise*	*Manu-facturing*	*Public enterprise*	*Manu-facturing*	*Public enterprise*	*Manu-facturing*	*Public enterprise*	*Manu-facturing*	*Public enterprise*
1973	109·2	101·0	7672	2212	89·2	91·6	0·699	0·641	—	—
1979	104·1	108·0	7107	2169	102·0	97·5	0·718	0·702	—	—
Average annual growth rate	(−)0·8	1·1	(−)1·3	(−)0·3	2·2	1·0	—	—	(−)0·6	0·9

Sources: Central Statistical Office, *National Income and Expenditure*, 1979 edition, 1986 edition; Department of Employment, *Employment Gazette*, February 1987. Labour's share is income from employment as a fraction of GDP before depreciation and stock appreciation and is estimated for the whole period for each sector as an average of the above two figures.

public enterprise high-flyers – gas, telecommunications and airways – also experienced large increases in output which can often drag up productivity whilst the below-par productivity growth in the 'also-rans', in Pryke's terminology, cannot wholly be explained by low sales growth.[4] In addition, productivity growth on some measures was declining in the public enterprise sector in the 1970s – though so also was productivity in manufacturing. The second argument is that the productivity level in British public firms is significantly less than in foreign firms in the same product area (Pryke, 1981, pp. 244–50; Shackleton, 1984, p. 63; Alford, 1988, pp. 48–9). For the 1970s there is a National Institute study (Smith *et al.*, 1982) of US and UK productivity, some of the data in which can be deployed to reinforce that point. Whereas output per head in US manufacturing was in the 1970s of the order of 2·8 times the level in British manufacturing (with construction at 1·6 and agriculture at 2·2), some of the major nationalised industries (gas, electricity, telecommunications, railways, coal) had a much worse comparative level of labour productivity. Such seems to underlie Pryke's conclusions that the performance of the industries during the 1970s was 'third rate', and that 'a substantial waste of resources is occurring within the public enterprise sector due both to technical inefficiency and to misallocation. The nationalised industries must not be judged too harshly because the private sector is also woefully inefficient. Nevertheless, even by British standards, their performance appears to be poor' (1980, p. 226; 1981, p. 257). This view has not really been questioned (cf. the title of the Institute of Fiscal Studies 1987 article by Molyneux and Thompson) and seems to echo the worries in the 1976 NEDO report about government control.

What needs to be established is whether output changes have truly distorted the Table 1 productivity growth comparison for UK manufacturing and public enterprise; second, and related, is what the pattern looks like over a long period; a third issue is whether the unfavourable international comparisons are sustained when one looks at periods in which fuel and transport were not nationalised. In Table 9.2, trends in productivity are highlighted for three subperiods determined by the cycle peaks of 1951, 1964 and 1973 (as used in the Matthews, Feinstein and Odling-Smee work on long-term British growth, 1982). The table shows that up to 1973 manufacturing output was growing at about 3% per annum on a long-term trend. This was slightly higher than for public enterprise at 2·7% per annum. However, labour-shedding was higher in the latter – its labour force was declining by 1% per annum *more* than in manufacturing. Thus the overall trend in labour productivity was higher in public enterprise. In the 1973–85 period output was falling in manufacturing, but the labour force declined very rapidly and the growth rate of labour productivity was slightly higher than in public enterprise – some 2·3% per annum. Nevertheless, over the whole 1951–85 period labour productivity growth was slightly behind that in public enterprise. Use of man-hours in the labour productivity measure does not alter these conclusions.[5]

Table 9.2 *Output and productivity in UK manufacturing and public enterprise 1951−85 (annual average % growth rates)*

	1951−64	1964−73	1973−85	1951−85
Manufacturing				
Output	3·2	2·9	(−)0·8	1·7
Labour	0·7	(−)1·1	(−)3·1	(−)1·1
Labour productivity	2·5	4·0	2·3	2·8
Capital	4·0	3·6	1·4	3·0
Capital productivity	(−)0·8	(−)0·7	(−)2·2	(−)1·3
Labour's share[a]	0·66	0·70	0·72	0·70
Total factor productivity	1·9	2·4	1·1	1·6
Public enterprise				
Output	2·7	2·7	0·9	1·9
Labour	(−)0·6	(−)2·3	(−)1·2	(−)1·3
Labour productivity	3·3	5·0	2·1	3·2
Capital	2·3	2·8	0·7	1·8
Capital productivity	0·4	0·1	0·2	0·1
Labour's share[a]	0·71	0·65	0·65	0·67
Total factor productivity	2·4	2·9	1·4	2·2

Notes: Definitions are the same as for Table 9.1 with series for subperiods spliced into each other to allow for changing coverage of each sector. The basic capital stock data is at 1963 replacement cost for 1948−63, at 1975 replacement cost for 1968−75, and at 1980 cost for 1975−85. For output, the weights and factor costs are 1980 for the 1975−85 period, 1975 for 1973−75, 1963 for 1949−56, and 1958 for the year 1948. The employment data 1948−68 refers to the UK and involves some changes in definitions in 1959 and in 1964. The post-1968 data refer to Great Britain only and involve a change in definition in 1971.

[a] Arithmetic average of the fraction for each year.

Sources: Central Statistical Office, *National Income and Expenditure*, 1960, 1967, 1971, 1979, 1986;

Department of Employment, *Employment Gazette*, July 1973, January 1982, February 1987 (Historical Supplement No. 1);

Department of Employment, *British Labour Statistics: Historical Abstract 1886−1968*, 1971, Table 132.

The more striking differences arise in the use of capital. In public enterprise the capital stock grew, over the long term, at approximately the same rate as output so that there was close to a zero growth in capital productivity over the whole period. In manufacturing, the capital stock grew consistently faster than output and the two were particularly out of line in the 1973−85 period. Capital productivity was declining at over 1% per annum on average over the whole post-war period. The net result is that total factor productivity growth per annum is some 0·6% higher in public enterprise over the long term. The source of this, we can now see, is twofold. First is the larger amount of labour-shedding in public enterprise in the 1950s and 1960s. This was mainly in coal and transport, supplemented by the other fuel industries in the 1960s. Second is the decline in capital productivity in manufacturing, which accelerated in the 1970s and 1980s, offsetting in this latter period the higher rate of growth of labour productivity.[6]

Returning to the short-term trends within 1973–85, it can be seen by comparing Tables 9.1 and 9.2 that the decline of capital productivity in manufacturing is consistent throughout, as is the virtually zero change in public enterprise. Also, the period 1973–79 shows a continuing higher labour productivity growth in public enterprise. Where the 1979–85 period shows a difference is in the substantial fall in the labour force in manufacturing (4·9% per annum), much bigger than previously and bigger than in public enterprise. Labour productivity growth is therefore considerably higher in manufacturing in these last six years and sufficiently higher to make for a larger increase in total factor productivity.

The UK public enterprise sector therefore does not have an inferior productivity growth record to that of private manufacturing. How does it compare internationally over time? Table 9·3 involves a labour productivity comparison of all the industrial sectors in the UK and the USA over a long period, based in part on the 1982 study by the National Institute (Smith *et al.*, 1982). By drawing on the earlier work of Rostas (1948) for the 1935–39 period and Paige and Bombach (1959) for 1950, we can encompass the period when the British nationalised sector had barely been born. Three points emerge. First is that over the whole post-war period, comparative sector productivity in the British and American economies has been stable. In the words of the National Institute study: 'For long periods ... the British bright spots have been agriculture and construction ... The laggards have been the extractive industries and public utilities' (p. 39). The latter, that is, as a group had an inferior relative output per head before nationalisation. Second it is clear that whilst the comparative labour productivity of manufacturing has not changed (nor that of agriculture and construction significantly) the UK public enterprise sector has advanced over the post-war period relative to the US industries in the same product area. US output per head for the broad group of extractive industries and utilities declined, taking UK = 100, from 769 in 1950, to 517 in 1968, to 323 in 1977. Transport declined from 458 to 240 to 213 and within that total railways and airlines have clearly been part of the UK improvement in relative labour productivity. From the more detailed figures available annually for 1968–77 we may see that both the gas industry and the electricity supply industry improved their relative productivity levels in practically every one of the nine years. The third point is that some of the improvements are of course simply structural – the rise in UK oil exploration in the 1970s clearly affecting the

Table 9.3 *Sector output per head 1938–77: US index (UK = 100)*

	1938	1950	1968	1970	1972	1975	1977
1 Agriculture	103	222	242	240	207	222	209
2 Extractive and utilities							
(a) Extractive	415	–	668	692	806	594	342
of which coal mining	380	374	855	892	1038	697	760
(b) Utilities	180	–	426	397	345	321	307
of which Gas	163	–	736	705	492	332	279
Electricity	193	–	406	371	345	354	457
Total	360	769	517	–	–	–	323
3 Manufacturing	215	292	289	285	293	282	291
4 Construction	115	150	206	163	165	165	170
5 Transport & communications							
(a) Transport	270–300	458	240	222	216	204	213
of which Railways	297	771	–	395	–	–	–
Airlines	–	388	–	–	152	–	–
(b) Communications	270	264	284	291	302	323	334
Total	280	412	262	251	250	252	264
6 Grand Total (all industry)	181	299	278	268	271	266	266

Note: The employment data underlying the calculations are generally total numbers of employees. The output data tend to refer to gross output for 1938 and net output for later years. Aggregates involve calculations using UK prices and weights. The 1938 figure for coal relates to tonnage per man-shift and the 1950 figure to tonnage per worker. All the other 1950 data on extractive and utilities exclude (for both countries) output sold within that sector. The data for airlines relate to ton-miles per employee.
Sources: 1968–77 data are taken from Smith *et al.*, National Institute of Economic and Social Research, 1982. The aggregate figure for all industry for all years is also taken from this source, Table 3.7. The 1950 data are from Paige and Bombach, 1959. The 1938 data from Rostas, 1948, and relate to various years in the period 1935–39.

UK figure for extractive industries – whilst in certain cases (coal, communications) the British performance, in labour productivity at least, has worsened relative to US.

This last point brings us to the question of capital productivity. Table 9.4 shows total factor productivity growth rates (using man-hours for labour) for the relevant sectors in the USA and the UK using the data in Griliches (1968) and the British sources already identified, together with data on mining productivity from Pryke (1981) and Molyneux and Thompson (1986).

Table 9.4 *Productivity growth in the USA and the UK 1950−85 (average annual %*
growth in total factor productivity)

	1950−65	1966−73	1973−85	1950−85
Manufacturing				
UK	1·9	2·4	1·3	1·8
USA	2·0	1·8	1·4	1·8
Mining				
UK	1·5	2·2	(−)1·0	0·9
USA	0·5	1·9	(−)4·3	−0·6
Gas, electricity and water				
UK	3·3	4·3	1·8	3·1
USA	3·7	2·4	1·2	2·6
Transport and communication				
UK	2·4	3·7	2·3	2·5
USA	1·0−2·7	1·6−3·0	0·1−2·3	0·9−2·6

Notes: The US data relate to 1949−66, 1967−73, 1974−85, 1949−85, and 'utilities'
is assumed to comprise gas, electricity and water. The UK data relate to 1951−64,
1964−73, 1973−85, 1951−85.
Sources: Pryke, 1981, Table 4.1; Matthews *et al.*, 1982; Molyneux and Thompson,
1986; Griliches, 1988; Millward, 1988 (see also Note 2).

Over the whole period 1950−85 productivity grew on average at 1·8% per
annum in manufacturing in both countries. In mining it grew at a consistently
higher rate in the UK. In gas, electricity and water there is not much difference in the first period, 1950−65, but thereafter and averaging over the
whole post-war period, annual productivity growth was higher in the UK.
The record in transport is usually, in every country, inferior to that in
communications. The separate figures for these two sectors in the USA have
not been aggregated in Table 9.4, but since the transport sector is clearly
bigger than communications by any measure then the overall productivity
growth in the UK is again higher than in the USA.[7] Of course, estimates of
productivity change are notoriously fragile. Nevertheless, the productivity
growth record of the transport and fuel sectors since coming under public
ownership in the UK bears comparison both with the privately owned
manufacturing sector in the UK and with the transport and fuel sectors in the
USA, where private ownership is much more extensive. The superior
productivity growth performance of the public enterprise sector recorded in
Table 9.1 for the 1974−79 period of the Labour government is therefore
consistent with the long-term trends. Given this, we can review the broad
trend of nationalised industries' price levels and finances in the context of
the government's macroeconomic policy on inflation.

4 Price inflation and nationalised industry deficits 1974-79

There is now little dispute that during the Heath government, 1970-74, price inflation was controlled more effectively in the public sector and that therefore nationalised industries' prices were held down relative to manufacturing and relative to the movement in their costs. The crude picture from Table 9.5 is that prices in manufacturing were rising in the 1970-73 period at nearly double the rate in nationalised industries. Official policy in the first two years of Conservative government represented no break from the 1964-70 Wilson government in that the industries were officially to be treated on a part to the private sector. None the less, it is clear that the Confederation of British Industry's declaration and initiative on price restraint in 1971 (requesting 200 of its members to limit price changes to 5% p.a.) was more readily enforceable by ministers who had in any case been exerting informal pressure on the nationalised industries from at least 1970. Moreover, the Stage 2 and 3 Price Codes of 1973 excluded the nationalised industries from the minimum profit provisions which provided a safety net for private firms earning less than an 8% rate of return; nor were the nationalised industries allowed to reduce deficits by raising prices more than cost increases.[8]

Table 9.5   *Price and cost inflation in the UK 1970-78 (annual % changes)*

	1970	1971	1972	1973	1974	1975	1976	1977	1978
Manufacturing									
Prices	7·1	9·1	5·2	7·4	22·6	22·2	17·3	19·8	9·1
Unit costs	8·1	8·7	4·9	8·9	24·9	21·9	16·7	20·6	7·3
Nationalised industry									
Prices	3·4	8·4	1·6	3·9	28·5	42·3	17·3	9·9	6·2
Unit costs	5·6	9·6	5·2	3·1	35·4	41·2	10·2	9·7	7·7

Source: *The Monthly Digests of Statistics* for the wholesale price index for all home sales of manufactured goods. A special price series was constructed for nationalised industries by aggregating, with revenue weights, the following indices calculated from the Annual Reports of the Corporations: average gas price per therm realised; average electricity revenue per kWh sold to all consumers; average of the postal and telecommunication tariff indices weighted by revenue; proceeds per saleable ton of coal; total revenue per load ton miles for BEA; for British Rail an average weighted by revenue of average fares per passenger mile and average receipts per net ton mile.

Unit costs relate to labour, fuel and other raw materials. Series on output, employment and earnings for nationalised industries were developed along the lines of the series for prices. These data were then used to estimate unit labour costs. Data on raw materials and fuel outlays of public corporations are published in the Blue Books. Hence unit input cost was calculated and added to unit labour costs. Unit labour costs in manufacturing were extracted from data in the *Employment Gazette*. Unit input costs in manufacturing were calculated as a residual from the data on prices, unit labour costs and profit rates. For details write to the author. I am grateful to R. Ward for research assistance in the compilation of these statistics.

By 1973 the Treasury was admitting the existence of price restraint policies in the public sector and this was picked up and reported by the Select Committee on Nationalised Industries (1st Report 1973/74 session). The problem was not deemed important enough to feature in Labour's programme and manifestos of 1974 but the November Review of the Price Code acknowledged 'a need for giving scope for higher price increases by nationalised industries ... [in order to make] ... progress towards the Government's objective of returning as many of the industries as possible to a position in which their deficits, and the accompanying public expenditure on subsidies, are eliminated' (p. 5). The broad idea was to approve price increases which would allow a surplus (after depreciation at historic cost) of 2% on turnover or 10% on net assets. The government, however, retained its powers to keep price increases to a level consistent with the traditional formula of allowable cost increases. The inflation White Paper of July 1975 acknowledged that the deficits had not been removed. A year later the government was reporting in *The Attack on Inflation: the Second Year* that the subsidies to support price restraint had been phased out, though an ambivalence about the balance between consumer interests and financial requirements is apparent in the June Command Paper on the Price Code (p. 9).

The government's restraint on public sector price increases seems to have continued.[9] Contemporary observers noted for example that it was not long after the 1978 White Paper had recognised the arm-twisting on prices that the government was announcing a freeze on electricity prices. In fact it proved to be a delay, pending an investigation, before the desired price increases were approved. In electricity generally the government continued to intervene in many areas connected with prices. The North Western Electricity Board, for example, reported in its 1976/77 annual report that the increase in standing charges was kept below that which would have been commercially desirable. In its next annual report it recorded that at the request of government the proposed increases in charges for reconnecting supplies following disconnection were not implemented. The Post Office in 1976 was warning that uncertainty about government attitudes to increases in prices was jeopardising the attainment of an economically viable parcel service. For several corporations it appears that price increases in the late 1970s above the general inflation level were frowned on. Increases in postal prices introduced in June 1977 were described by the Post Office as 'the smallest possible and much less than the rise in the retail price index'. By 1979 the chairman was recording an agreement with the government that postal prices would not increase over the period 1978/79–1982/83 more than the general inflationary trend in the UK, whilst for telecommunications the agreement was for an annual rise some 5% lower than general inflation. The 1976 annual report of British Rail indicates clearly the problem of reconciling the public-service obligation support price for passenger services with the financial constraints imposed on the corporation. In its 1978 report

British Rail was claiming that it had held its prices 'steady' – with a strong implication that the price increases had kept pace with inflation though more was warranted. The next annual report (p. 11) states: 'Remedial action, involving either real pricing, increased financial payments by Government or reduced operations by the closure of some loss-making services ... is crucial.'

How successful was the government in restoring the industries' finances? The annual rate of profit (including railway subsidies and before deducting interest payments but after capital consumption) on net fixed assets in the public corporation sector as a whole averaged zero in the 1950s. By the end of the 1960s, following more attention to financial matters, this had risen to 3%. This was of course much less than the company sector – then earning about 10%. In view of the secular decline in company sector profitability, especially if stock appreciation is deducted, the 3% figure is a reasonable benchmark. Given a capital output ratio of about 5 for the public corporation sector, this implies that profits should be of the order of 15% of value-added (net of capital consumption) – at least 15% given that the capital–output ratio was rising. If railway subsidies are excluded the relevant benchmark profit share of value-added is 8%, which was the 1969 figure. By 1972 gross trading profits for the public corporate sector, before subsidy, were only £1237 million, not even enough to cover estimated capital consumption of £1552 million. Even with subsidies included, profits accounted for only 3% of value-added. Future price increases would have to exceed any future cost increases by a considerable margin.

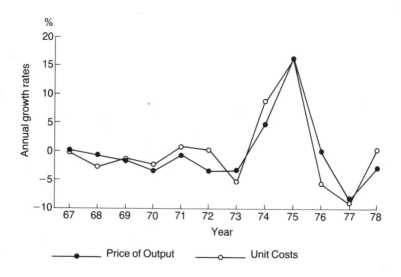

Fig. 9.1

The long-term trends in unit costs facing nationalised industries had two features. First was that labour productivity was growing faster than in manufacturing so that notwithstanding a much larger rise in wage inflation in the early 1970s, unit labour costs were still growing less than in manufacturing. Second was that the costs of fuel, raw materials and other items bought in by the nationalised industries were, however, growing more rapidly than in manufacturing, especially after the oil price rises of 1974, so that overall unit costs in the 1970s were rising, on a longer-term trend, at about the same rate in the two sectors. Figure 9.1 plots the annual growth rate of prices in nationalised industries relative to manufacturing; it shows the growth rate of relative prices. For the six years up to 1975 this growth rate lags behind the growth in relative unit costs. In fact, in the whole period up to 1978 in only one year (1976) did the percentage change in relative prices significantly exceed the percentage change in relative unit costs. The very large increases in nationalised industries' prices in 1974 (28%) and 1975 (42%) were actually, overall, slightly less than the rise in their unit costs (35% and 41% respectively). The effect on finances is shown in Figure 9.2. By 1976/77 subsidies and price increases had raised the profit share of income to 12% when subsidies are treated as revenue. It is clear, however, that price increases were playing a less important role than subsidies. The share net of subsidies rose to only 2% − well short of the 8% figure of the late 1960s. By 1979 the nationalised industries' profit, gross or net of subsidies, as a share of value-added had slumped. Their annual sales revenue as a group had again fallen below even operating costs and capital consumption.

There were of course considerable variations within the aggregate. In 1979 the rate of return on capital for the sector as a whole (after capital consumption but including subsidies) was less than 1%. But telecommunications were achieving (after depreciation at replacement cost) a return of 6.9% on net assets − above their target of 6% for 1976/77−1978/79. Posts were earning a trading surplus (after interest and replacement cost depreciation) of 2.3% on turnover − more than the target of 2%. Both the Giro and British Aerospace were also meeting their financial targets by 1978/79. British Transport Docks Board was earning 16.9% in 1978/79 though this was less than its target of 20%. None of the other public corporations, however, even by the time of the March 1978 White Paper, had a published financial target, though some had targets internally set and others in the transport area had the statutory break-even target adapted to include support grants. Pryke's data (1981, Table 13.2) on operating surpluses at the end of the 1970s confirm that the rate of profit in these other corporations was (apart from British Gas and National Freight) well below the level of the late 1960s. The British Electricity Boards' gross operating surplus was just under 40% of revenue in the late 1960s, whilst by the late 1970s it had fallen to 25%. Similar trends may be observed for the National Coal Board

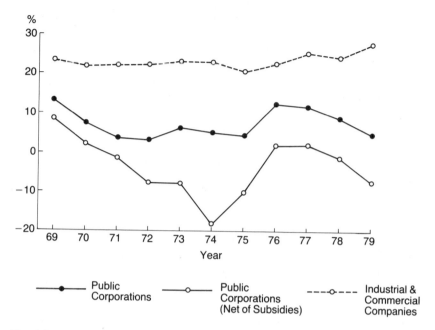

Fig. 9.2

(8% to approximately 4%), British Rail (1% to −16%), the Bus Groups (8% to −3%), British Airways (20% to 10%). Likierman (1979) reported that in July 1979, notwithstanding the White Paper injunction of March 1978, a lot of the corporations did not have published financial targets for 1978/79, and several of them had no target for future years. Indeed, the absence of any comprehensive standardised financial data in the White Paper itself is an indication of inadequate attention to financial monitoring.

5   Conclusions

The UK nationalised industries had a lot of achievements to their credit. Productivity growth in the period 1973−79 compares favourably with manufacturing and is consistent with their productivity record from 1950 to the 1980s. The inherited coal and railway industries in 1950 were much too big for their future role and a massive contraction and labour-shedding was achieved in the 1950s and 1960s. The gas and telecommunication industries showed a very large rise in output and productivity. At the same time the industries have been beset with problems in their finances. The overall financial performance of business organisations together with the set of prices and services which consumers face, is sometimes a surface reflection of the underlying productivity in the use of resources. But there is really no convincing evidence that the general trends in the nationalised industries' prices and finances in the post-war period were reflecting an underlying managerial incompetence.

There are two areas where the nationalised industries faced problems which became central in the 1970s. A fundamental requirement for a successful organisation is that its objectives are specified in such a way that performance can be monitored and judged. Definitions of success and failure must be part of the corporate plan. A second area relates to the fact that nationalised industries live in an economy dominated by modern large capitalist institutions which devote considerable attention to marketing their products and to the association of the company name with reliability and good quality. In the context of the 1970s and the commercial ambience always expected of the industries, this required the promotion of a corporate identity and the generation of some sense of pride in managers and workers in the organisation.

These issues are particularly important in terms of setting and achieving financial targets to underpin the statutory requirement to break even and in the way in which prices impinge on consumers. There is no doubt that the 1974–79 government and the earlier Wilson government of 1964–70 were aware of some of these issues. In this context the 1967 White Paper set out three guidelines. One was the reinforcement of the importance of financial targets so that the industries would know what was expected of them. Secondly, compensatory finance was to be arranged for activities which had a wider economic and social value than was reflected in profit consider-ations. Finally, the investment programmes were to be the focus of reviews of the state of each industry. The precise form of monitoring was not spelled out but in any case the whole set of instruments was overwhelmed by the price controls and financial deficits of the 1970s. As a result, the Select Committee on Nationalised Industries in 1973 requested the study which emerged from the NEDO in 1976 and which emphasised the strained relations between Boards and Ministries and the ability of both groups as well as civil servants to evade accountability for the performance of the industries.

In evaluating the policy of the 1974 government the first conclusion must then be the recognition of the horrendous heritage from the price restraint policy of the previous government. The restoration of the finances to the condition of the late 1960s required, given the underlying rise in costs, that the average level of prices in the nationalised industries would have to double over the three years 1974–77. It is to the government's credit that it went some way towards this. Where it can be criticised is in not fully recognising the difficulties in which the industries still found themselves by 1977. On the substantive issue of productivity in the use of resources, the industries could be defended and they clearly missed the opportunity this could have provided for improving public relations and developing a corporate identity. There is an air of complacency in the 1978 White Paper, perhaps stemming from relief that the statutory subsidies for deficits had at least been phased out;

on page 7 is a statement that the industries were in a much stronger position financially and yet the argument was not documented. The point is not that the government was wrong to reject NEDO's specific recommendations, but that it was wrong to believe that existing instruments, including the price increases of the mid-1970s, could deal with the problems identified by NEDO.

There were clear moves to improve accountability to Parliament and public in the form of requirements laid on the Boards to provide information on how they were measuring up to their objectives and to include in their annual reports summaries of the government's current instructions and guidance. In addition, a corporate plan was to be at the centre of industry –government discussions and financial targets were to be set for all corporations and supplemented by a new range of performance indicators. But the government did not address the main institutional issues; questions about vertical and horizontal disintegration into separately accountable units, the promotion of competition, or at least emulation, amongst public enterprises and with the private sector and the generation of distinct corporate identities.

Notes

1 See Rees (1979) and Heald (1980).

2 See Millward (1982) for a survey. In manufacturing, government-owned firms do less well; see Picot and Kaulmann (1989).

3 The main omissions are British Steel and British Leyland which were publicly owned for parts of the 1960s and 1970s and are here classified as part of manufacturing. They are more important as symbols of industrial policy in this period than in terms of their quantitative impact on the productivity measures here considered.

4 See Pryke (1980, 1981). On p. 241 of his 1981 book, Pryke states explicitly that the 'nationalised industries can only be regarded as efficient if they employ the minimum quantity of labour and other inputs to produce the goods and services they provide'. He then proceeds to consider the record of the industries in terms of the percentage change over time in labour productivity and total factor productivity. Pryke has also (1982) explored areas where private firms compete with the nationalised industries, and found that the latter had an inferior performance in terms of productivity levels. However, the activities in question were either marginal to the main business of the industries – sale of gas and electric appliances, Sealink – or, as in airlines, were not susceptible to proper total factor productivity comparisons, reliance having to be placed on partial measures like turnover per employee.

5 The superior labour productivity growth for manufacturing portrayed by the Treasury (1987) arises from excluding from the nationalised industry totals those industries which had been privatised by the end of the financial year 1987/88. This would exclude gas, telecommunications, airways and other high-growth industries. Productivity calculations using man-hours are available in Matthews *et al.* (1982) and Millward (1988). For manufacturing, these indicate man-hours growing more slowly than total employees in the 1951–64 period and declining more rapidly thereafter.

Using the output figures in Matthews *et al.* results in output per man-hour growing at 3·0% per annum for 1951–64, 4·6% per annum in the 1964–73 period and 2·6% per annum in the 1973–85 period. This growth is therefore some 0·3% points per annum higher than the data in Table 9.2 and largely reflects a 0·3% per annum decline in average hours worked per employee. An aggregate for public enterprises comparable with Table 9.2 is not directly available in Matthews *et al.* and Millward. Using employment shares in 1973 as weights, the growth rate of man-hours for the public enterprise sector was calculated and this yields labour productivity growth of 3·4% for 1951–64, 5·3% for 1964–73 and 2·3% for 1973–75. The overall growth of 3·5% is therefore still bigger than manufacturing at 3·2% per annum. (*N.B.* Millward, 1988, contains some typing errors: output growth in manufacturing in Table 2 should be −0·8% not −0·08% so that productivity growth is 1·3, weighted productivity growth is 0·41 and the residual is 0·45. Some of the calculations for labour hours in public enterprises for 1973–85 have been revised in the light of transposition errors where however the total figure for services is unaffected by these changes. The new figures relate to Table 5 labour growth rates and are −2·01 for gas, electricity and water, (−)1·3 for transport and −0·30 for communication. This has the effect of reducing the residual from 0·27 to −0·04.)

6　The other major sector of the economy (ignoring public services, where output is not measured) is commerce. Here output grew, like manufacturing, at about 3% per annum up to the mid-1970s and continued at about 2·2% per annum in the period up to 1985. The labour figure, in aggregate, did not decline like manufacturing and in the 1973–85 period actually increased at about 1·4% per annum. Despite a significant fall in hours worked in the latter period, the overall result is that labour productivity grew less than in manufacturing and the gap widened over time. Since the capital stock grew very rapidly in commerce (especially in banking and finance), the overall effect is that total factor productivity, using man-hours data, rose by only 1·7% 1951–64, 1·8% 1964–73 and actually declined at 1·1% per annum 1973–85 (cf. Matthews *et al.*, 1982, Table 8.3 and Millward, 1988, Table 5).

7　The productivity figures calculated by Kendrick (1987) for the USA are higher than those quoted by Griliches, which are based on National Bureau estimates. The effect is to put the fuel and transport record in the USA broadly in line with that in the UK − mining productivity grew at 0·6% per annum on average for the whole period 1950–85, gas, electricity and water at 3·5%, and transport and communications in the range 1·6–3·9%. But Kendrick's figures for manufacturing are also higher than Griliches' such that the excess of productivity growth in fuel and transport over manufacturing in the UK exceeds that in the USA. The source of the differences in the Griliches and Kendrick results lies partly in slightly different periods covered but other factors may also be at work.

8　See Millward (1976) for details.

9　See Annual Report and Accounts of the Post Office 1976/77 (p. 11), 1978/79 (pp. 8–9), the Electricity Council 1978/79 (p. 8), North West Electricity Board 1976/77 (p. 7), 1977/78 (p. 7), British Rail 1976 (pp. 4, 6), 1978 and 1979 (pp. 10, 11). See also Littlechild (1979, p. 24).

References

Alford, B. W. E. (1988), *British Economic Performance 1945–75*, Studies in Economic History for the Economic History Society, Macmillan, London.

Central Statistical Office, *UK National Income and Expenditure*, various years, HMSO.

Chancellor of the Exchequer (1978), *The Nationalised Industries*, Cmnd. 7131, March, HMSO.

Department of Employment (1971), *British Labour Statistics: Historical Abstract 1886–1968*, HMSO.

Department of Employment, *Employment Gazette*, various issues, HMSO.

Department of Industry (1974), *The Regeneration of British Industry*, Cmnd. 5710, August, HMSO.

Department of Industry (1975), *An Approach to Industrial Strategy*, Cmnd. 6315, November, HMSO.

Edmonds, F. (1987), *Another Bloody Tour*, Fontana, London.

Griliches, Z. (1988), 'Productivity puzzles and R & D: another non-explanation', *Journal of Economic Perspectives*, II, no. 4, Fall, pp. 9–22.

Heald, D. (1980), 'The economic and financial control of UK nationalised industries', *Economic Journal*, XC, June, pp. 243–65.

Jones, T. T. (1979), 'The Retail Price Index of nationalised industries 1962–78', UMIST Dept. of Management Sciences, Occasional Paper 7905, October.

Kendrick, J. W. (1987), 'Service sector productivity', *Business Economics*, XXII, no. 2, April, pp. 18–24.

Likierman, A. (1979), 'The financial and economic framework for nationalised industries, *Lloyds Bank Review*, October.

Littlechild, S. C. (1979), 'Controlling the nationalised industries: Quis custodiet ipsos custodes'. University of Birmingham, Faculty of Commerce and Social Science Series B Discussion Paper no. 56, August.

Matthews, R. C. O., Feinstein, C. H., and Odling-Smee, J. C. (1982), *British Economic Growth 1851–1973*, Clarendon Press, Oxford.

Millward, R. (1976), 'Price restraint, anti-inflation policy and public and private industry in the UK 1947–73', *Economic Journal*, LXXXVI, June, pp. 226–42.

Millward, R. (1982), 'The comparative performance of public and private ownership', in Lord Roll of Ipsden (ed.), *The Mixed Economy*, Macmillan, London.

Millward, R. (1988), 'The UK services sector, productivity change and the recession in long term perspective', *Services Industries Journal*, July, pp. 263–76.

Molyneux, R., and Thompson, D. J. (1986), *The Efficiency of the Nationalised Industries since 1978*, Institute of Fiscal Studies Working Paper no. 100.

Molyneux, R., and Thompson, D. J. (1987), 'Nationalised industry performance: still third rate?' *Fiscal Studies*, February, pp. 48–82.

National Economic Development Office (1976), *A Study of UK Nationalised Industries: Their Role in the Economy and Control in the Future*, November.

Paige, D., and Bombach, G. (1959), *A Comparison of National Output and Productivity of the UK and USA*, OEEC, London and Paris.

Picot, A., and Kaulmann, T. (1989), 'Comparative performance of government owned and privately-owned industrial corporations – empirical results from six countries', *Journal of Institutional and Theoretical Economics*, CXLV, pp. 298–316.

Prime Minister (1975), *The Attack on Inflation*, Cmnd. 6151, July, HMSO.

Prime Minister (1976), *The Attack on Inflation: The Second Year*, Cmnd. 6507, HMSO.

Pryke, R. (1980), 'Public enterprise in practice: the British experience of national-isation during the past decade', in W. J. Baumol (ed.), *Public and Private Enter-prise in a Mixed Economy*, Macmillan, London.

Pryke, R. (1981), *The Nationalised Industries: Policies and Performance since 1968*, Martin Robertson, Oxford.

Pryke, R. (1982), 'The comparative performance of public and private enterprise', *Fiscal Studies*, III, no. 2, pp. 68–81.

Rees, R. (1979), 'The pricing policy of the nationalised industries', *Three Banks Review*, no. 122, June.

Rostas, L. (1948), *Comparative Productivity in British and American Industry*, National Institute of Economic and Social Research, Cambridge University Press, Cambridge.

Secretary of State for Prices and Consumer Protection (1974), *Review of the Price Code: A Consultative Document*, Cmnd 5779, November, HMSO.

Secretary of State for Prices and Consumer Protection (1976), *Modifications to the Price Code*, Cmnd 6540, June, HMSO.

Select Committee on Nationalised Industries (1974), *Capital Investment Procedures,* 1st Report, Session 1973/4, HC 65, HMSO.

Shackleton, J. R. (1984), 'Privatisation: the case examined', *National Westminster Bank Review*, May.

Smith, A. D., Hitchens, D. M. W. N., and Davies, S. W. (1982), *International Indus-trial Productivity: A Comparison of Britain, America and Germany*, National Institute of Economic and Social Research, Cambridge University Press, Cambridge.

Treasury, HM (1967), *Nationalised Industries: A Review of Economic and Financial Objectives*, Cmnd 1337, November, HMSO.

Treasury, HM (1987), *Economic Progress Report*, no. 193, December, HMSO.

Industrial policy

1   The policy background

From the debates within the Labour Party during the period of opposition, a radical industrial policy emerged intended to increase the extent and effectiveness of government intervention in the economy. The relevance of that debate for this chapter is twofold. First, a major part of the parliamentary leadership of the Labour Party was opposed to the general thrust of the radical programme. It was only at the end of 1975 with the announcement of the industrial strategy that the policy stance became clear, though the controversy over the radical industrial policy may have conditioned the nature of the industrial strategy that emerged. The effective defeat of the radical industrial policy was signalled by the replacement of Tony Benn as Secretary of State for Industry in June 1975 by Eric Varley. Second, the two main parts of the framework of the radical industrial policy (planning agreements and the National Enterprise Board, hereafter NEB) were put in place, but were operated rather differently from the original intentions.

The two major instruments of the radical industrial policy were announced in *Labour's Programme 1973*. The first was the creation of a state-holding company (the NEB) with wide-ranging powers to acquire profitable private sector industrial companies. Shares acquired in return for financial assistance would be held by the NEB, and it would have a role in dealing with the collapse of 'lame ducks'. The list of tasks for the NEB was quite formidable, as can be seen from the section headings for a chapter in Labour Party (1973a), which ranged over planning for investment and growth promotion, jobs, industrial democracy, monopolies, concentration and social control, multinationals, joint ventures, public purchasing, renationalisation, modernisation, and value for public money. It was acknowledged though that 'the above is an impressive and extensive list of aims' (Labour Party, 1973a, p. 20), which could only be achieved over a long period. It was argued that to be fully effective the NEB had to acquire from the private sector a substantial base amongst the largest manufacturing firms, and

Labour Party (1973a) suggested that the take-over of some twenty to twenty-five companies over a five-year period would be required.

The second instrument was planning agreements intended to exert some control over decision making, with financial assistance made contingent on a planning agreement having been entered into. These agreements were intended to cover at least the 100 largest manufacturing firms and all major public enterprises, and would gather information on such matters as investment, prices, product development, marketing, exports and import requirements. This information was to be used 'to help the Labour government to identify and achieve its planning objectives and to plan for the redistribution of resources which will be needed to meet these objectives'. These agreements would 'provide a basis for channelling selective Government assistance directly to those firms which agree to help us to meet the nation's planning objectives' (Labour Party, 1973b).

An Industry Act was proposed to bring together and extend the powers for intervention, and indeed the Industry Act 1972 was extensively used within the industrial strategy (see below). A more controversial part of the proposed Industry Act derived from the view that 'the next Labour Government must be able to act, swiftly and *selectively*, directly at the level of the firm' (Labour Party, 1973b). The proposed Industry Act would provide a wide range of powers, including those to obtain any information deemed necessary from individual companies, to issue directives on matters such as prices, profits and investment programmes, and to assume control of any company which sought to frustrate the objectives of the government.

There were many influences at work behind these proposals, of which the main ones can be briefly indicated. There had been considerable disillusionment with the performance of the 1964–70 Labour government, especially its failure significantly to improve the growth performance of the British economy, and its use of deflationary measures. The behaviour of the private sector was viewed as having led to economic failure and inequalities. There were the perceived difficulties of ensuring that private companies co-operated with government policy, and the view that the National Plan had faltered through a lack of instruments to ensure private sector co-operation. Investment was seen as resistant to incentives and exhortation. There was also an awareness of the growth of industrial concentration and of multi-national enterprises, and the need to develop policies to offset the economic power which those changes represented.

The specific initial proposals for the nationalisation of twenty-five leading companies were quickly disavowed by the party leader, Harold Wilson.[1] The February 1974 election manifesto did not contain a specific number, but did propose to

take over profitable sections or individual firms in those industries where a public holding is essential to enable the Government to control prices, stimulate investment, encourage exports, create employment, protect workers and consumers from the activities of irresponsible multi-national companies, and to plan the national economy in the national interest.

(Labour Party, 1974)

The White Paper (Secretary of State for Industry, 1974) issued in August 1974 included a number of significant modifications to previous intentions.[2] Planning agreements were to be voluntary, based on consultations between the government and the company concerned.[3] The activities of the NEB were circumscribed in a variety of ways, as indicated below. The Industry Bill, published in January 1975, incorporated some further modifications of the original proposals. In particular, the provision for compulsory disclosure of information by firms was no longer connected with planning agreements. The NEB was established by the Industry Act, and its operations are reviewed in the next section. Planning agreements were legislated for, but as will be seen below they were virtually never used. Nationalisation was subject to its own legislation, and the three major nationalisations are discussed in Section 3. Section 4 discusses the industrial strategy, and this is followed by consideration of selective assistance. The final section provides some concluding remarks.

2 The National Enterprise Board in practice

The NEB was established in November 1975. Partly in response to the controversy preceding its establishment, a number of restrictions were placed on its operations. Its financial limit was initially set at £700 million, then raised in early 1978 by affirmative action in Parliament to £1000 million. The financial limit was raised to £3000 million at the end of 1978, though it was intended that about half of the increased finance would come from the private sector. The Secretary of State for Industry had to approve any acquisition of shares by the NEB which took its holding to over 30% of voting equity or if the value of the holding exceeded £10 million. Approval was also needed for loans, guarantees and joint ventures exceeding £25 million or if the NEB sought to acquire more than 10% of shares carrying unrestricted voting rights when existing directors did not give consent. Any loans provided by the NEB had to be at commercial interest rates.

The initial portfolio of the NEB was formed by the equity already owned by the government in eight companies, most of which had been rescued from bankruptcy through government intervention, though not all companies largely or completely owned by the government were transferred. The overall shareholdings of the NEB were dominated by the holdings in the companies initially transferred to it. By 31 March 1979, the NEB had received £777 million from public funds, of which £569 millions had been spent on acquiring BL,[4] £95 million on Rolls Royce and £78 million on acquisitions other than those from the government.[5]

Some indication of the time pattern of expenditure on the NEB is given in Table 10.1 (the cumulative total differs from that quoted in the last paragraph as the initial expenditure on BL was not assigned to the NEB). The government's plans in early 1979 were for continuing annual expenditure of around £250 million, a substantial part of which would be finance for BL and Rolls Royce. By March 1979, the NEB had shareholdings in over fifty companies,[6] with an average outlay of a little over £1 million a company. Many of the companies operated in high-technology areas, reflecting the identification of computers and microelectronics as priority areas.

In December 1977 the NEB was set the financial duty of earning a rate of return of 15−20% (excluding BL and Rolls Royce) by 1981, at which time, it was assumed, manufacturing industry would be obtaining a rate of return

Table 10.1   *Public expenditure relating to industrial policy (£ million)*

	1973/74	*1974/75*	*1975/76*	*1976/77*	*1977/78*	*1978/79*	*1979/80*[a]
National Enterprise Board	–	–	12	158	368	70	270
Selective Assistance	32	30	423	105	59	225	197
Shipbuilding[b]	282	294	231	157	− 35	66	60
Others[c]	448	196	105	46	35	35	40
Total of general support for industry	762	520	771	466	427	396	567
Selective assistance to industry in assisted areas[d]	50	58	74	35	34	92	67
Industrial innovation of which:	465	482	459	348	275	358	268
Aerospace	288	313	260	135	103	164	61
Nuclear	126	115	139	157	114	120	117

Notes:

[a]   Planned expenditure as of end-1978.

[b]   Refinancing of home shipbuilding lending, interest support costs of home shipbuilding lending, assistance to the shipbuilding industry. Negative figure for 1977/78 arises from the first of these three items.

[c]   Promotion of tourism, other support services, investment grants (which were £416m. in 1973/74, declined to £173m. in 1974/75, and then to zero).

[d]   Provided under Section 7 of Industry Act 1972, but only a relatively small part of expenditure on regional support and regeneration.

All figures in 1978 survey prices, except those for NEB which are in money terms.

Source: Chancellor of the Exchequer (1979).

of 20%. The rate of return earned by the NEB, before interest and taxation
and on a historic cost basis, but excluding BL and Rolls Royce, was:

1976 7·3%, 1977 11·4%, 1978 11·3%, 1979 (first half-year) 10·9%[7]

The overall rate of return for 1979 was 4·8%, but with the exclusion
of four loss-making companies and some green-field investments in initial
loss-making phase the rate of return was 18·1%.[8] The comparable rate
of return for manufacturing was 14·6% in 1975 and 14·9% in 1978.[9]
The well-known difficulties surrounding the measurement of the rate
of return are exacerbated for the NEB. It was operating during a period
of high and varying inflation, and its portfolio was dominated by companies which had been near to bankruptcy, both factors making the valu-
ation of assets employed particularly difficult. Further, there is the question
of what to include in costs, and the particular point here is the inclusion
or exclusion of costs associated with restructuring and with research and
development. The Committee of Public Accounts (1980) raised some
of these issues. Notably it argued that losses from closure of plants should
be included in the accounts on the basis that these losses arose from restructuring, which was one of the major roles for the NEB.

There were two distinct roles involved in the operations of the NEB.
The first role was rather akin to acting as a hospital for sick companies.
The assessment of this part of its work is largely an assessment of the
government rescue of the firms concerned. By late 1978, Parr (1979) argued
that of the eight companies transferred to the NEB, three (Ferranti, Brown
Boveri Kent and ICL) were performing well, and four (BL, Rolls Royce,
Herbert and Cambridge Instruments) continued to experience difficulties
(while the eighth, Dunford and Elliot, had been sold).

The major rescue undertaken by the Labour government was that of
BL. The difficulties of BL became apparent in the second half of 1974,
when it applied to the government for assistance; the government responded
by providing guarantees to the banks for up to £50 million. A committee
under Lord Ryder was appointed and reported within four months. It
argued that 'vehicle production is the kind of industry which ought to
remain an essential part of the UK's economic base' (p. 3) with BL supported as a major vehicle producer. It was estimated that nearly £1300
million over eight years at 1975 prices was needed from external sources
to finance viability, and 'a very large part of the funds can only be provided
by the Government and ... there is an overwhelmingly strong case for
the Government to provide the funds because of BL's importance to the
national economy' (Ryder Report, 1975, pp. 9–10). The justification for
government intervention was BL's position as a major exporter, producer
of import substitutes, and employer. The existing equity of BL was acquired
at a cost of £65m., and the government injected a further £200m. by the
acquisition of previously unissued equity. Subsequently, around £1000m. of

public money went to BL before the end of 1979 (Hindley and Richardson, 1983).

The government appears to have determined quickly that BL had to survive, which meant that government financial assistance had to be provided (see Expenditure Committee, 1975 for an indication of this). The immediate employment and balance of trade consequences of the disappearance of BL would appear to have been the major factor in that determination (cf. Central Policy Review Staff, 1975, especially pp. 110–11). In spite of the apparent haste of decision, it is difficult to see that any fundamentally different decision was ever likely. The disappearance of BL would have had an immediate impact on unemployment of around 170,000, with a further impact on suppliers, though partly offset by a rise in employment in other UK-based car factories. The balance of trade would have worsened significantly.[10] In the aftermath of the OPEC price rise, most car companies were in financial difficulties.[11] It would have been short-sighted to allow the disappearance of the only UK-owned car-producer in such circumstances, especially when most other countries were likely to support their car companies through the recession.

The major difficulties surrounding a government rescue such as that of BL do not necessarily derive from the losses incurred, since wider considerations such as employment and balance of trade may justify the rescue. It is rather that much of the relevant information has to be supplied by interested parties and that the 'soft budget' syndrome analysed by Kornai (1980) may apply. A company's survival appears to rely on securing government assistance rather than on improved products and productivity. Thus the pressures on a company to become financially viable may be diluted, especially since the government has already shown a willingness to supply finance.

There was a financial recovery by BL with positive pre-tax profits in 1976–78. However, the ambitious plans of Ryder soon appeared to have been over-optimistic, and were abandoned in November 1977 for a more modest corporate plan. Employment was cut drastically over the subsequent few years to reach 94,000 by the end of 1981.

The success or failure of some of the other rescues is more clear-cut. Alfred Herbert, a machine-tool manufacturer, can be classified as a failure. The Industrial Development Advisory Board (created to advise government on selective assistance) had counselled against assistance. Alfred Herbert became fully government-owned in 1975, and after a series of problems went into liquidation in 1980. The cost to the NEB had been £46·1 million. Ferranti, on the other hand, can be deemed a success. Financial difficulties in 1974 forced the company to apply to the government for assistance, leading to a loan and the purchase by the government of 62·5% of the equity, later transferred to the NEB. The company recovered and the NEB reduced its share of equity to 50% in 1978 (at a profit of nearly £1 million). The remaining 50% of shares were sold at 11% below the prevailing stock market price in July 1980 for £54m., which represented a £47m. profit.

The second role played by the NEB was the encouragement of relatively small firms and the creation of firms, particularly in some areas of high technology, with computers and microelectronics identified as priority sectors. The NEB sponsored the formation of a number of new companies, of which Inmos (a microchip company) wsa the best-known example and included INSAC Data systems (for the overseas marketing of British software), Nexos (office equipment) and British Underwater Engineering.

The NEB experiment came to an effective end soon after the change of government in May 1979. Many of the companies supported or owned by the NEB were sold off, and a much reduced NEB was merged with the National Research Development Council to form the British Technology Group. It is perhaps not surprising that in a high-risk activity there were a number of failures and some substantial successes. On the failure side, at least seven companies (in addition to Herbert) went into receivership. On the (commercial) success side, in the first ten months of 1981, the NEB holdings sold realised around £4m., of which £1·7m. represented profits on investments made.[12]

It is argued here that the second role of the NEB's operations (as identified above) should be given much more attention than the first role, even though the latter took up nearly 95% of the NEB's funds. Some organisation would have been required to oversee those companies rescued by the government anyway. It is, of course, possible to argue that such rescues should not have been mounted. Our view, as indicated in the above discussion of BL, is that many of the rescues were justified, even though mistakes were made and difficulties encountered. Thus the net addition of the NEB is represented by the second role. Further, this more entrepreneurial role for a state holding company is more in line with the original intentions and may provide more of a guide to a future role for state intervention. This role was carried on during the 1980s by local government through agencies such as the West Midlands Enterprise Board and the Greater London Enterprise Board. The operations of the NEB were subject to commercial criteria and to secure a return over a short time horizon but it still found outlets for its funds. This suggests that there was a gap in the provision of finance, particularly in the high-technology area, which the NEB helped to fill.

3 Nationalisation: British Shipbuilders, British Aerospace, BNOC

The three major nationalisations[13] in the period 1974/79 were undertaken for rather different reasons. But they did share the common feature that the companies acquired were not public utilities and were in competition with other companies.

The arguments for the nationalisation of the shipbuilding industry were a combination of the failure of private enterprise and the continuing government subsidies. 'A revitalised and modernised industry working through a central National Shipbuilding Corporation with resources for adequate research and development could move into the profitable areas of shipbuilding where future prosperity will be found' (Labour Party, 1973b).

British Shipbuilders came into existence in July 1977. Apart from the companies which were compulsorily acquired under the Act, several others were acquired by agreement. A year after nationalisation, British Shipbuilders was operating 30 shipyards, 19 repair establishments and 6 medium- and slow-speed diesel-engine companies, and controlled virtually all shipbuilding and marine engines manufacture, but only half of shiprepairing activity (*Trade and Industry*, 28 July 1978).

The British shipbuilding industry had been in decline throughout the post-war period (for figures see Thomas, 1983). British governments, like many others, had subsidised shipbuilding in a variety of ways, and the scale of assistance in the 1970s can be judged from Table 10.1. The experience of British Shipbuilders was rather more the management of decline than revitalisation.[14] It appears to have faced the common problem facing the amalgamation of independent companies with a range of factories and a variety of industrial relations practices. The subsequent privatisation of most of British Shipbuilders, generally through the sale of its constituent parts rather than as a whole, would suggest that there was no successful integration of the activities of the previously independent companies.

The aerospace industry was rather different in that it was perceived to have good future prospects. Though it had also been the recipient of extensive government assistance, this has been mainly for the development of new projects. The government was a large customer of that industry (directly for defence requirements or indirectly through British Airways). 'The continued existence of a privately owned airframe industry largely dependent on public money seemed increasingly absurd. Nationalisation would, it was claimed, legitimise that dependence and improve the accountability of publicly sponsored programmes' (Hayward, 1983, p. 193). In moving the second reading of the nationalisation Bill, Eric Varley argued that rationalisation was required to realise economies of scale and to avoid wasteful competition. Further, 'private sector firms [are] not able to finance the huge scale of current projects from their own resources' and 'an industry which depends for its existence and progress on public money on this huge scale cannot be called a genuine example of private enterprise'.[15] Nationalisation was seen as being able to resolve many control and accountability questions. The government as a customer of the aerospace industry was often purchasing on a cost-plus basis, which meant that some monitoring by the government over costs was required. Similarly, as a provider of financial assistance for research and development, the government would wish to have some control over expenditure.

British Aerospace (BAe) was formed from the British Aircraft Corporation, Hawker Siddeley and Scottish Aviation in April 1977; subsequently it was privatised in two stages in 1981 and 1985. The privatisation of BAe as a single entity suggests that the argument for a single British aerospace company was widely accepted (as is hinted in the parliamentary debates on the nationalisation Bill), and completes the government-sponsored rationalisation of the aerospace industry dating from the late 1950s.

On the basis of the limited evidence available, however, the ownership of the aircraft industry has had some effects on the formal relations between company and sponsoring departments, but has had little effect on the working relationships between the two parties. Strategically, of course, the interaction between the state and industry was effectively the same. At this level, however, the relationship was always determined by financial dependence and not ownership.

(Hayward, 1983, p. 197)

The formation of the British National Oil Company (BNOC)[16] was designed to enable the government to have a strong influence in the development of the offshore oil industry, and to gather and provide information which would enhance government control over private sector exploration and the rate of depletion.

Existing North Sea operators were required to conclude agreements with BNOC that gave the latter rights to participate in the developments (but not necessarily an ownership stake) and to purchase 51 percent of the resulting output at market prices ... By 1979, then, the activities of BNOC comprised two quite distinct types of operation. BNOC had quickly become a substantial exploration/development/production enterprise in its own right. In addition, however, it was also a major oil-trading enterprise, buying oil from other producers under the terms set out in the various participation agreements that had been concluded, and selling the product on into competitive markets.

(Vickers and Yarrow, 1988, pp. 319–20)

In many respects, BNOC could be said to have achieved the objectives with which it was charged.

4 Industrial strategy and the sector working parties

The industrial strategy was introduced in November 1975 following a tripartite meeting at Chequers. The title of the White Paper (*An Approach to Industrial Strategy*) suggests the tentative nature of the approach. Its 'procedure was conceived essentially as a dialogue between Government, management and unions conducted at both the industry and the national level, directed primarily to improving our medium-term prospects and operating to a timetable which tied in very closely with the annual spring Budget' (Lord, 1976, p. 11).[17] The industrial strategy built on existing institutional arrangements and was largely based on the National Economic

Development Office (NEDO). Sector Working Parties (SWPs) were tri-partite bodies established in key areas (often being the existing Economic Development Councils) to cover over thirty industries or sectors and in early 1979 there were thirty-nine SWPs.[18] The scope of the individual SWPs ranged from the broad (Food and Drink Manufacturing) to the relatively narrow (e.g. Drop Forgings). Selective assistance, discussed in the following section, could be provided under the Industry Act 1972 to help reduce problems identified by the SWPs. The SWPs only covered manufacturing industries, and only 40% of those industries.

The industrial strategy shifted the emphasis of policy away from a concern with redistribution of income towards production, particularly in the manufacturing sector. A joint statement by the Chancellor of the Exchequer and the Secretary of State for Industry (1975, p. 4) argued that

The Government intends to give greater weight and more consistently than hitherto, to the need for increasing the national rate of growth through regenerating our industrial structure and improving efficiency. For the immediate future this will mean giving priority to industrial development over consumption or even our social objectives.

There was a strong suggestion that short-term macroeconomic policy should take into account, if not be subordinated to, the medium-term industrial strategy. 'A microeconomic, self-regarding approach to the development of industrial policies can be vitiated if macroeconomic policies are not broadly benign' (Stout, 1978, p. 193).[19] Lord (1976) argued that previous governments 'have attached too much importance to 'fine tuning' in the interest of running the economy at maximum output and much too little weight to the importance for industry ... of having a stable economic and fiscal environment in which to operate and plan for the future' (p. 6).

There was an explicit rejection of the use of an overall national plan. 'The likelihood is that any plan which erected a single complete and mutually consistent set of industrial forecasts and targets would rapidly be falsified by events and have to be discarded' (Chancellor of the Exchequer et al. (1975), p. 7). Driver (1983) points out that the focus of the industrial strategy was on removing technical inefficiences, with the better direction of investment and the greater utilisation of resources, rather than on raising investment. He also pointed to the direction of state financial assistance being responsive to proposals from the SWPs, and the view that the greater utilisation of resources required reform of working practices, though with the intention of using existing workers more intensively to produce increased output, rather than reducing employment.

The industrial strategy highlights a number of difficulties which confront interventionist policies designed to speed up economic growth. The strategy was a medium-term one, and most of the fruits of such a strategy can only be expected to accrue after a number of years. The reform of working practices and other measures to raise productivity often involve a reduction of employment. There is likely to be a relative shift of resources away from private and social consumption towards investment and exports, though the absolute level of consumption need not fall in the presence of unutilised resources.

The industrial strategy was based on the identification of the difficulties facing particular sectors, to be followed by government assistance and other activities to reduce the constraints. Each of the SWPs set its own objectives, which were monitored by the NEDO staff. The objectives were much as expected, relating to such aspects as foreign trade performance and employment. Little work has been undertaken to establish the success or otherwise of the industrial strategy. Stout (1978) indicated that the work of the SWPs 'has so far been mostly in directions where controversy and conflict is small, and where quite a lot of improvement has been possible through analysis and the exchange of information' (p. 193). But 'progress has been slower in the investigation of ways of emulating the productivity of efficient producers both within Britain and abroad' and 'in reaching agreement about the rationalisation of output and its redistribution between companies' (p. 194). Stout suggests that even when net social benefit would arise from change, the implementation of change would be difficult because the SWPs did not represent enough of the producers and workers concerned.

A major objective of the industrial strategy was a reduction of import penetration, and Driver (1983) provides some evidence relevant to that objective. In a number of cases, it was possible broadly to link a sector working party with an industry as defined in official statistics. He compared the import penetration performances of each of 33 groups with the manufacturing average over the periods 1972–76 and 1977–79. Import penetration generally rises throughout these periods, and the success of the SWPs is judged in terms of the slowing down of the rise in import penetration. Of the 33 groups, 8 displayed an absolute decline of import penetration in the period 1977–79, 6 displayed import penetration rising at a slower rate than manufacturing as a whole, and the remaining 19 sectors at a faster rate. But the sectors had generally experienced import penetration rising at a faster rate than manufacturing as a whole during the earlier period of 1972–76. When improvement (or deterioration) of the performance of a sector is measured against the criterion that import penetration grows slower (or faster) relative to that for manufacturing in the second period than in the first period, then two-thirds of the sectors covered show an improvement. Driver calculates that, on average, the rate of increase of import penetration was slowed by just over 0·5% per annum in the industries covered by SWPs.

The government continued to reiterate its commitment to planning agreements, but acknowledged that 'progress in this important area of industrial policy which was announced by the government early in the passage of the 1975 Industry Bill as voluntary had been very disappointing'

(Eric Varley).[20] Only two planning agreements were concluded, neither of which had much impact on the companies concerned. One of these was with the nationalised National Coal Board, and the other was with the Chrysler car company in return for financial support. In December 1975, Chrysler was provided with financial assistance to cover losses and to finance future projects (up to a maximum commitment of £162·5m.) subject to a planning agreement.[21] In a number of respects, this should have proved an ideal test case for planning agreements. The company concerned was a large multi-national in a sector generally regarded as particularly important, with production facilities in a depressed area (Linwood in Scotland). However, three years later, Chrysler's UK operations were sold to Peugeot-Citroën, without the government or unions being informed until after the sale was agreed (Coates, 1980, p. 104). Although the planning agreement had given the government a veto over such a sale, 'in reality it [the government] had little choice. It could go along with the sale, and hope that British jobs would be safe, or veto it and see Chrysler UK close completely' (loc. cit.); and the government acquiesced in the take-over.

5 Selective assistance under the Industry Act 1972

The Industry Act 1972 empowered the government to provide selective financial assistance to industry, and the annual reports on that Act provide extensive details on selective assistance, while the report for 1976 reproduces a Department of Industry paper on the criteria for the provision of financial assistance. The amounts spent on selective assistance fluctuated considerably from year to year as can be seen from Table 10.1. This selective assistance includes assistance to individual firms, countercyclical investment schemes, and a number of sectoral schemes to encourage modernisation and rationalisation, many of which were in response to recommendations by the SWPs. Fifteen sectoral schemes were in operation at some stage during the period of the Labour government.[22]

The first such industry-wide scheme was that covering the wool textile industry. It was open for application between July 1973 and the end of 1975 and essentially completed by the end of 1977; it was followed by a second-stage scheme (open to application from November 1976 to December 1977). Some 30% of plants, accounting for 60% of the industry's employment received assistance. The scheme contained four elements: a 20% cash grant towards the buying of new machinery, a 30% grant for new buildings, interest relief grants for rationalisation and cash grants to companies and plants being closed down. Re-equipment grants were paid only for new machinery, where previously used capacity was scrapped. Government expenditure on grants totalled £16·6m. on 301 projects with associated investment by the industry of nearly £70m. This scheme was viewed as part of the industrial strategy, even though it had been started by the previous government. It is helpful that it was subject to an evaluation, summarised in *Trade and Industry*, 15 September 1978. Investment was dramatically higher (of the order of double) in 1973−75 than in the period 1970−72. A later unpublished work reported some regression analysis putting the increase of investment due to the two wool textile schemes at 25−50% (Gibbs, n.d.). The evaluation concluded that 'in all major respects the scheme has already brought about a most encouraging improvement in the performance of the industry' (*Trade and Industry*, 15 September 1978, p. 601).

The Accelerated Project Scheme (APS) was a countercyclical measure to bring forward investment during the period April 1975 to July 1976. It provided assistance at a public expenditure cost of nearly £72m. to 111 schemes on which the total financial outlays were over £560m.[23] The APS was replaced by the Selective Investment Scheme announced in December 1976 with an allocation of £150m. and closed in June 1979. By March 1980, grants of £106·5m. had been offered to 166 projects involving capital outlays of over £1000m. (from over 700 applications). The assistance provided was to be the minimum necessary to bring about benefits to the economy and varied between 3% and 20% of the project costs, averaging 10·5%. The Annual Report on the 1972 Industry Act for 1980 put the benefits derived from the investment assisted under this scheme as £700m. of orders for UK plants, equipment and construction industries (providing 90,000 person-years of work) and an annual primary benefit of £600m. to balance of payments for 1982 rising to over £950m. when all schemes are on-stream. It was officially estimated that 'about 20,000 permanent jobs are expected to be created and some 10,000 preserved by the selective investment scheme and the scheme which ran before it, the accelerated projects scheme'.[24]

Section 7 of the Industry Act 1972 permitted assistance to be given to projects (either new ones and expansions to create employment or modernisations and rationalisations which would safeguard employment) in the assisted areas. The government estimated that in the first three years of the industrial strategy, projects assisted in this way 'had involved the creation of 150,000 new jobs and the safeguarding of a further 90,000'.[25]

6 Concluding remarks

This chapter has concentrated on the aspects of Labour's industrial policy which could be considered innovative. Other aspects of industrial policy, notably policies on monopolies and mergers and on restrictive trade practices, continued unchanged, though there were major reviews of these policies towards the end of the period of government.[26] These reviews made some suggestions for policy change, notably some tightening of merger policy which it was suggested would roughly quadruple the proportion of mergers which were investigated. For restrictive practices policy, some strengthening of enforcement and new provision for control of some anti-competitive practices were recommended. The prices policy, discussed in Chapter 11, had significant impacts on the operation of firms, but its major implication for industrial policy came from the evolution of the Price Commission from a price control body into one of efficiency audit. Government support for industrial innovation continued much as before, with the exception of the NEB support for small high-technology firms. Public expenditure supporting research and development continued to be dominated by aircraft and aero-engine, space and nuclear projects (see Table 10.1), with the decline in support of aerospace research coming from the decline in expenditure on Concorde and the RB211.

One particular important aspect of the general approach of the radical industrial policy has been ignored above, namely the stress on the encouragement of workers' co-operatives and of industrial democracy more generally.[27] Assistance was given to three workers' co-operatives, all of which had been formed as a response to the financial difficulties of the capitalist firms from which they emerged. None of the co-operatives flourished, which is perhaps not surprising given the circumstances of their birth as co-operatives.

The debates on and proposals for industrial policy conducted during the years of opposition provided an inauspicious background. The divisions over policy led to confusion over what the policy was, and generated (perhaps avoidable) hostility from industrialists, whilst the resulting perceived need to mollify industrialists limited the scope of the industrial strategy. That hostility does, though, illustrate a basic dilemma. The perception within the Labour Party was that British industry had on the whole performed relatively badly, and a significant part of the responsibility for this was placed on industrialists. The improvement of industrial performance would then appear to require either the replacement of those industrialists by others of more appropriate outlook and skills or the elicitation of a better performance and different decisions from the current industrialists. In the short term, the former option is virtually impossible in that a pool of alternative industrialists does not exist. The Labour Party in opposition could be seen as having taken the latter route with a strong element of compulsion in seeking to enforce industrialists to make different decisions and to improve performance.[28] However, some degree of co-operation is also required, which may not be forthcoming with the aura of compulsion. But without the element of compulsion, the forces for change may be inadequate. Desai (1989) comments, in relation to the industrial policies of this period that 'modernisation involved a conflictual approach; after all some toes had to be stepped on. Instead the approach was to be on consensus.'

A successful industrial policy requires civil servants and others trained and committed to its implementation, and the radical industrial policy would have required a large number of people to operate planning agreements and the public ownership of twenty-five major companies. Further, as argued by

Taylor and Hussey (1982), 'many organisations either do not have corporate plans and therefore nothing which they can agree with government, or they produce plans in which top management has little confidence. To have a planning agreement, one presumably needs a plan.' The experience of France and Italy (amongst others) was cited to illustrate the possible beneficial effects of planning agreements and state holding companies. But the intellectual and institutional backgrounds in those countries were quite different from that in Britain: the state holding companies had been built up over several years. Thus there must be severe doubts as to whether the scale of operation indicated in *Labour's Programme 1973* would have been practical.

The radical industrial policy paid rather a lot of attention to institutions, and little to what the institutions would actually do. It was proposed that the NEB would have a portfolio of twenty to twenty-five major companies, but little was said as to how these companies would be run, or how their activities would be co-ordinated. Similarly, the planning agreements would have generated large amounts of information for the government, but little was said as to what would be done with the information obtained.

The radical industrial policy, intended to raise investment and improve international competitiveness, would have faced the difficulty faced by the industrial strategy, namely that a shift away from consumption must usually mean a shift away from wages. It may have been thought possible to finance higher investment out of profits. But in the circumstances of the 1970s there was little room for manoeuvre in that direction.

Two features of the industrial strategy stand out as potentially alleviating ingrained weaknesses of the British economy. First, there was an attempt by government to recognise the needs of manufacturing industry in the formulation of its macroeconomic policy, though we have no measure of how effective such recognition was (though Lord, 1976, p. 7 provides some examples). Second, the NEB helped to establish and sustain relatively small high-technology firms. The failure of British industry to develop new ideas, often produced in the UK, and the difficulties of raising finance for research have been frequently cited. One criticism which could be made is that the time horizon over which performance was judged was too short, though there are obvious dangers of continuing to put money into projects in the hope that something will eventually turn up.

The industrial policies considered in this chapter were only in full operation for three and a half years (November 1975 to May 1979). It is particularly difficult to evaluate their success or otherwise since the benefits of such policies can be expected to show through over a long time period and the policies were operated on a modest scale (as indicated by the expenditure figures in Table 10.1 and by estimates of the employment effects of the industrial strategy cited above). However, the evaluations quoted above indicate benefits from the industrial strategy, though a full assessment would need to pay more attention to the costs and to the indirect effects. In this section we have pointed to some significant, though unquantifiable, effects of the industrial strategy.

The question arises as to whether, in the light of the problems facing the UK economy in the 1970s (including the long-term relative decline and the general world recession), the industrial strategy should have been on a much larger scale. If it had been, then there would have been difficulties over availability of trained personnel and other resources and the industrial strategy would have become involved in more contentious issues.

Notes

I am grateful to Ciaran Driver for comments on an initial draft and for information and advice on the industrial strategy.

1 The story of the debates over the NEB proposals is given in Hatfield (1978), especially Chapters 8 to 10. See also Coates, 1980, Chapter 3.

2 See Hatfield (1978, Chapter 13) for the story of the battles over the contents of the White Paper on industrial regeneration.

3 For details on proposals for planning agreements, see Department of Industry (1975).

4 We use the term 'BL' throughout, even though the company was known as British Leyland Motor Company for part of the time.

5 The source is Committee of Public Accounts (1980).

6 From an answer to a parliamentary question, *Trade and Industry* (24 November 1978) lists forty-six companies in which the NEB had shareholdings on 15 November 1978. A further answer (*Trade and Industry* 30 March 1979) lists an additional eight companies in which NEB had shareholdings on 16 March 1979.

7 This rate of return was calculated before charging initial development costs of three high-technology subsidary companies: otherwise the rate of return would have been 8·6%.

8 Derived from Committee of Public Accounts (1980).

9 Derived from Committee of Public Accounts (1980).

10 In 1974, BL had domestic sales of £1595m. and exports of £485m. (Central Policy Review Staff, 1975, p. 7). If, in the short run, most of the exports were lost to UK producers and one-third of BL's domestic sales covered by imports, then the balance of trade loss would have eben around £1000m.

11 All major European car producers reported losses in 1974, of which BL's losses were the smallest in absolute terms (Central Policy Review Staff, 1975, p. 52).

12 Information on both failures and successes taken from answers to a number of parliamentary questions. In the case of failures, written answer dated 13 November 1980, and for successes written answer dated 25 November 1981.

13 The legislation was Aircraft and Shipbuilding Industries Act 1977 and Petroleum and Submarine Pipe-lines Act 1975.

14 Employment in shipbuilding and repairing (of which, British Shipbuilders was the major component) declined from 131,000 in 1980 to 77,000 in 1987.

15 Quotes taken from speech by Eric Varley reported in Official Reports, Parliamentary Debates, Commons, vol. 901 (1975).

16 For some further discussion see Vickers and Yarrow, 1988, pp. 316–25.

17 Alan Lord was second permanent secretary at the Treasury when he gave the lecture (delivered 10 November 1976) from which this quotation is taken.

18 This number is taken from the NEDO Analysis of Sector Working Party Reports, February 1979. Whilst most committees were called 'sector working parties', other labels were used.

19 David Stout was economic director of the National Economic Development Office when he wrote the paper from which this quote is taken.

20 Quoted in *Trade and Industry*, 25 November 1977.

21 For discussion of the history of the planning agreement with Chrysler and its implications for the general idea of planning agreements see Coates (1980, pp. 101–6).

22 For a listing and brief description see Annual Report on the Industry Act 1972 Year to 31st March 1980.

23 Information takes from the Annual Report on the Industry Act 1972 for year to 31st March 1980.

24 *Trade and Industry* 13 October 1978.

25 Answer to parliamentary question by Alan Williams, Minister of State, Department of Industry, reported in *Trade and Industry*, 24 November 1978, p. 383.

26 Review of Monopolies and Mergers Policy (1978) and Review of Restrictive Trade Practices Policy (1979).

27 For some discussion see Coates (1980, pp. 136–42).

28 Labour Party (1973b) proposed a state management consultancy service for this purpose. The Price Commission was used in the period 1977 to 1979 as an efficiency audit body and so in some respects acted to raise efficiency (cf. Chapter 11 on Prices Policy).

References

Annual Report on the Industry Act 1972 Year to 31st March 1976, HC 619, HMSO.
Annual Report on the Industry Act 1972 Year to 31st March 1979, Cmnd. 206, HMSO.
Annual Report on the Industry Act 1972 Year to 31st March 1980, Cmnd. 772, HMSO.
Central Policy Review Staff (1975), *The Future of the British Car Industry*, HMSO.
Chancellor of the Exchequer (1979), *The Government's Expenditure Plans 1979/80 to 1982/83*, Cmnd. 7439, HMSO.
Chancellor of the Exchequer and Secretary of State for Industry (1975), *An Approach to Industrial Strategy*, Cmnd. 6315, HMSO.
Coates, D. (1980), *Labour in Power?*, Longman, London.
Committee of Public Accounts (1980), *Sixth Report*, 1979/80, HC 446, HMSO.
Department of Industry (1975), *The Contents of a Planning Agreement*, HMSO.
Desai, M. (1989), 'Is Thatcherism the cure for the British disease?', in F. Green (ed.), *The Restructuring of the UK Economy*, Harvester Wheatsheaf, Hemel Hempstead.
Driver, C. (1983), 'Import substitution and the work of the sector working parties', *Applied Economics*, XV, pp. 165–76.
The Expenditure Committee (1975), *The Fourteenth Report: The Motor Vehicle Industry*, HC 617, HMSO.

Gibbs, J. (n.d.), 'An econometric analysis of Stages I and II', Mimeo.

Hatfield, M. (1978), *The house the Left built*, Gollancz, London.

Hayward, K. (1983), *Government and British Civil Aerospace*, Manchester University Press, Manchester.

Hindley, B., and Richardson, R. (1983), 'United Kingdom: pulling the dragon's teeth – the National Enterprise Board', in B. Hindley (ed.), *State Investment Companies in Western Europe*, Macmillan, London.

Kornai, J. (1980), *The Economics of Shortage*, North-Holland, Amsterdam.

Labour Party (1973a), *The National Enterprise Board: Labour's State Holding Company*, Labour Party.

Labour Party (1973b), *Labour's Programme 1973* (quotes in text taken from *Labour Weekly*, June 1973), Labour Party.

Labour Party (1974), *Let Us Work Together* (Manifesto for February 1974 General Election), Labour Party.

Lord, A. (1976), 'A strategy for industry', Ellis Hunter Memorial Lecture, University of York.

Parr, M. (1979), 'The National Enterprise Board', *National Westminster Bank Review*, February, pp. 51–62.

Review of Monopolies and Megers Policy (1978), *A Consultative Document*, Cmnd. 7198, HMSO.

Review of Restrictive Trade Practices Policy (1979), *A Consultative Document*, Cmnd. 7512, HMSO.

Ryder Report (1975), *British Leyland: the next decade*, HC 342, HMSO.

Secretary of State for Industry (1974), *The Regeneration of British Industry*, Cmnd. 5710, HMSO.

Stout, D. (1978), *'De-industrialisation and industrial policy'*, in F. Blackaby (ed.), *De-industrialisation*, Heinemann, London.

Taylor, B., and Hussey, D. (1982), *The Realities of Planning*, Pergamon Press, Oxford.

Thomas, D. (1983), 'Shipbuilding – demand linkage and industrial decline', in J. Williams, K. Williams and D. Thomas, *Why Are the British Bad at Manufacturing?*, Routledge & Kegan Paul, London.

Vickers, J., and Yarrow, G. (1988), *Privatization: an economic analysis*, MIT Press, Cambridge, Mass.

Prices policies

1 Introduction

The rates of inflation experienced in the UK and throughout the OECD area during the 1970s meant that the control of inflation was inevitably to the fore in economic policy-making. The incoming Labour government inherited a strongly inflationary climate. Between the second half of 1973 and the first half of 1974 the annualised rate of inflation was 17·1% in the UK and 15·2% in the largest seven OECD economies. In February 1974 the National Institute gave its optimistic forecast for the rise in the consumer price index between the fourth quarter of 1973 and the fourth quarter of 1974 at 13·8% with their pessimistic forecast as 17·8% (the out-turn was 11·1%).

Oil prices had quadrupled in late 1973. Under Stage 3 of the Heath government's pay policy, wages could rise by £2·25 per head per week or 7% (with a limit of £350 a year for any individual) plus 40p a week for each 1% rise of the retail price index (RPI) in excess of 7% above the index for October 1973. This threshold arrangement was permitted to 'safeguard employees' standard of living against the possibility of an exceptionally high rate of price increases during Stage 3' (Chancellor of the Exchequer, 1973), but with the rapid increase in oil prices and other inflationary pressures turned out to add significantly to the inflationary spiral. The Pay Board indicated that pay awards covering some 7½ million employees included threshold agreements, and after the demise of the Pay Board the National Institute estimated 10 million workers as being covered by such agreements. The RPI for October 1974 was over 17% higher than the October 1973 figure, and hence ten threshold payments were triggered (starting with the April RPI figure). At each stage, the price code permitted 50% of allowable costs to be passed through into prices, with the effect that profits would be squeezed with faster than expected rises in allowable costs (though we are not aware of any precise estimates of the impact of the price code on profitability).

The Labour government took office with Stage 3 of the Heath government's prices and incomes policy in force. Stage 1 had been introduced for a period of 90 days in November 1972 (later extended to the end of April 1973) with a freeze on most prices (other than fresh food), wages, dividends and rents. A Pay Board had been established to operate the wages policy.

On the prices side ... [a] separate body — the Price Commission — was set up and ... the requirements were more onerous for big firms than for small ones. Price controls were based on two principles: firms could apply for increases on the basis of 'allowable costs per unit'; also, they had a reference level of net profit margins — the average of the best two years of the last five — and were not to exceed that level. Distributors were not controlled by allowable costs, but by a combination of net profit margins and gross percentage margins.

(Blackaby, 1978, p. 381)

The various stages of the prices policy up to July 1977 under Conservative and Labour governments were modifications of this basic framework.

The general idea behind this approach was that a relatively small number of firms dominated an industrialised economy, and a significant impact on the general level of prices could be achieved by exerting control over their prices. Further, the prices of these large companies were seen as mainly cost-determined; at least the norm for price changes was taken to be cost changes. Commodities (such as fresh food) liable to substantial price fluctuations not directly related to cost fluctuations were excluded from regulation, despite their potential influence over wages.

The Pay Board was abolished in July 1974, as promised in the election manifesto. The Price Commission continued with a gradually evolving role and a significant change of purpose with the passage of the Price Commission Act 1977, and our discussion is divided into the two covering periods of before and after the passage of that Act.

The profitability of British industry had been declining for some years (the length and degree of the decline depending on the measure of profitability used). One effect of the price code under the Heath government had been to squeeze profitability further through the operation of the productivity deduction, as suggested above. This profit squeeze, taken with the effects of the world-wide recession from late 1973 onwards, meant that there was little room for reducing inflation by a downward pressure on profit margins, without accepting the consequences of widespread bankruptcies. A further complication was the increased significance of stock appreciation in total profits, placing a greater squeeze on liquidity. The first part of Table 11.1 provides figures on the share of profits in national income and the relative size of stock appreciation as part of profits. The first set of figures (for the period 1966—74) is taken from the 1975 issue of *Economic Trends*, and hence indicates the situation as perceived in the mid-1970s. The second set of figures comes from the 1982 issue of *Economic Trends*, and suggests that the profits squeeze was not as substantial as initially thought. The revival in profitability suggested by the figures is partly attributable to the landing

Table 11.1   *Measures of profitability*

	Gross trading profits (net of stock appreciation) as percentage of GDP		Stock appreciation as percentage of gross profits	
	(a)	(b)	(a)	(b)
1966	13·2	13·2	5·2	5·2
1967	13·1	13·1	1·9	1·9
1968	12·9	12·9	9·0	9·0
1969	11·6	12·8	11·6	10·2
1970	10·4	11·8	16·7	14·2
1971	10·8	12·6	14·2	12·1
1972	10·7	12·6	15·7	13·3
1973	9·8	12·5	29·8	22·1
1974	6·8	9·2	50·3	40·9
1975		8·3		35·6
1976		9·0		35·1
1977		13·0		19·0
1978		13·5		14·4
1979		12·6		26·1

Notes: (a) Figures calculated from data available in 1975.
         (b) Figures calculated from data available in 1982.

Source: Calculated from *Economic Trends*, Annual Supplements 1975, 1982.

	Rate of profit (as measured in 1975)	
	Before	After
	Stock appreciation	
1966	10·6	9·8
1967	10·6	10·2
1968	11·2	10·0
1969	9·9	8·5
1970	9·1	7·3
1971	8·9	7·4
1972	9·3	7·6
1973	10·3	6·6
1974	9·3	4·0

Source: *National Institute Economic Review* 1976 (based on figures given in *Trade and Industry*, 24 October 1975).

of North Sea oil. The recent trend in the rate of profit as perceived in 1975 is indicated by the second half of the Table.

During 1974 profit margins appeared to fall. The Price Commission observed that net profit margins had fallen to 50% of their reference level in the fourth quarter of 1974, compared with 71% in 1973 (and profit margins had previously hovered around the latter rate). The Commission observed that 'profits are not in general contributing to increased prices. Indeed, had profit margins been maintained at the level of a year ago, prices would have gone up more than they have ... the changes in the Stage 4 [price] Code designed to halt the erosion of profits were very much needed' (Price Commission, 1975a). The OECD economic survey of the UK similarly commented that changes in the price code were designed to aid higher levels of profits.

This chapter concentrates on the role of the Price Commission as a major part of the counter-inflationary strategy. Other chapters (notably Chapter 4 on incomes policies) deal with other aspects of that strategy. There are, of course, many decisions made by government such as those on indirect taxation and nationalised industry pricing which have an impact on the pace of inflation. It would be impossible to say what part was played by concern over inflation in such decisions. However, the reduction of value added tax from 10% to 8% in July 1974 appears to have been strongly influenced by both its direct impact on the rate of inflation and its indirect effect on inflation by reducing the number of threshold payments triggered.

Both Conservative and Labour governments used subsidies to help restrain prices. The Conservative government had focused on restraining nationalised industries' prices. Compensation from central government to nationalised industries for price restraint amounted to around £750 million in 1973/74, and over £1000m. in 1974/75 (expressed at 1978 prices: figures taken from Chancellor of the Exchequer, 1978). However, these price restraints were virtually eliminated during 1975/76. In consequence, nationalised industries' price rises were a significant component of inflation in 1975. The Price Commission (1975b) suggested that in the quarter of June–August 1975 nationalised industries' prices had risen by over 20% (against just over 4% in the private sector) and were responsible for over half of the rise in prices under the ambit of the Price Commission.

The Labour government introduced a range of subsidies on food, especially on bread, butter, cheese, flour, milk and tea. At 1978 survey prices, these food subsidies had an exchequer cost of over £900m. in 1974/75, falling to £502m. in 1976/77. From mid-1976 onwards, it was intended to phase out food subsidies by the end of the decade.

A number of voluntary agreements with retailers were drawn up to restrain prices. In June 1974, an agreement with food retailers was designed to have twenty items sold below normal price for a period of six months. In January 1976, a selective voluntary price restraint scheme was introduced

covering over fifty different product categories, with price rises to be kept
below 5% over a period of six months.

2 Price Commission 1974–77

The inherited Stage 3 of the prices policy lasted until December 1974, and
was succeeded by Stage 4 which eventually covered the period December
1974 to July 1976. Further amendments to the Price Code were made in
August 1976, and this 1976 Price Code remained in force until the end of
July 1977.

Stage 3 has continued the basic patterns of controls established under Stage 2.
These are the obligations to pre-notify price increases to the Commission; to
establish profit margin reference levels; and to report periodically particulars
of sales and profit margins. Distributors, who do not have to pre-notify price
increases, continue to have to establish and report upon their gross percentage
margins.

(Price Commission, 1974b)

Category I firms, numbering around 150, were required to pre-notify
price increases with 28 days' notice. Firms in manufacturing, public utilities,
posts and telecommunications, and services coming under Category II
were also required to pre-notify price increases but with only 14 days' notice.
Distributive, construction and professional services firms in category II were
only required to report. Category II firms numbered around 850.

The main changes in the price code between Stages 2 and 3 were:

(i)   the extension of the list of allowable cost increases, in particular to
       include increases in depreciation, introduced in part to encourage
       investment;
(ii)   safeguards to limit the reduction of profit margins, which were introduced
       to reflect the impact of the lower level of demand;
(iii) the extension of relief for low profits;
(iv)   new relief for under-utilised capacity;
(v)   increased powers for the Price Commission to reduce gross profit
       percentages where prices have risen substantially.

'Perhaps the fairest judgement on the balance of the changes [Stage 2 to 3]
is that they represent a tightening up of the administrative procedures and a
relaxation of the stringency of the rules under which price increases – or
some price increases – are calculated' (Price Commission, 1974a). The
Code was modified in May 1974 to restrict the frequency of price increases
(with at least three months between price changes), to restrict repricing of
shelf stock and to reduce the gross percentage margins of distributors.

The move from Stage 3 to Stage 4 took full effect on 20 December 1974
(with some changes backdated to 1 November). The main changes were:

(i)   a new scheme of investment relief whereby prices could be raised so as to generate 17½% (soon raised to 20%) of investment expenditure over a period of 12 months (or more);

(ii)   modification of the productivity deduction from 50% to an average of 20% (with variations between 8% and 35% depending on the proportion of costs accounted for by labour costs). This was the proportion of increase in labour costs which companies were required to absorb and not pass on into price increases. This change was intended to reflect a slower rate of growth of output and of productivity;

(iii) the introduction of further safeguards for loss-making and low-profitability firms.

The 1976 Price Code represented a further reduction in the stringency of price control, and could have permitted 'profit margins to double compared with their present [1976] level' (Price Commission, 1976). The investment relief was increased from 20% to 35%, and the provisions relating to depreciation of assets and appreciation of stocks recognised the effects of inflation. Further, the productivity deduction was abolished. However,

the Government do not expect that the changes in the price controls will by themselves lead to any early or appreciable increase in the general price level. Market forces have ensured that prices of many goods and services are now below the level which companies would be entitled to charge under the Price Code; but as economic recovery progresses, the Code will play an important part in keeping down the cost of living. By July 1977, when present powers to control prices expire, it is estimated that the proposed changes in the Code will probably have made a difference of about 1 per cent to the Retail Price Index.

(Chancellor of the Exchequer, 1976)

After August 1976, category I and II firms had the same obligations, and the size limits were raised to reflect the general rise in prices.

The Price Commission also acted (especially through its regional offices) rather like a 'consumer watchdog'. Each quarterly report of the Price Commission provides examples of cases where individuals had received price reductions or money back following the intervention of the Price Commission.

It is rather difficult to say much about the impact of the prices policies on the rate of inflation. The actual outcome needs to be compared with some counterfactual situation, the construction of which requires some theory of the inflationary process. A monetarist approach to inflation would clearly dismiss prices policies as of no consequence. Other approaches would stress the interaction between prices, wages, import prices and the exchange rate in the context of underlying conflict over income shares. The background here was one in which wages had been gaining at the expense of profits and in which commodity prices had risen drastically. In a situation where the claims of different groups are mutually incompatible, there is the prospect of a classic inflationary spiral. There were clear signs in the period 1973 to 1975 that an inflationary spiral was developing. In that context, a prices and incomes policy can be seen as having two roles. The first is to slow down at each stage the passing on of one set of price increases to the next (e.g. costs to prices, prices to wages). This does not resolve in itself the underlying problem, but can provide a breathing space for other adjustments to take place. The second role is to promote those adjustments. In the context of the 1970s the required adjustment was generally seen to be an increase in profitability.

As far as I am aware there has not been any published econometric evaluation of the impact of this era of price control though there have been a number concerned with the impact of wage control. Some unpublished work by Stephen Martin (of the University of York) has however failed to find any significant impact.

The calculations undertaken by the Price Commission were comparisons between actual price increases and announced price increases where the Commission intervened to restrict price increases. For Stage 2 (which is outside our period of interest), the Price Commission stated 'had there been no control and had enterprises increased prices to the full extent of their cost increases but no more – prices would have increased somewhat more than they have – in round terms by rather more than 11% instead of 10%' (Price Commission, 1974a). In that stage, the rejections, modifications, or withdrawals of price notifications were equivalent to more than a quarter of the price increases applied for.

In the period April 1973 to July 1977,

> the Commission dealt with over 32,000 [price increase notifications]. These came from about 1400 Category I and II manufacturing and service enterprises, divided into about 2400 units for profit-margin control purposes. The Commission also controlled the profit margins of about 350 large distributors in Category II, themselves divided into about 650 profit-margin units. In addition, the Commission's regional organisation had dealt with up to 17,000 smaller businesses in Category III. [In this period] the Commission modified, rejected or secured the withdrawal of about 6000 price increase notifications.
>
> (Price Commission, 1977a)

The scale of these interventions is indicated in Table 11.2.

The cumulative amount of interventions was just over £3½ billion during a period of 52 months, which averages out at £0·8 billion a year. In so far as some of these interventions concerned commodities sold to other firms (including retailers), the effect on final purchasers will have been greater. Further, competitors of producers subject to price control would find their prices influenced. The Price Commission (1977b) reported that amongst prices entering the retail price index, 29% were exempt from their control and 10% were imports, leaving 61% which were notifiable to the Price

Table 11.2 *Price Commission interventions*[a]

	Number of interventions	Amount of intervention[b] (£ millions)
Stage 2 (April–Oct. 1973)	546	507
Stage 3 (Nov. 1973–Dec. 1974)	2628	1613
Stage 4 (Dec. 1974–July 1976)	2084	892
1976 Code (Aug. 1976–July 1977)	787	541

Notes:
[a] The data from which the figures in this table are based are predominantly provided on a quarterly basis. Where a stage ends part-way through a quarter the figures for that quarter have been allocated pro rata to the two stages.
[b] The amount of intervention is the estimated reduction in prices for purchasers aggregated over interventions as a result of the difference between the price permitted by the Price Commission and the price initially announced by the company concerned.
Source: Calculated from Price Commission (1977a).

Commission. In the other direction, the notified price increases may have been inflated in anticipation of some reduction by the Price Commission. It is difficult to find a convenient aggregate with which to compare these price reductions. In 1974, GDP at market prices was £83 billion and in 1979 it was £192 billion. The direct impact of the Price Commission on the rate of inflation could be said to be of the order of 1% per annum (i.e. 0·8 as a proportion of 83). This could be multiplied up by consideration of indirect effect on other prices, on the exchange rate and on wages.

With distributors, where the control is over gross and net profit margins, it is impossible to give a similar estimate for the Commission's influence on prices. The Commission earlier argued that, since gross profit margins have been one or two percentage points below the level before the control began – roughly speaking the level in the 12 months to April 1973 – that reduction can be attributed to the control.
(Price Commission, 1977a)

The *National Institute Economic Review* no. 71 of February 1975 estimated that the price code 'may have reduced the price level by something of the order of 2 per cent below what it might have otherwise been' (pp. 31–2). The OECD argued that 'the continued application of price controls probably made a small contribution to the slowdown in prices. The importance of firms' notifications of price adjustments to the Price Commission was comparatively small in terms of the retail price index' (OECD, 1976, p. 7).

Table 11.3 reports the calculations of the OECD on the contributions to price increases during the 1970s. From those figures, it could be argued that there were years (notably 1974) when the inflationary pressures from unit labour costs and import prices were so strong that there was little that price control could do. In contrast, there were other years (for example, 1976) when price control could have had some impact.

Table 11.3 *Contributions to price increases (annual percentage increases)*

	1974	1975	1976	1977	1978
Unit labour costs	8·5	14·75	6·5	3·75	4·75
Other costs (including profits)	0·0	3·5	5·0	3·75	1·25
Import prices	10·25	4·5	4·5	4·5	1·0
Net indirect taxes	0·0	2·5	2·25	2·75	1·0
Residual	− 1·5	− 1·5	− 2·25	0·0	0·25
Consumers' expenditure deflator	17·25	23·5	16·0	14·75	8·25

Source: OECD (1979).

Evely (1976) reported on a survey of over a hundred firms carried out by the National Institute for the Department of Prices and Consumer Affairs in March 1976.

About two fifths of the 71 manufacturers and more than four fifths of the distributors considered that their current prices were about the same as they would have been if the Price Code had not been implemented, but [the table in this article] also shows that close on another two fifths of the manufacturers and all the remaining distributors reported that the Price Code had kept their prices down. The remaining one fifth of manufacturers thought that their current prices were higher than without the Price Code, partly because they had introduced price increases under its routine earlier than they might otherwise have done.

(Evely, 1976, p. 51)

But amongst the 47 firms making numerical estimates, on a weighted average basis, prices were 2 ½ % lower than they would have been. However, 'the consensus view emerging from the survey was that since the onset of the recession the dominant factor governing prices has been market conditions rather than the controls inherent in the Price Code' (Evely, 1976, p. 50), although this may tell us more about prices relative to costs, rather than the impact on the rate of change of prices.

In the context of the 1970s, price control policies could be seen as an essential complement to the wages policies. Some assurance that price rises will be constrained helps to restrain wage increases. There was a deliberate attempt by the government to use price control to support pay policy when it announced that it would

not allow firms which make excessive pay settlements to reflect these settlements in high prices to consumers. With every application to the Price Commission for a price increase, employers will have to notify details of any pay settlement underlying the application ... Where an employer breaks the pay limit, the whole pay increase will be disallowed for price increases.

(Chancellor of the Exchequer, 1975)

When wage and price constraint policies are successful, it may still be possible that there is no observable impact on price increases *relative* to wage increases. To the extent to which the existence of the Price Commission fostered lower expectations of inflation (and provided some reassurance that lower wage increases would lead to lower price increases rather than higher profits), it would have aided a lower rate of inflation without impacting on the relationship between prices and wages.

3 Price Commission activities after the 1977 Act

The activities of the Price Commission underwent a significant change of direction in August 1977, following the passage of the Price Commission Act 1977. The membership of the Price Commission was drastically changed (with only two members staying in place) and the mode of operation was changed. The purpose of the Price Commission was changed from a largely counter-inflationary body into one combining elements of efficiency audit (concerned with the level of costs and prices and the relationship between them) and commentator on competitive conditions.

In judging a proposed price increase or the level of prices and profit margin, the Commission was 'to have regard to all matters ... relevant with a view to restraining prices of goods and charges for services so far as that appears to the Commission to be consistent with the making of adequate profits by efficient suppliers of goods and services'. It was given a list of eight matters to take into account when judging prices, including the desirability of cost reductions through increased efficiency, of maintaining quality of goods and services, and of keeping a balance between demand and supply. A further matter to be considered was the promotion of competition between suppliers or when competition 'must be restricted or cannot be promoted (either because certain suppliers control a substantial share of the relevant market or for any other reason), by restricting prices and charges' (Price Commission Act 1977).

The role of the Commission as perceived by the Commission itself is conveniently summarised by the following.

We have to ask ourselves questions such as: Is the enterprise which is supplying the product an efficient one? Is the market fully competitive? Are the interests of purchasers adequately protected? In effect, the problem is to reconcile the public interest with the commercial health of provision of goods and services ... The Commission should not only be aware of it [the public interest] but on occasion should represent it ... One objective of the Price Commission is to develop machinery to identify market imperfections, building on work that has already been done by the Monopolies and Mergers Commission, and the Office of Fair Trading. This is not to say that market imperfections necessarily lead to inefficiency and unfair pricing, but only that they may do so.

(Price Commission, 1977b)

In this respect, the rationale underlying the Price Commission was similar to that for the Monopolies and Mergers Commission, namely that a position of market dominance allows the possibility of inefficiency and exploitation of consumers.

During the period August 1977 to May 1979, the Price Commission had two main tasks. First, large firms were required to give 28 days' notification of any intention to raise prices. The Commission selected some of the proposed increases for a 3-month investigation, during which prices were frozen or increases limited if profits fell below a specified level. The Price Commission made its recommendations to the Secretary of State for Prices and Consumer Affairs, who decided whether to impose restrictions on prices or profit margins for up to 12 months.

Second, the Secretary of State could direct the Commission to carry out investigations of anything concerning prices and charges in a sector or industry. There were no price restrictions during the investigation. But restrictions, which with parliamentary approval could last for any length of time, could be required afterwards by the Secretary of State within the constraint that the limits placed on the firms were not more restrictive than those proposed by the Price Commission.

In a period from August 1977 to its effective demise in May 1979 the Price Commission carried out forty-three investigations under either Section 4 or 5 of the Price Commission Act 1977 and sixteen examinations under Section 11. Eight of the investigations were concerned with public sector bodies, and to some degree the Price Commission began the type of investigations later carried out by the Monopolies and Mergers Commission under the Competition Act 1980.

There do not appear to have been any studies of the impact of the actions of the Price Commission. In particular, many of its reports made recommendations for government action and expressed hopes of improvements by the firms investigated, but there is no evaluation of whether these were followed up. In some cases (e.g. the report on the opticians Dolland & Aitchison concerning advertising by opticians), the essence of the recommendations has since been implemented, but it would seem unlikely that the Price Commission had much influence on the implementation.

The direct impact of the Price Commission on price increases in the period after August 1977 was small, with few cases where the proposed price increase was disallowed following an investigation. In many cases, however, further price increases during a specified period (up to 12 months) were restricted, though sometimes the restriction was conditional (e.g. unless there were substantial and unforeseen cost increases). In some other cases, the Price Commission indicated that decisions on future price increases would be influenced by whether the firm concerned took measures to rectify problems identified by the Price Commission.

The type of activities of companies which the Price Commission commented on adversely included:

(i)   the setting of prices without a clear relationship between prices and costs across a range of products. In some cases, there was the clear implication that relatively low prices were charged to powerful customers with the less powerful having to pay relatively high prices. In other cases, this lack appeared to arise more from management failure than deliberate action;

(ii) prices announced or structured in a manner which tended to confuse or exploit customers. This type of practice ranged over the use of recommended retail prices which bore little relationship to the eventual price through to the fuel cost adjustment used in the pricing of electricity;

(iii) restrictions on competition, which often arose from government legislation (e.g. sale of beer), but also included the joint negotiations between banks and a number of nationalised industries over charges for money transmission services conducted by the Committee of London Clearing Banks. The use of cumulative discounts, loyalty bonuses and so on were also generally condemned on the grounds of limiting competition and not being related to costs.

There do not appear to be any cases where a proposed price increase was disallowed because of high profits, though there were occasions where a period during which there would be no further price increases was linked with a high level of profits.

The conclusions and recommendations made by the Price Commission will have a familiar ring to anyone who has read reports by the Office of Fair Trading (OFT) or the Monopolies and Mergers Commission (MMC). The Price Commission had a broader remit in that an investigation could be triggered by a price increase notification rather than requiring evidence of a monopoly (one-quarter market-share) position. During this period the Price Commission was much more active than the MMC, and by way of comparison with the figures given above on the scale of activities of the Price Commission, in the period 1976 to 1978 ten monopoly references were made to the MMC.

The official perspective on the relationship between the Price Commission and the MMC was given in May 1978.

The Price Commission's investigations are not limited to markets where monopoly situations exist. We see its role as being to carry out short-term inquiries into the factors affecting pricing policies. It has to take account of a number of statutory criteria ... including the need to restrict prices and charges where 'competition must be restricted or cannot be promoted'. Some of the inquiries may reveal the need for a thorough investigation into structure and behaviour by the MMC with a view to long-term solutions ... We regard prices policy, operated along these lines, as essentially complementary to competition policy and in principle we consider that there would be advantage in bringing the MMC and the Price Commission together in due course.

(Review of Monopolies and Mergers Policy, 1978)

The document also recommended further study on the fusion of the Price Commission and the MMC to develop proposals.

4 Conclusions

The history of the Price Commission had two distinct phases. In the first phase, the Price Commission was heavily involved with counter-inflationary policies, whilst in the second phase its role was rather more akin to that of an efficiency audit. The evaluation of the Commission's role in each of these phases is heavily conditioned by one's prior views on the operations of a capitalist economy. In counter-inflationary policies, according to much macroeconomic theorising, there is little role for price control. Inflation is seen to arise from an excessive growth of the money supply or from the level of aggregate demand being pitched too high. However, it is widely recognised that the inflationary process is much influenced by expectations on the rate of inflation. From that perspective, the existence of a body such as the Price Commission can aid the lowering of inflationary expectations. But it is also argued that high rates of inflation tend to generate confusion and inaccurate expectations, and part of the role of the Price Commission was to reduce opportunities for producers to exploit that confusion.

When inflation is viewed as derived from a struggle over income shares then the role of a Price Commission is seen rather differently. The inflationary pressures, on that view, are reduced when the struggle over income shares is restrained. Such a reduction may come from the weakening of one (or more) sides in the struggle (e.g. through higher levels of unemployment reducing the power of trade unions) or from the acceptance by one (or more) sides of a lower income share. For whatever reason, as indicated in Table 11.1, the rate and share of profits had been squeezed in the late 1960s and early 1970s, and statements by the Price Commission suggest that it saw part of its role as the restoration of profit margins, which was partially achieved.

References

Blackaby, F. (1978), 'Incomes policy', in F. Blackaby (ed.) *British Economic Policy 1960–74*, Cambridge University Press, Cambridge.

Chancellor of the Exchequer (1973), *The Price and Pay Code for Stage 3: a consultative document*, Cmnd. 5444, HMSO.

Chancellor of the Exchequer (1975), *The Attack on Inflation*, Cmnd. 6151, HMSO.

Chancellor of the Exchequer (1976), *The Attack on Inflation: the second year*, Cmnd. 6507, HMSO.

Chancellor of the Exchequer (1979), *The Government's Expenditure Plans 1979/80 to 1982/83*, Cmnd. 7439, HMSO.

Evely, R. (1976), 'The effect of the price code', *National Institute Economic Review*, August, pp. 50–59.

OECD (1976), *United Kingdom*, Paris.

OECD (1979), *United Kingdom*, Paris.

Price Commission (1974a), Report for the period 1 September 1973 to 30 November 1973, HC 93, HMSO.

Price Commission (1974b), Report for the period 1 December 1973 to 28 February 1974, HC 56, HMSO.

Price Commission (1975a), Report for the period 1 December 1974 to 28 February 1975, HC 343, HMSO.

Price Commission (1975b), Report for the period 1 June to 31 August 1975 HC 631, HMSO.

Price Commission (1976), Report for the period 1 June to 31 August 1976, HC 641, HMSO.

Price Commission (1977a), Report for the period 1 June to 31 July 1977, Cmnd. 6950, HMSO.

Price Commission (1977b), Report for the period 1 August to 31 October 1977, HC 117, HMSO.

Price Commission (1978), Report for the period 1 August to 31 October 1978, HC 109, HMSO.

Review of Monopolies and Mergers Policy (1978), *A Consultative Document*, Cmnd. 7198, HMSO.

Labour market policies

1 Introduction

The increase in unemployment suffered by the United Kingdom over the 1974–79 period is often cited as evidence against the economic policies of the last period of Labour government. Figure 12.1 compares the British experience with that of some of its competitors, using the OECD's standardised measure of unemployment. The British unemployment rate rose from 2·9% to 5%, an increase which exceeded the figures for West Germany, Japan and

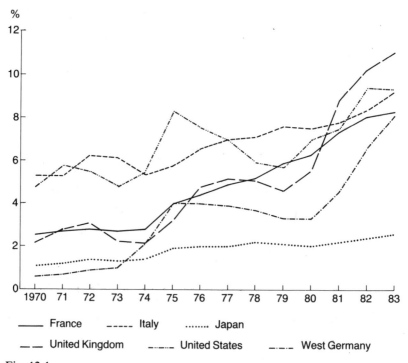

Fig. 12.1

the United States, but was less than the increase in France and Italy. The increase took place despite relatively slow growth of the labour force. Increases in the youth unemployment rate were particularly worrying (see Fig. 12.2). The UK's record was worse than the average for the seven major OECD economies, but it was not the worst by any means, as the graphs show. In the wake of the oil price shock at the beginning of the period, the structure of employment changed considerably, with a substantial decline in the share of manufacturing employment (2·3 percentage points) between 1974 and 1976, causing unavoidable adjustment problems. The 1974−79 unemployment record was one of the major obstacles to the government's re-election in 1979. This chapter considers some of the government attempts to cope with the problems presented by the labour market during Labour's terms of office.

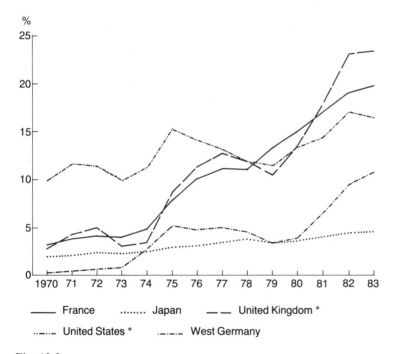

Fig. 12.2

The main responsibility for dealing with the rise in unemployment, which was particularly severe between 1974 and 1976, fell to macroeconomic policies, which are considered elsewhere in this book. This chapter concentrates on policies applied directly to the labour market, in particular, special employment measures and training support. Measures like the Temporary Employment Subsidy proliferated as the government attempted to find some way of increasing the impact of public spending on the level of employment, given the tightening constraints on its fiscal policy. Policy on training (and education) had the potential to improve the prospects of the unemployed in the short term and in the longer term the quality of the employed labour force. It should be noted that this focus neglects important matters such as the microeconomic impact of incomes policies, the transformation of the employment services, and incentives to participate in the labour force. Equal opportunity policies, arguably one of the successes of the Labour governments, are referred to briefly in Section 3.

Before turning to consider the chosen topics in more detail, it is useful to note some implications of attempts to measure shifts in the 'non-accelerating inflation rate of unemployment' (NAIRU), because they draw attention to factors apart from macroeconomic policy which influence unemployment. Layard and Nickell (1986), for instance, estimate that the NAIRU (calculated assuming balanced trade and using the adult male unemployment rate) increased from 4·2% in 1967−74 to 7·6% in 1975−79 (the corresponding actual average unemployment rate went up from 3·8% to 6·8%). The largest element of the increase (two percentage points) was contributed by the increase in the ratio of UK import prices to the world price of manufactures. Second was the impact of the increasing trade union mark-up estimated by the authors (1·6 percentage points), and third was the impact of increases in employers' labour tax rates (0·5 percentage points). While it would be wrong to attach too much importance to the particular numbers, given the wide margins of error which must be attached to any estimate of a NAIRU believed to move over time, the estimates of Layard and Nickell remind us of the relevance of tax policy and industrial relations policy to the state of the labour market. However, the connections are not straightforward. Despite the widespread view that the trade unions had unparalleled influence on economic policy during 1974−79, most of the increase in the trade union mark-up estimated by Layard and Nickell took place before 1974 (and was followed by an upward jump in 1980). Mismatch between the attributes of the unemployed (skills, regional location, industry of last attachment) and the attributes of vacancies was not a problem unique to this period, although there was a tendency for the number of the 'structurally unemployed' as a proportion of the workforce (but not as a proportion of the unemployed) to increase (Roper, 1986). Mismatch worsened from 1980. The reasons why the unemployment−vacancy relationship continued to deteriorate during the period (higher vacancy rates at any given unemployment rate) are not completely understood; movements in variables which may influence the speed of job matching, such as indices of mismatch and replacement rates, do not explain the trend fully. Layard (1986) has argued that the stringency of unemployment benefit eligibility tests was weakened. This goes some way towards an explanation, but does not account for why the trend was different in different industries.

2 Political background

The Labour Party came to power in 1974 after an election campaign which revolved around economic issues – the energy crisis, inflation, and industrial relations. Yet neither major party paid much attention in its campaign literature to the dangers of high unemployment nor to the training needs of the economy, both of which were to loom large during 1974–79. In the February 1974 Labour Party manifesto, the section on employment and expansion promised; 'we shall develop an active manpower policy with a powerful National Labour Board. In the longer term, redundant workers must have an automatic right to retraining: redundancy should then lead not to unemployment, but to retraining and job changing.' Apart from this there was remarkably little mention of unemployment. A similar line was taken in October 1974, when the manifesto promised, 'we shall transform the existing MSC into a powerful body, responsible for the development and execution of a comprehensive manpower policy', and repeated the pledge on retraining.

Thus the new government had a somewhat weaker commitment to changes in the national system of training than might have been expected from the discussions within the Labour Party in opposition. Apart from the 'automatic retraining' provision mentioned above, the Labour Party's 'Programme for Britain' in 1973 had argued for a massive expansion in the facilities for training and retraining and a National Manpower Board to supervise job placement and manpower planning. It had envisaged up to 2% of the workforce undergoing retraining at any one time and a new general training levy. However, training was not a salient issue in the political debate, and the Conservatives' Employment and Training Act (1973) had been given cross-party support. This Act had set up the Manpower Services Commission (MSC), which was to become central to the Labour government's labour market policies (and bore some resemblance to the National Manpower Service which had been promised by Labour in the 1970 election). The Employment and Training Act had weakened the grant-levy system; it excluded small firms and allowed exemptions for those firms deemed to be providing sufficient training themselves. It reduced the maximum proportion of payroll which could be levied from 4% to 1%. Despite some trade union opposition to these aspects of the Act, the basic structure established by it was accepted by the Labour government.

Hence Labour started off without strong commitments to change policy with respect to unemployment or training. The multitude of special employment measures which were introduced should be seen as reactions to unanticipated economic shocks. They did not fit into a coherent, forward-looking contingency plan for economic management. Policy development in training was somewhat different. A framework with substantial bipartisan support (but originated by the Conservatives) existed. It provided in the

MSC an organisation which could and did generate labour market initiatives without requiring an explicit government lead. It also proved to be a convenient vehicle for new instruments of employment policy. There was considerable devolution of power to professional experts and participation by trade unions and employers was encouraged. The tripartite structure of the MSC was characteristic of this period; the advantages and disadvantages of tripartism are discussed in Cassels (1989) and Middlemas (1983).

3 Employment policies

The first important new labour market measures introduced by the 1974–79 governments in the area of labour market policies concerned employment generation. The Regional Employment Premium was doubled in July 1974, packages to preserve jobs in the construction industry were put together, and selective assistance was granted to various firms and sectors. Amongst less piecemeal measures were (in descending order of size) the Temporary Employment Subsidy (TES), the Job Creation Programme (JCP), and the Recruitment Subsidy for School Leavers (RSSL) – details of these and other measures are given in the Appendix to this chapter. The emphasis was on job creation rather than reduced participation. TES had some of the features of the well-established Regional Employment Premium, but it was designed to stave off redundancies rather than to create new jobs. It started in assisted areas only but was extended to the whole country within two months. Originally announced as a temporary measure, the scheme was renewed repeatedly until 1979 with extensions in respect of the duration of subsidies, the minimum number required for the redundancies threatened, and the coverage of part-time workers. JCP set up job creation schemes run by local agents (mostly local authorities), involving detailed local administration: they had little or no training content. The schemes were supposed to generate temporary employment of social value. RSSL was a recruitment subsidy designed to help unemployed school-leavers. These schemes reflected the concern on the part of government about rising unemployment, a concern exacerbated by its uncertainty about the macroeconomic policies appropriate to reverse the rise.

How appropriate are such schemes as means to reduce unemployment? They have several desirable attributes. First, compared to other reflationary measures (e.g. tax cuts), they encourage the substitution of labour for capital (to a degree limited by the elasticity of labour demand). Second, they can be seen to have a direct impact on the number of jobs (though this can be misleading because of second-round effects). Third, they can be aimed at priority groups such as school-leavers or the long-term unemployed for whom the social costs of unemployment are likely to be particularly high. In most cases, employment increases for these groups are less likely to stimulate wage inflation, because their employment via special schemes is less likely to affect the bargaining behaviour of those already employed (it does not much reduce the competition from outsiders for existing employees' jobs). Fourth, the saving of unemployment and social security benefits and the generation of tax revenues can be weighed against the direct costs.

The size of Exchequer savings and thus the 'net cost per job' depend on a number of factors. First is the deadweight loss, the number of jobs supported which would have existed anyway without subsidy. Second, there are displacement effects. Subsidised *activities* can displace non-subsidised ones and thus reduce employment in firms competing with those receiving support (the 'domino effect'). If support is limited to workers in particular demographic groups, the subsidised *workers* may displace non-subsidised workers. Trade unions have long worried that subsidies to young workers do this, generating 'churning' within firms' workforces (Ryan, 1987).

A useful distinction can be made between subsidies paid according to the level or change in the number of employees recruited (a flow subsidy), and those paid according to the level or change in the number of workers actually employed (a stock subsidy). Layard (1979) points out that a stock subsidy is preferable to a recruitment subsidy, because it avoids the danger of increasing rates of labour turnover. Marginal subsidies are preferable because they minimise the government expenditure needed to achieve a given employment objective. TES was in principle a marginal stock subsidy, so it was well designed in this respect. Employment subsidies are particularly appropriate if the underlying cause of the rise in unemployment is believed to be an excessive real product wage and if the short-run wage elasticity of labour demand is negative. The duration of a subsidy scheme should in principle depend upon the speed with which the real product wage adjusts. This draws attention to two problems. First, the subsidies may slow down both macroeconomic and sectoral adjustment of the economy. Second, they may have to last a long time. Indeed, the real product wage might be excessive, not because of the slow adjustment of wages to shocks, but for other reasons, such as the existence of monopoly rents in particular industries accruing partly to labour, and an employment tax 'wedge' (Jackman and Layard, 1980 explore this issue from a theoretical standpoint). The danger of long-term subsidies is that their maintenance and increase may become an objective of collective bargaining.

What *were* the effects of special employment measures? A contemporary researcher claimed, 'the theoretical literature on national job creation subsidies has been extensive though contradictory and largely unpublished' (Buck, 1977/78). There have been several efforts to estimate them since, such as those by Layard (1979), Deakin and Pratten (1981) and Metcalf (1982), as well as by the Department of Employment itself. Some of the misgivings expressed about TES at the time, which applied to most of the special employment measures, have been summed up by Joel Barnett, the Chief Secretary to the Treasury during this period (Barnett, 1982, pp. 128–9):

One area of expenditure that caused me concern throughout was the many hundreds of millions spent on special employment measures. In 1977 I was faced with yet another package of measures that could have cost up to £1 billion. For several reasons it had to be handled with kid gloves ... I managed, however, to convince the Cabinet that the 'saving' of jobs, and unemployment benefit, could not reasonably be identified, as we could not be sure that jobs would definitely have been lost without the subsidies ... I also knew that many small and medium-sized firms in clothing manufacturing were obtaining substantial sums in TES when there was little likelihood of redundancies

Around 190,000 people were covered by TES in 1977 and 173,000 in 1978, but they were not distributed evenly across the economy. Table 12.1 presents the details. About 43% were located in textiles, clothing, and footwear (which were also beneficiaries of the Short-Time Working Compensation Scheme from May 1978). These were industries particularly open to foreign competition, and hence the displacement effects of the subsidy were likely to fall more on the workforce of firms overseas; indeed, there was a marked improvement in export performance and competitiveness with imports in these industries. This is why the European Commission severely curtailed it from 1978, insisting on a maximum percentage of a firm's workforce who could be subsidised and a cap on total expenditure well below the 1977/78 out-turn. In such industries, the effect of employment subsidies does not depend solely on the pure substitution effect; relatively price-elastic product demand allows a substantial scale effect, too (Deakin and Pratten (1981) estimated that price reductions accounted for about a quarter of the TES subsidy). This is why considerable savings could be made by the Exchequer. The Department of Employment estimated that, for every three jobs covered by TES, two were actually preserved after taking account of displacement effects. Deakin and Pratten also estimated about 1·2 jobs were preserved. This figure is less attractive, but follow-up surveys indicated that many of these jobs were preserved even after the exhaustion of TES benefits after twelve months (although it is impossible to prove that these would not have been available later without TES in the intervening period). Deakin and Pratten's estimates imply that employment in 1977−78 was perhaps 70,000 higher than it would have been without TES (and unemployment perhaps around 55,000 lower allowing for registration and participation effects). They calculated that the cost to the Exchequer was probably around 60% of the gross cost (£174m. in 1977/78, £133m. in 1978/79), less than some of the earlier predictions that the net cost would be negative and an official estimate in 1978 of 25%, but still evidence of good cost-effectiveness. Subsequent work (such as Turner *et al.*, 1987 and Stern, 1988) has shown that partial equilibrium calculations like these can be misleading. They neglect certain microeconomic feedback mechanisms such as differences in the spending patterns of the marginal workers employed and the upward pressure exerted on wages by reductions in some groups' unemployment.

Table 12.1   *Temporary Employment Subsidy: estimated number of jobs supported,
by industry, between 18 August 1975 and 31 March 1979*

Standard Industrial Classificaiton Order	Number of jobs supported	Share of jobs supported (%)	Industry's share[a] of all employees in employment (%)	Incidence of TES (3)/(4)
(1)	(2)	(3)	(4)	(5)
1 Agriculture, forestry, fishing	2,600	0·5	1·6	0·31
2 Mining and quarrying	2,500	0·5	1·5	0·33
3 Food, drink and tobacco	26,700	4·9	3·0	1·63
4 Coal and petroleum products	700	0·1	0·2	0·50
5 Chemical and allied industries	5,300	1·0	1·9	0·53
6 Metal and manufacture	16,400	3·0	2·0	1·50
7 Mechanical engineering	31,900	5·9	4·1	1·44
8 Instrument engineering	3,500	0·7	0·7	1·00
9 Electrical engineering	25,500	4·7	3·3	1·42
10 Shipbuilding and marine engineering	5,700	1·1	0·8	1·38
11 Vehicles	10,900	2·0	3·4	0·59
12 Metal goods n.e.s.	22,900	4·2	2·4	1·75
13 Textiles	117,900	21·8	2·1	10·38
14 Leather, leather goods and fur	8,300	1·5	0·2	7·50
15 Clothing and footwear	114,900	21·3	1·6	13·31
16 Bricks, pottery, glass, cement etc.	13,700	2·5	1·2	2·08
17 Timber, furniture etc.	29,600	5·5	1·2	4·58
18 Paper, printing and publishing	27,200	5·0	2·4	2·08
19 Other manufacturing industries	11,900	2·2	1·5	1·47
20 Construction	24,300	4·5	5·5	0·82
21 Gas, electricity and water	100	0·02	1·5	0·01
22 Transport and communication	4,000	0·7	6·4	0·11
23 Distributive trades	21,100	3·9	12·2	0·32
24 Insurance, banking and finance	600	0·1	5·2	0·02
25 Professional and scientific services	500	0·1	16·3	0·01
26 Miscellaneous services	11,600	2·2	10·4	0·21
27 Public administration and defence	–	–	7·1	–
All	540,300	100	100	1·00

Notes: All columns are subject to rounding errors.
   [a] Averaged for period March 1978 to March 1979.
Source: *Department of Employment Gazette*, November 1979, p. 1122.

However, the estimates are probably still useful as a guide to the short-run consequences of a scheme which was small in relation to total employment (less than 1% of jobs in manufacturing industry were probably attributable to TES), even if it was large in relation to other government measures.

The longer-term consequences are less clear. TES was supposed to buy time for employers to improve efficiency and reorganise production to compete more effectively; by staving off redundancies, it was expected to help employers obtain trade union co-operation in improving efficiency. Middlemas (1983), in his review of the work of the National Economic Development Council, reports that 'EDC and SWP chairmen confirmed that virtually no useful discussion about productivity could take place if they involved immediate redundancy'. However, as one would predict with any employment subsidy, the short-run effect of TES was to reduce labour productivity. A severe test was applied in the 1980/81 recession to the industries which had received TES support, a test which they largely failed, as many of the jobs supported disappeared. However, special employment measures (of the public employment type, at least) still do very well in model-based exercises when the criterion is the efficiency of government spending in increasing employment.

The Job Creation Programme (JCP), which developed into the Youth Opportunities Programme (YOP) and the Special Temporary Employment Programme (STEP), was designed to provide work doing jobs that otherwise would not be done. Unlike TES, which developed quite naturally from British experience with the Regional Employment Premium, JCP was partly the product of policy makers looking at experience abroad, particularly in Canada. It probably had smaller displacement effects than TES, because of the criteria established for the additionality of the output of approved schemes. It particularly helped unskilled youth, a group at high risk of unemployment. However, the manual work involved in many schemes meant that most beneficiaries were male. The non-employment benefits were questionable. The very fact that the work done was supposed to be work which would not otherwise be carried out implied that it was likely to be of low monetary value.

Deadweight effects were probably much larger for the RSSL/Youth Employment Subsidy which JCP and then YOP largely superseded. The Department of Employment found in its surveys that about 75% of firms admitted they would have hired the young people for whom they were receiving a subsidy regardless of the payments. The surveys also indicated that over 10% of the subsidised employees probably displaced other workers: young people tended to be substituted for married women and part-timers. The schemes had the disadvantages of a flow subsidy instead of a marginal stock subsidy.

The Small Firms Employment Subsidy (SFES) from July 1977 was supposed to help small firms create new jobs. The Department of Employment estimated that net new jobs were around 40% of the gross number created, but some of the displacement and competitive effects may have been underestimated, making this figure too high. SFES is a good example of the confusion which can arise in categorising policies – on the part of policy makers as well as observers. SFES was originally limited to Special Development Areas (SDAs), so it could be called a regional policy as well as an employment policy. But it was originally limited to manufacturing establishments, so it was an industrial policy, too, reflecting a view about sectoral needs and the size distribution of firms. It was subsequently extended to cover manufacturing firms anywhere, as long as they had up to 200 workers (a reduction in the 'small firms' element), and to cover non-manufacturing firms in SDAs (a reduction in the 'industrial' element).

The net effect of special employment measures cannot be measured with any great degree of certainty. However, using the estimates of displacement and deadweight effects made by the Department of Employment and others, and allowing for participation and registration effects, special measures (excluding aid to firms under Sections 7 and 8 of the Industry Act but including the Youth Opportunity Programme, considered in more detail below) probably reduced the unemployment count by about 20,000 in April 1976, 100,000 in April 1977, 130,000 in April 1978 and 100,000 in April 1979. The drop in 1979 was accounted for by the winding down of TES before the Short-Time Working Compensation Scheme (subsidising leisure instead of employment at the margin) took off under the subsequent government.

The Sex Discrimination Act of 1975 was one employment measure of the period which was not designed with a view to reducing the unemployment count. This law was designed to ensure equal employment opportunities for men and women. Thus it complemented the 1970 Equal Pay Act, which required equal pay for equivalent work by men and women by the end of 1975, by providing for women's access to equivalent work. Female relative earnings improved by 15% between 1970 and 1980 across nearly all occupations and industries, with most of the increase taking place between 1974 and 1976. This increase did not reduce the relative employment of females; on the contrary, it increased by about 18% (male employment actually fell slightly between 1974 and 1979). Zabalza and Tzannatos (1983) examined this phenomenon carefully and concluded that it cannot be explained by a shift of women from low- to high-paid sectors, nor by the flat-rate element of incomes policies during the period, nor by employment policy within the public sector alone. Instead, the anti-discriminatory legislation appears to have succeeded in increasing the relative demand for female labour at any given relative wage, eliminating a substantial fraction of the labour market discrimination the authors estimate afflicted women.

4 Training

The term 'training' is interpreted broadly here to include consideration of policy designed primarily to reduce youth unemployment. The main components of policy during the period were the development of the existing Training Opportunities Scheme (TOPS), support for industrial training via the Manpower Services Commission and the various Industrial Training Boards, and the introduction of the Youth Opportunities Programme.

TOPS had started in August 1972 as a rationalisation and extension of the government's existing vocational training schemes. It was soon expanded as planned to provide more openings for adult training, but never quite reached the undated target originally announced of 100,000 places per annum (the peak rate of completions was 98,964 in 1977). There were few other formal training opportunities available for adults apart from traditional apprenticeships. In 1974, about 134,000 people took these up; TOPS provided for about 45,000 other training opportunities. It was supposed to provide full-time training at a wide range of levels from semi-skilled work to management. A review of TOPS finished in 1978 concluded that the scheme should be geared more closely to the needs of the labour market; some of the skills taught had turned out to be very much in excess supply. Although adjustments were made in the programme to respond to this, TOPS remained an adjunct to conventional industrial training, partly as a remedial scheme and partly as a way of closing some of the bigger gaps in training provision. These gaps became more noticeable as the industries within manufacturing which historically had undertaken a high level of training contracted relative to the rest of the economy.

A survey was carried out by the Department of Employment to investigate the longer-term employment experience of a cohort of trainees leaving TOPS in June–July 1978 (McGill, 1981). This found that 60% were men, and most of them had completed courses related to occupations in manufacturing industry. Most women, on the other hand, had completed courses for clerical and commercial occupations. It is difficult to tell to what extent the courses addressed the most pressing skill shortages. The distribution across occupations and their skill-content level suggest that they were not particularly responsive to labour market needs. In the fifteen to seventeen months between finishing a TOPS course and being interviewed for the survey, only 6% failed to find work. Nearly 40 per cent found their first job using TOPS skills within a month. In this respect, their experience was better than that of the unemployed as a whole, but it must be remembered that many started TOPS courses better able to obtain employment than the typical unemployed worker; 22% of those who had been non-employed housewives at the time they joined TOPS failed to find a job at all. First jobs found were more likely to be with small firms (less than 100 people) than was the case for the average employee. This suggests two things. First, TOPS could be used by smaller firms, which were less able to maintain training for all their own skill needs. Second, larger firms, which could train internally, may have preferred to do so, to tailor employees' skills to their specific needs. The lack of training offered by recruiting firms is illustrated by the DE survey's findings on further training: only one-third of those interviewed who managed to find a job using TOPS skills received further training in their first job, and for most of them it lasted less than three weeks.

TOPS training accounted for a larger and larger proportion of formal training during the period, but did not take over from traditional training activities. It was never designed to do so. However, the state did take on more and more responsibility for financing traditional training organised by the Industrial Training Boards. By 1976, the MSC believed it was 'making good the gap' in training provision resulting from the reduction of industry's own contributions to the Boards (in the wake of the changes to the grant-levy system referred to earlier), although the Boards remained the delivery system. The increase in state funding had started as early as 1971, with finance for the first year of Engineering Industry Training Board apprentice-ships. At first, increases were viewed as a countercyclical measure, because employers tended to cut training expenditure in the face of greater pressure on profits. As the MSC established itself, it became accepted that government spending would remain important. MSC money accounted for one-twentieth of the Industrial Training Boards' income before 1974/75, but had increased to one-third by 1977/78. This development was attractive to both trade unions and employers: workers were less likely to have to finance training through accepting lower relative pay during their apprenticeships (a solution suggested by looking at West German experience), while employers did not have to contribute as much to finance training of workers who were vulnerable to 'poaching' (because of their apprentice certification). The outcome was temporary stabilisation of the proportion of workers in industry being trained through the Training Board network. Little progress was made, however, in terms of numbers or content of training (although 'training to standards' continued to spread). Figures 12.3a and 12.3b illustrate the pattern over time in manufacturing in general.

Measures to help young people became a major demand of trade unions as unemployment rose in the mid-1970s. This reflected the higher relative rates of youth unemployment, a problem throughout Europe at the time (de Montlibert, 1979), but particularly acute in France and Britain. Unemployment of school-leavers in Great Britain rose from 13,400 in October 1974 to a high point of 92,600 in October 1977, and then declined to 64,000 by October 1979 (see also Fig. 12.2 for figures for UK and other countries). It was largely pressure from the TUC whcih led the government to set up an MSC committee chaired by Geoffrey Holland, whose report argued for a unified scheme for youth, drawing on experience with the Work Experience Programme (WEP, from September 1976), designed to give young people a

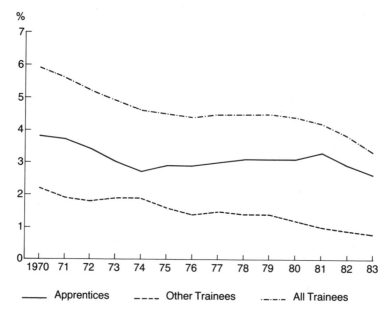

Fig. 12.3a

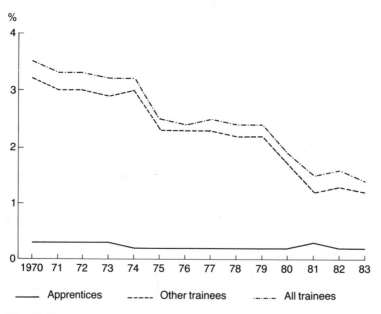

Fig. 12.3b

practical introduction to working life, and the Job Creation Programme (about half of the entrants to this programme had been aged 16–18). This led to the Youth Opportunities Programme (YOP) being set up in April 1978, offering young people aged 16–17 a variety of work and training opportunities of up to six-months' duration. Priority was to be given to unemployed school-leavers, so that they could be guaranteed a place on the programme by Easter of the year after they left school. In practice, 60% of YOP trainees had not had a job between leaving school and joining YOP. The schemes covered by YOP fell into five categories, of which Work Experience on Employers' Premises (WEEP), derived from the earlier WEP, was by far the most important, accounting for 65% of YOP trainees in 1978/79 (Bedeman and Harvey, 1981). The term 'trainee' denoted the fact that the young people on YOP were paid an allowance wholly financed by the MSC and were not regular employees, even though the work that they did was often indistinguishable from that of ordinary young unskilled workers. A survey of young people who had joined YOP between September 1978 and June 1979 found that large proportions of WEEP trainees did clerical and sales work. Vocational training was suggested but not required. In practice, it was uncommon. As far as basic skills concerned, only 18% were taught any mathematics as part of their training, and only 15% were given help with English. Only 10% were taught how to look for jobs, and few had access to the staff counselling and training in social skills which had also been envisaged. Although two-thirds of the YOP graduates agreed that they would need further training or qualifications if they were to acquire permanently the job they desired after sampling it on YOP, their overall response to the scheme was favourable. The majority felt that the experience had increased their chances of getting a job afterwards, that it had increased their self-confidence, and that it had helped them in getting on with other people. YOP satisfied the main criterion of young people themselves: it was better than being unemployed and doing nothing. The second criterion, that it should be a means of acquiring skills, was not met so successfully. YOP aimed much lower than apprenticeships or even most TOPS courses in content.

The number of young people on YOP grew rapidly (162,000 starts in 1978/79, 216,400 in 1979/80). As it did so, worries developed amongst trade unions about the size of its displacement effects (Ryan 1988). It proved fairly easy for employers to substitute YOP trainees for potential full-time, permanent recruits, and the expansion of YOP rapidly created a backlog in the monitoring of the many schemes run by private employers and other agents. YOP schemes were disproportionately concentrated in industrial sectors with low rates of union membership and amongst small firms, making supervision harder. However, the MSC stated clearly that YOP was designed to give a competitive edge to young people in the labour market (MSC, 1977). Moderate displacement effects and downward pressure on wage-rates were probably not unwelcome given the difficulties the young unemployed were having in stepping on to job ladders, and the persistent desire of the government to moderate pay claims.

Brief mention should be made of the implications for the labour market of educational policy in this period. The most important educational goal adopted was the development of a fully comprehensive system of secondary education and the ending of selection, but this did not have immediate ramifications for entrants to the labour force. Overall rates of participation in further and higher education hardly changed (19·8% in 1973/74 − a year still affected by the increase in the school-leaving age to 16 in 1972 − 21·6% in 1974/75, 21·4% in 1978/79). Finegold and Soskice (1988) draw attention to the OECD (1985) study which found that the United Kingdom was the only member of the OECD to experience a decline in the educational participation rate of the 16−19-year-old age-group in the latter half of the 1970s. A smaller proportion of school-leavers left school with no qualification at all (51% in 1973/74, 48% in 1978/79) but the proportion with one or more A-levels remained constant at around 15% (Pearson *et al.*, 1984 bring together data relating to educational attainment in this period).

However, ideas were afoot about the ways in which education could contribute better to the fulfilment of youthful aspirations, including economic ones. James Callaghan's speech at Ruskin College in October 1976, launching the 'Great Debate' on education, showed that thinking about curriculum reform, standards and assessment, the responsiveness of teacher training, and the relationship between school and working life was developing. Little of this came to fruition before the end of the decade, but it provided some ideas the Conservatives subsequently adopted in their more radical reforms (there is a parallel here with the Conservatives' New Training Initiative of 1981).

5   Conclusion

The causes of the rapid rise in unemployment at the beginning of Labour's tenure were not well understood at the time. There is still disagreement about the role of certain factors, such as trade union militancy, today. In these circumstances, the rapid introduction and extension of special employment measures were sensible experiments. They could be applied directly to the political and economic problem of the higher unemployment rate cost-effectively, an important consideration given the constraints on general fiscal expansion. The government may have overestimated the reduction in unemployment generated per pound of expenditure, but subsequent estimates for particular schemes still leave them scoring well in terms of their short-run effectiveness. The long-run dangers of inhibiting improvements in labour productivity (directly and by lessening the need for firms to respond to competitive pressures) were probably not fully appreciated. There was little analysis of how long in principle they should last, nor of the changes needed to remove the illness for which they were a short-term palliative. The recession which followed the period, together with the abolition of TES, meant that few of the long-run problems had to be faced. The 1979–83 government did not reject the concept of special employment measures out of hand, but concentrated on youth measures and short-time working compensation.

Training policy, on the other hand, was not particularly successful, particularly when measured against the Labour Party's original pledges. It was thrown off-course by the increase in unemployment. The MSC's growing expenditure, for instance, was increasingly devoted to schemes to generate employment or at least keep down the unemployment count. Marquand (1989) remarks that, by 1979, the Special Programmes cuckoo was filling most of the nest. In fact, the situation was not quite that extreme. Figure 12.4 shows how the composition of MSC spending developed over time.

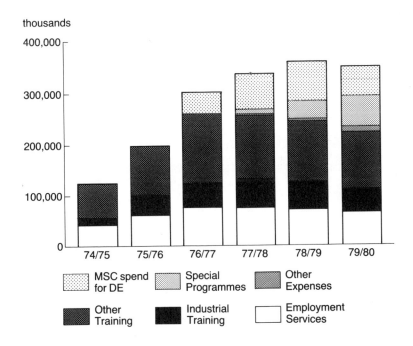

Fig. 12.4

Its total spending on its own account in 1979/80 was remarkably close to what had been projected in its first annual report (just under £293m. in 1974/75 prices, compared to a projection of £294m.). But YOP had little training content and the MSC had to try to compensate for industry's reduced contributions to the Industrial Training Boards. Sheldrake and

Vickerstaff (1987) take the view that 'the incoming Conservative government of 1979 inherited a set of training policies that were far from comprehensive, efficient or successful'. However, further deterioration in the British training effort had been resisted despite the distraction of the macroeconomic situation. On a more positive note, many new ideas first considered in the MSC during this period subsequently emerged in legislation. The experience with youth employment measures was a particularly useful foundation for the training and employment policies for young people adopted during the 1980s.

Appendix Employment and training measures, 1974 to 1979

Name and dates	Aims	Eligibility	Subsidy (in 1979 or at scheme end)	Notes
Temporary Employment Subsidy (TES) 18 Aug 1975 to 31 Mar 1979	To encourage companies to defer threatened redundancies.	Companies threatening redundancies affecting 10 or more workers, offered subsidy payable for a maximum of 12 months for each full-time job maintained.	£20 per week subsidy for each FT job maintained.	Supplement of £10 per worker payable to employers who exhausted TES, for 6 months.
Work Experience Programme (WEP) From Sep 1976	Employers asked to give young people a practical introduction to working life for a minimum of 6 months.		Young people on WEP received a allowance for which employers were refunded.	
Short-Time Working Compensation Scheme for Textile, Clothing and Footwear Firms 15 May 1978 to 31 Mar 1979	To encourage employers to adopt short-term working instead of making people redundant, employers reimbursed 75% of normal wages to those working short time, and employers NI contributions for workless days.			Introduced after TES support to firms in these sectors limited, after EEC intervention to 70% of labour force in applicant firm for first 6 months and 50% for second 6 months.
Job Creation Programme (JCP) 9 Oct 1975 to 31 Dec 1978 (approved applications continued throughout 1978)	Produced full-time, paid temporary (up to 12 months) employment for people who would otherwise have been unemployed.	Priority given to those aged 16–24 and over 50.		

Scheme	Purpose	Subsidy conditions	Amount	Notes
Recruitment Subsidy for School-Leavers (RSSL) Oct 1975 (applied to school-leavers of summer 1975 and December 1975)	To encourage employers in the private sector of industry and commerce and nationalised industries to give some preference to unemployed school-leavers.	Subsidy paid to companies employing school-leavers for maximum of 26 weeks.	£5 subsidy per school-leaver recruited per week.	Wound up on 30 September 1976, but in certain cases, ex-trainees, ex-rehabilitees, and ex-community employees were eligible for it until 31 Mar 1977.
Youth Employment Subsidy (YES) 1 Oct 1976 to 31 Mar 1978	A youth employment subsidy.	Paid for up to 26 weeks paid to any private sector or nationalised industry employer who recruited a young person (under 20 years old on 1 Oct 1976) who had been registered as continuously unemployed for 6 months or more.	£10 subsidy per week.	
Adult Employment Subsidy (AES) 7 Aug 1978 to 30 Jun 1979	Employers in industry and commerce and the nationalised industries received subsidy for employing unemployed persons.	Employers received subsidy for up to 26 weeks for everyone person aged over 19 and up to 64 (men) or 59 (women) and who had been registered unemployed for 12 months or more.	£20 subsidy per week.	9-month experimental period in Merseyside, Tyneside and Leeds; however, take-up of scheme disappointing.
Small Firms Subsidy (SFES) 1 Jul 1977 to 31 Mar 1980	Offered certain small manufacturing firms in the private sector a subsidy to encourage them to employ more people.	Firms with less than 200 employees offered a subsidy for up to 26 weeks for each extra full-time job over and above the number of jobs provided on a given base date. Part-time jobs of between 21 and 35 hours a week were counted as half, and those with less than 21 hours were excluded.	£20 subsidy per week. Originally only applied to Special Development Areas.	From 1 Jul 1979 extended to all assisted areas and Inner City Partnership areas, from 1 Jan 1979 to 30 Jun 1979 extended to the whole GB. Additionally small non-manufacturing firms in Special Development Areas, Development Areas and Inner City Partnerships eligible, but from 1 Jul 1979 only small manufacturing firms in the Special Development Areas and Development Areas were eligible.

Scheme	Purpose	Coverage	Allowance	Notes
Job Release Scheme (JRS) 3 Jan 1977 to 5 Apr 1982 1 Jul 1977 1 Mar 1978 1 May 1979 to 31 Mar 1980 6 Apr 1980	Enabled employed people in GB nearing statutory pensionable age to give up their jobs to make way for unemployed younger people and receive a weekly tax-free allowance.	Originally applied to employed and unemployed people within 1 year of NI retirement pension age in Assisted Areas. Restricted to persons in FT employment in Assisted Areas. Extended to all GB. Extended to cover men of 62 and 63 and disabled men of 60 and above. Eligibility age for non-disabled men reverted back to 64.	Allowance of £40 for married applicants with a dependent husband or wife, and £31·50 for all other applicants.	
Job Introduction Scheme (JIS) Introduced on a temporary basis in Jul 1977, accorded permanent status in 1980.	To encourage employers to give disabled people a trial of employment, where, in the judgement of the Disablement Resettlement Officer, the disabled person is prima facie suitable for the job but the employer has reasonable reservations about their ability to do it satisfactorily.	Scheme applied selectively, Disablement Resettlement Officers suggest scheme, employers do not apply for it.		In exceptional circumstances trial period can be extended to 13 weeks.
Youth Opportunities Programme (YOP) From 1 Apr 1978 with a projected lifespan of 5 years.	To improve employment prospects of unemployed young people aged 16–18 through the provision of work preparation and work experience schemes lasting up to 12 months.		£23·50 per week.	
Special Temporary Employment Programme (STEP) From 1 Apr 1978 with a projected lifespan of 5 years.	To provide FT temporary employment (up to 12 months) for unemployed people.	People aged 19 and over, with priority given to people aged 19–24 who have been unemployed for at least 6 months, and to people aged over 24 who have been unemployed for at least 12 months.		Incorporated the WEP.

Community Industry Scheme (CI) From spring 1972	To prepare for regular employment in as short a time as is practicable, unemployed people who find it difficult to obtain and keep jobs.	
Training	As part of special measures government began to provide special financial support for training in industry to combat the fall in the recruitment of young people to occupations requiring lengthy training.	
Scheme A	Provides grants to employers for training individuals.	Only available to employers who increase their labour force.
Scheme B	Provides grants to encourage off-the-job training.	For apprentices and technicians.
Scheme C	Provides grants for machinery and equipment, to increase the volume of off-the-job training at a semi-skilled level.	
Scheme D	Aims to help older workers, by making grants to employers.	Workers aged 45 and over who have been unemployed for 8 weeks or more, whether or not employer is increasing his labour force.
Training Opportunities Scheme (TOPS) From 7 Aug 1972	To offer an increased range of courses to men and women wishing to train for a new job, continuing courses available under the government vocational training scheme, and extending the range to include further education courses lasting 12 months or less, with an emphasis on people whose mobility is restricted.	Full-time training open to those who wish to acquire new skills whether employed or self-employed (provided they are willing to leave their present work), are out of work or otherwise outside the scope of employment but wishing to return to it. Candidates may undergo selection procedures to ensure they can make effective use of the course they wish to take.

Sources: House of Commons Library Research Division, Background Paper no. 92 'Unemployment', C. Barclay, P. Hutt, C. Neild and J. Tanfield, 1981. *Department of Employment Gazettes.* Manpower Services Commission Annual Reports.

Notes

The author is grateful to Sir John Cassels, Ken Mayhew, and participants at the conferences organised by the Editors for their advice and comments, and to Luci Francis for research assistance. However, the analysis and opinions expressed are entirely personal.

References

Barnett, J. (1982), *Inside the Treasury*, Deutsch, London.

Bedeman, T., and Harvey, J. (1981), 'Young people on YOP', *Employment Gazette*, LXXXIX, no. 8, August, Department of Employment.

Buck, T. W. (1977/78), 'Experiments with job creation subsidies', *Industrial Relations Journal*, VIII, no. 4, Winter.

Cassels, J. (1989), 'Reflections on tripartism', *Policy Studies*, IX, no. 3, Spring, pp. 6–19.

Deakin, B., and Pratten, C. (1981), *Effects of the Temporary Employment Subsidy*, Cambridge University Department of Applied Economics Occasional Paper No. 53, Cambridge University Press, Cambridge.

de Montlibert, C. (1979), *Youth and Employment in Europe*, Council of Europe, Strasbourg.

Finegold, D., and Soskice, D. (1988), 'The failure of training in Britain: analysis and prescription', *Oxford Review of Economic Policy*, IV, no. 3, pp. 21–53.

Jackman, R. A., and Layard, P. R. G. (1980), 'The efficiency case for long-run labour market policies', *Economica*, XLVII, August.

Layard, P. R. G. (1979), 'The costs and benefits of selective employment policies: the British case', *British Journal of Industrial Relations*, XVII, no. 2, July, pp. 187–204.

Layard, P. R. G. (1986), *How to Beat Unemployment*, Oxford University Press, Oxford.

Layard, P. R. G., and Nickell, S. J. (1986), 'Unemployment in Britain', in C. Bean, P. R. G. Layard and S. J. Nickell (eds), *The Rise in Unemployment*, Basil Blackwell, Oxford.

McGill, P. R. (1981), 'Post-training experience of TOPS trainees', *Department of Employment Gazette*, July, pp. 325–8.

Manpower Services Commission (1977), *Young People and Work*, MSC, London.

Marquand, J. (1989), *Autonomy and Change*, Harvester Wheatsheaf, Hemel Hempstead.

Metcalf, D. (1982), *Alternatives to Unemployment: Special Employment Measures in Britain*, Report no. 610, Policy Studies Institute, with the Anglo-German Foundation, September.

Middlemas, K. (1983), *Industry, Unions, and Government: Twenty One Years of NEDC*, Macmillan, London.

Organization for Economic Co-operation and Development (1985), *Education and Training after Basic Schooling*, OECD, Paris.

Pearson, R., Hutt, R., and Parsons, D. (1984), *Education, Training and Employment*, Institute of Manpower Studies Series, no. 4, Gower, Aldershot.

Roper, S. (1986), *The Economics of Job Vacancies*, Centre for Labour Economics Discussion Paper no. 252, London School of Economics.

Ryan, P. (1987), 'Trade unionism and the pay of young workers', in P. N. Junankar (ed.), *From School to Unemployment? The Labour Market for Young People*, Macmillan, London.

Ryan, P. (1989), 'Youth interventions, job substituting and trade union policy: Great Britain 1976–86', in S. Rosenberg (ed.), *The State and the Labor Market: Employment Policy, Collective Bargaining and Economic Crisis*, Plenum, New York.

Sheldrake, J., and Vickerstaff, S. (1987), *The History of Industrial Training in Britain*, Avebury Press, Aldershot.

Stern, J. (1988), *Methods of Analysis of Public Expenditure Programmes with Employment Objectives*, Government Economic Service Working Paper no. 103, May.

Turner, P. S., Wallis, K. F., and Whitley, D. (1987), 'Evaluating special employment measures with macroeconometric models', *Oxford Review of Economic Policy*, III, no. 3, Autumn, pp. xxv–xxxvi.

Zabalza, A., and Tzannatos, Z. (1983), 'The effect of Britain's anti-discriminatory legislation on relative pay and employment', Centre for Labour Economics Discussion Paper no. 155, London School of Economics.

Industrial relations

This period of Labour government was both initiated and terminated by industrial relations troubles. Brought to power in the election called by Edward Heath in the face of a coal miners' strike, the government was to suffer terminal electoral damage five years later from public service disputes in the so-called 'Winter of Discontent'. Throughout its term of office, industrial relations policies remained in the forefront. Most of these policies were to be unceremoniously scrapped by the government that followed. But how well conceived were they at the time, and how much can they teach us when reviewed in the knowledge of the subsequent dramatic policy change under Margaret Thatcher?

1 The inheritance

Until the late 1960s any idea of an industrial relations policy would have seemed odd. Peacetime governments up to then had been largely able to leave employers and trade unions to get on with collective bargaining on their own. Harold Wilson had first been forced to intervene with a statutory incomes policy. He also appointed a Royal Commission on Trade Unions and Employers' Associations under Lord Donovan to investigate the increasingly confused conduct and legal status of collective bargaining. The Commission reported in 1968 to the effect that there was relatively little action a government could take beyond encouraging employers to get their own houses in order (Donovan, 1968). But by then Wilson felt that the political pressure to be seen to be doing something about strikes was irresistible. A Bill proposing 'penal clauses' to regulate strike procedure provoked a backbench revolt and was abandoned. It was an experience which neither he, nor one of the leaders of the revolt, James Callaghan, were to forget (Jenkins, 1970).

For Mr Heath, however, the subject moved to the centre of the policy stage. His Industrial Relations Act 1971 was a radical and comprehensive measure, modelled in many respects upon American legislation, whereby written collective agreements could be enforced through a National Industrial Relations Court. Unions were liable for strike damages unless they were registered and followed correct procedures. It was a complex measure that immediately ran into difficulties. The union movement was adamantly opposed and the Trades Union Congress (TUC), at the cost of expelling twenty unions, enforced a successful campaign of deregistration. There was a general reluctance of employers to make use of their new legal powers, even to the extent of their protecting widespread, but now illegal, closed shops. In the few instances when the law was used the problems of enforcement were over-whelming. A tangled series of court cases resulted in widespread strikes and demonstrations, with union activists resisting court orders and refusing to pay the consequent fines. The Heath government, by 1972 keen on gaining union support for an incomes policy, must have felt it had unwittingly let loose an uncontrollable legislative monster (Weekes *et al.*, 1975).

It was not only through acute legal embarrassment that Heath learnt of the political power of British trade unions. He had the misfortune to take office at a time when the international economy was entering an inflationary phase which was to turn into a crisis in 1973. His attempts to reduce domestic in-flation resulted in a series of confrontations over wage claims. In early 1972 a coal strike precipitated an official state of emergency with much of industry reduced to working for only two or three days a week before it was settled. Later that year tripartite talks on pay restraint broke down and a statutory pay freeze was imposed. Subsequent stages of the 'counter-inflation' policy became more complex, with provisions intended to allow the miners extra money (Clegg, 1976). But, against a background of soaring petroleum prices, they were not sufficient. A coal strike was called for February 1974. Heath announced a General Election for later that month on the platform that the miners were challenging Parliament. He lost.

Quite apart from the disaster area that British industrial relations was becoming for governments, it was itself undergoing substantial change. The central diagnosis of the Donovan Report had been concerned with the level, form and coverage of collective agreements. In the private sector in Britain the preponderant form of agreement had long been nation-wide, industry-specific and 'multi-employer'. For various reasons many of these agreements had come to have limited effect, with individual employers choosing to add to the multi-employer agreements' provisions through workplace bargaining with shop stewards. Donovan had recommended that, where this was well established, it should be faced up to, and that employers should reform their procedures and control systems to achieve effective 'single-employer' bargaining, with formal site or company agreements. Although no legislative action was taken, employers were to move steadily in this direction. By the end of the 1970s multi-employer bargaining had so declined as to be of primary impor-tance for no more than a quarter of private sector employees.

Table 13.1 *Strike statistics and trade union density*

	Stoppages	Working days lost (w.d.l.) per 1000 employees	% strikes lasting <3 days	% of w.d.l. arising from strikes of >500,000 w.d.l.	% trade union density[b]
1960–64	2512	139	74	22	44
1965–69	2380	168	65	20	44
1970–73	2909	624	51	45	49
1974	2946	647	43	38	50
1974[a]	[3194]	[550]		[0]	
1975	2332	265	41	0	51
1976	2034	146	47	0	52
1977	2737	448	41	12	53
1978	2498	413	42	26	54
1979	2125	1273	42	72	55
1979[a]	[2400]	[380]		[62]	
1974–79	2445	532	43	42	53
1974–79[a]	[2528]	[359]		[20]	
1980–84	1363	484	54	67	50
1985–88	943	178	64	55	43

[a]   These figures are corrected using monthly data to cover the period between General Elections, from March 1974 until April 1979 inclusive, scaled up for a full twelve months. Sources of strike data were the *Employment Gazette*, September 1980 and DE private correspondence.

[b]   Average annual data expressing registered trade union membership as a percentage of employed and unemployed labour force excluding employers, self-employed and armed forces.

Sources: 1960–79, Bain (1983, p. 5); 1979–86, Kelly and Bailey (1989, p. 57). Estimated to 1988.

Partly as a result of these developments, the pattern of strikes was changing. The small spontaneous strike was tending to give way to larger disputes connected with more formal workplace bargaining. The incidence of strikes was spreading to an ever-broader range of industries. Above all, the public services' hitherto almost strike-free post-war record became only a memory after the start of the 1970s. The problem that for Wilson's first government had been unofficial private sector disputes became primarily one of large, official public sector strikes for Heath.

It is evident from Table 13.1 that there was a substantial rise in working days lost through disputes during the Heath years. The table also shows the upsurge in trade union membership during the same period. This was primarily a result of rising inflation, a growing public sector, and the increased tendency of employers to deduct their employees' membership dues on behalf of their unions.

On his return to power in 1974, Wilson thus had an unenviable inheritance. Hampered by the lack of a majority in the Commons until the autumn, his parliamentary position would continue to be weak. The trade union movement was more extensive and assertive than ever. His own largely token effort to regulate it had been rebuffed; Heath's radical attempt had met humiliation. Both governments had suffered from their attempts to restrain wage settlements, yet he now had to face unprecedented inflation, with the prospect of it being made worse by the 'Threshold' indexation provisions left over from Heath's Stage III pay policy.

The Stage III policy had permitted 'Threshold Agreements' whereby payments of up to 40p per week could be awarded for each 1% rise in the retail price index in excess of 7% from its position in October 1973. Such extra payments could be added to pay each month until October 1974. A sharp rise in the RPI first triggered payments in April 1974, and by November 1974 up to eleven instalments were possible. When the first payments became due it was estimated that only a minority of workers – 7 to 7½ million – had Agreements (Hughes, 1974). Since almost all the public sector was covered, there cannot have been more than a million private sector workers with Agreements by then. The Pay Board ruled that Agreements could not be made retrospective so that later Agreements were generally partial. Those low-paid private sector workers coming under Wages Councils were only partially covered or not at all. But in the better organised parts of the private sector pay settlements were already surging ahead after the February election when the government's commitment to its predecessor's norms was weakened (Brown, 1976). A safe summary would thus be that the Threshold Agreements were in the main used by the public sector to catch up with a private sector pay explosion. If Wilson had disowned them he would not only have undermined future pay restraint policies, he would have faced a public sector pay revolt which would have brought a Winter of Discontent four years early.

Wilson had, broadly, three sorts of policy approaches at his disposal: direct legislation to regulate collective bargaining; action by government as an employer in its own right; and broader political initiatives to change the context of industrial relations. These will be considered in turn.

2 Legislative action

The new government was determined to win the support of the trade union movement for its policies and Michael Foot, on the left wing of the party, was made Secretary of State for Employment. The 'Social Contract' was slow emerging, and it only gained real meaning with the £6 pay limit policy in mid-1975. But from the start it was understood that Labour would replace most of Heath's ill-fated Industrial Relations Act. More positively, it was proposed to provide employees and trade unions with new rights and also to extend and strengthen industrial democracy. It would be superfluous to describe these measures in detail, but it is necessary to explain some of the background.

British labour law is distinctive in that it provides trade unions with no clear right to strike under specified circumstances, as is the norm elsewhere. Instead the equivalent is achieved through the rather circuitous device of giving trade unions and employers' associations 'immunity' from being sued for damages arising from action 'in contemplation or furtherance of a trade dispute', in the cryptic language of the 1906 Trade Disputes Act. The Industrial Relations Act had, to a large extent, tried to cut the Gordian knot of legal interpretation of these immunities by providing registered unions with positive rights and by attempting to promote legally enforceable collective agreements.

Their recent tempestuous experience of the courts made the unions shy away from asking Labour to replace Heath's Act with something equally radical. Instead they were happy to see Labour legislate to reassert and extend the basic provisions of the revered 1906 Act. The wisdom of this should perhaps be judged in the retrospective knowledge that the damage done to trade unions by Thatcher's 'step by step' legislation of the 1980s also builds on the negative 'immunities' of the 1906 Act, substantially narrowing the basis on which unions can claim immunity. Be that as it may, as early as was possible the Trade Union and Labour Relations Act 1974 repealed Heath's Act. There were some changes and some clarifications, but essentially the corner-stone of union immunities and the non-enforcable character of collective agreements were restored (Lewis, 1983).

The second stage of Labour's legislation was the Employment Protection Act 1975 (EPA). This provided a new institutional basis for collective labour law and a medley of new rights for both individual employees and trade unions. In purging the previous regime, the 1974 government had swept aside the National Industrial Relations Court, the Commission on Industrial Relations (which had been the main consequence of the Donovan Report), the Pay Board, and the Registrar of Trade Unions and Employers' Associations. In their place was put the Advisory, Conciliation and Arbitration Service (ACAS), to which we shall return, the Central Arbitration Committee (CAC) to provide it with legal back-up, the Employment Appeal Tribunal to hear appeals from the industrial tribunals, and the Certification Officer, effectively replacing the Registrar. Unlike their predecessors, these four outlasted the government and were to continue, with altered powers, into the 1990s.

The varied new rights provided by the EPA can only be sketched. The right to complain to a tribunal against unfair dismissal was salvaged from the repealed Act and strengthened slightly to allow the tribunal to 'order' the reinstatement or re-engagement of an unfairly dismissed employee (or give compensation). There were new rights not to be dismissed because of pregnancy and to be reinstated after maternity. Various protections were provided for trade union activity. Dismissal for trade union activity or membership was outlawed. Time off was allowed for certain trade union duties and training. Unions seeking recognition from an employer were able to call on ACAS to investigate and make a recommendation, enforceable by the CAC. Unions could claim arbitration on 'recognised' terms and conditions or the 'general level' for comparable workers in the district. Employers were obliged to consult unions on proposed redundancies (following an EEC directive) and on industrial safety (altering the Health and Safety legislation drafted by the previous government). There was a legal obligation for employers to disclose to trade unions information necessary for collective bargaining.

The whole package of the EPA was, on the face of it, a major legal initiative, injecting positive legal rights into areas of union organisation and collective bargaining where they were hitherto unknown. To it should perhaps be added the substantial advances offered by the Sex Discrimination Act 1975 and the Race Relations Act 1976.

The third component of the Social Contract legislation was intended to promote industrial democracy. In marked contrast to the almost indecent haste with which the EPA had been introduced, movement towards this was so slow as to grind fruitlessly to a halt. The TUC had shown no more than a fitful interest in legislative support for having worker directors on company boards. As recently as 1967 a worker director scheme had been introduced with the renationalisation of the steel industry. The question was revived by the European Commission's 'fifth directive' proposal suggesting a company law requirement for worker representatives on supervisory boards. But the trade unions were ambivalent and divided on the question. One argument was that British collective bargaining with its strong workplace roots was already superior to European supervisory boards; another was that trade union independence would be compromised by participation in management.

In the end the government set up a committee under Lord Bullock to report on the question (Bullock, 1977). The committee produced a deeply divided report, with the employer representatives opposing the fairly radical proposals of the majority. When it was published, the employer response was furious and the trade union response lukewarm. After producing diluted legislative proposals in 1978 the government let the matter drop. It is here appropriate to note that the government sponsored another form of industrial democracy by assisting the employee buy-outs of substantial factories in Meriden, Kirkby and Glasgow. These were all unhappy failures (Eccles, 1981).

3   Consequences of the legislation

It is tempting to say that the most ambitious measures had least effect. At one extreme, the Bullock proposals never reached the statute book, although something very similar was briefly introduced by the Post Office in 1978. A detailed study of the early consequences of the Post Office experiment suggested that the introduction of worker directors had relatively little impact and won slight enthusiasm from the unions involved (Batstone *et al.*, 1984). It should be added, however, that the public debate on industrial democracy stimulated by Bullock may well have contributed to the undoubted increase in the use of consultative committees in the 1970s. A survey conducted at the end of 1977 found that of the 42% of manufacturing estbalishments with 50 or more employees that had joint consultative arrangements, 61% had introduced them in the previous five years (Brown, 1981). Their use has increased further in the 1980s.

Most of the new rights provided by the EPA appear to have had slight effect. The requirement to disclose bargaining information was so hedged about that it was judged as having an insignificant impact on bargaining behaviour (Gospel and Willman, 1981). The duty to consult in advance on redundancies was in practice easily side-stepped. Judges tended to take a very narrow view of organisational rights. The statutory recognition procedure was particularly vulnerable to judges' largely individualist values and a string of cases – including the long-running Grunwick dispute – saw the discretion given to ACAS whittled away. In any case, there is a wide gap between an employer's conceding recognition and his actually engaging in effective negotiations. Although the opportunity to press comparability claims was fairly heavily used, it was also cautiously interpreted (Jones, 1980). The maternity provisions have proved generally beneficial but were to be substantially weakened by the Conservatives in 1980.

There is a recurring theme from the now solid body of research into the impact of industrial relations legislation on behaviour. This is that it is of limited value to provide employees with rights unless either their employer is willing to comply with them or their trade union is strong enough to enforce compliance. An example of this inadequacy of unsupported legal rights is provided by the Health and Safety at Work Act (Dawson *et al.*, 1988). Another clear example is provided by the unfair dismissal protection, which also tends to reinforce disciplinary procedures and to undermine the ability of unions to resist dismissals (Dickens *et al.*, 1985). A review of union recognition and disclosure procedures concludes: 'Perhaps the major lesson which emerges from the experience of the 1970s is not to entertain too high expectations of what legislation can achieve in this area. Legislative procedures cannot substitute for union organising and recruitment activity' (Dickens and Bain, 1986).

One product of the EPA that has endured and quietly prospered has been

ACAS. A powerful academic case had been put for a central arbitration and conciliation service during the disorderly closing stages of Heath's Act (McCarthy and Ellis, 1973). It was argued that 'constructive mediation' could be used to facilitate reform where the law had failed. It is worth explaining the normal terminology here. What is generally termed 'third party intervention' divides between: 'conciliation', where the conciliator's object is to work behind the scenes to midwife an agreement; 'mediation', in which an explicit non-binding recommendation may be made by the mediator to get the antagonists off the hook; and a more formal process of voluntary 'arbitration', in which the parties agree from the start to accept the arbitrator's award as binding.

ACAS has taken the 'advisory' part of its remit seriously, publishing leaflets on good practice, commenting on legislative proposals, and pressing the merits of collective bargaining even in the face of government hostility during the 1980s. The old conciliation service of the Ministry of Labour had previously become hopelessly compromised by attempts to embroil it in implementing incomes policy. As defence against this, ACAS's governing council is composed of independent experts and nominees of the CBI and TUC, and it is expressly protected from ministerial direction. Most of its staff are concerned with conciliating the individual cases that are brought to them, generally running at well over 40,000 each year, the great majority for unfair dismissal. ACAS also has a panel of part-time arbitrators.

There may have been those who hoped that ACAS would come to occupy a central position in British collective bargaining, as arbitration does elsewhere in the English-speaking world. This has not happened. The number of cases dealt with has declined in recent years, more than halving from the 1976 level of 2800 in the subsequent decade, very much in line with the declining incidence of strikes. But this is not a sign of failure. There are substantial legal reasons why Britain has not tried to emulate, say, the USA and Australia in its use of third party intervention, and there is much to be said for its not aspiring to do so. ACAS has earned widespread respect among employers and trade unions and even, by the late 1980s, from a philosophically opposed government. It must be counted a substantial legislative achievement.

Although the institutional structure established by the 1974–79 government looks durable, the overall package of legislation was far from visionary. The hindsight of the 1990s is inevitably distorted, but one cannot help but ask whether the Trade Union and Labour Relations Act was not an act of complacency. Could not more have been done then to place union security on a firmer basis rather than return to relying on the judges' fickle interpretation of immunities? Could this not have been combined with measures on trade union government, thereby making a virtue of reform and denying the Conservatives the triumph of their subsequent balloting legislation? Nor, beyond ACAS, can much be said for the EPA, hastily put together and quickly confused by the courts, as previous experience suggested it might be. Would it not have been better to develop more carefully researched and more widely discussed, tailor-made packages of legislation linking up with, say, social security law, or company law, as appropriate?

Any assessment of legislation must take account of the fact that much of the effectiveness of a law lies not in its enforcement but in its symbolic signalling of public standards. The fact that minimum entitlements may not be fully observed does not mean that they are ineffective. Similarly, as Mrs Thatcher has shown in a negative way, the degree of sympathy towards collective bargaining indicated by legislation can have powerful demonstrative effects upon the style adopted by managers even if they make no use of the actual laws. Just as the public debate on Bullock probably stimulated consultative activity, so the content of the EPA probably bolstered employer support of collective bargaining. It probably encouraged the growth of trade unionism to what was to be its record level of 1979. Perhaps the main question is whether, with less haste and more debate, the job could have been done with greater persuasion and permanence.

4 The government as employer

In 1974 employment in the public sector was rising to its highest peacetime levels. With approximately 5 million in the public services and a further 2 million in the nationalised industries, the government was directly or indirectly responsible for nearly 30% of all UK employment. The public sector was approximately 80% unionised, so that it included almost half the membership of the TUC. It was, as has been noted, a workforce that was becoming increasingly strike-prone.

In sharp contrast to its successor, the 1974–79 government was largely inactive in its role as an employer. The previous Wilson government's National Board for Prices and Incomes had inquired deeply into employment practices across most of the public sector, and had been an important catalyst of innovation in, for example, local government, coal, and the steel industry. Heath's government, besides reorganising health and local government, had established the pay Review Bodies for doctors and dentists, 'top people', and the armed forces. Although his Pay Board in its brief life never established the same investigative style of its predecessor, it began to act primarily as an *ad hoc* review body for the public sector. But when Wilson returned, his government seemed to be fundamentally inhibited by the recent industrial conflicts and by the need to retain trade union support on incomes policy.

It would not be appropriate to stray into discussion of his government's industrial policy. But what stands out in retrospect is how little attention was given to the question of labour management in the state-owned industries as they struggled for competitiveness. It was particularly noticeable in those that had been recently natinoalised, such as British Leyland, British Steel, British Shipbuilders and British Aerospace, that the same poor management practices that had helped to force them into public ownership in the first place were carried on much as before, often with the same managers responsible. It was reflected in the short-sighted disorder of their pay systems, training practices, bargaining procedures and management development.

No doubt many of those managers would have blamed the obstructiveness of the unions with which they dealt. They would have pointed to the later impact of Edwardes and MacGregor, tackling the unions head-on with a vigour that the Labour government (perhaps any Labour government) would have neither allowed nor underwritten. But any attempt to shift the burden of blame to trade unions is weakened by major exceptions in the 1970s. The electricity industry continued to adapt smoothly to new technologies and the gas industry moved to North Sea gas with minimal discord. By contrast, the earlier defeat of the postal unions by Heath had not been enough to achieve substantial change in working practices because the Post Office management was incapable of taking advantage of it.

Defeating trade unions is neither necessary nor sufficient for achieving productive change. A surer recipe requires two preconditions. The first is product market circumstances that are sufficiently austere to require change, which in the public sector can to some extent be contrived. The second is the installation of management capable of implementing the major organisational upheaval required, including the changed labour practices which are a component, but usually not the major component. It is always possible that the ensuing negotiations with unions may involve strikes. Any change in a power relationship involves the risk of sanctions if expectations and aspirations cannot be adjusted by other means. But given the continuity of the employment relationship, it is both short-sighted and mistaken to believe that the defeat of the employees' trade unions is a necessary precondition for change.

This question is fundamental to an assessment of the 1974–79 Labour government's record. For whatever reason, the management of labour in much of the public sector was allowed to drift during its term of office. A common argument was later to be that only Thatcher could give management the resolve, the laws, and the resources to 'take on' and defeat the unions and thus achieve changed working practices. If we believe this we are close to saying that the drift under Labour was unavoidable, and even, more paradoxically, that no Labour government can be expected to have custody of a technologically effective public sector. But, as has been argued, 'taking on' unions as an end in itself carries substantial long-term costs and no necessary long-term gains. What is more important to the managements of state enterprises is the knowledge that they have the confidence of the government, and that in a dispute the government will not tacitly side with the unions with whom they deal. In its vagueness on this, the Labour government's record is vulnerable to criticism.

Heath's turbulent relations with his public sector mainly arose from his attempts to achieve pay restraint. The limited extent of his success is demonstrated by Figure 13.1 which shows how public sector earnings, having previously kept roughly in step with the private sector, moved ahead during his period in office. Under Labour, in the aftermath of the coal settlement and with the inherited 'Threshold Payments', for both the public corporations and public services (described in the figure as 'general government')

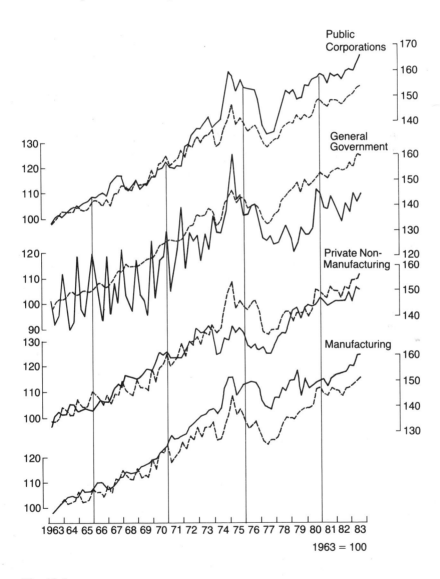

Fig. 13.1

pay levels surged ahead. They were to be brought back into line at first with the Social Contract incomes policy. But whereas the public corporations were soon to drift to a more favourable relative position in the late 1970s than they had previously experienced, the public services were to be dragged in the opposite direction. The fact that they fell so far behind was a major factor precipitating the public service unrest in the winter of 1978/79. Callaghan's 5% pay limit was doomed to rejection.

No attempt had been made by Labour to develop a specifically public services pay policy. The Review Bodies had been inherited from the Conservatives and continued in existence, as also did the increasingly suspect Pay Research Unit review system for Civil Service pay. All these relied on rough comparability with the rest of the economy. Labour added the dangerously rigid Edmund-Davies formula for the police, tying their pay to national average earnings, and compounded the problem by linking in the firemen after their strike of 1977/78.

Despite the position it was to be given in political demonology, the number of working days lost during the public service strikes of the Winter of Discontent was, as Table 13.1 shows, not substantial. It was the engineering industry stoppages later in 1979 that were to make it a heavy strike year. But the political embarrassment was acute and, in order to extricate himself, Callaghan established the Pay Comparability Commission under the chairmanship of Professor Hugh Clegg. Highly constrained by its terms of reference, it dealt rapidly with some 2½ million public service employees in eight reports, using management consultancy firms to carry out wage surveys and pick out comparable jobs. After its termination the Comparability Commission was to be widely charged with causing the inflation first encountered by the Thatcher government. Figure 13.1 suggests this to be spurious. By late 1980 the public services had been no more than temporarily returned to their traditional relative position. The 1974–79 government was not the first, and doubtless will not be the last, to pay dearly electorally for making its own employees bear the heaviest burden of a national incomes policy.

In its valedictory report the Comparability Commission drew a number of morals from its far-from-happy experience. One was that, rather than have different Review Bodies or *ad hoc* inquiries, a single body should carry out all public service pay analysis. In doing so it would have to, in effect, develop a common public service job evaluation system in order to guarantee consistency. Another moral was that existing industrial job evaluation techniques are not adequate, since they use measures of responsibility (as the nurses were to discover nine years later) unsuitable to the ethos of 'caring' professions. A third was that such a body should not have the responsibility of fixing binding awards, but of providing sound data for subsequent negotiation. Unless, that is, it is expressly desired to have an 'essential services' compulsory arbitration system. Another far-reaching conclusion was that it was dangerous to try to link pay and productivity by any mechanical formula; the setting of acceptable pay levels and the effective management of productivity are distinct, if connected, managerial tasks (Clegg, 1980). These are important lessons from which future governments should learn.

5   The political context

Looking back on any government's record there are some incidents which are redolent only of past battles, and others which can be seen to be foretastes of things to come. If the sponsored co-operatives and restored immunities were examples of the first, the Comparability Commission and the Social Contract pay policy have more promise. Like the Commission, the Contract was conceived in crisis, but from its experience important lessons can be learned.

In terms of the industrial relations practicalities of the time the Social Contract pay policy was dramatically successful. With its simple formula, clearly favouring the low-paid, the Social Contract, as both Table 13.1 and Figure 13.1 bear witness, brought down both pay settlements and strike levels. It is difficult to imagine its having been developed as boldly had not the influence of Jack Jones been so strong. As General Secretary of the Transport and General Worker's Union, he worked closely with Len Murray, the General Secretary of the Trades Union Congress.

To appreciate Jones' ambivalent attitude to what Thatcher was later to denigrate as 'corporatism', it is important that his career had developed far from his union's head office. A man of towering ability, he had started out as a dockers' shop steward in Liverpool where full-time officials were held in low esteem. As District Secretary in wartime and post-war Coventry and then Midlands Regional Secretary, he had done much to build up the position of shop stewards and, when he became General Secretary, he increased their representation on his union's national executive. He was thus established as the major figure behind the decentralisation of British trade union government when fears of the political consequences of hyperinflation forced him to the remarkable 'U-turn' of engineering the Social Contract, the most centralised period of pay-fixing ever experienced in peacetime Britain.

Perhaps this helps to explain why the Social Contract was conceived as a crisis measure, an aberration from the supposed virtues of 'free collective bargaining', rather than, as it might have been presented, a step towards a more united labour movement and an essential part of socialist economic strategy. The contrast with the steady and successful development of the Australian 'Accord' during the 1980s is notable. No research-orientated equivalent to the National Board for Prices and Incomes or the Pay Board was created to plumb the uncharted waters the policy was moving into.

The opportunity offered by Denis Healey, the Chancellor, to negotiate over income tax cuts in 1976 and 1977 was ducked, and with it the chance to develop a real, as opposed to nominal, incomes policy. Little was done to build up the TUC's role beyond that of holder of a veto, with the consequence that it was very largely the political whim of Callaghan, as Prime Minister, that fixed the disastrously low 'norm' of 5% for 1978/79.

The greatest opportunity for long-term institutional development that was missed was probably with the employers. The Confederation of British Industry had come into existence during the previous Wilson administration and had run an effective voluntary price restraint policy under Heath. It fought a successful campaign against the Bullock proposals and produced an important strategy document on 'The Future of Pay Determination' in 1977. The CBI was, and remains, seriously handicapped by its constitution, which inhibits its reaching authoritative decisions through which it might offer strategic leadership in any way comparable to most overseas counterparts. But, just as it was the creation of the National Economic Development Council that forced the pathologically individualistic British employers to create the CBI in the first place, so it is most likely to be an enhanced role in economic government that will trigger its constitutional reform. The CBI was (perhaps not unwillingly) excluded from the Social Contract, and with its exclusion went any chance of a co-ordinated approach to British collective bargaining and wage inflation. In the last weeks of the government, in the disorder of early 1979, the TUC and CBI separately published proposals stemming from informal talks, proposing an 'agreed economic assessment' and a 'national economic forum' as the basis for a bipartite approach to pay strategy. But, promising as that was, it was a consequence of governmental failure, and it was too late (CBI, 1979; TUC, 1979).

The recurring theme of this review of the 1974–79 government has been that of the damage done by its anxiety not to offend the trade union movement. The historical reasons for this anxiety are understandable enough. The fact that the government took so much policy straight from the unions behind the scenes inhibited the ability of both the TUC and the CBI to develop as actors and representative pressure groups in their own right and it prevented the government itself from pursuing a consistent strategy with regard to industrial relations. Unions are reactive, bargaining organisations, ill-prepared for writing the agenda for government. In attempting to placate, for tactical economic reasons, a largely unprepared trade union movement, the government did that movement lasting damage. It perpetuated the myth of the centrality of trade unions to the British inflationary process when, as the CBI itself was aware, a fragmented bargaining structure was a major contributor. By placing unions so centrally on the political stage, it prepared the way for the devastating Conservative reaction.

Note

The author is much indebted to the comments of Fred Bayliss, Hugh Clegg, Denis Healey, Bob Hepple, Bill McCarthy, Peter Nolan, Paul Ryan, Douglas Wass and a seminar at Queens' College, Cambridge.

References

Bain, G. S. (ed.) (1983), *Industrial Relations in Britain*, Oxford, Blackwell.

Batstone, E. V., Ferner, A., and Terry, M. A. (1984), *Unions on the Board*, Blackwell, Oxford.

Brown, W. A. (1976), 'Incomes policy and pay differentials', *Oxford Bulletin of Economics and Statistics*, XXXVIII, no. 1, pp. 27–49.

Brown, W. A. (ed.) (1981), *The Changing Contours of British Industrial Relations* Blackwell, Oxford.

Bullock, Lord (1977), Committee of Inquiry on Industrial Democracy, *Report* Cmnd. 6706, HMSO, London.

Clegg, H. A. (1976), *The System of Industrial Relations in Great Britain*, 2nd edn, Blackwell, Oxford.

Clegg, H. A. (1980), Pay Comparability Commission, *General Report*, Cmnd. 7995, HMSO, London.

Confederation of British Industry (1979), *Pay: the Choice Ahead*, CBI, London.

Dawson, S., Willman, P., Bamford, M., and Clinton, A. (1988), *Safety at Work: the Limits of Self-Regulation*, Cambridge University Press, Cambridge.

Dean, A. (1981), 'Public and private sector pay in the economy', in J. L. Fallick and R. F. Elliott (eds), *Incomes Policies, Inflation and Relative Pay*, Allen & Unwin, London.

Dickens, L., and Bain, G. S. (1986), 'A duty to bargain? Union recognition and disclosure', in R. Lewis (ed.), *Labour Law in Britain*, Blackwell, Oxford.

Dickens, L., Jones, M., Weekes, B., and Hart, M. (1985), *Dismissed*, Blackwell, Oxford.

Donovan, Lord (1968), Royal Commission on Trade Unions and Employers' Associations, *Report*, Cmnd. 3623, HMSO, London.

Eccles, T. (1981), *Under New Management*, London, Pan.

Foster, N., Henry, S. G. B., and Trinder, C. (1984), 'Public and private sector pay: a partly disaggregated study', *National Institute Economic Review*, no. 107.

Gospel, H., and Willman, P. (1981), 'Disclosure of information: the CAC approach', *Industrial Law Journal*, X, pp. 10–22.

Hughes, J. (1974), 'Are threshold agreements inflationary?', *The Banker*, October, pp. 1191–4.

Jenkins, P. (1970), *The Battle of Downing Street*, Charles Knight, London.

Jones, M. (1980), 'CAC and Schedule 11: the experience of two years', *Industrial Law Journal*, IX, March, pp. 28–44.

Kelly, J., and Bailey, R. (1989), 'British trade union membership, density and decline in the 1980s', *Industrial Relations Journal*, XX, no. 1, pp. 54–61.

Lewis, R. (1983), 'Collective labour law', in Bain (1983).

McCarthy, W. E. J., and Ellis, N. (1973), *Management by Agreement*, Hutchinson, London.

Trades Union Congress (1979), *The Economy, the Government and Trade Union Responsibilities*, TUC, London.

Weekes, B., Mellish, M., Dickens, L., and Lloyd, J. (1975), *Industrial Relations and the Limits of Law*, Blackwell, Oxford.

Redistribution

Labour Party General Election manifestos always promise redistribution, but the commitments to increased benefits for the poor and to higher taxes on those most able to pay were unusually prominent in the February 1974 manifesto. They reflected, in part, the opposition to the Conservative government's incomes policy which had led to the election. Labour's manifesto argued that only a 'much fairer distribution of the national wealth can convince the worker and his family and his trade union that "an incomes policy" is not some kind of trick to force him ... to bear the brunt of the national burden' (Labour Party, 1974, p.308). The emphasis on redistribution, aiming at 'a fundamental and irreversible shift in the balance of power and wealth in favour of working people and their families', also marked the dissatisfaction of some of its own supporters with Labour's 1964–70 policies.[1]

In 1974 urgent action was promised 'to strike at the roots of the worst poverty' and to redistribute income and wealth by changes in taxation. The outcomes of these objectives are the subject of this chapter. First, the results of the commitments to increase cash benefits are reviewed and considered in the light of evidence about the prevalence of poverty at the time, particularly in connection with the objective of dealing with the worst poverty. Then some of the most important changes in taxation are sketched, and evidence relevant to judging the success of the objective of shifting tax burden towards those most able to pay is outlined. Finally, after a digression on the impact of incomes policy, the overall redistributive effect of cash benefits and taxes is examined.[2]

1 Cash benefits

The first commitment was to help retirement pensioners, widows, the sick and the unemployed, by raising pensions and other benefits at once to £10 per week for single people and £16 for married couples. These benefits were then to increase annually in line with earnings.

Retirement pensions and unemployment and sickness benefits had been uprated equally since 1967, but in 1973 the Conservatives increased pensions more than unemployment and sickness benefits. Labour's first uprating, in 1974, set widows' and retirement pensions at £10 (£16 for couples) as expected. This was a record real increase of about 13% since the last uprating, bringing pensions as a proportion of average earnings up to their previous highest, 1965, value. But unemployment and sickness benefits, and the ordinary supplementary benefit rate, were increased in real terms by only 3%; they were a lower proportion of average earnings than they had been in 1971.

Labour's commitment to link benefits to earnings in subsequent upratings was not a major break with past practice. Between 1951 and 1973 national insurance benefits, and supplementary benefit, had increased roughly in line with earnings. Benefits for a single person (benefits for couples were about 60% higher) were about a fifth of male manual workers' average earnings. However, Conservative legislation only required benefits to be uprated after 1973 at least in line with price increases. This was a commitment to maintain, but not necessarily to increase, the real value of benefits as real earnings increased. Labour's commitment was therefore potentially more generous. In fact, Labour's 1974 legislation required long-term benefits to be increased in line with the greater of the increase in earnings or in prices, which was more generous than the manifesto commitment. But short-term benefits, despite the manifesto's suggestion of a link with earnings, were to be increased only in line with prices.

Prices rose by more than earnings in 1975–77, and so the fairly constant real values of benefits in that period were an increasing proportion of earnings. Earnings rose by more than prices in 1978, and so the gap between pensions and unemployment and sickness benefits, created by the Conservatives in 1973 and accentuated in Labour's 1974 uprating, increased to 24% (see Table 14.1).

Table 14.1   *Value of benefits 1971–78*

	Value in 1988 £			% of average earnings			RP/ USB	long-term/ ord. SB
	RP	USB	SB	RP	USB	SB		
Sept. 1971	30·89	30·89	27·20	17·5	17·5	16·9	1·00	1·09
Oct. 1973	33·46	31·74	28·33	17·5	16·6	16·1	1·05	1·14
July 1974	38·05	32·72	29·22	19·8	17·0	16·6	1·16	1·24
Apr. 1975	37·50	31·68	28·32	19·1	16·1	15·8	1·19	1·25
Nov. 1975	38·50	32·13	28·60	19·6	16·4	16·1	1·20	1·26
Nov. 1976	38·52	32·47	28·85	20·1	16·9	16·6	1·19	1·24
Nov. 1977	38·98	32·74	29·05	21·0	17·6	17·4	1·19	1·24
Nov. 1978	40·19	32·46	28·94	20·4	16·4	16·2	1·24	1·28

Note: Average earnings are of all men. RP: retirement pension, USB: unemployment and sickness benefits; SB: ordinary rate of supplementary benefit.
Source: Extracted from *Social Security Statistics*, 1988, Table 46.

This divergence between long- and short-term national insurance benefits was reflected in an increased divergence between the long-term and ordinary supplementary benefit rates.[3] By 1978 the long-term rate was 28% more than the ordinary rate. This was to protect pensioners claiming supplementary benefit, for it was not 'regarded as acceptable to increase supplementary pensions by less than the amount given to other pensioners' (DHSS, 1978, 14). The long-term unemployed were ineligible for the higher long-term supplementary benefit rates.

The different methods of uprating benefits therefore favoured certain categories of claimants. Pensions increased from 1973 to 1978 by 16% more than average earnings – by 20% in real terms. But unemployment and sickness benefit fell relative to average earnings, with a real increase of just over 2%.[4] Table 14.2 compares these changes, and the change in ordinary supplementary benefit, with those under preceding and succeeding governments. The outstanding feature is the increase in the value of pensions between 1973 and 1978.

Table 14.2   *Changes in values of benefits 1963–87*

		% change in real value			% change of proportion of average earnings		
		RP	*USB*	*SB*	*RP*	*USB*	*SB*
Labour	1963–69	15·3	15·1	18·9	−2	−4·31	0
Conservative	1969–73	11·6	5·9	8·1	−4	−9	−7·8
Labour	1973–78	20·11	2·3	2·2	16·1	−1·1	0·6
Conservative	1978–82	4·6	−1·4	5·9	6·3	0·6	4·5
Conservative	1982–87	−2·4	−2·4	−0·9	−10·1	−10·5	−11·8

Note: Benefit changes are between values at governments' last upratings. Average earnings are of male manual workers. Codes as for Table 14.1.
Source: Extracted from *Social Security Statistics*, 1988, Table 46.

1.1   *The State Earnings-Related Pensions Scheme*

Labour's 1974 manifestos proposed replacing the Conservatives' planned pension scheme, which had replaced the previous Labour government's plans, with another scheme. This was to provide increased pensions (in the future) related to past earnings, and fully protected against inflation. The State Earnings-Related Pensions Scheme (SERPS), presented in 1975, added an earnings-related pension to the basic flat-rate pension. Working-age people could 'contract out' of the additional component, and so pay lower contributions, by joining a private occupational pension scheme whose provisions were at least as good. The government undertook to supplement such private pensions, within limits, to protect their real value against inflation. The scheme as a whole, a compromise between previous proposals, was supported by the Conservatives.

Existing pensioners were unaffected. The supplement to the basic state pension was aimed at that half of the working population not already included in private schemes offering an occupational pension. It was intended to be redistributive. Pensions would be a higher proportion of earnings for those with lower than average earnings in the 20 'best years' of their working lives, and proportionally lower for those with higher than average earnings. The provision for contracting out, and other aspects of the scheme, made it difficult to estimate its likely redistributive effects. Introduced in 1978, the SERPS was to be fully operative by the turn of the century.

1.2 *New benefits*

Increasing existing benefits was the first priority in the February manifesto. The October manifesto reaffirmed the next priorities: to introduce new benefits to help families in poverty, and to increase the help given to disabled people.

Families had been helped by a combination of family allowances for children, except the first, and child tax allowances (of no value to parents with incomes below the tax threshold, of greatest value to those with the highest incomes). Family allowances were not increased in 1974, but remained at their 1969 rates. The increase in child tax allowances in the April 1974 budget left the real value of child support (for one- and three-child families) below its 1971 level and 28% below its 1952 peak, since when it had fallen by over 60% as a proportion of average earnings.

The manifesto had proposed to 'attack family poverty' by replacing the existing child support system with a new non-means-tested, tax-free, child benefit for all children, payable to mothers. This new benefit had all-party support, but it was indefinitely postponed in 1976, when the extension of family allowances in 1977 to the first child was announced. The government was concerned about the possible consequences for its incomes policy of reducing take-home pay by removing child tax allowances. Hostile reaction to the postponement led to the establishment of a TUC/Labour Party Liaison Committee working party which produced the child benefit scheme put into place in 1979, when child tax allowances were discontinued. The value of child support, in relation to average earnings, was then higher than it had been at any time in the 1970s, but lower than it had been in the 1960s. The October 1974 manifesto had added: 'We are also examining other ways of helping one-parent families', but little came of the examination.[5]

The non-contributory invalidity pension, paid from 1975, was for working-age people with insufficient national insurance contributions to qualify for invalidity benefit, introduced by the Conservatives in 1971 for those still unable to work after six months' receipt of sickness benefit.

A non-contributory attendance allowance for the disabled had also been introduced in 1971. In 1976 the Labour government introduced the invalid care allowance for those, except for married women, whose care for a severely disabled relative prevented them working and making national insurance contributions. The non-contributory invalidity pension and the invalid care allowance were both set well below normal long-term rates, and most recipients of them were no better off because their entitlements to supplementary benefit were reduced by an equivalent amount. A mobility allowance for those who could not walk was also introduced in 1976. The manifesto commitments to introduce new benefits for the disabled, and for families with children, had all been fulfilled by 1979.

1.3 Social security expenditure growth

The public expenditure cuts in 1976/77 and 1977/78 did not extend to the social security programme. It grew by an average of just under 6% a year – about three times faster than total public expenditure programmes. Table 14.3 shows the main features of this large increase. Some of the growth in expenditure on the family reflected the change from child tax allowances to child benefit. About half of the growth in total social security expenditure went to the elderly.

Table 14.3 *Increases in social security expenditure 1973/74 to 1978/79*

Expenditure on	Elderly	Family	Unemployed	Disabled and long-term sick	All social security
% increase 1973/74 to 1978/79	26·9	67·5	91·3	47·1	32·8
Increase as % of total rise in social security expenditure	46·4	20·8	16·6	14·8	(100)

Note: Expenditure is measured at 1978 survey prices.
Source: *The Government's Expenditure Plans 1979/80 to 1982/83*, Cmnd. 7439, pp. 148–53.

2 Poverty

The changes in benefits outlined above can be considered in the light of evidence on the prevalence of poverty commissioned by the Royal Commission on the Distribution of Income and Wealth (set up by the Labour government in August 1974).

One commissioned study, based on the 1975 General Household Survey, defined a poor family as one whose annual net income less housing costs was below 140% of its long-term supplementary benefit entitlement (Layard *et al.*, 1978).[6] Most of the 29% of families who were poor were elderly.

Two-thirds of all elderly families were poor, as were four-fifths of those without an occupational pension and not working. These data suggest that the government's concern to improve the state pension scheme for those without occupational pensions was well founded, and that the priority given to increasing pensions could be justified since most help was given to the largest group of poor families. Although 87% of non-working one-parent families were poor, one-parent families were only 6% of all poor families. Almost three-quarters of couples with more than two children, where the wife was not working (in paid employment!) and the husband had worked for less than 40 weeks in the year, were poor; but all families where the husband had worked for less than 40 weeks constituted just 8% of the poor in 1975. Half of the couples with a disabled man were poor, constituting 2% of all poor families.

Another study of poverty, based on the Family Expenditure Survey, investigated the depth of poverty suffered by poor families (Beckerman, 1979). The 'poverty line' chosen was the appropriate supplementary benefit scale rate for each family type, and the income measured was net disposable normal income less housing costs.[7] Defining poverty in that way, 4·4% of families (1·1m. families containing 1·74m. individuals) were poor in 1975. The 'poverty gap', the amount by which they fell short of the poverty line, totalled £248·5m. (0·25% of GDP). Subtracting benefits from incomes would have brought 30·6% of families (7·65m. families including 12·1m. individuals) below the poverty line; and the poverty gap would have been £5855m. (5·8% of GDP). The direct effect of social security benefits was therefore to reduce the numbers in poverty by 86% and the poverty gap by 96%. This appears to be an impressive reduction of poverty (although it is overstated to the extent that a lost of benefit would lead, in some cases at least, to an increase in the income from other sources of those who lost the benefit). However, the success of the system in reducing poverty varied considerably for different types of poor families.

Of the family types shown in Table 14.4, most poor families were over pension age and single-parent families constituted the smallest group of the poor. But the elderly families, on average, fell short of the poverty line each week by only £1·36 per adult equivalent,[8] whereas the poverty gap for single-parent families was £7·12. With a limited budget, there is apparently some choice between lifting as many families as possible above the poverty line, and helping those who have fallen furthest below it. These data suggest that the government's policies after 1975 were misdirected, if its intention was to help those in greatest poverty. A similar conclusion mgiht be drawn from the results of a subsequent investigation by Beckerman and Clark (1982) comparing the effects of increasing pensions or unemployment benefits by £100m. in the years 1974–76. Increasing pensions would have reduced the number of households in poverty by 56,000; increasing unemployment benefits would have reduced the number by only 19,000.

Table 14.4 *Poverty in 1975*

| | Before benefits | | After benefits | | Weekly poverty gap per |
	% of total poor	% of total poverty gap	% of total poor	% of total poverty gap	adult equivalent before benefits & after
Over pension age	71·0	70·9	54·7	23·2	£10·47	£1·36
Under pension age	29·0	29·1	45·3	76·8	£9·62	£4·73
Single adults						
No children	13·8	10·3	23·6	30·2	£10·53	£5·53
With children	5·1	6·1	4·2	11·3	£10·92	£7·12
Couples						
No children	3·8	4·2	5·5	9·4	£9·87	£4·58
With children	6·3	8·6	12·0	26·0	£7·76	£3·64
No. of poor families	7·65m		1·1m			
Poverty gap		£5855m		£248·5m		

Source: Extracted from Beckerman, 1979, Tables 3 and 4.

But when attention is directed to the depth of poverty, this outcome is reversed. Increasing pensions would have reduced the poverty gap by only £8m.; increasing unemployment benefit would have reduced it by £17m., more than twice as much.

2.1 *Means-tested benefits*
The poverty gaps discussed above are evidence that the supplementary benefits to which many families were entitled were not received, and raise the problem of the effectiveness of means-tested benefits. Over 20% of those eligible did not claim supplementary benefit during the 1970s; the estimated amount unclaimed in 1975 was about £240m. (Atkinson, 1989, p. 209). There are several reasons why means-tested benefits are not claimed, including ignorance of entitlement, the costs of claiming them − particularly when these costs are high in relation to the entitlement − and the stigma attached to their receipt. For whatever reasons, supplementary benefit was ineffective in helping a fifth of those families it was intended to help. This provides an argument against reliance on means-tested benefits for poverty relief.

Nevertheless, means-tested benefits are effective in the sense that they do not go to those who are judged to be not poor. The receipt of non-means-tested benefits is often sufficient to raise the families claiming them, and who would be poor without them, well above the poverty line. But Beckerman found that, in 1975, 17% of total benefits (including those not means-tested) went to families who would not have been poor if they had not received them. The proportion going to such non-poor families varied considerably between different benefits, from 5% of pensions to 62% of unemployment and sickness benefits and, most of all, 82% of family allowances and family income supplement. By definition, supplementary benefit goes to poor families only. Despite the hostility to means-tested benefits expressed in Labour's manifesto, the number of supplementary benefit recipients increased by about a tenth between 1973 and 1978.

Some of the trends which might have been expected in the light of the developments which have been sketched out above are shown in Table 14.5. The number of pensioners receiving supplementary benefit fell sharply in 1975, after the large increase in pensions in 1974, and then tended to rise in subsequent years; the number claiming in 1978 was 6% less than in 1973. The numbers of sick and disabled people receiving supplementary benefit steadily fell by over 20% over the five-year period, due to the fall in the numbers receiving contributory benefits in addition to supplementary benefits. But the increase in other groups more than offset these reductions. The number of single-parent recipients rose by about 100,000, an increase of over 40%. Unemployed families depending on supplementary benefit were consigned to the ordinary rate, 25% lower than the long-term rate in 1978 and with a real value almost the same as five years earlier. Their number increased by about 350,000 − two and a half times greater in 1978 than it had been in 1973. The manifesto commitments in relation to benefits were fulfilled with mixed success.

Table 14.5   *Recipients of regular supplementary benefit weekly payments (in thousands)*

	All	Pensioners	Unemployed	Sick/disabled	Lone parents
1973 (Nov.)	2680	1840	249	280	228
1975 (Nov.)	2790	1680	541	242	276
1978 (Nov.)	2930	1730	598	220	322
1987 (May)	4900	1730	1957	352	629

Source: *Social Security Statistics*, 1988, Table 34.30.

2.2   *Conflicting objectives?*

The relief of poverty is unlikely to be the only goal of social security policy. There may also be concern about its effects on people's behaviour; a desire to discourage the formation of single-parent families, and a fear of disincentive effects of unemployment benefit, for example. The possible conflict between different goals makes the assessment of policy in the light of only one of them inappropriate. It is interesting to note, however, that research undertaken for the DHSS 1978 review of supplementary benefits could find no justification in the needs of the claimants concerned for the difference between the ordinary and long-term rates (Supplementary Benefits

Commission, 1979, p.28), and that Nickell (1979) found that an increase in benefits for the long-term unemployed would involve negligible losses due to any disincentive effect. Atkinson *et al.* (1984), using 1972–77 data, demonstrated the difficulty of establishing any significant effect of benefits on the unemployment of other groups.

3 Taxes

In his first Budget Statement, Denis Healey spoke of the Labour government's aim to effect a 'deliberate and carefully considered redistribution of fiscal burdens so as to help those least able to bear them and place them on the shoulders of the better off' (Healey, 1974). Changes in income tax were particularly important for this objective.

When Labour came to office the highest marginal rate of tax on earned incomes was 75%, and there was a surcharge of 15% on investment income over £2000. The highest marginal rate of tax on investment income was therefore 90%, and this increased to 98% when the top rate on earnings rose to 83% in Labour's first Budget. A reluctance to impose a marginal rate of 100% on investment incomes probably explains the exemption of the 83% rate from the increase of 2 percentage points imposed on the nine other marginal rates on earnings in April 1975. The top rates of 83% and 15% surcharge remained unchanged throughout the period of the Labour government, but they (and the other marginal rates) were applied to lower bands of real income in 1978/79 than in 1973/74, as nominal tax brackets were increased by less than inflation (see Table 14.6).

Inflation also reduced the real value of tax thresholds; the single person's allowance fell by over a quarter between 1973/74 and 1976/77. A back-benchers' amendment to the 1977 Finance Bill required the real value of the allowance to be maintained in the absence of legislation to the contrary. Its real value increased in 1977/78 but fell again in 1978/79 to less than 80% of its 1973/74 level. This fall was, however, quite modest when compared to the fall in the real value of taxable incomes liable to some of the higher marginal rates, as Table 14.6 shows. Liability to the 70% rate began in 1978/79 at a taxable income which was little over half of its 1973/74 level.

The falls in the real value of the tax threshold and of income tax bands were exceeded by their falls in relation to earnings, continuing a long-run trend. In 1973/74 the personal allowance for a single person was just over a quarter of average earnings, only a little less than it had been in 1952/53. But the allowance for a married man had fallen by about three-quarters, relative to earnings, to under a half of average earnings. The fall in the value of child support, mentioned above in connection with benefits, was largely the result of the fall in the value of child tax allowances. In the twenty years after 1952/53, the tax threshold for a family with four children

Table 14.6   *Marginal rates of income tax 1973/74 to 1978/79*

Real value (1973/74 £) of slices of taxable income above which the marginal rates shown applied

| 1973/74 | | 1974/75 | | 1975/76 | | 1876/77 | | 1977/78 | | 1978/79 | |
£	%	£	%	£	%	£	%	£	%	£	%
										0	25
0	30	0	33	0	35	0	35	0	34	359	33
5000	40	3817	38	3061	40	2952	40	3106	40	3824	40
6000	45	4241	43	3402	45	3247	45	3624	45	4301	45
7000	50	5089	48	4082	50	3838	50	4142	50	4779	50
8000	55	5937	53	4762	55	4428	55	4660	55	5257	55
10000	60	6785	58	5442	60	5019	60	5177	60	5974	60
12000	65	8482	63	6803	65	5904	65	6213	65	6691	65
15000	70	10178	68	8164	70	7085	70	7248	70	7647	70
20000	75	12722	73	10205	75	8856	75	8284	75	8842	75
		16963	83	13606	83	11808	83	10873	83	11471	83

Real value of single person's allowance:

£595	£530	£459	£434	£489	£471

Source: *Annual Abstract of Statistics*, 116, 1980, Table 16.20 and RPI.

fell from 111% to 60% of average earnings. The relative values of the thresholds fell further between 1973/74 and 1978/79.[9]

An important consequence of the fall in the value of tax thresholds, widely discussed by the early 1970s, was that people whose low incomes qualified them for means-tested benefits were also liable to income tax. The combination of increasing tax liabilities and the withdrawal of those benefits as incomes rose meant that the highest implicit marginal income tax rates, which could exceed 100%, were to be found at certain bands of low rather than very high incomes. Although the number of people in this 'poverty trap' was not large, it seems likely to have been greater than the number of those facing the highest rate at the other end of the income scale. In 1978/79, only one and a half in a thousand income tax payers were liable to pay the highest marginal rate of 83% on earned income, and less than 3·3% paid more than the basic rate of 33% (Board of Inland Revenue, 1981, Table 16).

The proportion of income paid in tax depends on the average rate of tax. Table 14.7 shows the average rate schedule on earned incomes for single people in 1973/74 and 1978/79. Income tax became payable at just over a fifth, rather than a quarter, of average earnings, and the average tax rate increased at each of the other levels of earnings shown. At half average earnings the average rate increased by 20%; the increase was less for those

Table 14.7   *Income tax: average rates (single persons)*

| | *Multiple of average earnings:* | | | | | | | | | | | |
	0·25	0·5	1	2	3	4	5	6	7	8	9	10
1973/74	0	14·2	22·1	26	29·2	34·2	38·6	43	45·8	48·8	51·2	53·5
1978/79	4·6	17	25	29·5	37	44·5	50·5	56	59·6	62·5	64·8	66·6
% increase		20	13	13	27	30	31	30	30	28	27	24
(1988/89	5·3	15	20	25·1	30	32·6	34	35	35·7	36·3	36·7	37)

Source: *Annual Abstract of Statistics*, 1980, Table 16.20; and *Inland Revenue Statistics*, 1988, App. C.

with average and twice average earnings. Thereafter, the increases were greater, reaching 31% at five times average earnings and falling back to 24% at ten times.

However, Table 14.7 gives little guidance to the amount of income tax paid in practice. Other family types had higher allowances than the single person, and various deductions from total income may be made before taxable income is calculated. These deductions included the premiums for life insurance and pensions, and the interest payable on mortgages (all of which increase with income) as well as national insurance benefits. Nor was income tax the only tax levied on earned incomes, if national insurance contributions are considered to be a tax. Flat-rate contributions were replaced from 1975 by contributions linked to earnings, so that those who earned more (between certain limits) also paid more.

There were changes in other taxes too, and these were often designed to have a relatively favourable effect on the poor. VAT was reduced from 10% to 8% in 1974 in the effort to reduce price rises. It was raised later in the year to 25% for petrol; and in the following year the 25% rate was applied to items considered to be not essential, such as domestic refrigerators, or to be luxuries, such as furs and jewellery. In 1976 these higher rates were halved. Although VAT, like other taxes on expenditure, is not directly related to incomes, it is indirectly related through the different amounts and patterns of expenditure of different income groups. It is not easy to assess the effects on those different income groups of all the changes in direct and indirect taxation introduced by the Labour government, only some of which have been mentioned here. Ideally, the actual effects of the 1978/79 tax structure should be compared with those which the 1973/74 structure, suitably uprated, would have had in 1978/79. This ideal comparison has not been made. However, available evidence, particularly data published by the Central Statistical Office (CSO) on the effects of taxes and benefits on households' incomes, will be examined below.

4 Tax progressivity

The CSO's studies are based on the Family Expenditure Survey. There is a substantial degree of non-response to the FES, increasing with the age of the household head, and greater for households without children, for example. It seems to under-represent the top 1% of households, and investment and self-employment incomes are understated. However, it compares well with other surveys, and its deficiencies as a reliable source of information on households' incomes seem sometimes to have been exaggerated (Atkinson and Mickelwright, 1983).

The CSO assumes that taxes on expenditure fall entirely on consumers, by being added in full to the prices of the goods and services on which they are imposed. Direct taxes are assumed to result only in a reduction of the incomes of those obliged to pay them. Taxes whose incidence is particularly uncertain (eg. corporation tax) are not allocated to households. The CSO's studies for 1973 and 1978 each allocated about 75% of general government tax revenue to households.

The CSO's comparison of the effects of taxes and benefits in 1978 and 1973, the last full years of the Labour government and of its Conservative predecessor, groups the households surveyed in the FES into deciles, according to their incomes. When households are ranked according to their original incomes (i.e. incomes less direct cash benefits) their ranking corresponds to the number of adults in them and, even more markedly for all except the top decile, to the number of workers in them. The variation in household size and composition could be taken into account, at least roughly, by considering incomes per adult equivalent (as in Table 14.4 above) but such an analysis has not been made for 1973 and 1978. The problem raised by different household sizes, when comparing different deciles in the same year, is reduced when the objective is to compare the same decile in different years, and that is the objective here. Nevertheless, the assumptions and problems referred to above need to be kept in mind when considering the CSO's data.

Total tax payments as a proportion of households' gross incomes in 1973 and 1978 are shown in Table 14.8, with households ranked in quintiles according to their original income, and then by their disposable income.[10] Ranked in either way, the proportion of gross income paid in tax declined for the lowest quintile (and also for the next lowest when households are ranked according to their original income). The proportion paid by households with higher incomes was greater in 1978 than in 1973, and the increases in those proportions were greater, the higher the gross income. When examined by deciles the pattern is not so neat, mainly because of the increase in tax paid by households in the lowest decile as a result of the reduction of income tax thresholds. This increase might be considered to be particularly significant in judging whether the changed patter of tax payments showed an improvement. But the pattern between quintile suggests that, in comparison

Table 14.8   *Gross household income (current £) and total tax paid (%), 1973–78*

Households ranked by	Quintile									
	1		2		3		4		5	
	£	%	£	%	£	%	£	%	£	%
(a) original income:										
1973	1466	21·4	3065	30·7	4584	33·0	6133	33·0	10301	33·9
1978	3429	20·5	6309	29·4	9893	34·5	13523	35·4	21793	36·4
% change in tax rate		−3·98		−4·28		4·72		6·75		7·22
(b) disposable income:										
1973	1205	29·7	3087	32·5	4629	33·4	6168	32·6	10259	31·0
1978	3259	26·0	6470	33·1	10032	35·3	13609	34·9	21578	34·3
% change in tax rate		−12·50		1·75		5·67		7·10		10·73

Source: Derived from CSO, 1980, Tables 3 and 4.

with 1973, the tax system in 1978 did increase, relatively, the proportion of tax paid by those households with higher incomes.

Another study, designed to measure changes in the overall progressivity of the tax system for various types of family, provides a check on the CSO's results relating to deciles containing heterogeneous households. In this second study (Dilnot *et al.*, 1984) linear tax schedules were estimated for four family types. These schedules combine a constant marginal tax rate at all levels of income considered with a 'tax credit' which is set against the implied tax liability. These estimates take advantage of the fact that the marginal income tax rate of very few taxpayers in the UK exceeded the basic rate. The few for whom it did were excluded from the analysis, as were taxes on capital and corporation tax. Taxes not directly related to income, such as VAT, are related to it via an estimated linear relationship between income and expenditure on the taxed goods and services. Two different measures of tax progressivity were computed, and some of the results are reproduced in Table 14.9. For each household type considered, and on both measures, the tax system was more progressive in 1978 than in 1973.

5   The impact of incomes policies

Whatever success there was in redistributing the tax burden to the better-off has to be seen in the context of other developments affecting the distribution of incomes. The effects of the changes in benefits have to be considered, of course, and so do the effects of other changes to which the government's policies may have contributed. In particular, the government's incomes policy, designed primarily to restrain wage and salary increases,

Table 14.9   *Changes in tax progressivity 1968–82*

	Single	*Couples: wife working*	*Couples: wife not working*	*Couples: wife not working with 2 children*
1968	1·009 (1·006)	1·144 (1·097)	0·911 (0·925)	0·944 (0·920)
1973	0·940 (0·941)	0·908 (0·897)	0·883 (0·872)	0·877 (0·776)
1978	0·887 (0·904)	0·794 (0·771)	0·826 (0·833)	0·778 (0·615)
1982	0·901 (0·930)	0·824 (0·842)	0·830 (0·863)	0·750 (0·584)

Note: Lower values in this table indicate greater progressivity. The first value in each column shows the residual income progression (the ratio of the percentage change in income after tax to the percentage change in income before tax). The bracketed values show the reciprocal of the liability progression (the ratio of the percentage change in the tax liability to the percentage change in income before tax).
Source: Extracted from Dilnot *et al.* (1984) Table 7.

had at times the secondary objective of improving the relative position of the less well paid.

In 1974 the TUC had renewed its call for a national minimum wage of two-thirds of average male hourly earnings. The desirability of a minimum wage had been investigated by the previous Labour government. Barbara Castle, the Secretary of State for Employment and Productivity, described an interdepartmental report on the issue as 'the basis for a more informed discussion' (Department of Employment and Productivity, 1969, p. iii). One of the report's conclusions was that a national minimum wage would be less effective than selective social security benefits in the relief of poverty (ibid., p. 51). This conclusion was reinforced by Layard *et al.* (1978) who noted the lack of substantial overlap between low pay and poverty. They found that only one in five workers in the lowest decile of hourly earnings was also in the bottom decile of family incomes. And of workers in the bottom decile of family incomes, only one in five was in the bottom decile of earnings (Layard *et al.*, 1978, p. 24). However, an attempt to redistribute earnings towards the low-paid was made in the first two phases of incomes policy, from 1975 to 1977.

Shortly after the apparent failure of the 'Social Contract' to reduce wage increases in 1974/75, and Denis Healey's description of the 1975 Budget's income tax increases as 'an anti-inflationary surcharge' (15 March 1975, col. 317), Jack Jones proposed the introduction of an incomes policy allowing a maximum lump-sum (rather than a maximum percentage) increase in earnings. This proposal attracted some opposition, partly because it was seen to be a way of reducing wage differentials and favouring the low-paid, but it was adopted by the TUC which agreed Stage One of the pay policy with the government in July 1975. Those earning over £8500 a year were to have no increase at all in the year up to August 1976, and the increase for other employees was not to exceed £6 per week. Stage Two of the policy also had equalising elements. It was designed to reduce the overall increase in earnings from the 10% intended in Stage One to 5% for the year up to July 1977. Those earning between £50 and £80 a week (very roughly, between the lower and upper quartiles of all men's earnings) were to be allowed an increase of 5%. But those earning less than £50 were to be allowed more than 5% (a maximum weekly increase of £2·50) whereas those earning more than £80 were to get less than 5% (a maximum £4). Stages One and Two were directed at individuals' earnings, and had a potentially equalising impact on them. The following phases of the policy were directed at the earnings of bargaining groups, and it was hoped to keep the rise in overall earnings to a maximum of 10% in Stage Three, in the year up to July 1978, and to 5% in the following year.

Table 14.10 provides some information on the dispersion of men's gross weekly earnings during this period. The data relate to April of each year, and so do not correspond precisely to the phases of incomes policy outlined above; but between 1975 and 1977 there was some improvement in the relative pay of the bottom decile. This was reversed in the following years, so that the relative position of the bottom decile in 1978 appears just the same as it had been in 1974. The exception to this apparent stability in the distribution of men's earnings is at the highest decile of non-manual men. Their earnings fell from 175% of median non-manual men's earnings in 1970 to 167% in 1975 and to 163% in 1979. This fall could be associated with an increasing importance of non-pecuniary returns to the highest-paid over this period. The possible effects of incomes policy are only one of the determinants of relative earnings, and the efforts of researchers to identify the effects of the Labour government's apparently equalising incomes policies on the distribution of earnings have generally led to conclusions such as those of Elliott and Fallick (1981, p.260): 'The impact of incomes policies on the distribution of earned income is both uncertain and short-lived'.

6 Conclusion: the overall redistribution of incomes

Four-fifths of households' original incomes (before benefits and taxes) came from wages and salaries in 1973. Income from self-employment and from investments − rent, dividends, and interest, which go mostly to richer households − were about 12% and 8% of households' original incomes, and about 1 and 1·5 percentage points lower in 1978, when wages and salaries were about 82·5% of the total. These changes might have been expected to decrease the inequality of household incomes. However, other effects on the distribution of original incomes, including the rise

Table 14.10   *Dispersion of all men's gross weekly earnings*

	Median (£)	Percentage of median			
		Lowest decile	Lower quartile	Upper quartile	Highest decile
1973	£38·4	65·6	79·9	125·3	158·5
1974	£43·8	66·8	80·7	124·6	157·0
1975	£55·9	67·0	81·0	125·3	157·6
1976	£65·8	67·6	81·3	125·6	159·5
1977	£72·3	68·1	81·4	125·6	157·7
1978	£82·0	66·8	80·6	125·1	157·9
1979	£93·9	66·0	80·3	125·1	156·9

Source: *New Earnings Survey*, 1980, Table 15.

in unemployment, led to a less favourable distribution in 1978. All of the gains in the share of original income between 1973 and 1978 were made by the deciles in the top half, and the relative losses in the bottom half were greater, the lower the decile, as Table 14.11 shows.

Table 14.11 also shows the percentage change between 1973 and 1978 in each decile's share of income after all cash benefits and taxes. (A similar pattern is revealed when households are ranked by their disposable incomes.) The relative change is most marked at the bottom deciles, where there were relatively large percentage gains. (The increase in tax paid by the bottom decile, noted above, is more than outweighed by the increase in benefits received.) The greatest proportional loss was in the top decile. This change in the distribution of households' incomes between 1973 and 1978 is apparently due to the greater redistributive effects of cash benefits and taxes in 1978, and suggests that the government's cash benefits and tax policies did succeed in redistributing incomes.

7   A concluding note on wealth

There are systematic surveys of income which allow estimates of the impact of a government's policies on the distribution of income; these were drawn upon in the studies reported above. There are no such comprehensive estimates in the case of wealth, but it is difficult to avoid the conclusion that the government was not successful in redistributing wealth as the manifesto had promised, and these few comments relate to that failure.

Capital transfer tax (CTT), a tax on the transfer of wealth, began to replace estate duty from 1975/76. The intention was to block the avoidance of estate duty which arose from the exemption of life-time gifts. However,

Table 14.11   *Changes in the distribution of household incomes, 1973·78*

Decile	1	2	3	4	5	6	7	8	9	10
										(ranked by original income)
(a) Percentage share of original income:										
1973	0·082	1·23	3·93	6·66	8·45	10·16	11·81	13·83	16·84	27·01
1978	0·048	0·96	3·23	6·14	8·40	10·34	12·24	14·54	17·65	25·46
% change	−42	−22	−18	−7·80	−0·63	1·80	3·59	5·15	4·79	−2·04
(b) Percentage share of income after all cash benefits and taxes:										
1973	2·92	3·77	5·44	6·87	8·17	9·63	10·9	12·8	15·3	24·2
1978	3·47	4·05	5·57	6·71	8·18	9·68	11·1	13·0	15·4	22·8
% change	18·90	7·54	2·41	−2·30	0·09	0·52	1·76	1·09	1·20	−5·70

Source: Derived from CSO, 1980, Table 3.

the exemptions from CTT were steadily increased, and the real value of revenue from both taxes combined steadily fell. The £369m. collected in 1978/79 was less than a half of what had been collected in 1973/74. The revenue from capital gains tax did increase in real terms. It was 9% higher in 1978/79 than in 1973/74, and it had been even higher in the first two years of the government. But this tax, levied at a maximum rate of 30% of net gains, provided a principal means of avoiding tax on investment incomes. The Bank of England was one of the institutions which offered this tax-avoiding opportunity. Low-interest stocks were issued, providing a very low income each year, but a large capital gain when they matured. This way of converting investment income into capital gain made the almost confiscatory 98% tax rates on the highest investment incomes quite illusory. It was only one of the many ways of avoiding high income tax rates, but it is sufficient to illustrate the importance of considering the tax system as a whole when changes in progressivity are desired. One of the main reasons why the Labour manifesto's commitment to introduce a wealth tax was abandoned was that its connection with other parts of the tax system had not been worked out. The problems involved in fundamentally reforming the base of the tax structure, which would be required to tax wealth effectively, were not addressed by the Labour government.

The establishment of a Royal Commission on the Distribution of Income and Wealth was a potentially valuable innovation, but it did not investigate these problems. More generally, the Commission made no policy recommendations, and seems to have had no effect on the government's policies. It did publish a great deal of information. One of the first acts of the 1979 Conservative government was to abolish it.

Notes

1 An investigation of the 1964–70 period concluded that an improvement in the distribution of income was one of the Labour Government's main achievements – though, ironically, one that has received very little recognition from many of Labour's own supporters' (Stewart 1972, p. 111). Bosanquet and Townsend (1980, p. 1) remained critical of the record of 1964–70 and 1974–79.

2 Apart from a reference to incomes policies, the redistributive effects of other policies and changes in the provision of benefits in kind, such as the fairer distribution of resources between NHS regions resulting from the formual developed by the Resource Allocation Working Party in 1976, are not discussed here.

3 Supplementary benefit was available to those not in work whose income and other resources fell below a prescribed amount. The long-term rate was introduced in 1973 to incorporate the long-term addition, payable since 1967 to all claimants over pensionable age or claimants (except for the unemployed) who had been receiving supplementary benefit for two years or more. This addition recognised the greater needs, relative to resources, of long-term claimants previously met by discretionary payments.

4 Some of the unemployed also received an earnings related supplement. In November 1978 156,000 men received an average £9·34 and 53,000 women an average £6·49.

5 The married man's income tax allowance was given to single parents in 1975; there was a child interim benefit of £1·50 for the first child in 1976, and from 1977 a 50% addition to the child benefit paid for the first child, which resulted in an equivalent reduction in the entitlement of those claiming supplementary benefit; and, in 1979, the number of hours worked to be eligible for FIS was reduced from 30 to 24 hours.

6 All such studies require decisions on method. In particular, a measurable income concept must be chosen, and a 'poverty line' selected to separate those with lower incomes (the poor) from those with higher incomes (the non-poor). In this case, net annual income includes earned and unearned income, occupational and state pensions, all other state cash benefits, imputed rent minus gross mortgage interest, and rent and rate rebates, *less* income tax and NIC. Housing costs (rent, imputed rent, and rates) were deducted because supplementary benefit recipients received housing costs in addition to the scale rates. 'Family' means parent(s) and dependent children.

7 Normal income covers cases where the current income of those out of work for less than 13 weeks is considered to be less than normal.

8 For example, the addition of 62% to the single householder's supplementary benefit rate for a spouse, and 29% for a child aged 0–5, implies that a couple with a child of 2 were reckoned as 1·92 'adult equivalents'.

9 The single person's allowance fell from 26·4% to 20·4% of average earnings, the married man's from 34·3% to 31·8%.

10 The ranking of households will be somewhat different, depending on whether they are ranked by their original incomes, their gross incomes (including cash benefits), or by their disposable incomes (incomes after direct taxes have been paid), as the relative positions of individual households change. In the 1973/1978 comparison, the CSO ranked households first by original income, and then by disposable income.

References

Atkinson, A. B. (1989), *Poverty and Social Security*, Harvester Wheatsheaf, London.

Atkinson, A. B., and Mickelwright, J. (1983), 'On the reliability of the income data in the Family Expenditure Survey 1970–1977', *Journal of the Royal Statistical Society*, CXLVI, pp. 33–61.

Atkinson, A. B., Gomulka, J., Mickelwright, J., and Rau, N. (1984), 'Unemployment benefit, duration and incentives in Britain. How robust is the evidence?', *Journal of Public Economics*, XXIII, reprinted in Atkinson (1989), pp. 159–80.

Beckerman, W. (ed.) (1972), *The Labour Government's Economic Record: 1964–1970*, Duckworth, London.

Beckerman, W. (1979), 'The impact of income maintenance payments on poverty in Britain, 1975', *Economic Journal*, LXXXIX, pp. 261–79.

Beckerman, W., and Clark, S. (1982), *Poverty and Social Security in Britain since 1961*, Oxford University Press, Oxford.

Board of Inland Revenue (1981), *The Survey of Personal Incomes 1978–79*, HMSO, London.

Board of Inland Revenue (1988), *Inland Revenue Statistics 1988*, HMSO, London.

Bosanquet, N., and Townsend, P. (eds) (1980), *Labour and Equality*, Heinemann, London.

Central Statistical Office (1980), 'The effects of taxes and benefits on household income, 1978', *Economic Trends*, CCCXV, pp. 99–130.

Department of Employment and Productivity (1969), *A National Minimum Wage*, HMSO, London.

DHSS (1978), *Social Assistance. A Review of the Supplementary Benefit Scheme in Great Britain*, HMSO, London.

DHSS (1988), *Social Security Statistics 1988*, HMSO, London.

Dilnot, A. W., Kay, J. A., and Morris, C. N. (1984), 'The UK tax system, structure and progressivity, 1948–1982', *Scandinavian Journal of Economics*, LXXXVI, pp. 150–65.

Elliott, R. F., and Fallick, J. L. (1981), 'Incomes policies, inflation, and relative pay an overview', in J. L. Fallick and R. F. Elliott (eds), *Incomes Policies, Inflation and Relative Pay*, Allen & Unwin, London.

Healey, D. (1974), House of Commons Debates (Hansard), 26 March, col. 295.

Labour Party (1974), *Let Us Work Together*, reprinted in *The Times Guide to the House of Commons. February 1974*, pp. 305–11, Times Newspapers, London.

Layard, R., Piachaud, D., and Stewart, M. (1978), *The Causes of Poverty. Royal Commission on the Distribution of Income and Wealth Background Paper no. 5*, HMSO, London.

Nickell, S. J. (1979), 'The effect of unemployment and related benefits on the duration of unemployment', *Economic Journal*, LXXXIX, pp. 34–49.

Stewart, M. (1972), 'The distribution of income' in Beckeman (1972), pp. 75–117.

Supplementary Benefits Commission (1979), *Response of the Supplementary Benefits Commission to Social Assistance. A Review of the Supplementary Benefit Scheme in Great Britain* SBA Paper no. 9, HMSO, London.

15   *John Bowers*

Regional policy

This chapter is concerned with regional policy as conventionally defined to encompass the set of incentives and controls on the location of investment and employment within Great Britain. Almost every element of public expenditure and most fiscal instruments can be considered to have a differential regional impact and it is possible to argue that the Labour governments of the 1970s were aware of this and that therefore a commitment to regional development affected decisions taken over a wide range of policy making. Whether this was in fact so will not be established until government papers are available for inspection, but in any case it does not feature in this chapter. We have drawn the boundaries very narrowly, excluding both industry-specific aid where the regional element was very important (e.g. aid to shipbuilding) and also economic development in Northern Ireland. Policy was separately administered in the province and subjected to separate legislation. Ulster was a problem for governments of the 1970s and the 'Troubles' obviously had an economic dimension but it was not merely a regional problem nor in the sense that the term is used here, primarily so.

1   The policy framework

The regional policy framework operated by the Labour government at the end of the 1960s comprised five major elements:

(i)   an employment subsidy, the Regional Employment Premium (REP);
(ii)   powers to build factories and industrial estates in assisted areas for sale or rent with associated powers to undertake environmental improvements (e.g. the clearance of derelict land) in order to attract industry to those areas;
(iii)   controls on location decisions through the administration of Industrial Development Certificates (IDCs);

(iv) automatic subsidies for investment in assisted areas in the form of differential investment grants; and

(v) discretionary financial assistance given in a variety of forms of soft loans and grants.

This regional policy was directed at raising economic activity in three categories of assisted areas: Intermediate Areas, Development Areas and Special Development Areas. The two former categories were distinguished primarily by levels of unemployment (see Fig. 15.1). While current unemployment was also a factor in defining Special Development Areas, anticipated unemployment arising from heavy dependence on the declining industries of coal and shipbuilding was the major factor.

While the Heath government had started by attacking this policy

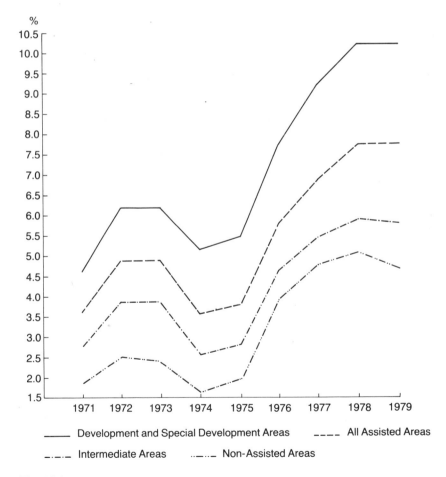

———— Development and Special Development Areas ＿ ＿ ＿ ＿ All Assisted Areas

＿.＿.＿ Intermediate Areas   ...＿... Non-Assisted Areas

Fig. 15.1.

framework, rising unemployment caused a change of mind. As a result the regional policy framework inherited by the Labour government in 1974 was similar to and in some respects stronger than that of the late 1960s. REP had survived although the real value of payments had been eroded by inflation and it was under threat of termination. Powers to finance the provision of advance factories and clean up industrial dereliction under the Local Employment Act 1972 were essentially identical to powers under previous Acts. The requirement for an IDC for investment in assisted areas had been abolished. However, since the granting of a certificate had previously been more or less automatic this was arguably a change of no consequence. Outside assisted areas the exemption limit for IDC control had been raised in 1972 to 15,000 ft^2 floorspace except in the South-East where it was raised to 10,000 ft^2.

The investment incentives in existence in 1974 were authorised under the Industry Act 1972. The automatic element was the Regional Development Grant (RDG), the discretionary element being known generally as Regional Selective Assistance (RSA).

Investment in Manufacturing, Mining and Quarrying, and Construction qualified for RDG at a rate of 20% (22% in Special Development Areas). Receipt of RDG did not reduce the volume of capital expenditure qualifying for tax allowances. Unlike the Investment Grants of the late 1960s there was no differentiation by type of expenditure − although mining works and purchases of vehicles other than mobile machinery were excluded.

Comparison of the strength of regional incentives in 1974 with those in operation in the late 1960s is made difficult by the different incentive packages in both assisted and non-assisted areas. Using a 10% discount rate Melliss and Richardson (1976) found slightly lower differences between assisted and non-assisted areas in discounted cash flow for a building project but a substantially higher differential for plant and machinery − implying a higher differential for a 'typical' mixed project. However, at the same discount rate the ratio of gross to net-of-tax-and-grant yields in development areas in 1974 were lower than in the late 1960s for both industrial buildings and plant and machinery. The Heath reforms thus provided somewhat lower incentives to capital investment overall but a stronger inducement to locate that investment in assisted areas. In the light of the conclusions of academic studies of regional policy in the 1960s: that it worked in shifting investment but in the process created a bias towards capital intensity, this might be seen as a sensible reform − though whether it was so by intention is unclear.

RSA was available under Section 7 of the Industry Act. There were two categories of qualifying projects. In category 'A' came new projects and expansions which created additional employment; in category 'B' came projects which, while creating no new jobs, maintained or safeguarded existing employment. Category 'A' projects qualified for loans at dis-cretionary rates, including interest-free periods or alternatively interest relief grants. The authorities had the option of providing assistance in the form of share capital. For a move to an assisted area a grant of up to 80% of removal costs, including statutory redundancy payments, could be paid. A removal grant could also be paid to service industries moving to an assisted area, provided that move created additional employment and was not serving a purely local market. For category 'B' projects, loans at commercial rates of interest or share capital were the only available options. Service industries also qualified under this category provided they were not serving purely local needs.

While RSA was similar in form to that available under previous legislation it was considerably broader in scope. 'The powers are wider in that they enable the Secretary of State to give assistance in virtually any form and in virtually any circumstances where the assistance is likely to provide, maintain or safeguard employment in the Assisted Areas' (Field and Hills, 1976). Specific innovations were the abandonment of any strict employment creation rule, the extension of the assistance to mobile service industries, and the introduction of Interest Relief Grants which permitted the Department of Industry to give the equivalent of a concessionary loan with less call on the public purse and with fewer stringent safeguards on public money.

Thus in March 1974 the incoming Labour government inherited a fairly strong basic framework for regional policy. At the end of April the Minister for Industry made the following House of Commons statement:

One of the Government's first priorities is to achieve a high rate of new investment, particularly in manufacturing industry. No one can say that over the whole post-war period our performance has been satisfactory in this respect. Equally, we must make a sustained effort to eliminate the disparities in employment which have built up over the years between Scotland, Wales and the assisted areas of England and other parts of the country. Our broad intention is to continue and develop the financial and other incentives now available for the location of new industry and the expansion of existing industry in the assisted areas.

Against this background, we have been considering the system of incentives we have inherited from our predecessors in the Industry Act 1972. This Act gives us wide powers, which we intend to use to the full in promoting investment, the modernisation of industry and regional regeneration.

Thus, industry can be assured that the existing system of regional development grants will be maintained, although within this framework adjustments may, of course, have to be made from time to time. We certainly do not intend to cause the same hiatus in investment as was created by the previous Government from 1970–72, when they abolished the system of investment grants.

- (House of Commons, Parliamentary Debates, vol. 872, session 1974, cols. 347–8)

This commitment was fulfilled. The continuity of policy was maintained but the various reforms all served to increase the strength and scope of regional powers.

The initial changes introduced reversed the elements of weakening of the policy of the late 1960s that the Heath government had made. REP was extended beyond its deadline of September 1974, and the rates doubled. As a percentage of average male manual wages this restored its value to that of 1969.

IDC exemption limits were lowered at the same time although, outside of the South-East, they remained above the levels of the late 1960s. Rates of RDG were not altered and indeed remained constant throughout the period, but the expenditure limit on RSA in accordance with the provisions of the 1972 Industry Act was raised by £100 million in February 1975 and again by £100 million to £350 million in January 1976. Finally, in August 1974, the boundaries of assisted areas were altered. Merseyside and parts of North Wales became Special Development Areas, Edinburgh and Cardiff were made Development Areas and Chesterfield became an Intermediate Area.

The 1975 Industry Act widened the operation of Section 7 of the 1972 Act on RSA. Constraints were removed on the use of equity holdings as a form of assistance. The Secretary of State was no longer required only to take equity if assistance could be given in no other form. Nor was he constrained to acquire no more than half of the issued equity capital or to dispose of it as soon as he believed it reasonable to do so. These changes were part of the Industrial Strategy conferring required powers on the NEB. The Act also removed the constraint that type B assistance could only be given if it could not appropriately be provided from other sources. Finally, RSA could be given outside of the normal guidelines 'in appropriate cases, for example where a company is facing acute financial difficulty' (Annual Report under the Industry Act 1972, July 1976, paragraph 16). With these modifications the judgement of Field and Hills quoted above is certainly true.

A check on the developing powers to promote regional development was administered almost immediately after the 1975 Act came into operation with the public expenditure cuts of July 1976. Payment of RDG on applications received after 31 March 1977 were deferred for three months and the mining and construction industries were deprived of eligibility for grants. The deferral of RDG payments was discontinued from December 1977 and the deferred payments cleared by mid-February 1978, Of greater significance was the abolition of REP with effect from 2 January 1977.

Another casualty of the cuts was probably the limits of expenditure on RSA. No further increases in expenditure limits were announced after 1976, with the consequence that its significance as an incentive would be eroded by inflation. There were probably other factors involved in this decision. Increasing emphasis was being given to assistance to specific industries under Section 8 of the 1972 Industry Act as amended by the 1975 Act. The limit on Section 8 expenditure was increased from £850 million to £1000 million in May 1978, that is, to almost three times the limit on RSA. The implications of Section 8 for regional policy are discussed below. The other factor was the emergence of a European dimension to regional policy. A scheme of guarantees against risk of exchange rate fluctuations on loans to firms from the European Investment Bank was introduced in January 1978, and in addition the government negotiated an agency agreement for EIB loans below the normal limit of £2·5 million. At a nominal interest rate of 9·5% for seven years against a UK MLR rate of 12·5%, these loans were 'soft'.

The rules for operations of RSA under Section 7 of the 1972 Industry Act were clarified in a Department of Industry Paper, *Criteria of Assistance to Industry* issued in January 1976. The main concern of this paper was with the criteria for government rescue operations which, with the collapse of British industry, was of immediate moment. Section 7 assistance was to be available in assisted areas for the purchase of assets from a receiver under category 'A' since the purchaser was to be deemed to be creating new employment (paragraph 27). An appendix explained that applications for selective assistance were assessed in the light of three criteria:

(1) Viability defined to mean a company's ability 'after receiving RSA on a once and for all basis' to maintain profitability without continuing subsidies other than RDG and REP available to all enterprises. As noted above REP was in fact abolished a year later.
(2) A benefit to employment either by creating new (category A) or maintaining existing (category B) employment.
(3) The provision by the applicants of the greater part of project costs from outside the public sector.

While (2) could be said to be already understood to apply, (1) and (3) may be construed as restrictions on the operation of Section 7.

2 Expenditure on regional policy

Annual expenditure on the four major elements of policy, namely employment subsidies, environmental improvements and automatic and discretionary investment incentives is detailed in Table 15.1. At current prices, total expenditure for the first year of Labour government, 1974–5, was double that of the previous year and peaked in 1976/77, falling back in 1977/78 to the level of 1974/75 and remaining at roughly that level until 1979/80. The major cause of the fall was the abolition of REP; investment incentives fell slightly in 1977/78, rose a little in 1978/79 and only fell back somewhat in 1979/80. The rise in expenditure in 1978/79 was the result of discretionary payments to the Ford Motor Company.

At 1972/73 out-turn prices, the peak year is 1975/76 when expenditure was £134m. above the last year of the Heath government. The fall thereafter was more drastic and by 1979/80 expenditure was only 52% of that of 1973/74. Automatic investment incentives were back to the 1973/74 level, RSA had fallen by £38m. but again the principal cause of reduction in expenditure was the loss of REP.

Disaggregation by type of assisted area is only feasible for some types of

Table 15.1   *Public expenditure on regional policy (£m, current prices)*

| | Payments to firms | | | | | |
	Automatic payments[a]	Discretionary payments[b]	REP	Infrastructure[c]	Total	Total at 1972/73 prices[e]
1972/73	75·9	57·4	100·0	58·3	291·6	291·6
1973/74	136·8	69·8	106·0	31·2	243·8	308·5
1974/75	228·2	57·3	154·0	47·7	487·2	376·2
1975/76	330·4	79·2	213·0	70·1	692·7	442·6
1976/77	410·1	43·0	216·0	40·2	709·3	383·9
1977/78	393·9	45·0	–	42·3	481·2	217·0
1978/79	417·5	103·2[d]	–	51·2	571·9	230·8
1979/80	330·8	68·4[d]	–	55·4	454·6	160·8

Notes

[a]   Regional Development Grant plus Investment Grants under Part 1 of the Industrial Development Act 1966. This Act ws repealed in 1971. The last payments were made in 1978/79.

[b]   Under Sections 3 and 4 of the Local Employment Act 1972 and Section 7 of the Industry Act 1972.

[c]   Local Employment Act 1972. Expenditure on factory building, plus grants to local authorities for clearance of derelict land and for the provision of basic services.

[d]   Includes large payments to the Ford Motor Company.

[e]   Derived by deflating the figures by the national accounts deflator for gross domestic fixed capital formation except for REP where the deflator for income from employment is used.

expenditure and for some years. REP was only paid in Development and Special Development Areas, where it would be proportional to manufacturing employment. RDG, the other major head of expenditure, was available in Intermediate Areas only for industrial buildings. Of the RDG paid to development areas of both kinds, Special Development Areas received on average 44% of the payment but constituted only 35% of the number of employees covered. If the qualifying capital expenditure was distributed between SDAs and DAs according to the distribution of employees, SDAs should have received (as a result of the difference in grant rates) 38·5% of the payments. With RSA under Section 7 of the 1972 Industry Act a similar bias is visible. Thus over the period 1974–77, SDAs received 37% of payments but constituted only 22% of employees in the areas at risk. The comparable figures are: Development Areas 35% of payments and 42% of employees. Intermediate Areas 28% of payments and 36% of employees. There is thus some evidence that the differentiation between types of assisted area achieved the intended results in terms of the allocation of investment.

3 Effects of policy

Data for investment in manufacturing industry by region, although not by
category of assisted area, is available from 1971. This is summarised in
Figure 15.2. For purposes of analysis we consider two regional aggregates:
'development regions' consisting of the regions of Great Britain that contain
most of the Development Areas (the South-West DA is a small part of its
region and is perforce ignored) and assisted regions containing the
preponderance of DAs, SDAs and IAs. At constant prices, manufacturing
investment (gross domestic fixed capital formation) fell sharply between
1971 and 1972, recovered a little until 1974, fell again until 1976 and then
recovered, slightly exceeding the 1971 level in 1979. Thus much of the
period of most active regional policy of the Labour governments, 1974–76,
took place against a slump in manufacturing investment. Over this period,
as a result presumably of the aggregate influence of regional policy measures,
the share of investment taking place in the development and assisted regions
rose. After 1976 the share fell (Figure 15.2). The increase in share over the
period 1974–77 as a whole was in fact sufficient to enable investment in
these regions to grow despite the national decline. After 1976 with the
weakening of regional policy, the performance of the development and

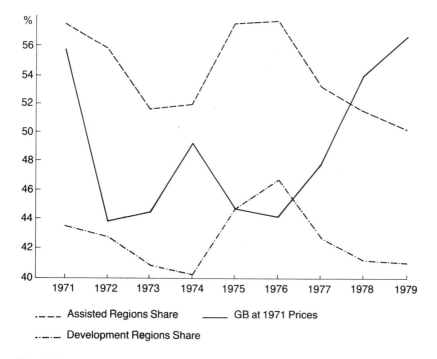

Fig. 15.2

assisted regions was again inferior to the rest of the nation, investment falling in 1976–77 against a strong rise elsewhere and rising less rapidly in 1977–79.

How far this evidence of success of regional policy in 1974–76 was attributable to the strengthening of that policy by the Labour government is unclear. There is a substantial delay between investment decisions and implementation and some at least of the additional investment in 1974–76 must have been the result of decisions taken in earlier years. In fact during this period payments equivalent to £60m. investment under the Investment Grants Act 1966, abolished in 1971, were made.

Most of the academic work on the evaluation of regional policy concentrates not on the intermediate objective of investment but the final objective of employment creation in assisted areas. The major studies of policy in the 1960s are those of Moore and Rhodes (1973b, 1976a, 1976b). Their main work uses shift-share analyses of employment growth and attributes the regional component[1] to the impact of regional policy which is apportioned between the main policy instruments (investment incentives, IDC control, REP) by regression analysis. For periods of active regional policy defined by the policy instruments in operation: 1960–63, 1964–67, 1967–71, Moore and Rhodes find increasing success in manufacturing sector job creation in Development Areas, the respective rates, for constant pressure of demand, being 14·7, 20·5 and 26·0 thousands per annum. Short-run Keynesian and longer-run base multipliers are applied to these numbers to give the total impact of policy on job creation. Between 1960 and 1971 the total regional policy effect is estimated at 300,000 jobs created. IDC control and investment incentives are seen as the most important policy instruments with REP of considerably less significance (Moore and Rhodes 1976a).

A further study (Moore et al., 1977) extended the analysis to 1976. The conclusion was that in the period 1972–76 regional policy was effective but less so than in the late 1960s, creating, at constant demand pressure, 17,200 jobs per annum against 26,000 in 1967–71. For the regions of North, Scotland and Wales total jobs created are estimated at 46,000. At the level of unemployment prevailing in the late 1960s another 40,000 would have been added (i.e. the impact of the recession reduced the effectiveness of policy by 47%). Demand pressures aside, the reduced effectiveness of policy is attributed to three factors:

(i)   a weakening of IDC control (as measured both by higher limits outside of the South-East and by a lower rate of refusals);

(ii)   the maturity of policy. 'Regional subsidies, like devaluation are equivalent to an exogenous shock which will raise the level of employment and investment in Development Areas relative to other areas but will not secure a permanent acceleration in the growth of relative employment and investment' (op. cit., p. 75);

(iii) the continuing decline in UK manufacturing employment. Presumably this factor is not wholly picked up by their cyclical variable (the national unemployment rate).

The authors estimate that REP created 30–60,000 jobs between 1967 and 1971 and a further 10,000 between 1971 and 1976. The abolition of REP was forecast to result in a loss of 17–35,000 jobs in Development Areas by 1980. Had the payments continued, a further 6–10,000 jobs would have been created instead.

The Moore and Rhodes methodology is open to a number of objections. Shift-share analysis is subject to index number problems. Their assumption that in the absence of policy, industries in the assisted areas would grow at national rates (i.e. that the regional problem is one of poor industrial structure) is only valid if industry growth rates are independent of base-year distribution. Weeden (1974) shows that this does not hold for the set of industries and regions in the UK. But this mis-specification is certainly not of sufficient moment to overturn the conclusion that in the late 1960s assisted areas were doing better than could be expected which in any case is confirmed by other evidence, such as industrial movement data (Moore and Rhodes, 1976b). However it undermines conclusions on the size of policy effects. The conclusions on the timing of effects can also be questioned. The assumptions about the speed and mode of operation of IDC control are in conflict with the findings of Bowers and Gunawardena (1977–78).

4 Regional policy and devolution

As part of the government's devolution policy, RSA powers under Section 7 of the Industry Act and the advance factory and environmental provisions under the Local Employment Act were transferred in 1975 to the Scottish and Welsh Office. At the end of that year the Scottish and Welsh Development Agencies were set up with substantial grant-in-aid (initially £9 million for the Scottish DA and £7 million for the Welsh DA), and with wide powers to promote industrial developments in their respective countries. The powers under Section 7 of the Industry Act (RSA) and the Local Employment Act powers were henceforth exercised by these agencies on behalf of their secretaries of state. In 1976 a Development Board for Rural Wales was created as a counterpart to the Highlands and Islands Development Board in Scotland.

No similar development agencies were created for the English regions. Instead, under Section 3 of the Industry Act 1975, the Secretary of State for Industry was empowered to direct the National Enterprise Board to exercise his Section 7 powers. It could be argued that this arrangement was not a comparable move since the NEB was concerned primarily with general restructuring of British Industry using powers under Section 8 of the 1972

Act as extended by the 1975 Act, and that in consequence the English assisted areas were relatively disadvantaged.

In terms of offers of RSA — this being a more relevant statistic than actual payments which are subject to many intervening factors — there is no evidence of any development agency effect. The average share for Scotland and Wales is more or less identical for the four years after the creation of the agencies (46·2%) to that for the three years preceding their creation (46·5%) but there are very large year-to-year fluctuations.

Information on fixed capital formation is given in Table 15.2 where comparison is with Northern England, a composite of the standard regions of North, North-West, and Yorkshire and Humberside. Both areas experienced declining shares of manufacturing investment over the period but the share of Northern England fell more sharply than that of Scotland and Wales. The definition of manufacturing capital formation was changed in 1981 and the regional impact of this change is unclear. If the comparison is restricted to the period 1977–80 then both areas lost 2 percentage points as compared with the position in 1971–76. The Scottish verdict of 'not proven' would seem appropriate given the limited data.

Devolution, however, involved more than the control of the discretionary incentives for manufacturing investment. The Scottish and Welsh Offices assumed responsibility from 1976 for a substantial proportion of Central Government Capital Expenditure. Table 15.2 contains data on some major categories. It is fairly clear that devolution led to an increased share of capital expenditure on Economic Services, at least until the Public Expenditure cuts of 1980–81. Much of this expenditure was on infrastructure — roads, water and so on. There is no evidence of increased shares of expenditure on Education and Health. With Housing and Community Development, total UK expenditure at current prices fell from £2·1 billion to £0·5 billion between 1980 and 1982. Welsh expenditure declined in proportion but Scottish expenditure largely escaped the cuts, falling only from £312 million in 1980 to £229 million in 1982. Devolution no doubt was the main force in insulating Scotland here. There is no evidence, however, that prior to this holocaust either country was gaining at the expense of Northern England.

The introduction of development agencies represented a new departure in regional policy, involving information and co-ordination of activities rather than subsidies and grants. This has been continued under the Conservative government with some success. To this extent our analysis probably understates the significance of the innovation.

Table 15.2 Shares of gross domestic fixed capital formation (%)

	Manufacturing		Housing & Community Development		Education and Health		Economic Services	
	N. England	Scotland & Wales	N. England	Scotland & Wales	N. England	Scotland & Wales	N. England	Scotland & Wales
1971	39·6	17·9	25·2	17·5	26·1	15·4	28·5	19·7
1972	37·1	18·7	24·3	16·8	24·4	15·9	25·6	20·6
1973	33·8	18·0	24·3	16·4	24·5	15·4	27·6	17·2
1974	35·5	16·4	22·9	16·6	25·3	16·2	23·5	21·4
1975	37·9	19·5	21·2	17·8	26·6	16·7	22·9	22·6
1976	38·3	19·3	22·0	15·6	27·1	18·4	21·9	25·2
1977	35·8	17·1	22·1	16·1	26·2	17·8	22·7	29·4
1978	35·5	15·4	23·6	16·3	25·6	17·5	20·2	32·6
1979	34·3	16·1	24·6	18·4	28·4	16·8	19·1	32·5
1980	34·3	16·4	24·2	20·6	28·5	15·1	20·5	28·9
1981	29·8[a]	18·3[a]	22·6	26·4	28·7	17·4	23·9	23·8
1982	28·9[a]	16·6[a]	13·9	56·4	29·9	17·9	20·0	24·5
Mean 1971–76	37·0	18·3	23·5	16·8	25·7	16·3	25·0	21·1
Standard deviation	2·09	1·04	1·78	0·79	1·11	1·13	2·67	2·70
Mean 1977–82	33·1	16·7	21·8	25·7	27·9	17·1	21·1	27·0
Standard deviation	2·98	0·90	4·00	15·5	1·64	1·05	1·83	5·28
Mean 1977–80	35·0	16·3	23·6	17·9	27·2	16·8	20·6	30·9
Standard deviation	0·79	0·70	1·10	2·10	1·49	1·21	1·51	1·97

Note: [a] New definition.
Source: CSO Regional Trends.

5   Some issues on policy

The conclusions about regional policy in 1974–79 are as follows:

(i)   In terms of financial incentives and the scope of discretionary instruments, policy was strengthened in 1974–76;

(ii)   after 1976 the policy was substantially weakened by the abolition of REP, loosening of IDC limits, tightening of the criteria for RSA and failure to raise RSA expenditure limits in line with inflation;

(iii)   IDC control was operated less stringently throughout the period than had been the case under Labour governments in the 1960s.

(iv)   there is evidence of success of policy in the period 1974–76 in comparison both with the early 1970s and 1977–79, but the achievements were less than in the late 1960s.

A number of questions arise from these conclusions: namely, why was the policy weakened after 1976? Why was REP abolished? Why were IDC controls applied less stringently?

(i)   *IDC control*

Regional policy as developed and operated in the late 1960s generated a considerable debate not merely on whether it worked, which has been considered, but on the appropriateness of the instruments chosen, the geographic scope of assistance, the efficiency with which resources were used, and the external consequences of policy. Many of these issues have no obvious impact on policy of the 1970s and will not be discussed here. They are surveyed elsewhere (MacLennan and Parr, 1979; Armstrong and Taylor, 1985).

The arguments about the detailed consequences of policy have to be assessed against a background of its overall cost. The view which received wide coverage in government and academic circles in the early 1970s was that regional policy was essentially costless: generating additional national resources but absorbing none. This was most clearly expressed by Moore and Rhodes in evidence to the Trade and Industry Sub-committee of the Expenditure Committee (Moore and Rhodes 1973a), endorsed by the Committee in its report and clearly viewed favourably by the civil servants giving evidence to the Committee. More specifically, the argument was that when operated in conjunction with a national policy of demand management aimed at maintaining full employment, regional policy will lead to increased output in Development Areas without leading to a loss of employment and output in the fully employed regions (op. cit., p. 447). This argument has its basis in the Phillips curve. By reducing the dispersion of demand levels (unemployment) between labour markets, regional policy could shift the national curve towards the origin, thus permitting a higher level of activity for any rate of inflation (Bowers *et al.*, 1970).

Moore and Rhodes (1973a) added to this idea a view on the balance of payments. In the absence of regional policy, full employment could only be achieved by creating excess demand in the South-East which would suck in imports. Equalising demand across the regions would shift the balance of payments constraint as well as the national Phillips curve. The extra public expenditure required for regional incentives could be covered from the extra resources generated by the policy. Most of the expenditure was transfer payments in any case. Any real resource cost (for administration and infrastructure provision) was covered by the higher level of activity that the expenditure facilitated.

IDC control, if it leads to the abandonment of investment refused a certificate, provided an exception to this doctrine since manufacturing capacity and probably competitiveness would be lost in the process. The perfect regional policy was thus one which worked entirely on incentives provided by resource transfers. The Select Committee took evidence from industry in 1972 and heard instances of investment being abandoned because of control. This consideration probably explains the decision of the Heath government to reduce the effectiveness of IDC control. While the Labour government initially reversed this process the growing collapse of manufacturing industry both in production and investment raised the importance of lost investment. In a climate of de-industrialisation the price of effective IDC control was probably judged to be too high.

(ii) *REP*

Even before its introduction REP was a subject of considerable controversy and with subsequent experience views polarised. In its favour it was argued that it helped to offset the capital bias in the regional policy package. An extreme neoclassical view was that as a labour subsidy it was the only defensible instrument since the problem was that of immobile labour whose price was kept above market clearing levels while capital as a factor was mobile and the capital market competitive (Archibald, 1972). This view entailed rejection of many of the assumptions on which the case for regional policy was based − economies of agglomeration and external diseconomies of location − and was not widely held, but the idea that the bias towards capital was undesirable when the regional problem was unemployed labour was more generally acceptable. Against this was the idea that REP served to maintain inefficient firms in production, thereby inhibiting the restructuring of the economies of assisted areas which was necessary if the regional problem was ultimately to be solved (Mackay, 1976). The view of industrialists as revealed to the Sub-Committee on Trade and Industry was that REP was a partial compensation for the higher costs of locating in assisted areas rather than in the South-East and Midlands (House of Commons, 1973). It did not lead, as was its presumed intention, to higher employment levels. The study by Moore and Rhodes (1976a) suggested that the employment effects of REP were modest and certainly well below the sanguine hopes expressed at the time of its introduction. Bowers and Gunawardena (1977–78) found it a powerful instrument for creating approvals in Development Areas although mainly for small projects. The Heath government proposed to phase it out from 1974. Despite its reintroduction and uprating it remained on sufferance. A new factor in the equation was conflict with the EC.

Articles 92–4 of the Treaty of Rome give the European Commission power to review and if necessary call for the modification and withdrawal of any aid granted to specific firms. Specific exception is made to aid to promote the development of areas where the standard of living is particularly low or where there is substantial unemployment and to aid to facilitate specific activities where the common interest is not affected.

The EC developed its interpretation of these articles during the course of the 1970s and in doing so came in conflict with UK governments on a number of occasions. By a decision of 1971 it subjected aids in the central area of the Community to a ceiling of 20% grant equivalent and attempted to classify much of the UK DAs and IAs as central. Following conflict with the Heath government and its successor this attempt was postponed, but from January 1975 DAs and SDAs were classed in a group that placed a 30% grant equivalent as a maximum; IAs were to be subjected to the 20% ceiling. EC rules for regional aids required that they relate solely to the initial cost of investment, that they should be measureable in advance, and should be of determinable geographic and industrial incidence. REP failed to satisfy these criteria. Apart from measurement difficulties it was unacceptable in being by intention a permanent and continuing subsidy available equally for employment sustained by replacement investment as for new investment.

REP was 'a minor but potentially troublesome element in renegotiation discussions' (MacLennan, 1979) and once the issue of membership was finally settled it was clear that it would ultimately have to go. The July 1976 measures provided the opportunity for this to happen without the government seeming to bow to the EC.

(iii) *The run-down of regional policy*
Three factors are clearly central to an explanation of the decision to reduce the strength of regional policy: the July crisis which necessitated cuts in public expenditure and thereby destroyed the argument that policy was costless; the collapse of manufacturing industry which simultaneously reduced the supply of mobile manufacturing investment – the base on which regional policy operated – and accorded greater weight to maintaining employment and investment in industry regardless of its precise location; and rising national unemployment which reduced the significance attached to unemployment in the assisted areas even though it did not reduce the absolute size of unemployment differentials.[2] These factors are jointly if not severally sufficient. Regional policy as developed in the 1960s and

early 1970s was appropriate to a different world from that emerging in the late 1970s. Two other factors however are worth brief comment.

First the Industrial Strategy under Section 8 of the Industry Act did not in any sense replace regional policy nor, except that it was in competition for public expenditure, did it undermine it. The share of assisted areas in the expenditure on industry-specific and general schemes in the period 1977–79 was close to their share of total employment.

Of arguably greater importance, however, was the evidence that the nature of the problem was changing with major job losses in the inner cities, including especially the cities of London and Birmingham, both outside the assisted areas. There is little evidence that regional policy was responsible for these losses: they arose either from plant closures or short-distance moves to new towns or outer suburban sites. That was certainly the case for London, where only 9% of the employment decline over 1966–74 was due to movement to assisted areas (Dennis, 1978). Massey and Meegan (1978) found similarly that 89% of job losses in major cities were lost to the economy as a whole and that of the remaining 11% only a little over a half went to assisted areas. They attribute the job losses to the process of de-industrialisation entailing a de-skilling of the workforce. The inner cities suffered particularly from this process because in manufacturing they specialised in processes involving manual skills.

The possibility remains of course that regional policy prevented inner cities from attracting unskilled jobs that were on offer although there is no evidence to support this contention. The real significance of the issue is that it changes the dimensions of the problem of the distribution of industry and reduces the significance of regional differences as such. If regional policy is not a cause of the inner-city problem, it is not a treatment either.

The Labour government can take the credit for shifting the approach to urban problems from that of urban development and dispersal allied to the building of new towns to that of urban regeneration. This shift dates from 1976. Initially promoted by revitalising the Urban Programme established in the late 1960s — expenditure rising from £1·3m. in 1975/76 to £4·94m. in 1978/79 — the approach was consolidated in the Inner Urban Areas Act 1978 which gave designated authorities additional powers of economic development including the right to declare Industrial Improvement Areas. This Act formed the basis of the inner-city policy of the first Thatcher government. Unlike regional policy, inner-city policy survived the 1979 election.

Notes

1   $\Sigma_i \, W_{ir}(g_{ir} - g_{in})$ where subscripts i refer to a set of industries, r is the assisted region, n is the nation, g is growth rate of employment, and W base year employment weight.

2 A regression of assisted area unemployment rates on those of non-assisted areas in 1966–79 gives:

Development Areas (including SDAs) $\quad U_{DA} = 2\cdot45 + 1\cdot49\ U_N \quad R^2 = 0\cdot96$

Intermediate Areas $\quad\quad\quad\quad\quad\quad\ U_I\ = 1\cdot23 + 0\cdot94\ U_N \quad R^2 = 0\cdot97$

Rising unemployment thus increases the absolute difference between DAs and the rest of the country but reduces the ratio. With intermediate areas, both the absolute difference and the ratio are reduced.

References

Archibald, G.C. (1972), 'On regional economic policy in the United Kingdom', in M. Peston and B.A. Corry (eds), *Essays in Honour of Lord Robbins*, Weidenfeld & Nicolson, London.

Armstrong, H., and Taylor, J. (1985), *Regional Economics and Policy*, Phillip Allan, London.

Bowers, J.K., and Gunawardena, A. (1977–78), 'Industrial Development Certificates and regional policy', *Bulletin of Economic Research*, XXIX, pp. 112–22, XXX, pp. 1–13.

Bowers, J.K., Cheshire, P.C., and Webb, A.E. (1970), 'The change in the relationship between unemployment and earnings increases: a review of some possible explanations', *National Institute Economic Review*, no. 54.

Dennis, R. (1978), 'The decline of manufacturing employment in Greater London 1966–74', *Urban Studies*, XV, pp. 63–73.

Field, G.M., and Hills, P.V. (1976), 'The administration of industrial subsidies', in Whiting (1976).

House of Commons (1973), *Expenditure Committee (Trade & Industry Sub-Commitee), Minutes of Evidence*, 4th April.

MacLennan, D., and Parr, J.B. (1979), *Regional Policy, Past Experience and New Directions*, Martin Robertson, Oxford.

MacLennan, M.C. (1979), 'Regional policy in a European framework' in MacLennan and Parr (1979).

Mackay, R.R. (1976), 'The impact of the Regional Employment Premium', in Whiting (1976).

Massey, D. (1979), 'In what sense a regional problem?', *Regional Studies*, xiii, pp. 233–43.

Massey, D.B., and Meegan, R.A. (1978), 'Industrial restructuring versus the cities', *Urban Studies*, xv, pp. 273–88.

Melliss, C.L., and Richardson, P.W. (1976), 'Value of investment incentives for manufacturing industry 1946 to 1974', in Whiting (1976).

Moore, B., and Rhodes, J. (1973a), 'The economic and Exchequer implications of regional policy', Memorandum 24, Minutes of Evidence (from October 1972 to June 1973) and Appendices, Regional Development Incentives, House of Commons Expenditure Committee (Trade and Industry Sub-Committee), Session 1972–73, London.

Moore, B.C., and Rhodes, J. (1973b), 'Evaluating the effects of British regional economic policy', *Economic Journal*, LXXXIII, pp. 87–100.

Moore, B.C., and Rhodes, J. (1976a), 'A quantitative analysis of the effects of the regional employment premium and other regional policy instruments', in Whiting (1976).

Moore, B.C., and Rhodes, J. (1976b), 'Regional economic policy and the movement of manufacturing firms to development areas', *Economica*, XLIII, no. 1, pp. 17–31.

Moore, B.C., Rhodes, J., and Tyler, P. (1977), 'The impact of regional policy in the 1970s', *Centre for Environmental Studies Review*, no. 1 (London), pp. 67–77.

Weeden, R. (1974), 'Regional rates of employment growth: an analysis of variance treatment', *National Institute of Economic and Social Research Regional Papers III*, London.

Whiting, A. (ed.) (1976), *The Economics of Industrial Subsidies*, HMSO, London.

Summary and appraisal

1 Introduction

The period 1974–79 – indeed, for most people the 1970s more generally – is one which is redolent of economic failure. During these years economic growth slowed to a snail's pace, inflation reached levels unparalleled in modern British history, staple industries entered the first phase of what was to prove for many their terminal decline, unemployment rose to levels without precedent in post-war experience whilst the period ended in the turmoil of the 'Winter of Discontent'. This is a catalogue, certainly, of bitterly disappointing outcomes but disappointing economic performance was far from being confined to the United Kingdom. As the summary in the table (Table 16.1) shows, indicators of economic performance in the advanced countries generally indicate a deterioration in the 1970s from the 1960s and a marked deterioration in 1974–79. Everywhere, output growth slowed and unemployment and inflation rose. In most cases, the balance-of-payments performance worsened. In the United Kingdom, the deterioration in growth performance came on top of an already weak performance by G-7 standards, whilst the extent of the worsening in both inflation and balance-of-payments performance was more marked in the UK than in most other countries.

The question that sets the agenda for this chapter is how far these outcomes could have been avoided, or at least mitigated, by better policies – but policies that would have been feasible in the circumstances. In responding to this question we refer extensively and as occasion demands to earlier chapters in the book, elaborating on points established in them. But we have consciously not sought to provide the reader with a listing of chapter summaries. Rather, in what follows, we proceed from a general but brief review of the principles of policy appraisal we have followed to an account that highlights three principal features of the period: the initial inheritance of the system of threshold agreements from the previous government, the 1976 crisis in the foreign exchange market, and the 1978 decision to pursue a 5% incomes-policy norm. The reasons for highlighting these particular

Table 16.1   *Economic performance in the G-7 countries*

	Output growth % p.a.	Unemployment %[a]	Inflation % p.a.[b]	Balance of Payments current a/c surplus in % GDP[c]
Canada				
1960s	5·4	4·7	3·1	−1·5
1970s	4·9	6·6	8·1	−1·2
1974−79	4·2	7·2	8·2	−2·2
USA				
1960s	4·2	4·6	2·9	0·6
1970s	3·0	6·0	7·2	0·2
1974−79	3·1	6·6	7·8	0·3
Japan				
1960s	10·6	1·3	5·2	0·2
1970s	4·7	1·7	8·0	0·6
1974−79	4·6	1·9	5·7	0·3
France				
1960s	5·5	1·5	4·2	0·3
1970s	3·9	3·7	9·2	−0·3
1974−79	3·1	4·5	10·4	−0·6
West Germany				
1960s	4·4	0·9	3·3	0·8
1970s	2·9	2·5	5·4	0·9
1974−79	2·7	3·6	4·3	1·0
Italy				
1960s	5·8	5·1	4·3	1·7
1970s	3·0	6·2	14·1	0·2
1974−79	2·3	6·6	16·9	−0·2
UK				
1960s	2·9	1·6	3·9	−0·3
1970s	2·4	3·7	13·4	−0·7
1974−79	2·0	4·5	16·3	−1·3

Notes:
[a]   National definitions
[b]   GDP deflator
[c]   Unweighted average of annual figures.

Sources: OECD *National Accounts 1960−1986; Main Economic Indicators, Historical Statistics.*

features will become evident as we proceed. After reviewing what was in effect the government's general demand-management strategy, we then turn to a consideration of the 'supply side' and the government's policies for this. This is not all that is covered in this book, however, nor does it cover all the aims a Labour government might have in prosecuting economic policy; so we turn finally to consider these other aspects, necessarily somewhat over-shadowed by the principal action of the period.

2 Policy appraisal

Any attempt to evaluate or appraise policy invokes, explicitly or otherwise, a counterfactual alternative. A clear example of this in a formal, model-based context can be found in Chaper 6; but the point applies quite generally. Unless the counterfactual is clearly specified, there is always a danger that policy and outcome will be conflated, vitiating the possibility of drawing any useful conclusions. But there is a variety of scenarios that can be considered as appropriate counterfactuals. What we have chosen to do in appraising the policies of the period is to set as the counterfactural what we suppose would have been feasible alternative courses of action given the economic and political circumstances of the time. This is different from drawing lessons for economic policy in unrestricted circumstances or those which it might be supposed may face a future Labour government, instructive as these exercises may be. A danger with the kind of appraisal we seek is that of taking too narrow a view of the range of feasible alternatives, for then one will be driven too close to the position that policy was what it had to be and could not, except in the smallest detail, have been otherwise. What sets out to be appraisal degenerates into a litany of excuses. We hope to have avoided both this risk and the opposite danger of over-indulging benefit of hindsight in what follows. We aim, in any event, to discuss the issues raised with sufficient clarity that the reader can exercise his or her own judgement on the issues.

3 Difficult beginnings

Chapter 1 supplies a narrative account of our period, starting with a description of the Labour government's inheritance from the previous administration and the strain in the international as well as the domestic environment. The beginning of the period is dominated by the effects of the OPEC oil price rises – a quadrupling of the costs of a vital raw material – an event which, coming on top of large increases in commodity prices in general, promised to provide a testing combination of problems with inflation, the balance of payments and unemployment. The need to pay four times as much as before for a vital import required an increase in output to sustain the same level of real income; yet there was every likelihood that a balance-of-payments scramble among the developed countries would induce recession and a loss of output. All of this in fact seems to have been as well understood by the government and its advisers as by anyone (see Chapters 2 and 7), though arguably policy was for a while predicated on too optimistic an assessment of the extent to which the advice dispensed by the OECD and the IMF would be followed by others.[1] That advice was sensibly (but in the event vainly) dedicated to avoiding an internecine balance-of-payments scramble by the developed countries which could only exacerbate, rather than smooth, the real income consequences of the oil price rise. Understanding the nature of the problems posed by the international environment was one thing, however; being able to determine a coherent response to them was another.

Some of the consequences of the OPEC decision were indeed already manifest in the circumstances of the government's own election to office. The rise in oil prices had stengthened the hand of the miners' union; the government, arriving in office in circumstances of industrial turmoil, had in effect been elected to buy it off. Another consequence of the OPEC shock was to turn the Heath administration's 'threshold agreements' form of incomes policy into a doomsday machine. As explained by Paul Ormerod in Chapter 4, a system of wage indexation such as the threshold agreements, implies that an inescapable rise in import prices is turned into a spiralling increase in wage settlements and inflation. The Italian 'scala mobile' system of wage indexation produced a similarly catastrophic inflation result.

Nothing, of course could be done about the OPEC shock itself, nor was Britain's international position strong enough to allow her to modify the international response significantly (though she did the right things – see Chapter 7). But the threshold agreements were a piece of domestic policy and one that was singularly inappropriate for the circumstances. Should the government have reneged on those agreements, therefore? Paul Ormerod (Chapter 4) thinks that they should and Christopher Allsopp (Chapter 2) terms them an 'economic disaster'. Nevertheless we are inclined to argue that in this case there was no feasible alternative to continuing with them. The circumstances in which the government was elected, both narrowly political (the government initially had no majority in parliament at all and even after October 1974 a majority of only 3) and more broadly (with its 'mandate' to avoid industrial turmoil) suggest that it could not in fact have moved against the trade unions, which is how reneging on the agreements would have been construed. Moreover it can be argued that since the threshold system was itself introduced to forestall aggressive wage demands which anticipated price rises to come, abolition of the system would merely have led to an alternative form of indexation enforced through militant bargaining backed up by strikes. (This seems to be William Brown's view – see Chapter 13.) In this respect, it is hard to see that in its early days the government had very much room for manoeuvre − much 'policy space' in which to affect the outcomes. One of the prerequisites for more effective policies was that it should be able itself to create or otherwise acquire a less constrained policy space.

4   Enlarging the policy space

The inauspicious beginnings did in fact lead to an enlargement of the policy space and economic performance improved. By the beginning of 1976 inflation was already falling fast, the balance of payments was improving, public expenditure was being brought under control and the government's authority had been strengthened as a result of the favourable popular verdict on the revised terms for entry into the Common Market (which, moreover, enabled the Prime Minister to remove Mr Benn from control of the highly controversial industrial policies with which Labour had assumed office).

How far the defeat of inflation was due to the large rise in unemployment and how far independently to the successful negotiation of the Jones−Foot incomes policy compact is not entirely clear: Paul Ormerod (Chapter 4) points out that later experience (in 1980/81) indicates the potential for a rise in unemployment to cool the inflationary climate. The traditional logic for incomes policy was that it reduced the extent of the unemployment necessary to achieve a given reduction in inflation and this belief was certainly important at the time, correct or not. Moreover, the government's deep concern with unemployment throughout the period can in our view be strongly defended, both on moral grounds and by reference to the longer-term costs of substantial shocks to unemployment which, experience has subsequently confirmed, can have the effect of raising the unemployment rate at which inflation can be brought under control (the non-accelerating inflation rate of unemployment − NAIRU). At the same time, although wage inflation had peaked a few months before Stage One of the Labour government's incomes policy came into operation, it is unlikely that the short-run course of wage inflation was unrelated to the introduction of the policy, even if the rise in unemployment was a necessary condition for it to appear to 'bite'.

The chapters here on public expenditure policy and monetary policy indicate that in both areas − with cash limits in the 1976 budget and tighter monetary policies − the government had moved decisively towards policies more appropriate to an inflationary climate and a period of slow growth. Indeed the retrenchment and austerity implied appears to have been accepted before the foreign exchange market crisis of 1976 had reached its height (see Chapter 2) and the additional steps enjoined by the IMF stabilisation loan appear to have added little of significance. The popular attribution of the credit for these achievements to the IMF is simply misplaced.

It can be argued, though, that the policy reforms were conditioned by the long-drawn-out foreign exchange crisis and it is surely true that the crisis stiffened the resolve to see through the adaptation of the government's monetary and fiscal stance. But the proposition that the crisis itself was induced by earlier unreformed policies and was proof positive of their irresponsibility is another story again. It is true that, at least against the dollar, the exchange rate was probably overvalued by the end of 1975; this was certainly believed to be so in influential parts of the policy-making machinery at the time and the model-based calculations of policy effects presented in Chapter 6 of this book lend support to the idea that past policies had left the exchange rate substantially overvalued. But there is also evidence to support the view that the convulsion in the foreign exchange market was in part a 'confidence crisis' unrelated to the 'fundamentals'. For, indeed, all the obvious fundamentals – the inflation rate, the money supply, the current account – were moving in a favourable direction at the time and there were the additional factors that by 1976 the prospective value of North Sea oil to the exchanges was understood and the government's hand had been strengthened politically by the results of the Common Market entry referendum. This is a case in which it *is* illuminating to use the benefit of hindsight in interpreting events; for it is now much clearer than it was (see, e.g., the issue of the *Oxford Review of Economic Policy* for September 1989) that the foreign exchange market has a considerable capacity to depart from the levels warranted by the fundamentals and that *pace* Friedman's (1953) view, self-interested profit-seeking does not ensure that current values always stay close to the equilibrium. The capacity of the market to deliver a misleading verdict on policy is one thing, however; whether this excuses the government from blame in its policy stance in 1976 is a different matter. For a corollary of the view that markets may display 'bandwagoning' behaviour is that the authorities may have an opportunity to influence events by providing the markets with a firm steer, backed up or signalled by taking appropriate action. Partly as the result of internal disagreements and partly because of lack of experience with and understanding of confidence crises in foreign exchange markets with non-fixed parities, the government in 1976 failed to act on such an understanding; indeed, the only message the government seems to have communicated to the market was that it was not, initially, averse to a depreciation. It then failed to convince the markets that it really believed the rate had fallen sufficiently far and in effect connived at its own subsequent embarrassment. The government was also facing, it should be noted, strong pressure from the UK Treasury and Federal Reserve, which wanted to see significant tightening of public expenditure and monetary policy (Fay and Young, 1978).

5   Squandering the fruits?

The government's policy reforms brought progressive improvement once confidence had returned, leading to a heady period in 1977–78 when it seemed the corner had been turned. In the light of the debacle that then ensued the question must be asked whether the government was culpable for squandering the gains that it had itself made. Two decisions in particular stand out for attention in this light: first, there was the decision to uncap sterling in the autumn of 1977; then there was the decision to set the norm in the 1978 phase of incomes policy at 5%, the proximate 'cause' of the 'Winter of Discontent'.

The first of these decisions foreshadowed the oscillation of policy between monetary and exchange rate targets that was to recur in later years. The argument at the time was straightforward; the reflux of confidence in sterling was so great as to lead to an upward pressure on the exchange rate that conflicted with the unofficial exchange rate target that had been adopted. To deflect the exchange rate pressure required a fall in the rate of interest that would be immediately expansionary (and was so, in so far as interest rates were in fact reduced) and would threaten the preservation of the (recently adopted) monetary target. In a world of high capital mobility it is not in general possible to target the money supply and the exchange rate independently so in this sense the dilemma was inescapable and reflected a policy inconsistency. The way in which it was resolved at the time seems to have reflected the belief that it was important to maintain the credibility of the monetary target with foreign exchange markets, not so much because of any immediate inflationary threat (though the appreciation of the exchange rate would have reduced the extent of price rises) as for the sake of the role it could play in future, possibly more stressful, periods as a key part of the counter-inflationary bulwark the government had set in place. There is little more that can be said. Since it neither had, nor was thought to have, any completely reliable alternative means of controlling inflation the government was obliged to value monetary targets and to solve its dilemma as it did: the exchange rate target of that time was not itself considered as a counter-inflationary policy, but was inspired by 'real-side' (competitiveness) considerations.

The incomes policy decision represents a different, and surely more culpable choice. It appears to have been taken on Prime Ministerial initiative and (not only in retrospect) to embody an element of *folie de grandeur* (or as Healey, 1989, has put it, the decision was 'typical of the hubris which can overcome a successful government towards the end of its term' (p. 398)). It seems to have been an attempt to crown success with more success, when the path of greater wisdom might have been to let up. That the norm was set so low of course reflected a belief that incomes policy must be seen as encouraging a continuing fall in inflation. From the October 1977 Budget, however, fiscal policy was being significantly relaxed as the government sought to use the opportunity provided by the improvement in inflation and the balance of payments to reduce unemployment, and — not for the first time or the last — the reflation seems to have been too strong. The implication of Paul Ormerod's analysis is that wage pressure was bound to rise as unemployment fell, though whether this is sufficient alone to account for the strength of the wage push is not so clear. Thus it seems unlikely that even a slightly higher norm than that dictated by mechanical arithmetical considerations would have been feasible. In the event the reservations previously expressed by trade union leaders were more than borne out by the strength of grass-roots feeling evinced during the Winter of Discontent. The question that needs to be posed, therefore, is whether the incomes policy had not altogether outlived its usefulness.

6   The emphasis on incomes policy

In the overt design of the government's demand-management policies — that is the mix of fiscal, monetary and incomes policy — incomes policy played a key role. It also commanded a large amount of policy time and the energies and imagination of those, policy makers and others, who were involved. It has to be asked whether it was worth it. The traditional conception of incomes policy saw it as a necessary adjunct to the acceptance of the goal of full employment; managing demand so as to preserve full employment meant that unemployment could no longer act as a check on wages and prices. Put in another way, in a static classical model, guaranteeing full employment amounts to targeting the quotient of nominal wages to prices, not the absolute nominal quantities themselves: to solve this problem incomes or wages policy supplied the correct formal solution — conditional on its feasibility. The early post-war experiments with incomes policy have usually been thought of as successful, as were phases at least of the incomes policy experiments of the 1960s Labour governments. There have always been successful incomes policy experiments functioning abroad — in Sweden, formerly at least in The Netherlands, latterly in Australia. However, conditions in the UK in the 1970s did not seem conducive to sustained success; William Brown points to the spread of plant-level bargaining in this period, and whilst there was a critical period when the Jones—Foot policy had some success, backed up by austere demand policies, the Winter of Discontent demonstrated that this was not sustainable in conditions of reflation. Even had a relaxation of the norm been found which could have deflected that particular period of turmoil there is really no indication that the cost of such a formula would have been other than the postponement of the formal disintegration of the policy. Thus in retrospect the experience seems to show that policy design in which incomes policy — at least of the 'centralised' type practised in Britain both in the 1970s and before — plays a key role is not the way to go. Moreover, William Brown argues in Chapter 13, that adherence to these policies damaged the trade unions as well as the governments. However, it is important to add a qualification to this negative judgement: although the incomes policy emphasis was formally a key part of policy design, the damage caused by the weakness of the policy was contained by adherence to an eclectic 'belt-and-braces' approach to counter-inflationary policy in which, for the bulk of the period at least, incomes policy and demand-management policy pulled in the same direction; but persistence with the policy was certainly exhausting, a drain on ministers' and policy advisers' time, and it made a major contribution to the government's political downfall.

7   The supply side

Our judgement on the governments' demand management does not suggest spectacular failure, or indeed given the circumstances any clear presumption of worse-than-average performance. With industrial policy, the judgement has to be harsher. More than elsewhere industrial policy was the scene of the Labour Party's own civil war, resulting in vacillations between extremes in policy statements and an essentially sterile and unproductive policy period. The government succeeded in getting rid of the (politically and economically) least feasible elements of the package they inherited from the years of opposition, but in practice industrial policy turned out to be a curious mixture of innocuous-sounding (and innocuous in effect) 'sector working parties' on the one hand and expensive industrial 'bail-outs', of sometimes questionable permanent value, on the other. Malcolm Sawyer (Chapter 10) points out some mitigating features: some successes for the NEB in restructuring and in its innovative role, the strong political forces behind the 'bail-outs', some suggestive evidence in favour of the success of the sector working parties. Still, relative to aspirations the overall verdict has to be one of failure. This failure is the more piquant for the fact that, whatever the defects of its prescription, the diagnosis of the problem by the Left in the policy statements issued in opposition at least had the merit of recognising that British economic problems are more deep-seated than can be treated simply by tricks from the demand-management toolbox. Indeed this is nowadays common ground. However, the effect of the ill-considered policy prescription offered, together with the related Left–Right disputes, was to produce an interlude of expensive non-policy, nearly (though not wholly) unrelieved by any successes. In the other areas of policy that are nowadays identified as 'supply side', the Labour government did relatively little, with no radical restructuring of tax rates and work incentives and little enough spent on training – though here, as Alex Bowen's Chapter 12 shows, there were some useful initiatives.

8 Other policies

What we have discussed above are the principal arms of demand and supply management policy. What of the record outside this sphere? Where these were identified with a strong emphasis on trade union involvement, subsequent interventions in the 1980s seem to have produced clear reversals of the previous position. In some other policy areas, this identification was less pronounced and elements of policy continuity seem more in evidence. Regional policy, for example (see John Bowers's discussion in Chapter 15) was adjusted, in ways that were broadly similar to what happened in other countries, to the new conditions brought about by the rise in the general level of unemployment and the decline in footloose manufacturing industry. At the same time there was a promising innovation in respect of policy towards inner-urban areas. These themes were continued under the subsequent administrations. Robert Millward (Chapter 9) shows that the record of the nationalised industries was far better than popularly supposed, though policy here was marked by a failure to project success where it occurred and a failure to instil a management ethos appropriate to the commercial ambience of these industries. These weaknesses helped pave the way for the denationalisations of the 1980s. The labour market policies analysed by Alex Bowen in Chapter 12 suggest that these were at least partly successful in terms of their own, limited, objective: moreover, the objective of creating jobs has a ready rationale in a period of rapid industrial rundown, workforce displacement and likely rises in the NAIRU, with all their longer-term consequences. For this reason, similar policies were followed by other governments in the leading industrial countries at this time. Even in the 1980s, a variety of job subsidy schemes continued. International economic policy, analysed here by George Zis and Andrew Scott (Chapters 7 and 8), is for the UK mainly a matter of relationships with the EC. That these did not proceed well is documented by Andrew Scott; George Zis criticises the government for a lack of leadership over the issue of the EMS, but this was an issue on which the government's opinion was very much in line with the views expressed by experts from outside – although the reasoning offered for the decision not to participate varied from one to another. A Labour government should be expected to make some progress in the direction of redistributing income and wealth (even if it is not capable of bringing about 'a fundamental and irreversible shift'). Alan Gillie (Chapter 14) shows that there were some important gains; despite the rise in unemployment, there were large percentage gains for the lowest deciles of households by income, and a large proportional loss for the highest decile, between 1974 and 1978. Moreover, the much-touted higher marginal rates of income taxation were paid only by an extraordinarily small proportion of taxpayers. In the sphere of industrial relations, as William Brown argues in Chapter 13, the government demonstrated little innovative vision either in the legislation it enacted or in its role as employer, although the creation of ACAS must be regarded as a significant and positive achievement and the much-vilified Comparability Commission suggested some useful lessons. More fundamentally, however, the government's pervasive deference to the trade union movement did both government and trade unions great damage: it offered a role in policy-making to institutions that were not equipped for the task, and ultimately it laid them open to the attacks of the Conservative government in the 1980s.

9   A prelude to Thatcherism?

For some the most damaging thing that might be said about the Labour governments of Mr Wilson and Mr Callaghan in the 1970s would be that by example or by incompetence they set the scene for Thatcherism. Both views exist: thus Coates (1980) argues that the policies of the latter-day Labour government laid the foundations for monetarism, whilst Holmes (1985) emphasises policy mistakes, from which Mrs Thatcher and her advisers drew their own lessons. We do not think that matters are quite so simple. It is possible to be misled by rhetorical incidents such as the well-known speech by James Callaghan to the Labour Party conference in 1976 and by the occasional desire of Conservative ministers to share their difficulties with the opposition by pinning the credit for an innovation on their predecessors. As we see it, the Labour governments essentially made their way pragmatically to policy settings appropriate for an inflationary era, lowering the premium on full employment and raising that on beating inflation by fiscal and monetary means; their monetary targets and cash limits can be distinguished (see the chapters by David Cobham and by Peter Jackson) from the successor devices employed by the Thatcher administrations. The basis for arguing that irresponsible government policies led to a bail-out by the IMF is weak, as we have discussed above. Whether Mrs Thatcher and her colleagues drew the right lessons for a future period of government is a topic for another book. But it is hard to forbear from pointing out that, despite the very severe deflation of the early 1980s, the Thatcher government has not managed to eliminate inflation but has presided over a massive rise in the NAIRU; while the late 1980s also witnessed recurring periods of sterling crisis and a clear example of the kind of excessive reflation that was supposed to be a phenomenon of the 1960s and 1970s.

10   Conclusions

When the Labour government relinquished office in 1979 inflation was lower (though rising) than it had been in 1974, growth had been resumed and unemployment (though higher) was falling. The balance of payments was far stronger, the exchange rate steady. Of course in the interval Labour had presided over a violent inflationary spasm, a severe recession and a foreign exchange crisis; growth in productivity and real personal disposable income had been low. But the determinants of much of the poor performance lay outside the control of the Wilson and Callaghan governments, either in the international environment or in the legacy from the past. At the same time there was a turmoil of unreconciled ideas about the way the economy worked and the kinds of policy that were most appropriate which made policy making more contentious. Nor was the temper of the Labour Party itself or society at large conducive to consensual understanding of the problems and their solution. Despite a large-scale and in some ways innovative incomes policy experiment, the government did not move closer to resolving the country's enduring inflation/unemployment problem and it failed to accelerate the underlying growth of the economy: but it was not unique among British governments before, or since, in these respects either. What it did do, was to move pragmatically to adapt policy to the new environment of higher inflation and slower growth and whilst it is possible to argue that this could have been done more quickly, or less expensively, it seems fair to claim that the Labour governments left the economy and the policy-making machinery in better condition in 1979 than they had found them in 1974.

Notes

1 Healey (1989) admits as much, confessing of the policy implementation early in the period, 'This was a mistake ... It is not possible for a country like Britain to grow alone when the rest of the world is contracting' (p. 393).

References

Coates, D. (1980), *Labour in Power? A Study of the Labour Government 1974–9*, Longmans, London.

Fay, S., and Young, H. (1978), 'The day the £ nearly died', *Sunday Times*, 14, 21 and 28 May.

Friedman, M. (1953), 'The case for flexible exchange rates', in M. Friedman (ed.), *Essays in Positive Economics*, University of Chicago Press.

Healey, D. T. (1989), *The Time of My Life*, Michael Joseph, London.

Holmes, M. (1985), *The Labour Government 1974–79*, Macmillan, London.

Appendix A *Mark Wickham-Jones*

A calendar of events

Abbreviations

ASLEF Associated Society of Locomotive Engineers and Firemen
AUEW Amalgamated Union of Engineering Workers
BP   British Petroleum
BR   British Rail
CBI   Confederation of British Industry
EEC   European Economic Community
FT   *Financial Times*
IMF   International Monetary Fund
MLR   Minimum Lending Rate
NCB   National Coal Board
NEB   National Enterprise Board
NEC   National Executive Committee (of the Labour Party)
NEDC National Economic Development Council
NIC   National Insurance Contributions
NIESR National Institute of Economic and Social Research
NUM   National Union of Mineworkers
NUR   National Union of Railwaymen
NUS   National Union of Seamen
OECD Organisation of Economic Co-operation and Development
PLP   Parliamentary Labour Party
PSBR Public Sector Borrowing Requirement
RPI   Retail Price Index
TGWU Transport and General Workers' Union
TUC   Trades Union Congress

1974

January
1   Three day-week, declared by the Conservative government in response to the miners' overtime ban, begins.

February

5 NUM announces a strike for 10 February after 81% of miners vote in favour of action.

7 Prime Minister, Edward Heath, calls a General Election for 28 February.

8 Labour Party manifesto rejects statutory incomes policy and stresses the need for national unity and greater state intervention to solve the economic crisis.

15 Retail Price Index figures show that prices are rising faster than at any time since the index began in 1947 after a 1·9% increase in January.

17 Harold Wilson, Leader of the Labour Party, makes the Social Contract between the Labour Party and the trade unions a major theme of the election.

25 January's trade figures show the worst visible deficit ever recorded for a single month: £383 million.

28 General Election results in a hung parliament where Labour have more seats (5) than the Conservatives.

March

4 After failing to get Liberal Party support Heath resigns and Wilson becomes Prime Minister of a minority Labour government.

6 Pay Board reports that the miners are due exceptional increases and the government helps resolve the dispute by authorising an offer outside the Stage III pay policy as miners accept an increased offer from the NCB which averages 29%.

7 Government announces the end of the three-day week.

26 Denis Healey, Chancellor of the Exchequer, introduces his first Budget. Effect is said to be slightly deflationary though there is some redistribution as public spending and taxes rise. TUC reacts favourably to the Budget but the CBI says that the high level of taxation will hinder expansion.

April

1 Michael Foot, Employment Secretary, refuses to break the Stage III guidelines of the Heath government pay policy by allowing increases in London weighting allowances.

May

14 Healey tells the annual dinner of the CBI that the government supports the private sector.

20 Tony Benn, Industry Secretary, reports to the TUC–Labour Party Liaison Committee on his industrial strategy plans. Some colleagues are alarmed at the radical extent of these, as are the CBI and others when the plans are leaked to the press.

24 First threshold pay increases occur under Heath's Stage III incomes policy (after the RPI increases 3% in April) and give 6–7 million workers up to an extra £1·20 a week.

June

21 RPI increase triggers a threshold increase of 80p per week for 8–10 million workers.

26 TUC General Council approves the Social Contract in the form of voluntary wage restraint coupled with social justice in the document *Collective Bargaining and the Social Contract.*

K

July

11   Eric Varley, Energy Secretary, says that the government will take a major share in oil and gas operations in the North Sea where necessary as well as taxing profits. A state oil company (British National Oil Corporation) will be formed.

19   RPI rise in June results in a 40p threshold payment.

22   Healey has a mini-budget to lower inflation and reflate the economy which is estimated to add £200 million to demand and £340 million to the PSBR for 1974/75. The measures include a VAT cut of 2%.

23   OECD *Economic Outlook* forecasts recession and record inflation for the UK and is sceptical about the Social Contract.

25   Benn offers financial aid to ex-Beaverbrook newspaper workers to begin a new independent paper, the *Scottish Daily News*, as a co-operative.

26   Social Contract comes into operation as Stage III of Heath's incomes policy and statutory restraint end.
     Loans and grants for former Norton Villiers Triumph workers to set up the Meriden Motorcycle Co-operative are agreed by Benn.

31   The Trade Union and Labour Relations Bill is enacted repealing the 1971 Industrial Relations Act, extending workers' rights and abolishing the National Industrial Relations Court.

August

1   *CBI Industrial Trends* reports a collapse in business confidence and suggests it is largely caused by rising costs, liquidity problems, political and economic uncertainty and increased government intervention. Investment intentions are falling. *The Times* says it is 'one of the gloomiest surveys ever'.

15   Benn launches the White Paper *The Regeneration of British Industry*, though the final form owes much to Wilson who has moderated earlier drafts.

16   Increase in the RPI leads to a 40p threshold rise for 10 million workers.

September

4   TUC Annual Congress votes by a large majority to support the Social Contract after the AUEW, which was planning to vote agianst, comes under pressure and agrees to abstain.

18   Wilson calls a General Election for 10 October.

23   Healey claims that inflation is down to 8·4% (annual rate from a three-month base).

October

1   Healey, in Washington, suggests an extension of IMF arrangements for re-cycling oil surpluses but appears to receive little support.

10   General Election results in an outright Labour win with a small majority of 3.

17   Jack Jones, leader of the TGWU, asks unions to be moderate over pay because of the worsening economic crisis.

18   RPI increase leads to a 40p threshold increase.

November

5   AUEW leaders vote by 27 to 25 against a left-wing proposal for a wage increase of £18 per week. This vote is seen as a big boost for the Social Contract.

12 Autumn Budget aims to improve the profitability and liquidity of firms through £1500 million of aid. The Price Code is eased and corporation tax is reduced by relief on stock appreciation. These measures put up the PSBR by £800 million but in any case it is now far higher than the March estimate. CBI does not think that Healey has done enough to help industry.

15 Rise in the RPI results in the final two threshold payments.

December

5 NIESR predicts price rises over 20% in the coming months largely due to the failure of the Social Contract.

6 Government says it will take an equity stake in British Leyland which has run into severe financial trouble.

31 Government rescues Burmah Oil, which has a critical liquidity problem, by guaranteeing Burmah's borrowings. Burmah agrees to a 51% government share in North Sea oil operations.

1975

January

6 Financial Times 30 Share Index reaches lowest level for 21 years at 146.

21 Len Murray, TUC General Secretary, says that pay increases must not be based upon likely or expected price rises.

31 Government publishes Industry Bill which includes plans for the NEB and planning agreements. The government proposes to extend public ownership to profitable areas of manufacturing. TUC support the Bill, wanting to see strong union representation on the NEB and quick action. CBI attacks proposed measures as dangerous.

February

13 NUM accepts 35% pay increase. One leader, Arthur Scargill, says triumphantly that it is a breach of the Social Contract.

19 Figures are published which indicate that wages increased by a record 29% in 1974.

28 Bank of England suspends the corset controls on bank lending after two years. FT 30 Share Index closes at 301·8 having doubled in 8 weeks.

March

18 Government decides to recommend a vote to stay in the EEC i the forthcoming referendum after the Cabinet votes 16 to 7 in favour of remaining a member.

April

15 Budget is aimed at redirecting resources to improve the balance of payments and reduce the PSBR. Demand is reduced by £300 million and 2·75% is added to the RPI. Measures include tax increases and cuts of £900 million in public spending. *The Times* says that Healey has 'finally and totally broken with post war economic orthodoxy'. Murray and Jones are disappointed while the CBI shows relief that it was a tough budget.

18 Inflation reaches a new peak of 25·4% a year (on a six-month base).

23 Healey says that if the Social Contract does not work further spending cuts may yet be needed.
24 Ryder Report on British Leyland is published proposing a new structure and the injection of up to £900 million of public money over three years. Government accepts it and will take a majority shareholding.
26 Special Labour Party Conference votes for withdrawal from the EEC by a 2 to 1 margin.

May
2   Pound falls to $2·3375 and the weighted average effective depreciation since December 1971 ends the week at 23·1%, having fallen 1·4% since the budget. (All further figures for the pound show either the dollar exchange rate or the effective depreciation against other major currencies since December 1971.)
9   Tony Crosland, Environment Secretary, announces that 'the party is over' and that councils must curb spending.
17 Jones makes crucial speech at the TGWU rally telling workers that they may have to accept a flat across-the-board pay rate increase.
30 NUR leaders reject 27·5% arbitration offer and a call for strike if BR does not meet demands for 30–35% pay increases (see 20 June).

June
5   EEC referendum results in a large vote to stay in Europe (67·2% Yes and 32·8% No).
9   Bank for International Settlements report argues that British unions must accept a cut in real consumption.
10 After the referendum Wilson reshuffles government. In what is widely seen as demotion Benn is swapped with Eric Varley at the Department of Energy. Benn hesitates but accepts.
11 TUC economic committee gives some support to Jones's flat-rate plan for incomes while the NIESR warns of faster inflation to come without some form of incomes policy.
13 Inflation reaches an annual rate of 36·3% on a six-month base.
17 AUEW conference rejects the Social Contract as pound reaches low of $2·2720.
20 Cabinet decides in principle to go for a voluntary pay policy.
    NUR accepts 30% from BR and cancels strike.
22 Jones says that collective bargaining could be suspended for a year if the government will take action on prices.
23 TUC–Labour Liaison Committee fails to reach agreement over pay policy. TUC wants tight price controls but the government says these are not feasible.
25 TUC General Council accepts the need for a flat-rate increase in pay policy provided it is part of the principles for a new version of the Social Contract. Other principles include price targets, price controls, and action on unemployment.
30 Sterling continues to do down, after falling 1·3% in a day to £2·1920 and an effective depreciation of 28·9%. Pressure is clearly mounting on the government which still hopes for a voluntary deal with the trade unions.

July

1 Healey announces measures to restore confidence in sterling and to reduce inflation. These include pay limits, price controls, the use of cash limits for government wage bills and some other public spending. A pay policy will be developed soon, hopefully with TUC support. Pound responds by moving up to $2·2100.
TGWU conference votes in favour of Social Contract although it opposes statutory wage control.

3 TUC economic committee meets Healey and accepts the need for a pay policy when he makes it clear that proposals must be agreed or they will be enforced. £6 emerges as the likely limit following Jones's flat-rate plan.

8 Government meets the TUC economic committee and reaches a broad consensus over the TUC pay and prices plan although Healey still wants statutory back-up powers.
NUM conference decides to seek £100 per week wage and not to demand it. A major threat to the pay policy is removed.

9 TUC General Council adopts the pay policy document *The Development of the Social Contract*, which accepts the £6 limit, by 19 votes to 13.

11 Government publishes the White Paper *The Attack on Inflation* with details of the pay policy. Basic limit is £6 per week with nothing for those earning over £8500 a year. The Price Code will be used to stop any breaches of the limit being passed on in prices. Some other price restraints further placate the unions.

24 Unemployment rises above 1 million for the first time sicne 1940, with an unadjusted total of 1·036 million.

31 Varley refuses further aid for Norton Villiers Triumph including the Meriden Motorcycle co-operative which has run into financial trouble. (It soon goes into liquidation.)

August

1 £6 pay policy comes into operation.

5 Peter Shore, Trade Secretary, announces that an independent inquiry into industrial democracy will be set up. (Sir Alan Bullock is appointed chairman of it in December.)
Foot gives details of a Temporary Employment Subsidy which will pay £10 per week to firms for each person kept employed who would otherwise be sacked.

12 House of Commons Trade and Industry Sub-Committee publishes a report critical of the Ryder plan for British Leyland.

September

3 TUC Annual Congress votes for the £6 pay policy by 6·9 million votes to 3·4 million.

29 Labour Party Conference votes overwhelmingly to support the £6 pay week pay policy.

October

9 Official figures show a 2·5−3% fall in real disposable income in the second quarter of 1975, the biggest fall for 20 years.

November

3   In talks with the government over possible financial aid, Chrysler places the onus on the government to give help to its British subsidiary (see 12 December).

          Wynne Godley, a Cambridge economist tells the House of Commons Expenditure Committee that public expenditure is not properly controlled.

5   An NEDC meeting at Chequers heralds a shift in priorities away from public expenditure and towards industrial regeneration. There is also a shift away from direct intervention and towards co-operation and indirect measures. NEDC will set up 30 sectoral working parties.

7   Government applies to the IMF for a $2 billion loan, $1·2 billion from the oil facility and $0·8 from the first tranche.

8   Lacking funds and with no further aid from the government the *Scottish Daily News* closes.

15–17   Leaders of the six leading Western industrial nations meet at Rambouillet in France for a three-day summit. They issue a 15-point declaration of principles of economic co-operation and give a commitment to economic recovery.

19   Joel Barnett, Chief Secretary to the Treasury, says that pay policy will have to be tough after July 1976. A government survey of 6000 pay settlements under the current policy shows no major breaches.

25   Government cuts bread subsidy by 0·5p per loaf — the first reduction since food subsidies were introduced last year.

December

8   Rumours that the IMF will make a ban on import controls a condition of the $2 billion loan to Britain are denied. There is pressure on the UK not to restrict trade and the US government is concerned about import controls.

12   Government agrees to give aid to Chrysler with £162·5 million in loans, grants and guarantees. 8000 jobs out of 25,000 are to be lost. A split Cabinet accepts the deal reluctantly. Chrysler will give a declaration of intent.

1976

January

1   IMF directors agree to loans of $2 billion to Britain.

February

12   Healey announces a package to encourage investment and attack unemployment by creating 70,000 jobs at a cost of £220 million.

19   Public expenditure White Paper shows cuts of £1 billion for 1977/78 and £2·4 billion for 1978/79 from previous plans.

March

5   Pound falls below $2 for the first time and ends the day at $1·9820 with an effective depreciation of 31·5%. Fall follows Bank of England sale of sterling.

10 Government is defeated in a debate on the public expenditure White Paper by 284 votes to 256 with 37 Labour abstentions.

Despite Bank intervention the pound falls further to $1·9145 and an effective depreciation of 33·8%. The pound has fallen 6% in a week.

11 Government wins a confidence motion, after defeat of 10 March, by 297 votes to 280.

15 At EEC Finance Ministers meeting Healey denies that the fall in sterling was engineered in order to gain a competitive trading advantage.

16 Harold Wilson announces his surprise resignation as Prime Minister.

23 Unemployment falls for the first time in almost two years to 1·18 million (seasonally adjusted).

April

1 Pound falls heavily against the dollar amidst reported concern over UK's economic prospects and industrial relations troubles at British Leyland as well as uncertainty over the Labour leadership and the future course of economic policy. It ends at $1·8840 and an effective depreciation of 35·3%.

5 James Callaghan becomes Prime Minister, beating Michael Foot by 176 votes to 137.

6 Healey introduces a 'conditional' Budget where most of the tax cuts are linked to a new pay norm of 3% being accepted by the TUC. Cash limits now apply to 75% of government spending.

7 Initial union reaction to the 3% pay norm is that it is too low.

Labour formally loses its majority in the House of Commons though major defeats remain unlikely given the number of minor party MPs.

9 Treasury issues a statement saying that there is 'no economic justification' for the extent of sterling's fall as it touches $1·8380.

29 Price Commission announces that inflation has been halved in nine months from 30% to 13%.

May

5 Government and TUC agree on pay formula which will add 4·5% to wages. Maximum increase will be £4 and minimum £2·50. This meets the conditions of the Budget. Employers give a cautious welcome.

13 NUM leaders vote for new pay policy and dealers say that this helps to steady sterling.

28 Pound falls to $1·7585. The reason for this drop appears to be adverse foreign sentiment over the Budget.

June

2 Pound falls 3 cents to $1·7248 and an effective depreciation of 41·1%. Over $3000 million of reserves have been used in supporting it over three months. Healey says Britain 'must keep its nerve and not panic'.

7 Healey announces a stand-by credit of $5·3 billion, borrowed for six months central banks and the Bank for International Settlements. The pound rises four cents to $1·7573.

16 Special TUC meeting supports pay policy by 9·3 million votes to 0·5 million.

22   US Treasury warns Britain of the need to change policies and reduce government deficit if it wants international aid.
30   Government publishes White Paper *The Attack on Inflation: the second year* with details of new policy. The Price Code is altered to allow increases in corporate profitability. Healey says next round will have to be more flexible.

July
3   Healey says public spending cuts may be needed to keep economic recovery moving steadily.
14   Callaghan and Healey stress to PLP and TUC that government survival depends on public spending cuts such as those now being considered.
19   Cabinet begins to allocate spending cuts.
22   Healey announces £1 billion of spending cuts. A limit on money supply growth is declared, as is a rise of 2% in National Insurance contributions from April 1977 to raise £1 billion.
28   Despite the cuts the TUC and Labour NEC formally endorse a new phase of the Social Contract. They agree to develop industrial democracy and indicative planning.
30   CBI tells PM of its opposition to the July measures and especially the NIC increase. It accuses the Government of bad faith and withdraws its investment initiative plans.

August
1   New pay policy comes into force.
13   July visible trade deficit of £524 million is the highest for 20 months and the second worst ever.

September
7   Labour's NEC publishes a policy document which calls for public ownership for four main clearing banks and seven insurance companies.
8   TUC Annual Congress votes for the pay policy but also a return to free collective bargaining next year, amidst warnings of rank-and-file revolt if pay restraint continues.
     Pound comes under pressure on news of a threatened seamen's strike at $1·7720 despite Bank support.
9   Bank of England stops supporting the pound. This may be an attempt to put pressure on the seamen or simply reflect the cost of continued support. Pound falls to $1·7480.
10   Bank raises MLR by 1·5% to 13%, a record peak last seen in November 1973.
16   Bank of England tightens monetary policy by calling for £350 million of special deposits. Pound rises to $1·7380.
20   Statistics indicate that first stage of the pay policy has halved the rate of growth of earnings to 14% and there have been no major breaches of it.
22   Seamen's strike is averted as NUS accepts pay offer.
26   Healey rules out the introduction of general import controls.
27   Labour Party Conference votes against government White Paper on public expenditure and supports councils who refuse to implement cuts.

28 Pound falls a record 4 cents to $1·6370 (depreciation of 45·5%). Healey postpones departure to the IMF Conference. Callaghan makes speech attacking conventional reflation.

29 Healey announces that he is to apply to the IMF for $3·9 billion to finance the balance of payments and repay the short-term credit from June. Pound gains 3 cents to $1·6675 with reported Bank of England support.

30 Healey gets support for his policies from the Labour Conference. However the Conference also votes for nationalisation of the 'big four' banks.

October

7 MLR is increased by 2% to a record 15% and the Bank calls for a further 2% special deposits to control money supply growth.

25 Following a *Sunday Times* article claiming to give the terms already agreed for the IMF loan including a sterling rate of $1·50, the pound falls 5 cents to $1·5950. Both the IMF and the US Treasury deny the story. Callaghan says he wants to end sterling's reserve role.

26 Unemployment figures fall for the first time since March 1976 to 1·25 million (seasonally adjusted).

27 Labour Party NEC votes against further spending cuts and the Party seems extremely divided.

November

2 IMF team arrives in London for talks over the loan.

4 Labour loses two out of three by-elections and is now clearly a minority government.

5 Treasury gives the IMF forecasts which show the PSBR at £11 billion for 1977, £2 billion above the July estimate.

16 Harold Lever, a Cabinet member, tries to reach an agreement with the US government in Washington to deal with the sterling balances.

18 Government tightens squeeze on bank lending by reintroducing the corset to control the money supply.

23 Cabinet begins discussion on the terms for the IMF loan.

28 William Simon, US Treasury Secretary, comes to London and discusses the terms of the loan with Healey and Lever.

29 Government withdraws commitment to a wealth tax.

December

2 Cabinet accepts the need to reduce spending in order to get the IMF loan.

7 Healey says he hopes for a safety net agreement to protect sterling.

11 Healey admits that IMF measures will be unpopular but says that the government is determined to get it right this time. In December opinion poll support for Labour falls to 34% with the Conservatives at 49·9%.

15 Healey announces economic package as part of the IMF loan. Public spending is to be cut by £1 billion in 1977/78 and £1·5 billion in 1978/79 in order to reduce the PSBR by £2 billion in 1977/78 and £3 billion in 1978/79. Indirect taxes are up and the government is going to sell part of BP to raise £0·5 billion. The Letter of Intent to the IMF will also include targets for domestic credit expansion.

21 In debate on economic measures 27 Labour MPs vote against the govern-
    ment, which wins by 219 to 51 votes as most Conservatives abstain.
29 Pound rises to highest level for three months to $1·7055 and 44% effective
    depreciation.

1977

January
3   IMF grants standby credit of $3·9 billion to Britain, the largest credit ever
    made.
10 Bank for International Settlements backed by various countries announces
    availability of a medium-term credit facility of $3 billion for Bank of England
    as security against withdrawal of foreign official sterling balances.
13 Bank of England eases squeeze on bank lending by releasing £1·1 billion from
    special deposits.
26 Bullock Report into industrial democracy is published which recommends that
    companies with over 2000 employees should be compelled to accept equal
    numbers of worker representatives onto their boards.
28 Callaghan promises to introduce legislation based on the Bullock Report by the
    summer.

February
2   *The Times* says that the CBI will lose enthusiasm for industrial strategy unless
    there is some compromise and flexibility regarding industrial democracy.
15 Callaghan retreats from his commitment to legislation on the Bullock Report
    in the face of opposition from the CBI.
16 TUC tells Healey that it cannot agree to pay policy before the Budget.

March
1   Effective sterling exchange rate index rebased. (Figures given below are index
    figures on December 1971 = 100.)
2   The NEB and the government threaten not to give further aid to British Leyland
    unless strikes which have laid off 28,000 end (see 15 March).
15 British Leyland management and unions give strikers an ultimatum to return to
    work or be dismissed as 46,000 are now laid off (see 21 March).
21 Normal working is resumed at British Leyland but the NEB is concerned by
    the extent of funding that the company has required.
23 Government survives almost certain defeat in a no-confidence motion by 24
    votes with the support of 13 Liberal MPs. This vote marks the beginning of
    the Lib—Lab pact.
29 Healey introduces a further 'conditional' Budget. Income tax cuts are made
    from 35% to 33% on the basic rate but linked to a pay policy being agreed.
    Concessions are equal to a 4·5% pay rise. City reaction to the Budget is mainly
    favourable.
31 Prospects for a third year's pay policy are jeopardised by the low norm of 4—5%
    which Healey wants, and by union reaction to the Budget.

April

5 Albert Booth, Employment Secretary, says that employers and unions may distribute increases within an agreed level for phase three which is unlikely to be more than 10%.

17 Jones, critical of the Budget, rejects a formal pay deal for Phase Three but warns against a free for all. Joe Gormley, the miners' leader, has also rejected a phase three deal.

24 Healey says that a 'single-figure pay/prices equation' will be needed for phase three.

May

2 Murray and Hugh Scanlon, President of the AUEW, express cautious support for the Social Contract but say that phase three must be more flexible.

4 AUEW leaders reject third stage of pay policy and call for a return to free collective bargaining. Vote is seen as very damaging to the policy.

5 Government withdraws 5·5p increase in petrol tax following pressure from Liberal MPs.

12 Bank of England extends the corset controls on the growth of bank lending for another six months.

13 In the twelfth cut of the year the Bank reduces MLR to 8%, the lowest rate since the summer of 1973.

17 At the CBI annual dinner Healey says that it will be up to the private sector to ensure that a more flexible pay policy is not abused.

June

1 The NEB gives clearance for British Leyland to resume capital spending beginning with investment in the new Mini.

14 Government is defeated in the committee stage of the Finance Bill over personal tax allowances. This includes the 'Rooker–Wise' amendment where these two Labour MPs joined the Opposition to tie the level of tax relief to the cost of living.

22 TUC General Council votes by 19 to 4 to honour Stage Two of the pay policy, especially the twelve-month rule, but wants a return to free collective bargaining after 31 July.

July

6 TGWU votes for a return to free collective bargaining and against the twelve-month rule despite the advice of leaders. This action is regarded as ending hopes for a formal agreement between the government and trade unions.

12 Healey meets the trade unions for a final round of talks but no agreement is reached. TUC says that a third year of pay restraint is not possible in the face of rank-and-file opposition.

15 Healey announces economic package and guidelines on pay; income tax will be cut to 34% not 33% as proposed in the Budget. Healey calls for a pay limit of 10% and for a twelve-month gap between increases. Price controls mean that firms will not be able to pass on over-10% pay rises in price increases.

25 Government gives another £100 million for British Leyland provided company satisfies NEB of progress in improving industrial relations.

27   Bank of England cuts sterling's informal link with the dollar and it rises to $1·7370. Bank has held sterling down since March. More attention will be paid to the effective index rate since 1971 now at 61·7.

August
11   Bank suspends the corset introduced in the autumn of 1976 as the money supply seems under control.
26   NIESR says that the government should pay off the outstanding debt to the IMF and begin to reflate the economy.

September
6   PM hints at possible reflation at the TUC Annual Congress but says that the government will not be deflected from controlling inflation.
7   TUC Annual Congress votes in favour of twelve-month rule while supporting free collective bargaining by a majority of 2·8 million votes.
14   Record current account surplus for August is announced (£316 million) caused partly by a sharp fall in imports. It is the first trade surplus since July 1972. FT index rises to an all-time high of 549·2, 5·6 points above previous high of May 1972.
16   RPI shows a significant slow-down in the annual rate of inflation in August from 17·6% (for July) to 16·5%.
20   Unemployment figures reach a new post-war peak of 1·39 million (adjusted figure) or 6·0%.
22   Government withdraws export credit guarantees from James Mackie and Sons as a sanction because its pay increases have breached the pay policy guidelines.

October
3   Labour Party Conference supports the government's economic policy by a large margin.
14   Bank of England cuts minimum lending rate to 5%.
25   After four poor months, unemployment falls by 12,000 to 1·38 million (seasonally adjusted).
26   Healey introduces a mini-Budget which involves limited reflation of £1 billion in current year and £2·2 billion in the next, pushing the PSBR up to £7·5 billion in 1977/78.
31   Bank of England ceases to intervene in the foreign exchange markets to hold sterling down because of continued inflows of foreign currency which could endanger domestic monetary targets. Effect is that pound rises 6 cents to $1·8405 (index of 64·6), which is the highest level for 18 months.

November
2   Reserves rise by $3·04 billion during October to a record of $20·2 billion.
10   An opinion poll shows that 87% of people support the 10% pay policy.
14   National strike by firemen begins in support of 30% pay claim. Troops are called in (see 21 December).
16   Average earnings show an 8·8% rise in earnings in the year to September but many workers may be holding back before settling.

25 Bank raises MLR by 2% to 7% following the end of Bank intervention over sterling.

December
21 TUC General Council votes by 20 to 17 not to support the firemen's strike (see 12 January).

1978

January
1 Callaghan says that he wants wage increases limited to 5% by 1979.
3 Pound rises nearly 4·5 cents to highest level for nearly two years of $1·9635.
12 Government publishes White Paper for public expenditure with planned public spending increases of 2·25% in 1978/79, 2% in 1979/80, 2% in 1980/81 and under 1% in 1981/82.
   The firemen's strike is called off.
26 The government says that it is to repay $1 billion of the IMF loan early.

February
1 Michael Edwardes, the new chairman, says that British Leyland is to cut its workforce by 12,500. Shop stewards and managers support him.
7 The House of Commons votes for a clause that all future government contracts should involve companies adhering rigidly to the 10% pay guidelines.
8 NUM accepts 10% pay increase after initially seeking 92%.
17 RPI shows inflation is in single figures − 9·9% for the year to January − for the first time since October 1973.

March
3 PSBR is well below forecast at 3610 million in the first nine months of 1977/78 − the lowest level for 4 years.
15 Albert Booth, Employment Secretary, announces a £300 million package of measures to help create 400,000 jobs by March 1979.
21 The Government publishes the White Paper *The Challenge of North Sea Oil* listing four uses for the revenues: industrial investment, improving economic performance, investment in energy and improved infrastructure.
29 Jones retires and Moss Evans becomse TGWU General Secretary.

April
3 British Leyland gets government support for a revised £1·3 billion investment programme including an injection of £850 million of state funds over 4 years.
11 The Budget is aimed at a limited stimulation of the economy with tax cuts, pension and benefit increases, and larger company tax allowances. $1 billion is repaid to the IMF.

May
2 Terry Duffy is elected President of the AUEW to replace Scanlon and end left-wing control of the union.

8   The Opposition forces a cut of 1p in the basic rate of income tax in an amendment to the Finance Bill.
23   After a long delay the government publishes a White Paper on industrial democracy. PM says that he hopes for legislation in the next session. Employers are still critical of any scheme.
25   Bank of England abandons market-related formula for determining MLR. The rate will be decided administratively.
      The termination of the Lib–Lab pact is announced.

June
8   Market pressure and the low level of gilt sales force the government to introduce a package of restrictive monetary and fiscal measures in order to cut money supply growth. The corset is reactivated, MLR rises by 1% to 10% and National Insurance contributions are increased by 2·5%.
22   Price Commission warns that inflation will start to rise from the end of the year because of wage and commodity price increases.
28   Government reduces proposed increase in National Insurance contributions to 1·5% because of Liberal pressure.
30   Callaghan warns that wage guidelines will be reduced in the coming year despite union discontent.

July
6   Miners vote against further pay policy.
18   TUC General Council meets government but fails to reach agreement over pay.
      Unemployment begins to rise for the first time in ten months, to 1·31 million adjusted or 5·6%.
19   CBI tells the government that it wants pay policy but without sanctions on firms that break it.
21   Government publishes White Paper *Winning the Battle against Inflation* with details of the next stage of the pay policy. Government sets a 5% limit for pay with some limited exceptions and room for productivity deals. The aim is to get inflation below 7·5%.

August
1   1978/79 pay round begins. The government is reported as being optimistic but the TUC is opposed to a formal deal and the 5% limit.
10   It is reported that the French firm Peugeot Citroën is to pay £220 million for the European operations of Chrysler Corporation, meaning that Chrysler is in breach of its agreement with the government (see 28 September).
17   The government is to extend the corset in the autumn until June 1979 to meet money supply targets.
24   Ford unions claim a pay rise over 5% (see 21 September).

September
6   TUC Annual Congress votes against any pay limits.
7   Callaghan announces that despite widespread expectations there will be no autumn election.

20 Figures show that wages increases on average by 14·2% in 12 months of Stage Three. Department of Employment says that 99% of settlements from major groups are within policy guidelines.
21 Ford workers strike after rejecting 5% pay offer (see 31 October).
28 Government approves Peugeot take-over of Chrysler.

October
2 Labour Party Conference votes against government's 5% pay policy by 4·0 million to 1·9 million votes. Government says it will stick by policy.
17 Government holds talks with the TUC and there are hints of a wider package of measures.
36 Government and the CBI discuss a possible new package of measures including tighter price controls which the CBI opposes.
30 Government repays another $1 billion to the IMF.
   Pound reaches its highest level since September 1975 at $2·1045 and index of 63·3.
31 Unions reject a new Ford offer of 16·5% (see 22 November).

November
6 Government approves a 22% pay rise for the firemen under special case deal which ended the strike earlier in the year.
7 Bakers go on strike until 17 December when they get 14% pay rise.
14 Talks between the government and the TUC result in a joint statement on pay and prices. However the TUC General Council has a tied vote at 14-all and rejects publication of the new guidelines. Healey says that the 5% remains in force.
22 Ford workers accept 16·5% after a nine-week strike.
28 Government announces decision to blacklist Ford following pay settlement. Government departments will not place contracts and discretionary aid will be reassessed.
30 Times Newspapers suspends publication after the failure to reach agreement with the unions over new technology.

December
5 Government decides not to join the new European Monetary System.
7 Government plans to raise NEB loan limit to £4·5 billion.
12 Unions representing 1 million workers in the National Health Service and local authorities reject the 5% pay offer and call for a programme of industrial action in the new year.
13 Government loses vote in the Commons over the pay policy sanctions by 285 to 283.
14 Government says that it is abandoning discriminatory sanctions against private companies.
20 Ford give a formal undertaking to the Price Commission that it will not pass on in higher prices more than 5% of the recent pay award.

1979

January

3 Lorry drivers begin an unofficial pay strike.
10 Callaghan returns from foreign summit and questions whether there is a crisis in Britain though lorry drivers' strike has had a major impact.
11 TGWU make road haulage dispute official.
16 Government relaxes wages policy in a bid to avoid a series of crippling strikes in public services. Cabinet agrees a three-point package with help for the low-paid, comparability for the public sector, and tougher price controls. ASLEF hold the first of a series of one-day strikes.
18 Cabinet accepts voluntary code of the TGWU for picketing, which has become a major issue in the strikes, rather than declare a state of emergency.
19 Government further relaxes pay guidelines when it says that it will not prevent road haulage firms from increasing prices to cover higher wage costs.
22 1·5 million public service workers stage a 24-hour strike for a £60 per week minimum wage.
25 Healey spells out the serious economic consequences of high pay claims. Taxes and unemployment may rise.
30 Nearly half the hospitals in Britain are said to be giving only emergency cover because of a strike by hospital ancillary workers.

February

3 Callaghan eases pay guidelines for local authority workers.
7 Bank raises MLR by 1·5% to 14%.
14 A joint government–TUC statement *The Economy, Government and Trade Union Responsibilities* is published which aims to get unemployment below 5% in three years. Unions give a series of guidelines on picketing.

March

1 Referenda on devolution are held in Scotland and Wales. Both fail to get adequate support for the legislation to be passed.
28 Government loses a confidence motion by 311 to 310 votes as previous allies, the Liberals, and more recent allies, the Scottish Nationalists, vote against it. General Election is called.

April

3 'Care and maintenance' Budget is passed by the government with the agreement of the opposition.

May

3 General Election is held and results in victory for the Conservative Party with 339 seats and an overall majority of 43.

Sources

The Times (and *Daily Telegraph*)
National Institute Economic Review
Economic Trends

Economic Progress Report
Scottish Economic Bulletin
Bank of England Quarterly Bulletin
British Journal of Industrial Relations
Geoff Foote, *A Chronology of Post War British Politics*, (Croom Helm, London, 1987)
David Butler and Gareth Butler, *British Political Facts 1900–1985* (London, Macmillan, 1985)
Robert Taylor, 'The Winter of Discontent' (*Contemporary Record*, I, no. 3)
Barbara Castle, *The Castle Diaries 1974–1976*, (Weidenfeld & Nicolson, London, 1980)

Appendix B

Basic statistics

Table B.1: Output, income and consumption, 1970–85

	Levels (£m., 1985 prices)				Annual rate of change (%)			
	GDP (at factor cost, average estimate)	Real personal disposable income (RPDY)	Private consumption (C)	Government consumption (G)	GDP	RPDY	C	G
1970	231,350	172,304	156,336	55,827	1·99	3·91	2·78	1·66
1971	234,999	174,548	161,208	57,483	1·58	1·30	3·12	2·97
1972	241,428	189,208	171,052	59,909	2·74	8·40	6·11	4·22
1973	259,998	201,147	179,852	62,500	7·69	6·31	5·14	6·31
1974	255,797	199,554	177,233	63,666	-1·62	-0·79	-1·46	1·87
1975	253,651	200,484	176,273	67,219	-0·84	0·47	-0·54	5·58
1976	260,596	200,168	176,853	68,053	2·74	-0·16	0·33	1·24
1977	267,260	195,753	176,016	66,926	2·56	-2·21	-0·47	-1·66
1978	275,376	210,065	185,950	68,466	3·04	7·31	5·64	2·30
1979	282,782	221,826	193,794	69,943	2·69	5·60	4·22	2·16
1980	276,495	225,084	193,806	71,050	-2·22	1·47	0·01	1·58
1981	273,462	222,456	193,832	71,269	-1·10	-1·17	0·01	0·31
1982	278,420	221,941	195,561	71,826	1·81	-0·23	0·89	0·78
1983	288,703	228,126	204,318	73,282	3·69	2·79	4·48	2·03
1984	293,909	232,568	207,927	73,897	1·80	1·95	1·77	0·84
1985	304,933	238,804	215,535	73,955	3·75	2·68	3·66	0·08

Table B.2 *Output and productivity, 1970–85*

| | Levels (1975 = 100) | | | | Annual rates of change (%) | | | |
| | Output | | Productivity[a] | | Output | | Productivity | |
	Production industries	Manufacturing industry	Whole economy	Manufacturing industry	Production industries	Manufacturing industry	Whole economy industry	Manufacturing
1970	97·77	98·42	94·55	88·84	0·48	0·30	2·00	0·46
1971	97·30	97·44	97·15	90·88	−0·48	−1·00	2·74	2·30
1972	99·06	99·51	99·75	95·92	1·81	2·12	2·80	5·54
1973	107·85	108·77	103·34	104·22	8·88	9·31	3·58	8·65
1974	105·74	107·39	101·48	102·59	−1·96	−1·27	−1·79	−1·57
1975	100·00	100·00	100·00	100·00	−5·43	−6·88	−1·46	−2·52
1976	103·28	101·87	102·85	105·17	3·28	1·87	2·84	5·17
1977	108·67	103·84	105·69	107·07	5·22	1·93	2·76	1·81
1978	111·72	104·43	108·54	108·16	2·80	0·57	2·57	1·02
1979	116·06	104·33	110·27	108·71	3·88	−0·09	1·71	0·50
1980	108·44	95·27	107·92	104·35	−6·57	−8·69	−2·24	−4·01
1981	105·04	89·56	110·15	108·03	−3·14	−6·00	2·17	3·52
1982	107·03	89·75	114·73	115·24	1·90	0·22	4·26	6·68
1983	111·02	92·31	119·68	124·90	3·72	2·85	4·19	8·38
1984	111·25	96·16	120·79	132·11	0·21	4·16	1·44	5·77
1985	117·23	98·52	123·76	136·05	5·37	2·46	1·63	2·99

Note: [a] Output per person employment not taking into account part-time working or hours of work.

Table B.3 *Fixed investment, 1970–85*

	Levels (£m. 1985 prices)				Annual rate of change (%)			
	Total fixed investment	Dwelling investment	Investment other than in dwellings	Investment in manufacturing	Total fixed investment	Dwelling investment	Investment other than in dwellings	Investment in manufacturing
1970	51564	12292	39272	10666	2·53	−9·22	−9·22	8·86
1971	52517	13396	39121	9757	1·85	8·98	−0·38	−8·52
1972	52401	13777	38624	8496	−0·22	2·84	−1·27	−12·92
1973	55818	13513	42305	9149	6·52	−1·92	9·53	7·69
1974	54465	12727	41738	10036	−2·42	−5·82	−1·34	9·70
1975	53383	13042	40341	9181	−1·99	2·48	−3·35	−8·52
1976	54277	13457	40820	8761	1·67	3·18	1·19	−4·57
1977	53307	12811	40496	9154	−1·79	−4·80	−0·79	4·49
1978	54914	12913	42001	9763	3·01	0·80	3·72	6·65
1979	56450	13363	43087	10136	2·80	3·48	2·59	3·82
1980	53416	12379	41037	8761	−5·37	−7·36	−4·76	−13·57
1981	48298	10247	38051	6579	−9·58	−17·22	−7·28	−24·91
1982	50915	10899	40016	6360	5·42	6·36	5·16	−3·33
1983	53476	12247	41229	6422	5·03	12·37	3·03	0·97
1984	58075	12571	45504	7810	8·60	2·65	10·37	21·61
1985	60283	11928	48355	8735	3·80	−5·11	6·27	11·84

Table B.4 Employment, unemployment, prices and earnings 1970–85

	Employment[a] 000s	Unemployment[b] 000s	Retail prices 1975 = 100	Retail price inflation	Earnings levels		Earnings inflation	
					Manufacturing	Whole economy	Manufacturing	Whole economy
1970	22479	532·00	54·29	6·52	47·78	46·38	12·76	12·59
1971	22139	746·30	59·28	9·18	53·13	51·69	11·20	11·46
1972	22137	668·17	63·71	7·48	59·69	57·94	12·34	12·09
1973	22679	444·98	69·53	9·13	67·67	65·39	13·38	12·85
1974	22804	554·37	80·61	15·94	79·34	76·91	17·23	17·62
1975	22723	977·90	100·00	24·05	100·00	100·00	26·05	30·02
1976	22557	1116·17	116·62	16·62	116·60	113·01	16·60	13·01
1977	22631	1198·76	135·18	15·91	128·56	124·74	10·26	10·37
1978	22789	1110·17	146·26	8·20	147·34	140·71	14·60	12·81
1979	23173	1052·00	165·93	13·45	170·88	162·57	15·98	15·53
1980	22991	1698·93	195·84	18·03	200·30	195·53	17·22	20·28
1981	21892	2371·73	219·11	11·88	226·97	220·90	13·31	12·97
1982	21414	2669·87	237·95	8·60	252·31	241·62	11·16	9·38
1983	21067	2832·13	248·75	4·54	274·91	262·03	8·96	8·45
1984	21238	2982·77	261·22	5·01	298·97	278·09	8·75	6·13
1985	21506	3057·90	277·01	6·04	326·21	301·45	9·11	8·40

Notes:
[a] Excludes H M Forces, self-employment and those on government training schemes.
[b] Adult unemployment. Figures show the seasonally adjusted fourth quarter monthly average.
Source: CSO Public Database, October 1989.

Table B.5 *Trade and the balance of payments*

	Visible exports 1975 = 100	Visible imports	Visible trade balance (£m)	Current account balance (£m)	Terms of trade 1975 = 100
1970	81·1	81·9	−14·0	821·0	118·6
1971	86·0	85·7	210·0	1114·0	119·7
1972	85·7	95·7	−742·0	203·0	121·1
1973	97·2	108·9	−2566·0	−996·0	106·8
1974	104·3	109·4	−5233·0	−3186·0	92·8
1975	100·0	100·0	−3257·0	−1526·0	100·0
1976	110·0	106·4	−3959·0	−963·0	97·7
1977	119·0	108·6	−2324·0	−175·0	100·1
1978	122·1	113·7	−1593·0	936·0	105·9
1979	127·4	124·6	−3398·0	−550·0	110·2
1980	129·0	117·9	1353·0	2820·0	114·3
1981	127·8	113·1	3350·0	6628·0	114·6
1982	131·3	119·5	2218·0	4587·0	113·0
1983	134·3	129·8	−1075·0	3758·0	111·4
1984	145·2	144·6	−4580·0	1885·0	110·4
1985	153·4	149·2	−2346·0	3203·0	110·9

Source: CSO Public Database, October 1989.

Table B.6 *Exchange rates and interest rates*

	Exchange rates[a]			Interest rates	
	$ rate	DM rate	Effective rate (1975 = 100)	Treasury bill rate[b]	Long rate (20 years)[c]
1970	2·3960	8·7360	128·1	6·9300	9·2100
1971	2·4440	8·5300	127·9	4·4600	8·8500
1972	2·5020	7·9750	123·3	8·4800	8·9000
1973	2·4526	6·5400	111·8	12·8200	10·7100
1974	2·3402	6·0490	108·3	11·3000	14·7700
1975	2·2198	5·4470	100·0	10·9300	14·3900
1976	1·8046	4·5510	85·7	13·9800	14·4300
1977	1·7455	4·0510	81·2	6·3900	12·7300
1978	1·9197	3·8500	81·5	11·9100	12·4700
1979	2·1225	3·8880	87·3	16·4900	12·9900
1980	2·3281	4·2270	96·1	13·5800	13·7800
1981	2·0254	4·5560	95·3	15·3900	14·7400
1982	1·7489	4·2430	90·7	9·9600	12·8800
1983	1·5158	3·8700	83·3	9·0400	10·8000
1984	1·3364	3·7900	78·8	9·3300	10·6900
1985	1·2976	3·7840	78·7	11·4900	10·6200

Notes:
[a] Averages.
[b] Last Friday.
[c] Average (see CSO *Economic Trends* (AS), 1989 for precise definition).
Source: CSO *Economic Trends* (AS), 1987 and Public Database, October 1989.

Author index

Subject index